A Framework for Human Resource Management

Second Edition

Gary Dessler

Florida International University

Prentice
Hall

Upper Saddle River, New Jersey 07458

Library of Congress Cataloging–in–Publication Data

Dessler, Gary
    A framework for human resource management / Gary Dessler. — 2nd ed.
       p. cm.
  Rev. ed. of: Essential of human resource management. c1999.
  Includes bibliographical references and index.
  ISBN 0-13-091282-4
    1. Personal management.   I. Title: Human resource management.
    II. Dessler, Gary, 1942– Essentials of human resource management. III. Title.

HF5549.D43788   2001
658.3—dc21   2001021306

Acquisitions Editor: Melissa Steffens
Editor-in-Chief: Jeff Shelstad
Assistant Editor: Jessica Sabloff
Marketing Manager: Shannon Moore
Managing Editor (Production): Judy Leale
Production Editor: Keri Jean
Permissions Coordinator: Suzanne Grappi
Associate Director, Manufacturing: Vincent Scelta
Manufacturing Buyer: Diane Peirano
Design Manager: Pat Smythe
Designer: Janet Slowik
Interior Design: Jill Little
Cover Design: Janet Slowik
Cover Illustration/Photo: Susan Leopold
Manager, Print Production: Christy Mahon
Composition: Rainbow Graphics
Full-Service Project Management: Rainbow Graphics
Printer/Binder: Hamilton

Credits and acknowledgments borrowed from other sources and reproduced, with permission, in this textbook appear on appropriate page within text.

Prentice
Hall

10 9 8 7 6 5 4 3 2 1
ISBN 0-13-091282-4

Brief Contents

Contents

Section 2 Training, Development, and Compensation

Section 3 Managing Employee Relations

A Framework for Human Resource Management provides students and practicing managers with a brief and a lucid review of essential HR management concepts and techniques in a highly readable and understandable form. As expected, it has been used successfully in several situations: in modularized undergraduate and graduate courses that necessarily blend several topics (such as management and HR, or HR and OB); in college courses (such as those offered in quarters or shortened semesters) in which the professor wants a relatively brief treatment of HR; in more specialized HR courses such as "HR in high-technology companies"; and by practicing managers who want to update their HR skills with a brief and intensive review of the subject. The book's basic mission is to provide readers with a consise review of HR's core concepts and techniques, supported, for those who want it, by a complete multimedia and Internet-based learning package. Because all managers have personnel-related responsibilities, this book is aimed at all students of management, not just those who will someday be human resource managers.

The chapter titles are unchanged from the successful previous edition, but a number of other changes have been made. The research and topics throughout all chapters have, of course, been updated to reflect the latest findings and thinking in the HR field, and, in addition, a number of topics have been expanded in response to reviewer suggestions. Expanded coverage includes employment at will and dot-com company pay, for instance. Additional examples (including more small-business and global examples) have been added throughout the text. Because of the rapid deployment of computerized techniques and information technology in HR, many more examples of HR technology, and Web-based HR are integrated throughout all chapters. Modern managers are constantly coping with an implementing change, and so the general topic of change and, specifically, examples of how HR management concepts and techniques can be useful in managing change have also been expanded.

I am, as usual, indebted to a great many people for their assistance and support in creating this book. At Prentice Hall, Natalie E. Anderson, editor-in-chief, first proposed this book to me, and was helpful in developing its basic content and theme. Melissa Steffens, managing editor, was very helpful in working with me as the writing progressed, and Shannon Moore, marketing manager, enthusiastically supported the project, provided important input from potential adopters, and gave me much-needed input and support. It is safe to say that I would not have even considered writing this book without the ongoing support and advice that I have always received from the professionals in Prentice Hall's sales representative organization. I appreciate my wife, Claudia, tolerating the many evening and weekend hours that I had to spend writing this book, and last, but by no means least, I appreciate the support and lessons learned from my son, Derek.

Chapter 1

Managing Human Resources Today

When you finish studying this chapter, you should be able to:

■ *Answer* the question "What is human resource management?"

■ *Discuss* the components of the changing environment of human resource management.

■ *Describe* the nature of strategic planning.

■ *Give* examples of human resource management's role as a strategic partner.

INTRODUCTION

At the Port of New Jersey, one dock supervisor who has worked there for 43 years recently said, "This is not Marlon Brando's waterfront anymore and never will be [a reference to the actor's classic portrayal of a longshoreman in the movie *On the Waterfront*]. They used to say that this was a place where the men were made of iron and the ships were made of wood. . . . Now the only way most of us get exercise is by going to the health club."[1]

That's because on the docks today they're hiring brains, not brawn. Workers who once spent days in a ship's hold using hooks to manually move the cargo up to the dock today do computerized checks of inventory, and steer 10-story cargo cranes to load and unload containers. Ships that took three months and 500 men to unload 30 years ago are unloaded in 24 hours by 10 people today. At the Port of New Jersey and at many companies today, managers know what some of their competitors don't: In today's supercompetitive world, it's usually the company's employees—its "human resources"—that give the firm its competitive edge.

HUMAN RESOURCE MANAGEMENT AT WORK

What Is Human Resource Management?

Human resource (HR) management refers to the practices and policies you need to carry out the personnel aspects of your management job, specifically, acquiring, training, appraising, rewarding, and providing a safe and fair environment for your company's employees. These practices and policies include, for instance:

Conducting job analyses (determining the nature of each employee's job)

Planning labor needs and recruiting job candidates

Selecting job candidates

Orienting and training new employees

Managing wages and salaries (how to compensate employees)

Providing incentives and benefits

Appraising performance

Communicating (interviewing, counseling, disciplining)

Training and developing

Building employee commitment

And what a manager should know about:

Equal opportunity and affirmative action

Employee health and safety

Grievances and labor relations

Why Is HR Management Important to All Managers?

Why are these concepts and techniques important to all managers? Perhaps it's easier to answer this by listing some of the personnel mistakes you *don't* want to make while managing. For example, you don't want

To hire the wrong person for the job

To experience high turnover

To find employees not doing their best

To have your company taken to court because of your discriminatory actions

To have your company cited under federal occupational safety laws for unsafe practices

To allow a lack of training to undermine your department's effectiveness

To commit any unfair labor practices

Carefully studying this book can help you avoid mistakes such as these. More important, it can help ensure that you get results—through others. Remember that you could do everything else right as a manager—lay brilliant plans, draw clear organization charts, set up modern assembly lines, and use sophisticated accounting controls—but still fail, by hiring the wrong people or by not motivating subordinates, for instance. On the other hand, many managers, whether presidents, generals, governors, or supervisors, have been successful even with inadequate plans, organization, or controls. They were successful because they had the knack for hiring the right people for the right jobs and motivating, appraising, and developing them. Remember as you read this book that getting results is the bottom line of managing and that, as a manager, you will have to get these results through people. As one company president summed it up:

> For many years it has been said that capital is the bottleneck for a developing industry. I don't think this any longer holds true. I think it's the workforce and the company's inability to recruit and maintain a good workforce that does constitute the bottleneck for production. I don't know of any major project backed by good ideas, vigor, and enthusiasm that has been stopped by a shortage of cash. I do know of industries whose growth has been partly stopped or hampered because they can't maintain an efficient and enthusiastic labor force, and I think this will hold true even more in the future.[2]

Line and Staff Aspects of HRM

All managers are, in a sense, HR managers, because they all get involved in activities such as recruiting, interviewing, selecting, and training. Yet most firms also have a separate human resource department with its own human resource manager. How do the duties of this departmental HR manager and his or her staff relate to line managers' human resource duties? Let's answer this question by starting with a short definition of *line* versus *staff* authority.

Line Versus Staff Authority

Authority is the right to make decisions, to direct the work of others, and to give orders. In management, we usually distinguish between line authority and staff authority. **Line managers** are authorized to direct the work of subordinates—they're always someone's boss. In addition, line managers are in charge of accomplishing the organization's basic goals. (Hotel managers and the managers for production and sales are generally line managers, for example. They have direct responsibility for accomplishing the organization's goals. They also have the authority to direct the work of their subordinates.) **Staff managers**, on the other hand, are authorized to assist and advise line managers in accomplishing these goals. HR managers are generally *staff managers*. They are responsible for advising line managers (such as those for production and sales) in areas such as recruiting, hiring, and compensation.

In general, firms have an average of one HR employee for each 100 people in the workforce, although that ratio declines as total employment rises. And, HR and line managers generally share responsibility for most HR activities. For example, in about two-thirds of the firms responding to one survey. HR and line departments shared responsibility for skills training.[3]

Line Managers' Human Resource Management Responsibilities

According to one expert, "The direct handling of people is, and always has been, an integral part of every line manager's responsibility, from president down to the lowest-level supervisor."[4]

For example, one major company outlines its line supervisors' responsibilities for effective human resource management under the following general headings:

1. Placing the right person in the right job
2. Starting new employees in the organization (orientation)
3. Training employees for jobs that are new to them
4. Improving the job performance of each person
5. Gaining creative cooperation and developing smooth working relationships
6. Interpreting the company's policies and procedures
7. Controlling labor costs
8. Developing the abilities of each person
9. Creating and maintaining departmental morale
10. Protecting employees' health and physical conditions

In small organizations, line managers may carry out all these personnel duties unassisted. But as the organization grows, line managers need the assistance, specialized knowledge, and advice of a separate human resource staff.[5]

Human Resource Department's HR Management Responsibilities

The human resource department provides the specialized assistance that the line managers need.[6] A summary of the HR positions you might find in a large company, along with their salaries, is presented in the organization chart in Figure 1.1. As you can see, HR positions include compensation and benefits manager, employment and recruiting supervisor, training specialist, employee relations executive, safety supervisor, and industrial nurse. Examples of job duties include:

Recruiters: Maintain contact within the community and perhaps travel extensively to search for qualified job applicants.

Equal employment opportunity (EEO) representatives or affirmative action coordinators: Investigate and resolve EEO grievances, examine organizational practices for potential violations, and compile and submit EEO reports.

Job analysts: Collect and examine detailed information about job duties to prepare job descriptions.

Compensation managers: Develop compensation plans and handle the employee benefits program.

Training specialists: Plan, organize, and direct training activities.

Labor relations specialists: Advise management on all aspects of union–management relations.[7]

HR managers' priorities tend to shift with changing times (for instance, with the relative availability of job applicants). Recently, 65% of the HR managers surveyed listed recruiting, selection, and placement among their top three priorities. Other high priorities included training and development, employee benefits, compensation, and employee/labor relations.[8]

THE CHANGING ENVIRONMENT OF HR MANAGEMENT

To better understand HR's role in organizations today, it's useful to understand how companies are changing, and the trends that are causing these changes to occur. For instance, as you are undoubtedly aware, organizations today are under increasing pressure to be more competitive—thus, health maintenance organizations (HMOs) are squeezing more productivity out of hospitals, companies are downsizing, and universities are working hard to boost enrollment and faculty productivity. Globalization of competition and deregulation are two trends accounting for this pressure to be more competitive. Other trends affecting organizations today include diversity and other workforce changes.

Workforce Diversity

The composition of the workforce will continue to become more diverse as women, minority-group members, and older workers flood the workforce.[9] For example, women represented 42.1% of the civilian U.S. labor force in 1979 and 46% in 1994, and they are expected to represent 48% in the year 2008.[10] Related to this, about two-thirds of all single mothers (separated, divorced, widowed, or never married) are in the labor force today, as are almost 45% of mothers with children under age three. The human resource department will increasingly be called upon to help companies accommodate these employees, with new child care and maternity leave provisions, for example, and with basic skills training where such training is required.

Changes in racial composition will be even more dramatic. For example, between 1992 and 2005 people classified as Asian and other (including Native American) in the workforce will jump by just over 81%, whereas the number of employees classified as black will rise 25.2%, and as white will rise 15%. In the same period, workers classified as white will have declined as a percentage of the civilian labor force from 87.6% in 1979 to 85.5% in 1992 to a projected 17% in 2008. The number of Hispanics in the civilian labor force will jump by almost 64% in the next 10 years.[11]

The labor force is also getting older. The median age of the labor force in 1979 was 34.7 years. This has risen continuously since then to 37.8 years in 1995, and is projected to go to 40.5 years in 2005.[12] This is due mostly to the aging of the baby boom generation, those born between 1946 and 1964, because baby boomers now comprise just over half the U.S. labor force.[13]

Increased diversity will place heavy demands on the HR management function.[14] For example, there will be a shortage of workers aged 25 to 34, "while the career opportunities in management for workers in the 35 to 44 age cohort may be constrained by the abundance of more experienced members of the 45 to 54 age cohort."[15] At the same time, today's Generation Xers, those born between 1963 and 1981, reportedly often crave more benefits such as free time and "flextime" than their baby boom parents ever did.[16] With more females in the workforce, an upswing in the number of dual-career couples will force more employers to establish child care facilities on or near company premises and to accommodate the travel, scheduling, and moving needs of dual-career employees.

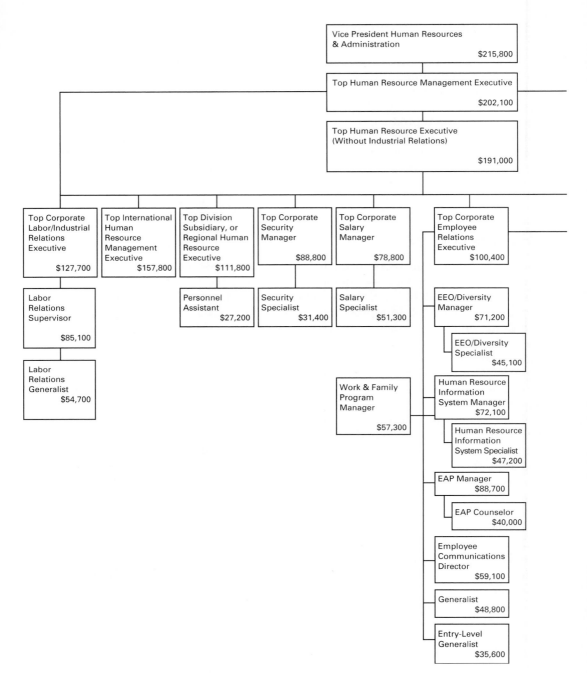

FIGURE 1.1 Typical Positions and Salaries Within a Large HR Department

Source: Reprinted with permission from *Bulletin to Management (BNA Policy and Practice Series)* 48, no. 38, pp. 300–301 (September 18, 1997). Copyright 1997 by The Bureau of National Affairs, Inc. (800-372-1033) <http://www.bna.com>.

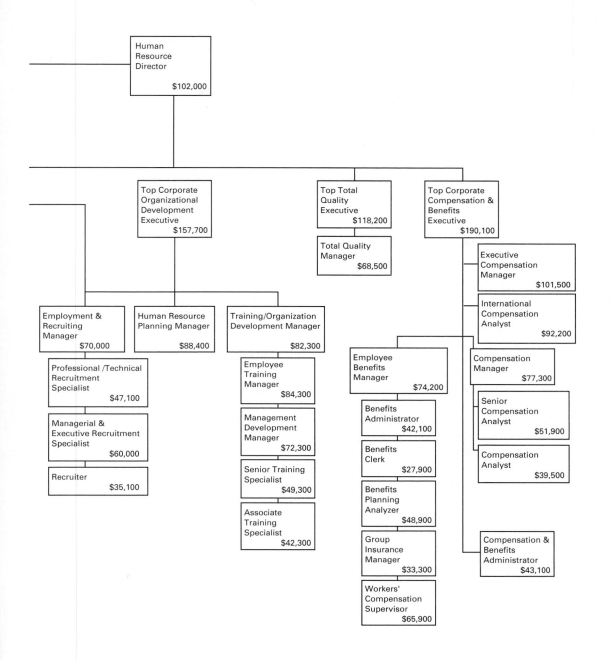

Human Resource Director
$102,000

Top Corporate Organizational Development Executive
$157,700

Top Total Quality Executive
$118,200

Total Quality Manager
$68,500

Top Corporate Compensation & Benefits Executive
$190,100

Executive Compensation Manager
$101,500

International Compensation Analyst
$92,200

Employment & Recruiting Manager
$70,000

Human Resource Planning Manager
$88,400

Training/Organization Development Manager
$82,300

Professional /Technical Recruitment Specialist
$47,100

Managerial & Executive Recruitment Specialist
$60,000

Recruiter
$35,100

Employee Training Manager
$84,300

Management Development Manager
$72,300

Senior Training Specialist
$49,300

Associate Training Specialist
$42,300

Employee Benefits Manager
$74,200

Benefits Administrator
$42,100

Benefits Clerk
$27,900

Benefits Planning Analyzer
$48,900

Group Insurance Manager
$33,300

Workers' Compensation Supervisor
$65,900

Compensation Manager
$77,300

Senior Compensation Analyst
$51,900

Compensation Analyst
$39,500

Compensation & Benefits Administrator
$43,100

Globalization

Globalization refers to the tendency of firms to extend their sales or manufacturing to new markets abroad. For U.S. firms, this globalization is manifesting itself in many ways. U.S. exports are reaching new markets, with big gains to countries ranging from Uruguay and Mexico to the Netherlands, Hungary, and Kuwait.[17] Production is becoming globalized, too, as manufacturers around the world put manufacturing facilities where they will be most advantageous.

Why is globalization important to managers, including HR managers? In part because it means increased competition. Throughout the world, firms that formerly competed only with local firms—from airlines to carmakers to banks—have discovered that they must now face an onslaught of new foreign competitors. From tapping the global labor force to formulating selection, training, and compensation policies for expatriate employees, managing globalization will thus be a major HR challenge in the next few years.

Trends in the Nature of Work

At the same time, work—what people do and how they do it— is changing, too. For example, technological changes, including information technology and the Internet, have allowed companies to relocate operations to locations where wage rates are lower; for instance, Hertz Rent-A-Car's reservation operation is now centered in Oklahoma City.[18]

Another notable trend is the shift to service jobs and to knowledge work and the stress on human capital. First, there has been a shift from manufacturing jobs to service jobs in North America and Western Europe. Today more than two-thirds of the U.S. workforce is employed in producing and delivering services, not products. In fact, the manufacturing workforce declined over 12% during the 1980s. Of the 21 million or so new jobs that will be added to the U.S. economy to 2008, virtually all will be in such service industries as computer and data processing, health services, and engineering services.[19]

And (as at the New Jersey port) these jobs, in turn, will demand new types of knowledge workers and new human resource management methods to manage them.[20] As *Fortune* magazine put it, today "practically every package deliverer, bank teller, retail clerk, telephone operator, and bill collector in American works with a computer."[21] In fact, most jobs today demand a level of expertise far beyond that required of most workers 20 or 30 years ago, so that human capital is quickly replacing machines as the basis for most firms' success. As a result, the distinguishing characteristic of companies today and tomorrow, say many experts, is the growing emphasis on human capital—the knowledge, education, training, skills, and expertise of a firm's workers.[22] As *Fortune* magazine said:

> Brain-power . . . has never before been so important for business. Every company depends increasingly on knowledge—patents, processes, management skills, technologies, information about customers and suppliers, and old-fashioned experience. Added together, this knowledge is intellectual capital.[23]

For managers, the challenge of fostering intellectual or human capital lies in the fact that such workers must be managed differently than were those of previous generations. As one expert put this, "the center of gravity in employment is moving fast from manual and clerical workers to knowledge workers, who resist the command and control model that business took from the military 100 years ago."[24] Workers like these, in other words, cannot just be ordered around and closely monitored. New human resource management systems and skills—new incentives, new selection techniques, and new appraisal methods, for instance—are required to select and train such employees and to win their self-discipline and commitment.

THE CHANGING ROLE OF HR MANAGEMENT

Not surprisingly, HR's role is changing, to adapt to these trends.

How HR Has Evolved

HR has gone through several phases. In the early 1900s, "personnel" first took over hiring and firing from supervisors, ran the payroll department, and administered benefit plans. It was a job consisting largely of ensuring that procedures were followed. As technology in such areas as testing and interviewing began to emerge, the personnel department began to play an expanded role in employee selection, training, and promotion.[25]

The emergence of union legislation in the 1930s led to a second phase in personnel management and a new emphasis on protecting the firm in its interaction with unions. The discrimination legislation of the 1960s and 1970s triggered a third phase. Because of the large penalties that lawsuits could bring to a company, effective personnel practices became more important. In this phase (as in the second phase), the personnel department continued to provide expertise in areas such as recruitment, screening, and training, albeit in a more expanded role. Notice, though, that whether dealing with unions or equal employment, personnel gained status as much for what it could do to protect the organization from problems as for the positive contribution it made to the firm's competitiveness.

Today, personnel is speeding through a fourth phase, and its role is shifting from protector and screener to planner and change agent. The metamorphosis of *personnel* into *human resource management* reflects the fact that in today's flattened, downsized, and competitive organizations, highly trained and committed employees, not machines, are often a firm's best competitive key.

This all means that it's more important than ever to hire the right people and to effectively train and motivate them. And this, in turn, demands a more effective HR system. Based on one review, for instance, best HR practices for many of today's firms include highly selective hiring, teamwork and decentralized decision making, high pay, extensive training, reduced status distinctions, and extensive information sharing among employees and management, all built on a foundation "that relies on people as a source of competitive advantage and on a management culture that embraces that belief."

By one estimate, effectively managing the HR system can translate into improved financial returns to the firm, estimated in some cases to be over $20,000 per employee.[26] At employers such as the pharmaceutical firm Merck & Company, HR helps employees adapt to the increased pressures in their downsized departments by helping them learn to prioritize tasks and reduce job stress.[27] A survey by a management consulting firm of over 1,000 North American companies found that successful organizations use many HR practices to help employees become more productive. These practices include leadership training, technical training, mentoring programs, and career workshops.[28]

HR and Technology

The HR function is therefore changing. For one thing, it's going high-tech. Thus, many firms are installing intranet portals to facilitate "self-service HR." At Dell Computer Corporation, for instance, a section of the firm's intranet is dedicated to "manager tools." Here, about 30 automated Web applications (including executive search reports, hiring tools, and automated employee referrals) let managers unilaterally perform HR tasks that previously required direct participation by HR. The intranet also allows Dell employees to administer their own 401(k) plans, check job postings, and monitor their total compensation statements, for instance.[29]

Data warehouses are another example. A data warehouse is a large repository of information gleaned from various databases throughout an organization. In one state agency, for example, state managers can, from their desktop computers, easily find the average salary for each occupation, the agencies doing the most or least hiring, and who pays the highest salaries.[30]

Technology is helping companies streamline other HR tasks. Electronic performance support systems (EPSS) are an example. These performance support systems help workers perform tasks. Electronic performance support systems "are sets of tools that effectively automate training, documentation, and phone support, integrate this automation into applications, and provide support that's faster, cheaper, and more effective than the traditional methods." For example, a computer company might use an EPSS to improve its technical service function. When you call the computer serviceperson, an EPSS consisting of questions with several possible answers (such as "what operating system does the computer system use?") opens on the technician's screen, guides the technician's questions, and helps the person arrive at a solution. Systems like these have simplified training in many firms, as we'll see in Chapter 5.[31]

HR is also growing more professionalized. For example, certification exams administered twice a year for the Society of Human Resource Management test knowledge of HR practices (such as staffing and appraisal), knowledge of business including financial analysis, and knowledge of change management techniques including problem solving and organizational transformation.[32]

HR and Responsiveness

Many of the management changes occuring today are aimed at making the enterprise more responsive to product innovations and technological change. Thus, downsizing, flattening the pyramid, empowering employees, and organizing around teams are aimed in part at making it easier for decisions to be made and for the company to respond quickly to its customers' needs and its competitors' challenges.

HR can play a crucial role. At Levi Strauss, HR helped create the firm's new team-based alternative manufacturing system. This ties employees' compensation incentives to team goals and, along with Levi's new flexible-hours program, helps inject more flexibility into the firm's production process.[33] We'll see many other examples throughout this book of how HR practices can help to boost a firm's flexibility and responsiveness.

HR and Service

Employee behavior is particularly important in service firms such as banks and retail establishments. If a customer is confronted by a tactless salesperson, all the firm's other efforts will have been wasted. Service organizations have little to sell but their good service; that makes them uniquely dependent on their employees' attitudes and motivation—and on HR management.

HR, therefore, plays a crucial role in service firms.[34] It has been noted, for instance, that there are "quite a few [employees] who lack the temperament, maturity, social skills, and tolerance for frequent contact" that customer service jobs require, and that the first step in avoiding this problem is screening and selection.[35] A study of service firms illustrates the HR–service link. The researchers found that progressive HR practices such as facilitating employees' career progress, developing orientation/training/socialization programs for new employees, and eliminating conditions on the job that inhibit task performance appear to improve employees' customer service as well as the overall quality of that service from the customers' point of view.[36] This idea is probably best summed up by Fred Smith, the chairman and founder of FedEx, whose philosophy is "people–service–profits." In other words, use progressive HR practices to build employee commitment and morale; employees will then provide excellent customer service, which in turn will generate profits.

HR and Employee Commitment

Competition and the need to be more responsive puts a premium on employee commitment. As the vice president of human resources at Toyota Motor Manufacturing in Georgetown, Kentucky, put it:

> People are behind our success. Machines don't have new ideas, solve problems, or grasp opportunities. Only people who are involved and thinking can make a difference. . . . Every auto plant in the U.S. has basically the same machinery. But how people are utilized and involved varies widely from one company to another. The workforce gives any company its true competitive edge.[37]

Building employee commitment—aligning employees' and employers' goals so that employees want to do their jobs as if they own the company—takes a multi-pronged effort, one in which HR plays the central role. For example, two-way communications foster commitment; and, firms such as FedEx and Toyota have programs that guarantee two-way communications and fair treatment of all employees' grievances and disciplinary matters.

HR and Corporate Strategy

Perhaps the most striking change in HR's role is its growing involvement in developing and implementing strategy. Strategy—the company's plan for how it will balance its internal strengths and weaknesses with external opportunities and threats in order to maintain a competitive advantage—was traditionally a job for the company's operating (line) managers. Thus, the president and his or her staff might decide to enter new markets, drop product lines, or embark on a five-year cost-cutting plan. Then the president would more or less leave the personnel implications of that plan (hiring or firing new workers, hiring outplacement firms for those fired, and so on) to be carried out by HR management.

Today, things have changed. Strategies increasingly depend on strengthening organizational competitiveness and on building committed work teams, and these put HR in a central role. In a fast-changing, globally competitive, and quality-oriented industrial environment, it is often the firm's employees themselves, its human resources, who provide the competitive key. It is now increasingly common to involve HR in the earliest stages of developing and implementing a firm's strategic plan, rather than letting HR just react to it. We thus turn next to strategic planning and HR's strategic role.

STRATEGIC PLANNING AND HR MANAGEMENT

The Nature of Strategic Planning

Managers engage in three levels of strategic decision making; these are summarized in Figure 1.2.[38]

At the first level, many firms consist of several businesses; for instance, PepsiCo includes Pepsi, Frito-Lay, and Pizza Hut. PepsiCo therefore needs a *corporate-level strategy*. A company's corporate-level strategy identifies the portfolio of businesses that, in total, comprise the organization and the ways in which these businesses relate to each other.

At the next level down, each of these businesses (such as Pizza Hut) is guided by a *business-level/competitive strategy*. A competitive strategy identifies how to build and strengthen the business's long-term competitive position in the marketplace.[39] It identifies, for instance, how Pizza Hut will compete with Dominos or how Wal-Mart will compete with Kmart.

Finally, each business is itself composed of departments, such as manufacturing, sales, and human resource management. *Functional strategies* identify the basic courses of action that each of the business's departments will pursue in order to help the business attain its competitive goals.

Although companies pursue three types of strategies, the term *strategic planning* is usually reserved for the company's corporate-level, organizationwide strategic planning process. Specifically, strategic planning outlines the type of business the firm will be, given the firm's external opportunities and threats and its internal strengths and weaknesses. Deciding whether Mom and Pop's Supermarket will compete head to head with Enormous Markets by building similar superstores or instead will continue with its small local gourmet market is a typical strategic planning problem.

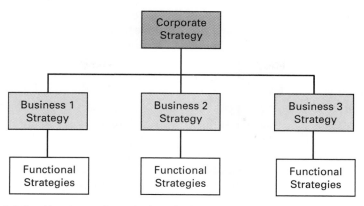

FIGURE 1.2   Relationships Among Strategies in Multiple-Business Firms

The manager's strategic plan ideally seeks to balance two sets of forces: the firm's external opportunities and threats on the one hand, and its internal strengths and weaknesses on the other. For example, IBM bought the Lotus software firm, in part to acquire the Lotus Notes networking programs. Sensing the opportunities and threats presented by the Internet's growing popularity and by IBM's relative lack of expertise in networking software, IBM Chair Louis Gerstner apparently decided to diversify. IBM bought Lotus to position IBM to compete more effectively with other, Internet-based means of linking or networking companies and individuals.

In any case, the three levels of strategic decision making should be interrelated and mutually supportive. For example, let's consider IBM's Lotus acquisition. At the corporate organizationwide level, the acquisition represents an attempt to reposition the giant corporation to compete more effectively in the age of networking computers. After deciding to acquire Lotus, Gerstner then had to make a business-level strategic decision regarding how to organize IBM's new networking business and in particular how to compete with other firms making similar products. In this case, John Manzi, the head of Lotus, proposed to Gerstner the merger of Lotus with IBM's other software divisions, with Manzi in charge; Gerstner rejected this suggestion, deciding to keep Lotus and its Lotus Notes software separate and to let Manzi leave the firm.

Corporate- and business-level strategic decisions like these in turn help determine what IBM's functional strategies should be. For example, IBM's push into networking has production strategy implications because it may require phasing out several hardware manufacturing facilities and consolidating the firm's network program design facilities in fewer locations. Similarly, IBM's marketing and sales efforts may have to be increasingly organized around a networking sales effort. The HR function will also have to accomplish its share: For instance, there will be facilities to be closed, new ones to be staffed, and new network program designers to be recruited and hired.[40]

Building Competitive Advantage   Companies try to achieve competitive advantages for each business they are in. A **competitive advantage** can be defined as any factors that allow an organization to differentiate its product or service from those of its competitors to increase market share.[41]

There are several ways to achieve competitive advantage. One way, *cost leadership*, means the enterprise aims to become the low-cost leader in an industry. For example, Wal-Mart is a typical industry cost leader: It maintains its competitive advantage through its satellite-based distribution system and grew large in its early days by keeping store location costs to a minimum by placing stores on low-cost land outside small to medium-sized towns.

Differentiation is a second example of a competitive strategy. In a differentiation strategy, a firm seeks to be unique in its industry along dimensions that are widely valued by buyers.[42] Thus, Volvo stresses the safety of its cars, Apple stresses the usability of its computers, and Mercedes Benz emphasizes reliability and quality. Like Mercedes Benz, firms can usually charge a premium price if they successfully stake their claim to being substantially different from their competitors in some coveted way.

Human Resources as a Competitive Advantage   Low-cost, high-quality cars like those of Toyota and Saturn aren't just a result of sophisticated automated machines. Instead, they are a result of intensely committed employees all working hard and with self-discipline to produce the best cars that they can at the lowest possible cost. In today's intensely competitive and globalized marketplace, in other words, maintaining a competitive advantage means having a highly committed and competent workforce.

Managing Human Resources Today   At no time in our history has that been more true than it is today. An example can help illustrate this. An expert at Harvard University studied manufacturing facilities that had installed computer-integrated manufacturing systems.[43] The idea of computer-integrated manufacturing is to use computers to integrate product design, manufacturing, and storage to give a firm a competitive edge.

Surprisingly, this expert discovered that computer integration was not in itself associated with either producing a wider range of products or improved changeover times. Instead, what he found was that:

> The flexibility of the plants depended much more on people than on any technical factor. Although high levels of computer integration can provide critically needed advantages in quality and cost competitiveness, all the data in my study point to one conclusion: operational flexibility is determined primarily by a plant's operators and the extent to which managers cultivate, measure, and communicate with them. Equipment and computer integration are secondary.[44]

Other experts make the same point. Strategic planning experts K. C. Prahalad and Gary Hamel say that competitive advantage lies today in being able to tap the company's special skills or *core competencies*, "in management's ability to consolidate corporate-wide technologies and production skills, such as Sony's expertise in miniaturation, into competencies that empower individual businesses to adapt quickly to changing opportunities."[45] As yet another expert puts it:

> In a growing number of organizations human resources are now viewed as a source of competitive advantage. There is greater recognition that distinctive

competencies are obtained through highly developed employee skills, distinctive organizational cultures, management processes, and systems. This is in contrast to the traditional emphasis on transferable resources such as equipment . . . Increasingly, it is being recognized that competitive advantage can be obtained with a high quality workforce that enables organizations to compete on the basis of market responsiveness, product and service quality, differentiated products, and technological innovation.[46]

Strategic Human Resource Management

The fact that employees today are central to achieving competitive advantage has led to the creation of **strategic human resource management.**[47] This has been defined as "the linking of HRM with strategic goals and objectives in order to improve business performance and develop organizational cultures that foster innovation and flexibility."[48] Put another way, it is "the pattern of planned human resource deployments and activities intended to enable an organization to achieve its goals."[49] Strategic HR means accepting the HR function as a strategic partner in the formulation of the company's strategies, as well as in the implementation of those strategies through a set of internally consistent HR activities such as recruiting, selecting, training, and rewarding personnel.[50]

Whereas strategic HR reflects HR's partnership role in the strategizing process, the term *HR strategies* refers to the specific HR courses of action the company plans to pursue to achieve its aims. Thus, one of FedEx's primary aims is to achieve superior levels of customer service and high profitability through a highly committed workforce. Its overall HR strategy is thus aimed at building a committed workforce, preferably in a nonunion environment.[51] The specific components of FedEx's HR strategy follow from that basic aim: to use various mechanisms to build healthy two-way communications; to screen out potential managers whose values are not people oriented; to guarantee to the greatest extent possible fair treatment and employee security for all employees; and to institute various promotion-from-within activities aimed at giving employees every opportunity to fully utilize their skills and gifts at work.

Figure 1.3 illustrates the interplay between HR strategy and the company's business plans and results. Ideally, HR and top management work interactively to formulate the company's overall business strategy. The company's strategy then provides the framework within which HR activities such as recruiting and appraising must be integrated. If this integration is successfully implemented, it should produce the needed employee competencies and behaviors, which in turn should contribute to the business's effectively implementing its strategies and achieving its goals. Notice that it is in clarifying the company's strategy and formulating its HR practices that management has the most direct influence: It can only hope to influence its employees' behavior through the practices it implements.[52] Let's now take a closer look at HR's role as a strategic partner.

HR's Role as a Strategic Partner

Personnel/HR's long history of having a staff or advisory function has left it with a somewhat impoverished reputation: Some still tend to view it as less than it is. For example, one view is that HR is strictly operational and that HR activities are not

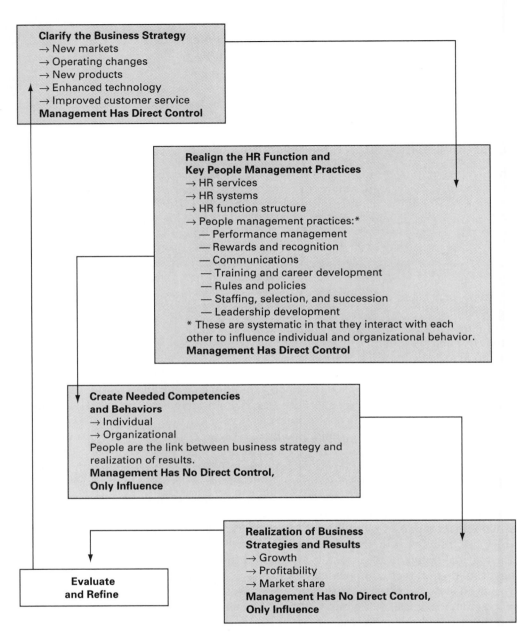

FIGURE 1.3 Key Components of the HR Strategy Model

Source: From Timothy J. Galpin and Patrick Murray, "Connect Human Resource Strategy to the Business Plan," *HRMagazine*, March 1997. Reprinted with the permission of *HRMagazine*, published by the Society for Human Resource Management, Alexandria, VA.

strategic at all.[53] According to this line of reasoning, HR activities simply "involve putting out small fires—ensuring that people are paid on the right day; the job advertisement meets the newspaper deadline; a suitable supervisor is recruited for the night shift by the time it goes ahead; and the same manager remembers to observe due process before sacking the new rep who didn't work out."[54]

A more sophisticated (but perhaps no more accurate) view of HR is that its role is simply to "fit" the company's strategy. In this view HR's strategic role is to adapt individual HR practices (recruiting, rewarding, and so on) to fit specific corporate and competitive strategies. In this view, top management crafts a corporate strategy, such as to purchase another company, and then HR is told to create the HR programs required to successfully implement that corporate strategy.[55] As two strategic planning experts have argued, "the human resources management system must be tailored to the demands of the business strategy."[56] The idea here is that "for any particular organizational strategy, there is purportedly a matching human resource strategy."[57]

A third view of HR management is that it is an equal partner in the strategic planning process. Here, HR management's role is not just to tailor its activities to the demands of business strategy, nor, certainly, just to carry out operational day-to-day tasks such as ensuring that employees are paid. Instead, the need to forge a company's workforce into a competitive advantage means that human resource management must be an equal partner in both the formulation and the implementation of the company's organizationwide and competitive strategies.[58]

HR's Role in Formulating Strategy   Formulating a company's overall strategic plan requires identifying, analyzing, and balancing two sets of forces: the company's *external opportunities and threats* on the one hand and its *internal strengths and weaknesses* on the other.

This is one area in which strategic HR management plays a role. For example, HR management can play a role in what planners call *environmental scanning*—in other words, identifying and analyzing external opportunities and threats that may be crucial to the company's success. For example, in 1995, both United Airlines and American Airlines considered and then rejected the opportunity to acquire USAir, a smaller and relatively weak airline. Although both American and United had several reasons for rejecting a bid, HR considerations loomed large. Specifically, both American and United had doubts about their abilities to successfully negotiate new labor agreements with USAir's employees, and both felt the problems of assimilating them might be too great.

Similarly, HR management is in a unique position to supply competitive intelligence that may be useful in the strategic planning process. Details regarding competitors' advanced incentive plans, opinion survey data from employees that elicit information about customer complaints, and information about pending legislation such as labor laws and mandatory health insurance are some examples. Furthermore:

> From public information and legitimate recruiting and interview activities, you ought to be able to construct organization charts, staffing levels and group missions for the various organizational components of each of your major competitors. Your knowledge of how brands are sorted among sales divisions and

who reports to whom can give important clues as to a competitor's strategic priorities. You may even know the track record and characteristic behavior of the executives.[59]

HR also participates in the strategy formulation process by supplying information regarding the company's internal strengths and weaknesses. For example, IBM's decision to buy Lotus was probably prompted in part by IBM's conclusion that its own human resources were inadequate to enable the firm to reposition itself as an industry leader in networking systems, or at least to do so quickly enough. Similarly, Wells Fargo acquired Crocker National [Bank] Corporation, and approximately two months later it surveyed 1,500 Crocker employees to discover any problems as quickly as possible.

The strengths and weaknesses of a company's employees—its human resources—can have a determining effect on the viability of the firm's strategic options: Some in fact build their strategy around an HR-based competitive advantage. For example, in the process of automating its factories, farm equipment manufacturer John Deere developed a workforce that was exceptionally talented and expert in factory automation. This in turn prompted the firm to establish a new-technology division to offer automation services to other companies.[60] As another example, the accounting and consulting firm Arthur Andersen developed unique human resource capabilities in training. The firm's Illinois training facility is so sophisticated that it provides the firm with a competitive advantage, enabling it to provide fast, uniform training in-house and so "react quickly to the changing demands of its clients."[61]

HR's Role in Executing Strategy   HR management also plays a central role in executing a company's strategic plan. For example, FedEx's competitive strategy is to differentiate itself from its competitors by offering superior customer service and guaranteed on-time deliveries. Because basically the same technologies are available to UPS, DHL, and FedEx's other competitors, it's FedEx's workforce—its human resource—who necessarily provide FedEx with a crucial competitive advantage. This puts a premium on the firm's HR processes, as discussed earlier, and on the firm's ability to create a highly committed, competent, and customer-oriented workforce.[62]

HR management supports strategic implementation in numerous other ways. For example, HR is today heavily involved in the execution of most firms' downsizing and restructuring strategies, through outplacing employees, instituting pay-for-performance plans, reducing health care costs, and retraining employees. For example, when Wells Fargo went on to also acquire First Interstate Bancorp, HR played a strategic role in the implementation—for instance, in merging two "wildly divergent" cultures and in dealing with the uncertainty and initial shock that rippled through the organizations when the merger was announced.[63]

The Strategic Future of the HR Department   Ironically, although the need for HR is obviously great and growing, the future of the HR department itself sometimes seems in doubt. Human resource departments will face further downsizing and "reengineering," says one expert, "as they face pressure from senior management to add value to the organization or have their functions contracted out."[64]

The belt-tightening in HR reflects two related causes: downsizing and outsourcing. At Sears Roebuck and Company, for instance, downsizing/reorganizing of the HR department resulted in slashing the corporate HR department from 700 to about

200 employees. HR responsibilities that had previously been dispersed at 32 U.S. locations were consolidated in one Atlanta office as part of this downsizing.[65] Outsourcing is having an impact, too. For example, in one survey, about 71% of respondents said they were outsourcing one or more[66] HR activities such as temporary staffing, recruiting, benefits administration, payroll, or training.[67] Cost reduction was the most commonly cited explanation.[68]

What can HR departments do to keep themselves from getting outsourced out of existence? For one thing, HR can't focus just on traditional maintenance and administrative functions such as recruiting, testing, and payroll. To paraphrase one HR consultant, if an HR department focuses only on maintenance and administration, it's going to become an endangered species, because outsourcing firms can do a better job of handling such tasks. Today, says this expert, the HR department needs to focus more on activities that add value to the firm's bottom line—activities such as strategic planning, change management, corporate culture transition, and development of human capital.[70]

Does strategic HR influence company performance? Yes, as noted previously, research findings show that effective HR management does translate into higher productivity, cash flow, and market value.[71] In this book we'll look more closely at how to accomplish this.

THE PLAN OF THIS BOOK

The following is a brief overview of the chapters to come:

Chapter 2: Managing Equal Opportunity and Diversity. What you'll need to know about equal opportunity laws as they relate to human resource management activities such as interviewing, selecting employees, and evaluating performance appraisals

Part I: Recruiting and Placing Employees

Chapter 3: Personnel Planning and Recruiting. How to analyze a job and how to determine the job's requirements, specific duties, and responsibilities, as well as what sorts of people need to be hired and how to recruit them

Chapter 4: Testing and Selecting Employees. Techniques such as testing that you can use to ensure that you're hiring the right people

Chapter 5: Training and Developing Employees. Providing the training and development necessary to ensure that your employees have the knowledge and skills required to accomplish their tasks

Part II: Appraising and Compensating Employees

Chapter 6: Appraising Performance. Techniques for appraising performance

Chapter 7: Compensating Employees. How to develop equitable pay plans, including incentives and benefits, for your employees

Part III: Employee Rights and Safety

Chapter 8: Managing Labor Relations and Collective Bargaining. Concepts and techniques concerning the relations between unions and management, including the union-organizing campaign; negotiating and agreeing on a collective bargaining agreement between unions and management; and managing the agreement

Chapter 9: Managing Careers and Fair Treatment. Ensuring fair treatment through discipline, grievance, and career management processes

Chapter 10: Protecting Safety and Health. The causes of accidents, how to make the workplace safe, and laws governing your responsibilities in regard to employee safety and health

REVIEW

Summary

1. Staffing, personnel management, or human resource management includes activities such as recruiting, selecting, training, compensating, appraising, and developing.

2. HR management is a part of *every* line manager's responsibilities. These HR responsibilities include placing the right person in the right job and then orienting, training, and compensating the person to improve his or her job performance.

3. The HR manager and his or her department carry out several functions. First, the manager exerts *line authority* in his or her unit. He or she exerts a *coordinative function* to ensure that the organization's HR objectives and policies are coordinated and implemented. And he or she provides various *staff services* to line management; for example, the HR manager or department assists in the hiring, training, evaluating, rewarding, promoting, and disciplining of employees at all levels.

4. Changes in the environment of HR management are requiring HR to play a more major role in organizations. These changes include growing workforce diversity, rapid technological change, globalization, and changes in the nature of work, such as the movement toward a service society and a growing emphasis on education and human capital.

5. One consequence of changes in the work environment is that HR management must be involved in both the formulation and the implementation of a company's strategies, given the need for the firm to use its employees as a competitive advantage.

6. Strategic human resource management may be defined as "the linking of HRM with strategic goals and objectives in order to improve business performance and develop organizational cultures that foster innovation and flexibility." HR is a strategic partner in that HR management works with other top managers to formulate the company's strategy as well as to execute it.

Key Terms

human resource management	line manager	strategic human resource management
authority	staff manager	
	competitive advantage	

Discussion Questions and Exercises

1. Explain what HR management is and how it relates to line management.

2. Give several examples of how HR management concepts and techniques can be of use to all managers.

3. Compare the work of line and staff managers; give examples of each.

4. Working individually or in groups, develop a list showing how trends such as workforce diversity, technological trends, globalization, and changes in the nature of work have affected the college or university you are now attending or the organization for which you work.

5. Working individually or in groups, develop a list of examples showing how the new management practices mentioned in this chapter (worker empowerment, flatter organizations, and team work) have or have not been implemented to some extent in the college or university you are now attending or in the organization for which you work.

6. Working individually or in groups, interview an HR manager; based on that interview, write a short presentation regarding HR's role today in building a more responsive organization.

7. Why is it important for a company to make its human resources into a competitive advantage? How can HR contribute to doing so?

8. What is meant by *strategic human resource management*, and what exactly is HR's role in the strategic planning process?

APPLICATION EXERCISES

Case Incident: Jack Nelson's Problem

As a new member of the board of directors for a local bank, Jack Nelson was being introduced to all the employees in the home office. When he was introduced to Ruth Johnson, he was curious about her work and asked her what her machine did. Johnson replied that she really did not know what the machine was called or what it did. She explained that she had been working there for only two months. She did, however, know precisely how to operate the machine. According to her supervisor, she was an excellent employee.

At one of the branch offices, the supervisor in charge spoke to Nelson confidentially, telling him that "something was wrong," but she didn't know what. For one thing, she explained, employee turnover was too high, and no sooner had one employee been put on the job than another one resigned. With customers to see and loans to be made, she explained, she had little time to work with the new employees as they came and went.

All branch supervisors hired their own employees without communication with the home office or other branches. When an opening developed, the supervisor tried to find a suitable employee to replace the worker who had quit.

After touring the 22 branches and finding similar problems in many of them, Nelson wondered what the home office should do or what action he should take. The banking firm was generally regarded as a well-run institution that had grown from 27 to 191 employees during the past eight years. The more he thought about the matter, the more puzzled Nelson became. He couldn't quite put his finger on the problem, and he didn't know whether to report his findings to the president.

Questions

1. What do you think is causing some of the problems in the bank home office and branches?

2. Do you think setting up an HR unit in the main office would help?

3. What specific functions should an HR unit carry out? What HR functions would then be carried out by supervisors and other line managers?

Source: From *Supervision in Action,* 4/e by Claude S. George, © 1985. Adapted by permission of Prentice Hall, Inc., Upper Saddle River, NJ.

TAKE IT TO THE WEB

 For Internet exercises, updates to chapter material, and more, visit the Dessler Web site at

www.prenhall.com/dessler

ENDNOTES

1. Ronald Smothers, "They're Hiring on the Docks: Brains, Not Brawn," *New York Times* (May 4, 2000): 23.

2. Quoted in Fred K. Foulkes, "The Expanding Role of the Personnel Function," *Harvard Business Review* (March/April 1975): 71–84. See also Warren Wilhelm, "HR Can Make the U.S. a Global Leader," *Personnel Journal* (May 1993): 280.

3. "Human Resource Activities, Budgets & Staffs, 1999–2000," *BNA Bulletin to Management* 51, no. 25 (June 29, 2000): S1–S6.

4. See Robert Saltonstall, "Who's Who in Personnel Administration," *Harvard Business Review* 33 (July/August 1955): 75–83, reprinted in Paul Pigors, Charles Meyers, and F. P. Malm, *Management of Human Resources* (New York: McGraw-Hill, 1969), pp. 61–73. For a recent review, see, "Special Survey Report: Human Resources Outlook," *BNA Bulletin to Management* (January 28, 1998): 1–20.

5. Saltonstall, "Who's Who in Personnel Administration," p. 63.

6. For a detailed discussion of the responsibilities and duties of the human resource department, see Mary Zippo, "Personnel Activities: Where the Dollars Went in 1979," *Personnel* 57 (March/April 1980): 61–67; and "SHRM-BNA Survey No. 62, Human Resource Activities, Budgets, and Staffs: 1996–1997," *BNA Bulletin to Management* (June 26, 1997): 1–20.

7. U.S. Department of Labor, Bureau of Labor Statistics, *Occupational Outlook Handbook,* Bulletin 2250, 1986–1987 Edition, pp. 45–47.

8. "Human Resource Priorities and Outlook," *BNA Bulletin to Management* (February 3, 2000): S1–S20.

9. Gerald Ferris, Dwight Frank, and M. Carmen Galang, "Diversity in the Workplace: The Human Resources Management Challenge," *Human Resource Planning* 16, no. 1: 41–51. See also, "Immigrants in the Workplace," *BNA Bulletin to Management* (August 15, 1996): 260–61; and "The 1998–2000 Job Outlook in Brief," *Occupational Outlook Quarterly* 44, no. 1 (spring 2000).

10. Howard Fullerton, Jr., "Another Look at the Labor Force," *Monthly Labor Review* (November 1993): 31–40; "The American Workforce, 1994–2005," *BNA Bulletin to Management* (January 4, 1996): 4–5.

11. *Ibid.,* p. 4.

12. *Ibid.,* p. 38.

---

13. *Ibid.*, p. 37.

14. Except as noted, this section is based on Charles Greer, *Strategy and Human Resources* (Upper Saddle River, NJ: Prentice Hall, 1995), pp. 49–52.

15. *Ibid.*, p. 50.

16. Gillian Flynn, "Xers vs. Boomers: Teamwork or Trouble?" *Personnel Journal* (November 1996): 86–89.

17. *Ibid., The World Almanac*, p. 207.

18. See Greer, *Strategy and Human Resources*, pp. 52–53; Brian Stanko and Rebecca Matchette, "Telecommuting: The Future Is Now," *B and E Review* (October/December 1994): 8–11; "Part-Time Employment," *BNA Datagraph Bulletin to Management* (July 7, 1994): 212–13.

19. "Charting the Projections: 1998–2008," *Occupational Outlook Quarterly* (winter 1999–2000): 2–4.

20. Rachel Moskowitz and Drew Warwick, "The 1994–2005 Job Outlook in Brief," *Occupational Outlook Quarterly* 40, no. 1 (spring 1996): 2–41.

21. Bryan O'Reilly, "Your New Global Workforce," *Fortune* (December 14, 1992): 63.

22. Richard Crawford, *In the Era of Human Capital* (New York: Harper, 1991), p. 10.

23. Thomas Steward, "Brain Power," *Fortune* (June 3, 1991): 44.

24. Drucker, "The Coming of the New Organization," *Harvard Business Review* (January–February 1988): p. 45.

25. This discussion is based on William Berliner and William McClarney, *Management Practice and Training* (Homewood, IL: Irwin, 1974), p. 11.

26. Brian Becker and Mark Huselid, "Overview: Strategic Human Resource Management in Five Leading Firms," *Human Resource Management* 38, no. 4 (winter 1999): 287–301.

27. Charlene Marmer Solomon, "Working Smarter: How HR Can Help," *Personnel Journal* (June 1993): 54–64.

28. "Human Capital Critical to Success," *Management Review* (November 1998): 9.

29. "Human Resource Goes High-Tech: The 1999 HR Technology Conference and Exposition," *BNA Bulletin to Management* (October 14, 1999): S1–S4.

30. Bill Roberts, "HR Is Linked to Corporate Big Picture," *HRMagazine* (April 1999): 103–10.

31. Craig Morton, "What Is the EPSS Movement and What Does It Mean to Information Designers?" http://www.chesco.com/~cmarion/PCD/EPSSimplications.html.

32. Brenda Sunoo, "Certification Enhances HR's Credibility," *Workforce* (May 1999): 71–80.

33. Jennifer Laabs, "HR's Vital Role at Levi Strauss," *Personnel Journal* (December 1992): 37. For other examples, see for instance, Michael Donahue, "Do Your Human Resources Add Value?", *Management Accounting* (June 1996): 47–48.

34. See, for example, Benjamin Schneider and David Bowen, "The Service Organization: Human Resources Management Is Crucial," *Organizational Dynamics* 21, no. 4 (1993): 39–52.

35. Karl Albrecht and Ron Zemke, *Service America!* (Homewood, IL: Dow Jones-Irwin, 1985), p. 101.

36. Schneider and Bowen, "The Service Organization," p. 43.

37. Commerce Clearing House, "HR Role: Maximize the Competitive Advantage of People," *Ideas and Trends in Personnel* (August 5, 1992): 121. For additional examples, see, "Key to Success: People, People, People," *Fortune* (October 1997): 232.

38. Patrick Gunnigle and Sara Moore, "Linking Business Strategy and Human Resource Management: Issues and Implications," *Personnel Review* 23, no. 1 (1994): 63–84. See also Jopseph Martocchio, *Strategic Compensation* (Upper Saddle River, NJ: Prentice Hall, 2001), pp. 9–15

39. Arthur Thompson and A. J. Strickland, *Strategic Management* (Homewood, IL: Irwin, 1992), p. 38.

40. For a description of the need for an effective and integrated strategy see, for example, Erhard Valentin, "Anatomy of a Fatal Business Strategy," *Journal of Management Studies* 31, no. 3 (May 1994): 359–82.

41. Gunnigle and Moore, "Linking Business Strategy and Human Resource Management," p. 64.

42. Michael Porter, *Competitive Strategy* (New York: The Free Press, 1980), p. 14.

43. David Upton, "What Really Makes Factories Flexible?" *Harvard Business Review* (July/August 1995): 74–86.

44. *Ibid.*, p. 75.

45. C. K. Prahalad and Gary Hamel, "The Core Competence of a Corporation," *Harvard Business Review* (May/June 1990): 82.

46. Greer, *Strategy and Human Resources*, p. 105.

47. For a discussion see, for example, Jay Galbraith, "Positioning Human Resource as a Value-Adding Function: The Case of Rockwell International," *Human Resources Management* 31, no. 4 (winter 1992): 287–300; Augustine Lado and Mary Wilson, "Human Resource Systems and Sustained Competitive Advantage: A Competency-Based Perspective," *Academy of Management Review* 19, no. 4 (1994): 699–727; and John Delery and D. Harold Doty, "Modes of Theorizing in Strategic Human Resource Management: Tests of Universalistic, Contingency, and Configurational Performance Predictions," *Academy of Management Journal* 39, no. 4 (1996): 802–35.

48. Catherine Truss and Lynda Gratton, "Strategic Human Resource Management: A Conceptual Approach," *The International Journal of Human Resource Management* 5, no. 3 (September 1994): 663.

49. P. Wright and G. McMahan, "Theoretical Perspectives for Strategic Human Resource Management," *Journal of Management* 18, no. 2 (1992): 292; and Mark Huselid et al., "Technical and Strategic Human Resource Management Effectiveness as Determinants of Firm Performance," *Academy of Management Journal* 40, no. 1, (1997), pp. 171–88.

50. See Michael Sheppeck and Jack Militello, "Strategic HR Configurations and Organizational Performance," *Human Resource Management* 39, no. 1 (spring 2000): 5–16.

51. Although still largely nonunionized, FedEx's pilots did vote to join the Airline Pilots Union in 1995.

52. Based on Timothy Galpin and Patrick Murray, "Connect Human Resource Strategy to the Business Plan," *HRMagazine* (March 1997): 99–104.

53. For a discussion, see Peter Boxall, "Placing HR Strategy at the Heart of Business Success," *Personnel Management* 26, no. 7 (July 1994): 32–34.

54. *Ibid.*, p. 32.

55. Randall Schuler, "Human Resource Management Choices and Organizational Strategy," in Randall Schuler, S. A. Youngblood, and V. L. Huber (eds.), *Readings in Personnel and Human Resource Management*, 3rd ed. (St. Paul, MN: West, 1988).

56. For a discussion, see Truss and Gratton, "Strategic Human Resource Management," pp. 660–71.

57. *Ibid.*, p. 670.

58. For a discussion see, for example, Randall Schuler, Peter Dowling, and Helen DeCieri, "An Integrative Framework of Strategic International Human Resource Management," *Journal of Management* 19, no. 2 (1993): 419–59; Vida Scarpello, "New Paradigm Approaches in Strategic Human Resource Management," *Group and Organization*

Management 19, no. 2 (June 1994): 160–64; Sharon Peck, "Exploring the Link Between Organizational Strategy and the Employment Relationships: The Role of Human Resources Policies," *Journal of Management Studies* 31, no. 5 (September 1994): 715–36; and Mark Youndt et al., "Human Resource Management, Manufacturing Strategy, and Firm Performance," *Academy of Management Journal* 39, no. 4, (1996): 836–66.

59. William Henn, "What the Strategist Asks from Human Resources," *Human Resource Planning* 8, no. 4 (1985): 195; quoted in Greer, *Strategy and Human Resources*, pp. 117–18.

60. Greer, *Strategy and Human Resources*, p. 105.

61. *Ibid.*, p. 117.

62. Delery and Doty, "Modes of Theorizing . . ." *op. cit.*

63. Samuel Greengard, "You're Next! There's No Escaping Merger Mania!" *Workforce* (April 1997): 52–62.

64. "Human Resource Departments Fight for Their Future," *BNA Bulletin to Management* (January 25, 1996): 25.

65. *Ibid.*

66. "Core HR Functions Are Being Given Away as More Employers Join Outsourcing Trend," *BNA Bulletin to Management* (June 8, 2000): 177.

67. "Outsourcing Gains Attention," *BNA Bulletin to Management* (June 5, 1997): 180–81.

68. *Ibid.*

69. "HR's Value Measured in Terms of Strategy, CEO Says," *BNA Bulletin to Management* (April 10, 1997): 113.

70. "The Shifting Role of HR Departments," *BNA Bulletin to Management* (May 16, 1996): 1. For similar comments see, for example, Michael Donahue, "Do Your Human Resources Add Value?", *Management Accounting* (June 1996): 47–48; "HR Faces Challenge of Adding Value," *BNA Bulletin to Management* (April 24, 1997): 136; and Bernard Tyson, "Kaiser's HR Services Get a Shot in the Arm," *Personnel Journal* (September 1996): 87–90.

71. Mark Huselid, Susan Jackson, and Randall Schuler, "Technical and Strategic Human Resource Management Effectiveness as Determinants of Firm Performance," *Academy of Management Journal* 40, no. 1 (1997): 171–88.

Chapter 2

Managing Equal Opportunity and Diversity

When you finish studying this chapter, you should be able to:

■ *Summarize* the basic equal employment opportunity laws regarding age, race, sex, national origin, religion, and handicap discrimination.

■ *Explain* the basic defenses against discrimination allegations.

■ *Present* a summary of what employers can and cannot do with respect to illegal recruitment, selection, and promotion and layoff practices.

■ *Explain* the Equal Employment Opportunity Commission enforcement process.

INTRODUCTION

Hardly a day goes by without news reports of equal opportunity–related lawsuits at work: Home Depot USA agreed to pay $65 million and change its personnel practices to settle a class action suit that alleged discrimination against women in hiring for sales and management positions at its West Coast division stores.[1] Salomon Smith Barney recently offered settlements ranging from $1,000 to $100,000 to almost 2,000 current and future female employees who had filed a sexual harassment class action suit.[2] A California jury awarded $120 million in punitive damages to 17 black bakery workers in one recent case.[3] Coca-Cola recently agreed to settle a race bias suit brought by thousands of its employees.[4] Even the federal government hasn't been immune. It recently agreed to pay $508 million to a class of over 1,100 women who alleged that the Voice of America and the U.S. Information Agency had denied them jobs because of their gender.[5] Understanding and managing equal opportunity and diversity at work is a crucial management job.

The number of employment discrimination cases brought to America's federal courts has doubled in the past three years, and the number of attorneys specializing in the field has tripled since 1990.[6] No wonder almost 40% of employers responding to one survey report that they now carry employment practices liability insurance, and that understanding equal employment law is essential for all managers today.[7] In this chapter, we'll look more closely at the equal employment opportunity laws with which employers are required to comply. Then, in the following chapters, we'll turn to applying this information to activities such as recruiting.

EQUAL EMPLOYMENT OPPORTUNITY LAWS

Background

Legislation barring discrimination against members of minority groups in the United States is nothing new. For example, the Fifth Amendment to the U.S. Constitution (ratified in 1791) states that "no person shall . . . be deprived of life, liberty, or property, without due process of the law." But as a practical matter, Congress and various presidents were reluctant to take dramatic action on equal employment issues until the early 1960s. At that point, "they were finally prompted to act primarily as a result of civil unrest among the minorities and women" who eventually became protected by the new equal rights legislation and the agencies created to implement and enforce it.[8]

Title VII of the 1964 Civil Rights Act

What the Law Says **Title VII of the 1964 Civil Rights Act** was one of the first of these new laws. Title VII (as amended by the 1972 Equal Employment Opportunity Act) states that an employer cannot discriminate on the basis of race, color, religion, sex, or national origin. Specifically, it states that it shall be an unlawful employment practice for an employer:[9]

1. *To fail or refuse to hire or to discharge an individual* or otherwise to discriminate against any individual with respect to his or her compensation, terms, conditions, or privileges of employment, because of such individual's race, color, religion, sex, or national origin.
2. *To limit, segregate, or classify his or her employees or applicants for employment* in any way that would deprive or tend to deprive any individual of employment opportunities or otherwise adversely affect his or her status as an employee, because of such individual's race, color, religion, sex, or national origin.[10]

The EEOC The **Equal Employment Opportunity Commission (EEOC)** was instituted by Title VII; it consists of five members, appointed by the president with the advice and consent of the senate. Each member of the EEOC serves a term of five years.

Establishing the EEOC greatly enhanced the federal government's ability to enforce equal employment opportunity laws. The EEOC receives and investigates job discrimination complaints from aggrieved individuals. When it finds reasonable cause that the charges are justified, it attempts (through conciliation) to reach an agreement eliminating all aspects of the discrimination. If this conciliation fails, the EEOC has the power to go directly to court to enforce the law. Under the Equal Employment Opportunity Act of 1972, discrimination charges may be filed by the EEOC on behalf of an aggrieved individual, as well as by the individuals themselves. In one recent year, the EEOC won a record $307.3 million in benefits for discrimination victims.[11] This procedure is explained in more detail later in this chapter.

Executive Orders

Under executive orders issued in the Johnson administration, employers who do business with the U.S. government have an obligation beyond that imposed by Title VII to refrain from employment discrimination. Executive Orders 11246 and 11375 don't just ban discrimination; they require that contractors take **affirmative action** to ensure equal employment opportunity (we will explain affirmative action later in the chapter). All firms with contracts over $50,000 and 50 or more employees must develop and implement such programs. The orders also state a policy against employment discrimination based on age or physical handicap, in addition to race, color, religion, sex, or national origin. These orders also established the **Office of Federal Contract Compliance Programs (OFCCP)**, which is responsible for implementing the executive orders and ensuring the compliance of federal contracts. For example, the OFCCP recently reached a settlement involving Triad International Maintenance Company, an aviation contractor, which agreed to pay over $240,000 to settle claims that women and blacks were subjected to a "perversely hostile work environment," including racial slurs.[12]

Equal Pay Act of 1963

The **Equal Pay Act of 1963** (amended in 1972) made it unlawful to discriminate in pay on the basis of sex when jobs involve equal work—equivalent skills, effort, and responsibility—and are performed under similar working conditions. However, differences in pay do not violate the act if the difference is based on a seniority system, a merit system, a system that measures earnings by quantity or quality of production, or a differential based on any factor other than sex.

Age Discrimination in Employment Act of 1967

The **Age Discrimination in Employment Act (ADEA) of 1967**, as amended, made it unlawful to discriminate against employees or applicants for employment who are 40 years of age or older, effectively ending most mandatory retirement.

One-fifth of the court actions filed by the EEOC recently have been ADEA cases. (Another 30% have been sex discrimination cases.) This act is a *favored statute* among employees and lawyers because it allows jury trials and double damages to those proving "willful" discrimination.[13]

Vocational Rehabilitation Act of 1973

The **Vocational Rehabilitation Act of 1973** requires employers with federal contracts over $2,500 to take affirmative action for the employment of handicapped persons. The act does not require that an unqualified person be hired. It does require that an employer take steps to accommodate a handicapped worker unless doing so imposes an undue hardship on the employer.[14]

Vietnam Era Veterans' Readjustment Assistance Act of 1974

The provisions of the **Vietnam Era Veterans' Readjustment Act of 1974** require that employers with government contracts of $10,000 or more take affirmative action to employ and advance disabled veterans and qualified veterans of the Vietnam era. The act is administered by the OFCCP.[15]

Pregnancy Discrimination Act of 1978

Congress passed the **Pregnancy Discrimination Act (PDA)** in 1978 as an amendment to Title VII. The act broadened the definition of sex discrimination to encompass pregnancy, childbirth, or related medical conditions. It prohibits using these for discrimination in hiring, promotion, suspension or discharge, or any other term or condition of employment.[16] Basically, the act says that if an employer offers its employees disability coverage, pregnancy and childbirth must be treated like any other disability and must be included in the plan as a covered condition.[17] The U.S. Supreme Court ruled in *California Federal Savings and Loan Association* v. *Guerra* that if an employer offers no disability leave to any of its employees, it can (but need not necessarily) grant pregnancy leave to a woman who requests it when disabled for pregnancy, childbirth, or a related medical condition, although men get no comparable benefits.[18]

Federal Agency Guidelines

The federal agencies charged with ensuring compliance with the aforementioned laws and executive orders issue their own implementing guidelines. The overall purpose of these **federal agency guidelines** is to specify the procedures these agencies recommend employers follow in complying with the equal opportunity laws.

Uniform Guidelines on Employee Selection Procedures   Detailed guidelines to be used by employers have been approved by the EEOC, Civil Service Commission, Department of Labor, and Department of Justice.[19] These uniform guidelines supersede earlier guidelines developed by the EEOC alone. They set forth "highly recommended" procedures regarding such matters as employee selection, record keeping, preemployment inquiries, and affirmative action programs. As an example, the guidelines specify that any employment selection devices (including but not limited to written tests) that screen out disproportionate numbers of women or minorities must be *validated.* The guidelines also explain in detail *how* an employer can validate a selection device. (This procedure is explained in Chapter 5.) The OFCCP has its own *Manual of Guidelines.*[20]

The American Psychological Association has published the latest *Standards for Educational and Psychological Testing*, and many experts expect that this document, which represents a consensus among testing authorities, "will be used in court to help judges resolve disagreements about the quality of . . . validity studies that arise during litigation."[21]

EEOC Guidelines   The EEOC and other agencies also periodically issue updated guidelines clarifying and revising their positions on matters such as *national origin discrimination* and *sexual harassment.*[22] For instance, the EEOC issued guidelines on the 1991 Civil Rights Act, the Americans with Disabilities Act, and sexual harassment.[23]

Historically, these guidelines have fleshed out the procedures to be used in complying with equal employment laws. For example, recall that the ADEA prohibited employers from discriminating against persons over 40 years old because of age. Subsequent EEOC guidelines stated that it was unlawful to discriminate in hiring (or in any way) by giving preference because of age to individuals within the 40-plus age bracket. Thus, if two people apply for the same job, and one is 45 and the other is 55, you may not lawfully turn down the 55-year-old candidate because of his or her age and expect to defend yourself by saying that you hired someone over 40.[24] (However, hiring, say, a 53-year-old, may be defensible.)

Sexual Harassment

The EEOC's guidelines on **sexual harassment** state that employers have an affirmative duty to maintain a workplace free of sexual harassment and intimidation.[25] Harassment on the basis of sex is a violation of Title VII when such conduct has the purpose or effect of substantially interfering with a person's work performance or creating an intimidating, hostile, or offensive work environment. The Civil Rights Act of 1991 added teeth to this by permitting victims of intentional discrimination, including sexual harassment, to have jury trials and to collect compensatory damages for pain and suffering and punitive damages in cases in which the employer acted with "malice or reckless indifference" to the individual's rights.[26]

The **Federal Violence Against Women Act of 1994** provides another avenue women can use to seek relief for violent sexual harassment. It provides that a person "who commits a crime of violence motivated by gender and thus deprives another" of her rights shall be liable to the party injured. In 1998, a female administrative assistant successfully sued under this act when an officer of her corporate employer became verbally abusive and his requests for sex became "increasingly threatening."[27]

The EEOC guidelines define sexual harassment as:

> unwelcome sexual advances, requests for sexual favors, and other verbal or physical conduct of a sexual nature that takes place under any of the following conditions:
>
> 1. Submission to such conduct is made either explicitly or implicitly a term or condition of an individual's employment.
> 2. Submission to or rejection of such conduct by an individual is used as the basis for employment decisions affecting such individual.

3. Such conduct has the purpose or effect of unreasonably interfering with an individual's work performance or creating an intimidating, hostile, or offensive work environment.[28]

Based on one recent U.S. Supreme Court decision, sexual harassment does not apply solely to relations between males and females: Employees can file discrimination suits claiming sexual harassment by people of their own sex.[29] (In this particular case, a worker on an offshore oil rig claimed that his male supervisors restrained him several times while another worker harassed him and that he ultimately had to quit out of fear of being raped.)

Two 1998 U.S. Supreme Court decisions have further clarified the law on sexual harassment. The decisions will make some harassment lawsuits against employers easier to win and limit the exposure of those employers who take steps to have in place anti-harassment policies.[30]

In the first case, *Burlington Industries* v. *Ellerth*, the employee accused her supervisor of *quid pro quo* harassment. She said she was propositioned by her boss and threatened with demotion if she did not respond. The threats were not carried out, and she was in fact promoted. In the second case, *Faragher* v. *City of Boca Raton*, the employee accused the employer of condoning a hostile work environment: She said she quit her lifeguard job after repeated taunts from other lifeguards. The Court ruled in favor of the employees in both cases.

The Court's decisions have several important consequences for employers. They make it clear that in a *quid pro quo* case (explained in more detail next) it is *not* necessary for the employee to have suffered a tangible job action (such as being demoted) to win the case. Furthermore, the Court spelled out an important defense against harassment suits: The employer must show that it took "reasonable care" to prevent and promptly correct any sexually harassing behavior and that the employee unreasonably failed to take advantage of the employer's policy.

How can an employer help minimize its liability for such suits? To show reasonable care, it is crucial that the employer have a policy against sexual harassment, including a publicized and effective complaint procedure that all employees are aware of and can take advantage of. Furthermore, if the employer knows (or should reasonably know) that harassment is occurring, it should take immediate steps to stop it.

There are three main ways an employee can prove sexual harassment.

Quid Pro Quo   The most direct way an employee can prove sexual harassment is to prove that rejecting a supervisor's advances adversely affected the employee's tangible benefits, such as raises or promotions. For example, in one case the employee was able to show that continued job success and advancement were dependent on her agreeing to the sexual demands of her supervisors. She showed that after an initial complaint to her employer she was subjected to adverse performance evaluations, disciplinary layoffs, and other adverse actions.[31]

Hostile Environment Created by Supervisors   It is not always necessary to show that the harassment had tangible consequences such as a demotion or termination. For example, in one case the court found that a male supervisor's sexual harassment had substantially affected a female employee's emotional and psychological ability to the point that she felt she had to quit her job. Therefore, even though no direct threats or promises were made in exchange for sexual advances, the fact that the advances interfered with the woman's performance and created an offensive work environment were enough to prove that sexual harassment had occurred. On the other hand, the courts do not interpret as sexual harassment any sexual relationships that arise during the course of employment but that do not have a substantial effect on that employment.[32] In a recent decision, for instance, the U.S. Supreme Court held that sexual harassment law doesn't cover ordinary "intersexual flirtation." In his ruling, Justice Antonin Scalia said courts must carefully distinguish between "simple teasing" and truly abusive behavior.[33]

Hostile Environment Created by Co-workers or Nonemployees Advances do not have to be made by the person's supervisor to qualify as sexual harassment: An employee's co-workers (or even the employer's customers) can cause the employer to be held responsible for sexual harassment. In one case, the court held that a sexually provocative uniform the employer required led to lewd comments and innuendos by customers toward the employee; when she complained that she would no longer wear the uniform, she was fired. Because the employer could not show that there was a job-related necessity for requiring such a uniform and because the uniform was required only for female employees, the court ruled that the employer, in effect, was responsible for the sexually harassing behavior. EEOC guidelines also state that an employer is liable for the sexually harassing acts of its nonsupervisor employees if the employer knew or should have known of the harassing conduct.

What the Employer Should Do As summarized in the *HR in Practice* box, employers can take steps (such as issuing a strong policy statement) to minimize liability if a sexual harassment claim is filed against the organization and to prevent such claims from arising in the first place.

What the Employee Can Do Any employee who believes he or she has been sexually harassed can also take several steps to address the problem.

The steps to take are based in part on how courts define sexual harassment. For example, "hostile environment" sexual harassment generally means the workplace was permeated with discriminatory intimidation, ridicule, and insult sufficiently severe or pervasive to alter the conditions of employment. Courts in these cases look at such things as whether the discriminatory conduct is frequent or severe; whether it is physically threatening or humiliating, or a mere offensive utterance; and whether it unreasonably interferes with an employee's work performance.[34] In turn, whether an employee subjectively perceives the work environment as abusive is related to such things as whether the employee welcomed the conduct or immediately made it clear that the conduct was unwelcome, undesirable, or offensive.[35] The steps an employee can take include:

1. File a verbal contemporaneous complaint or protest with the harasser and the harasser's boss stating that the unwanted overtures should cease because the conduct is unwelcome.
2. Write a letter to the accused. This may be a polite, low-key letter that does three things: provides a detailed statement of the facts as the writer sees them; describes his or her feelings and what damage the writer thinks has been done; and states that he or she would like to request that the future relationship be on a purely professional basis. This letter should be delivered in person, with a witness if necessary.

What Employers Should Do to Minimize Liability in Sexual Harassment Claims

1. Take all complaints about harassment seriously. As one sexual harassment manual for managers and supervisors advises, "When confronted with sexual harassment complaints or when sexual conduct is observed in the workplace, the best reaction is to address the complaint or stop the conduct."[36] If complaints are not taken seriously, or it's risky to complain, or perpetrators are unlikely to be punished, then the firm's employees are likely to experience considerably higher levels of harassment.[37]

2. Issue a strong policy statement condemning such behavior. The EEOC's standards today say an effective anti-harassment policy should contain: a clear explanation of the prohibited conduct; assurance of protection against retaliation for employees who make complaints or provide information related to such complaints; a clearly described complaint process that provides confidentiality and accessible avenues of complaint as well as prompt, thorough, and impartial investigations; and clear assurance that the employer will take immediate and appropriate corrective action where harassment has occurred.[38] An example, presented in Figure 2.1, states, for example, that "such behavior may result in . . . dismissal."

3. Inform all employees about the policy prohibiting sexual harassment and of their rights under the policy.

4. Develop and implement a complaint procedure.

5. Establish a management response system that includes an immediate reaction and investigation by senior management. The likelihood of employer liability is lessened considerably when the employer's response is "adequate" and "reasonably calculated to prevent future harassment."[39]

6. Begin management training sessions with supervisors and managers to increase their awareness of the issues.

7. Discipline managers and employees involved in sexual harassment.

8. Keep thorough records of complaints, investigations, and actions taken.

9. Conduct exit interviews that uncover any complaints and that acknowledge by signature the reasons for leaving.

10. Republish the sexual harassment policy periodically.

11. Encourage upward communication through periodic written attitude surveys, hot lines, suggestions boxes, and other feedback procedures to discover employees' feelings concerning any evidence of sexual harassment and to keep management informed.[40]

The company's position is that sexual harassment is a form of misconduct that undermines the integrity of the employment relationship. No employee—either male or female—should be subject to unsolicited and unwelcome sexual overtures or conduct, either verbal or physical. Sexual harassment does not refer to occasional compliments of a socially accepted nature. It refers to behavior that is not welcome, that is personally offensive, that debilitates morale, and that, therefore, interferes with work effectiveness. Such behavior may result in disciplinary action up to and including dismissal.

FIGURE 2.1 Sample Sexual Harassment Policy

Source: © 1991 by CCH Incorporated. All Rights Reserved. Reprinted with permission from *Sexual Harassment Manual for Managers and Supervisors.*

3. If the unwelcome conduct does not cease, file verbal and written reports regarding the unwelcome conduct and unsuccessful efforts to get it to stop with the harasser's manager and/or the human resource director.
4. If the letters and appeals to the employer do not suffice, the accuser should turn to the local office of the EEOC to file the necessary claim.
5. The employee can also consult an attorney about suing the harasser for assault and battery, intentional infliction of emotional distress, and injunctive relief and to recover compensatory and punitive damages if the harassment is of a serious nature.

Selected Court Decisions Regarding Equal Employment Opportunity

Several early court decisions helped to form the interpretive foundation for EEO laws such as those involving sexual harassment. Some important decisions are summarized in this section.

Griggs **v.** *Duke Power Company*　*Griggs* (1971) was a landmark case because the Supreme Court used it to define unfair discrimination. In this case, a suit was brought against the Duke Power Company on behalf of Willie Griggs, an applicant for a job as a coal handler. The company required its coal handlers to be high school graduates. Griggs claimed that this requirement was illegally discriminatory because it wasn't related to success on the job and because it resulted in more blacks than whites being rejected for these jobs.

Griggs won the case. The decision of the Court was unanimous, and in his written opinion Chief Justice Burger laid out three crucial guidelines affecting equal employment legislation. First, the Court ruled that discrimination on the part of the employer need not be overt; in other words, the employer does not have to be shown to have intentionally discriminated against the employee or applicant—it need only be shown that discrimination took place. Second, the court held that an employment practice (in this case requiring the high school diploma) must be shown to be *job related* if it has an unequal impact on members of a **protected class**. In the words of Justice Burger:

> The act proscribes not only overt discrimination but also practices that are fair in form, but discriminatory in operation. The touchstone is business necessity. If an employment practice which operates to exclude Negroes cannot be shown to be related to job performance the practice is prohibited.[41]

Third, Burger's opinion clearly placed the burden of proof on the employer to show that the hiring practice is job related. Thus, the *employer* must show that the employment practice (in this case, requiring a high school diploma) is needed to perform the job satisfactorily if it has a disparate impact on (unintentionally discriminates against) members of a protected class.

Albemarle Paper Company **v.** *Moody*　In the *Griggs* case, the Supreme Court decided that a screening tool (such as a test) had to be job related or valid—that is, performance on the test must be related to performance on the job. The 1975 *Albemarle* case is important because the Court provided more details regarding how an employer should validate its screening tools—in other words, how it should prove that the test or other screening tools are related to or predict performance on the job.[42] In the *Albemarle* case the Court emphasized that if a test is to be used to screen candidates for a job, then the nature of that job—its specific duties and responsibilities—must first be carefully analyzed and documented. Similarly, the Court ruled that the performance standards for employees on the job in question should be clear and unambiguous, so the employer could intelligently identify which employees were performing better than others.

In arriving at its decision, the Court also cited the EEOC guidelines concerning acceptable selection procedures and made these guidelines the "law of the land."[43] Specifically, the Court's ruling had the effect of establishing the detailed EEOC (now federal) guidelines on validation as the procedures for validating employment practices.[44]

The Civil Rights Act of 1991

Subsequent Supreme Court rulings in the 1980s (such as **Wards Cove Packing Company v. Atonio**, which involved packing employees in Alaska) had the effect of limiting the protection of women and minority groups under equal employment laws; this prompted congress to pass a new Civil Rights Act. The **Civil Rights Act of 1991 (CRA 1991)** was signed into law by President Bush in November 1991. The effect of CRA 1991 was to reverse several decisions (including *Wards Cove*). In fact, the effect was not just to roll back the clock to where it stood prior to these Supreme Court decisions. The effect was to add legislation that makes it even more important that employers and their managers and supervisors adhere to both the spirit and the letter of EEO law. We summarize some of the act's main provisions in the following sections.

Burden of Proof (*Wards Cove*)

Prior to *Wards Cove*, the equal employment litigation process basically went like this: The plaintiff (say, a rejected applicant) had to demonstrate that an employment practice (such as a test) had a disparate or adverse impact on a particular group. For example, a requirement that employees be able to lift heavy weights might unintentionally discriminate against women.[45] Then, once the plaintiff showed such disparate impact, the *employer* had to show that the challenged practice was job related for the position in question. For example, the employer had to show that the "lift heavy weights" requirement was actually required for the position in question, and that the business could not run efficiently without the requirement. In *Wards Cove*, the Supreme Court said that the burden of proof was no longer on the employer to prove that the requirement (lifting heavy weights) was a business necessity. The employer had to show only a business justification, and then the burden shifted back to the plaintiff. The latter then had to prove that the requirement was put in to intentionally discriminate against the members of his or her minority group. This was difficult for plaintiffs to do.

The Civil Rights Act of 1991 rejects the Court's position and turns the EEO clock back to where it was prior to *Wards Cove* with respect to this matter. With the passage of CRA 1991, the burden is once again on the employer to demonstrate business necessity, not merely business justification.

Money Damages Section 102 of the 1991 Civil Rights Act provides that an employee who is claiming *intentional discrimination* can ask for (1) compensatory damages and (2) punitive damages, if it can be shown the employer engaged in discrimination "with malice or reckless indifference to the federally protected rights of an aggrieved individual."[46] (See also the *Global Issues in HR* box.)

This is a marked change from the conditions that prevailed until 1991. Victims of intentional discrimination who had not suffered financial loss and who sued under Title VII could not then sue for compensatory or punitive damages. All they could expect was to have their jobs reinstated (or be awarded a particular job). They were also eligible for back pay, attorney's fees, and court costs.

Finally, the Civil Rights Act of 1991 states that:

> An unlawful employment practice is established when the complaining party demonstrates that race, color, religion, sex, or national origin was a motivating factor for any employment practice, even though other factors also motivated the practice.[47]

In other words, an employer cannot avoid liability by proving it would have taken the same action—such as terminating someone—even without the discriminatory motive.[48] If there is any such motive, the practice may be unlawful.

The Americans with Disabilities Act

The **Americans with Disabilities Act (ADA)** aims to reduce or eliminate serious problems of discrimination against disabled individuals. The Senate Committee on Labor and Human Resources estimated that 43 million U.S. workers have some type of disability and that two-thirds of those between the ages of 16 and 64 are unemployed although they want to work. Testimonials such as those of a severely arthritic woman who was refused employment by a college because a trustee thought "normal students shouldn't see her" and a blind Harvard law school student who was rejected for employment three different times from each of 600 corporations convinced lawmakers of the need for the ADA.[49]

The act prohibits employers from discriminating against qualified disabled individuals. It also says employers must make "reasonable accommodations" for physical or mental limitations unless doing so imposes an "undue hardship" on the business.

The definitions of the act's pivotal terms are important in understanding its impact. For example, specific disabilities aren't listed; instead, the EEOC's implementing regulations provide that an individual is disabled if he or she has a physical or mental impairment that substantially limits one or more major life activities. They also provide that an impairment includes any physiological disorder or condition, cosmetic disfigurement, or anatomical loss affecting one or more of several body systems, or any mental or psychological disorder.[50] On the other hand, the act sets forth certain conditions that are not to be regarded as disabilities, including homosexuality, bisexuality, voyeurism, compulsive gambling, pyromania, and certain disorders resulting from the person's currently using illegal drugs.[51]

Simply being disabled doesn't qualify someone for a job, of course. Instead, the act prohibits discrimination against qualified individuals—those who, with (or without) a reasonable accommodation, can carry out the essential functions of the job. This means that the individual must have the requisite skills, educational background, and experience to do the essential functions of the position. A job function is essential

Enforcing the 1991 Civil Rights Act Abroad

The 1991 Civil Rights Act marked a substantial change in the geographic applicability of equal rights legislation. Congressional legislation generally only applies within U.S. territorial borders unless specifically stated otherwise.[52] However, CRA 1991 specifically expanded coverage by amending the definition of *employee* in Title VII to mean a U.S. citizen employed in a foreign country by a U.S.-owned or -controlled company.[53] At least theoretically, therefore, U.S. citizens now working overseas for U.S. companies enjoy the same equal employment opportunity protection as those working within U.S. borders.[54]

Two factors limit the wholesale application of CRA 1991 to U.S. employees abroad, however. First, the civil rights protections are not universal or automatic because there are numerous exclusions. For example, an employer need not comply with Title VII if compliance would cause the employer to violate the law of the host country. (For instance, some foreign countries have statutes prohibiting the employment of women in management positions.)

A more vexing problem is the practical difficulty of enforcing CRA 1991 abroad. For example, the EEOC investigator's first duty in an extraterritorial case is to analyze the finances and organizational structure of the respondent, but in practice few, if any, investigators are trained for this duty and no precise standards exist for such investigations.[55] Similarly, one expert has argued that U.S. courts are "little help in overseas investigations, because few foreign nations cooperate with the intrusive enforcement of U.S. civil law."[56] It is possible, therefore, that in this case CRA 1991's bark will be considerably worst than its bite and that, as one expert says, "Congress' well-meaning effort to leave no American uncovered by U.S. antidiscrimination law will not have its intended effect."[57]

when, for instance, it is the reason the position exists, or because the function is so highly specialized that the person doing the job is hired for his or her expertise or ability to perform that particular function.

If the individual can't perform the job as currently structured, the employer is required to make a reasonable accommodation unless doing so would present an undue hardship. *Reasonable accommodation* might include redesigning the job, modifying work schedules, or modifying or acquiring equipment or other devices to assist the person in performing the job. Court cases illustrate what "reasonable accommodation" means. An employee who worked as a door greeter at a Wal-Mart store was diagnosed with and treated for back problems. When she returned to work she asked her employer if she could sit on a stool while on duty and the employer rejected her request, contending that standing was an essential part of the greeter's job. She sued, but the federal district court agreed with the employer that the door greeters must act in an "aggressively hospitable manner," which can't be done sitting on a stool.[58]

In another case, the court held that the employer did not discriminate against a blind bartender by requiring her to transfer to another job because she was unable to spot underage or intoxicated customers.[59] On the other hand, one U.S. Circuit Court of Appeals held that punctuality was not an essential job function for a laboratory assistant who was habitually tardy; the court decided he could perform the job's 7½ hours of data entry even if he arrived late.[60] In another case, an employee argued that her depression-related sleeping on the job qualified as a disability and that she should not have been fired; the U.S. Court of Appeals disagreed, saying the sleeping difficulties were only sporadic.[61] HIV-positive individuals are generally considered ADA disabled, whether or not they are symptomatic.[62]

Legal Obligations Related to the ADA   The ADA imposes numerous legal obligations on employers. These include (but are not limited to) the following:

- Employers may not make preemployment inquiries about a person's disability, although employers may ask questions about the person's ability to perform specific job functions.
- Employers should review job application forms, interview procedures, and job descriptions and in particular identify the essential functions of the jobs in question.
- Employers must make a reasonable accommodation unless doing so would result in undue hardship.

ADA complaints are flooding the EEOC and the courts. However, the chances of prevailing in ADA cases are against the plaintiff: employers prevailed in almost 96% of federal circuit court decisions in one recent year.[63] Employees are failing to show that they are disabled and qualified to do the job.[64] One expert points out that just because an employee has a disability does not mean that he or she is protected under the ADA. Instead, employers should ask questions such as Does the employee have a disability that substantially limits a major life activity? Is the employee qualified to do the job? Can the employee perform the essential functions of the job? Can any reasonable accommodation be provided without creating an undue hardship on the employer? An impairment must be permanent or of significant duration, says another expert, to be qualified as an ADA disability.[65]

For example, the U.S. Supreme Court recently decided (*Murphy* v. *United Parcel Service*) that a person whose disability was mitigated by medication could not claim a disability as a limitation if he had not taken his medication.[66] In light of recent U.S. Supreme Court decisions, one expert advises "don't treat employees as if they are disabled." If they can control their conditions (for instance, through medication), they usually won't be considered disabled. However, if they are treated as disabled by their employers (for instance, with respect to the jobs they're assigned), they'll normally be "regarded as" disabled and protected under the ADA.[67]

State and Local Equal Employment Opportunity Laws

In addition to the federal laws, all states and many local governments also prohibit employment discrimination.

In most cases, the effect of the state and local laws is to further restrict employers regarding their treatment of job applicants and employees. In many cases, state equal employment opportunity laws cover employers that are not covered by federal legislation (such as those with fewer than 15 employees).[68] Similarly, some local governments extend the protection of age discrimination laws to young people as well, barring discrimination not only of those over 40, but those over 17 as well; for instance, it would be illegal to advertise for "mature" applicants because that might discourage some teenagers from applying. The point is that many actions that might be legal under federal laws are illegal under state and local laws.[69]

State and local equal employment opportunity agencies (often called human resources commissions, commissions on human relations, or fair employment commissions) play a role in the equal employment compliance process. When the EEOC receives a discrimination charge, it usually defers it for a limited time to the state and local agencies that have comparable jurisdiction. Then, if satisfactory remedies are not achieved, the charges are referred back to the EEOC for resolution.

Summary

Selected equal employment opportunity legislation, executive orders, and agency guidelines are summarized in Table 2.1.

DEFENSES AGAINST DISCRIMINATION ALLEGATIONS

What Is Adverse Impact?

Adverse impact plays a central role in discriminatory practice allegations. Under the Civil Rights Act of 1991, a person who believes he or she has been unintentionally discriminated against need only establish a prima facie case of discrimination; this means showing that the employer's selection procedures had an adverse impact on a protected minority group. *Adverse impact* "refers to the total employment process that results in a significantly higher percentage of a protected group in the candidate population being rejected for employment, placement, or promotion."[70]

What does this mean? If a minority or other protected group applicant for the job feels he or she has been discriminated against, the applicant need only show that the selection procedures resulted in an adverse impact on his or her minority group. (There are several ways to do this, for example, by showing that 80% of the white applicants passed the test, but only 20% of the black applicants passed; if this is the case, a black applicant has a prima facie case proving adverse impact.) Then, once the employee has proved his or her point, the burden of proof shifts to the employer. It becomes the employer's task to prove that its test, application blank, interview, or the like, is a valid predictor of performance on the job (and that it was applied fairly and equitably to both minorities and nonminorities).

Discrimination law distinguishes between disparate *treatment* and disparate *impact*. *Disparate treatment* "requires no more than a finding that women (or protected minority group members) were intentionally treated differently . . . because of their gender," according to a recent appeals court decision. *Disparate impact* claims do not require proof of discriminatory intentions. Instead, the plaintiff must show that there's a significant disparity between the proportion of (say) women in the available labor pool and the proportion hired, and that there's an apparently neutral employment practice (such as word-of-mouth advertising) that is causing the disparity.[71]

Bringing a Case of Discrimination: Summary   Assume that an employer turns down a member of a protected group for a job based on a test score (or some other

TABLE 2.1   Summary of Important Equal Employment Opportunity Actions

Action	What It Does
Title VII of 1964 Civil Rights Act, as amended	Bars discrimination because of race, color, religion, sex, or national origin; instituted EEOC
Executive orders	Prohibit employment discrimination by employers with federal contracts of more than $10,000 (and their subcontractors); establish office of federal compliance; require affirmative action programs
Federal agency guidelines	Indicate policy covering discrimination based on sex, national origin, and religion, as well as employee selection procedures; for example, require validation of tests
Supreme Court decisions: *Griggs* v. *Duke Power Co.*, *Albemarle* v. *Moody*	Rule that job requirements must be related to job success; that discrimination need not be overt to be proved; that the burden of proof is on the employer to prove the qualification is valid
Equal Pay Act of 1963	Requires equal pay for men and women for performing similar work
Age Discrimination in Employment Act of 1967	Prohibits discriminating against a person 40 or over in any area of employment because of age
State and local laws	Often cover organizations too small to be covered by federal laws
Vocational Rehabilitation Act of 1973	Requires affirmative action to employ and promote qualified handicapped persons and prohibits discrimination against handicapped persons
Pregnancy Discrimination Act of 1978	Prohibits discrimination in employment against pregnant women, or related conditions
Vietnam Era Veterans' Readjustment Assistance Act of 1974	Requires affirmative action in employment for veterans of the Vietnam War era
Wards Cove v. *Atonio*, *Patterson* v. *McLean Credit Union*	Made it more difficult to prove a case of unlawful discrimination against an employer
Martin v. *Wilks*	Allowed consent degrees to be attacked and could have had a chilling effect on certain affirmative action programs
Americans with Disabilities Act of 1990	Strengthens the need for most employers to make reasonable accommodations for disabled employees at work; prohibits discrimination
Civil Rights Act of 1991	Reverses *Wards Cove, Patterson,* and *Martin* decisions; places burden of proof back on employer and permits compensatory and punitive money damages for discrimination

employment practice, such as interview questions or application blank responses). Further assume that the person believes that he or she was discriminated against due to being in a protected class and decides to sue the employer.

All he or she has to do is show that the employer's test had an adverse impact on members of his or her minority group. Once the person has shown the existence of adverse impact to the satisfaction of the court, the burden of proof shifts to the employer, who then has to defend against the charges of discrimination.

There are then basically two defenses that the employer can use: the bona fide occupational qualification (BFOQ) defense and the business necessity defense. Either can be used to justify an employment practice that has been shown to have an adverse impact on the members of a minority group.[72] (A third defense is that the decision was made on the basis of legitimate nondiscriminatory reasons, such as poor performance, having nothing to do with the alleged prohibited discrimination.)

Bona Fide Occupational Qualification

One approach an employer can use to defend against charges of discrimination is to claim that the employment practice is a **bona fide occupational qualification (BFOQ)** for performing the job. Specifically, Title VII provides that:

> it should not be an unlawful employment practice for an employer to hire an employee . . . on the basis of religion, sex, or national origin in those certain instances where religion, sex, or national origin is a bona fide occupational qualification reasonably necessary to the normal operation of that particular business or enterprise.

For example, age is a BFOQ when federal requirements impose a compulsory age limit, such as when the Federal Aviation Agency sets a ceiling of age 64 for pilots. Actors required for youthful or elderly roles or persons used to advertise or promote the sales of products designed for youthful or elderly consumers suggest other instances when age may be a BFOQ. As another example, a bus line's maximum-age hiring policy for bus drivers has been held to be a BFOQ by the courts. The court said that the essence of the business is safe transportation of passengers, and given that, the employer should strive to employ the most qualified persons available.[73] Yet Supreme Court decisions such as *Western Airlines, Inc.* v. *Criswell* seem to be narrowing BFOQ exceptions under ADEA. In this case the Court held that the airline could not impose a mandatory retirement age (of 60) for flight engineers, even though they could for pilots.

Business Necessity

The **business necessity** defense requires showing that there is an overriding business purpose for the discriminatory practice and that the practice is therefore acceptable.

It's not easy to prove that a practice is a business necessity.[74] The Supreme Court has made it clear that business necessity does not encompass such matters as avoiding inconvenience, annoyance, or expense to the employer. The Second Circuit Court of appeals held that business necessity means an "irresistible demand" and that to be retained the practice "must not only directly foster safety and efficiency" but also be essential to these goals.[75] Similarly, another court held that:

> The test is whether there exists an overriding legitimate business purpose such that the practice is necessary to the safe and efficient operation of a business; thus, the business purpose must be sufficiently compelling to override any racial impact; and the challenged practice must effectively carry out the business purpose it is alleged to serve.[76]

Thus, it is not easy to prove that a practice is required for business necessity. For example, an employer cannot generally discharge employees whose wages have been garnished merely because garnishment (requiring the employer to divert part of the person's wages to pay his or her debts) creates an inconvenience for the employer. On the other hand, the business necessity defense has been used successfully by many employers. Thus, in *Spurlock* v. *United Airlines,* a minority candidate sued United Airlines, stating that its requirements that a pilot candidate have 500 flight hours and a college degree were unfairly discriminatory. The Court agreed that these requirements did have an adverse impact on members of the person's minority group. However, the Court held that in light of the cost of the training program and the tremendous human and economic risks involved in hiring unqualified candidates, the selection standards were required by business necessity and were job related.[77]

Attempts by employers to show that their selection tests or other employment practices are valid represent one example of the business necessity defense: The employer is required to show that the test or other practice is job related—in other words, that it is a valid predictor of performance on the job. Where such validity can be established, the courts have often supported the use of the test or other employment practice as a business necessity. Used in this context, the word *validity* means the degree to which the test or other employment practice is related to or predicts performance on the job; validation is discussed in Chapter 4.

ILLUSTRATIVE DISCRIMINATORY EMPLOYMENT PRACTICES

A Note on What You Can and Cannot Do

Before proceeding, we should clarify what federal fair employment laws allow and do not allow you to say and do. Most federal laws, such as Title VII, do not expressly ban preemployment questions about an applicant's race, color, religion, sex, age, or national origin. In other words:

> With the exception of personnel policies calling for outright discrimination against the members of some protected group, it is not really the intrinsic nature of an employer's personnel policies or practices that the courts object to. Instead, it is the result of applying a policy or practice in a particular way or in a particular context that leads to an adverse impact on some protected group.[78]

For example, it is not illegal to ask a job candidate about her marital status (although at first glance such a question might seem discriminatory). You can ask such a question as long as you can show either that you do not discriminate or that the practice can be defended as a BFOQ or business necessity.

In other words, inquiries and practices such as those summarized on the next few pages are not illegal per se. But, in practice, there are two good reasons most employers avoid such questionable practices. First, although federal law may not bar asking such questions, many state and local laws do. Second, the EEOC has said that it disapproves of such practices as asking women their marital status or applicants their age. Therefore, simply asking such questions may raise a red flag that draws the attention of the EEOC and other regulatory agencies. Employers who use such practices thus increase their chances of having to defend themselves against charges of discriminatory employment practices.

Recruitment

Word of Mouth   You cannot rely on word-of-mouth dissemination of information about job opportunities when your workforce is all (or substantially all) white or all members of some other class such as all female, all Hispanic, and so on. Doing so might reduce the likelihood that others will become aware of the jobs and thus apply for them.

Misleading Information   It is unlawful to give false or misleading information to members of any group or to fail to refuse to advise them of work opportunities and the procedures for obtaining them.

Help Wanted Ads   "Help wanted—male" and "Help wanted—female" advertising classifieds are violations of laws forbidding sex discrimination in employment unless sex is a BFOQ for the job advertised.[79] Also, you cannot advertise in any way that suggests that applicants are being discriminated against because of their age. For example, you cannot advertise for a "young" man or woman.

Selection Standards

Educational Requirements   An educational requirement may be held illegal when (1) it can be shown that minority groups are less likely to possess the educational qualifications (such as a high school diploma), and (2) such qualifications are also not job related. For example, in the *Griggs* v. *Duke Power Company* case, a high school diploma was found both unnecessary for job performance and discriminatory against blacks. Unnecessary prerequisites (such as requiring a high school diploma where one is not required to perform the job) reportedly remains a problem today.[80]

Tests   According to former Chief Justice Burger:

> Nothing in the [Title VII] act precludes the use of testing or measuring procedures; obviously they are useful. What Congress has forbidden is giving these devices and mechanisms controlling force *unless they are demonstrating a reasonable measure of job performance.*

Tests that disproportionately screen out minorities or women and are not job related are deemed unlawful by the courts. But remember that a test or other selection standard that screens out a disproportionate number of minorities or women is not *by itself* sufficient to prove that the test *unfairly* discriminates. It must also be shown that the tests or other screening devices are not job related.

Preference to Relatives   You cannot give preference to relatives of your current employees with respect to employment opportunities if your current employees are substantially nonminority.

Height, Weight, and Physical Characteristics   Maximum weight rules for employees don't usually trigger adverse legal rulings. However, some minority groups have a higher incidence of obesity, so employers must ensure that their weight rules aren't adversely impacting those groups. Similarly, "few applicants or employees will be able to demonstrate an actual weight-based disability" (in other words, that they are 100% above their ideal weight or there is a physiological cause for their disability). Few are thus entitled to reasonable accommodations under the ADA. In practice, however, studies do suggest that employers may treat overweight female applicants and employees to their disadvantage, and this needs to be closely monitored.[81]

American Airlines was recently sued by the EEOC, allegedly for asking questions about an applicant's medical history and medical condition before he was hired. Under the ADA, "employers are generally prohibited from asking questions about applicants' medical history or requiring pre-employment physical examinations." However, such questions and exams can be used once the job offer has been extended to determine that the applicant can safely perform the job.[82]

Arrest Records You cannot ask about or use a person's arrest record to disqualify him or her automatically for a position because there is always a presumption of innocence until proof of guilt. In addition, arrest records in general have not been shown valid for predicting job performance, and a higher percentage of minorities than nonminorities have been arrested.

Application Forms Employment applications generally shouldn't contain questions pertaining, for instance, to applicants' disabilities, workers' compensation history, age, arrest record, or U.S. citizenship. Personal information required for legitimate tax or benefit reasons (such as who to contact in case of emergency) are best collected after the person has been hired.[83]

Sample Discriminatory Promotion, Transfer, and Layoff Procedures

Fair employment laws protect not just job applicants but current employees as well.[84] Therefore, any employment practices regarding pay, promotion, termination, discipline, or benefits that (1) are applied differently to different classes of persons; (2) have the effect of adversely affecting members of a protected group; and (3) cannot be shown to be required as a BFOQ or business necessity may be held to be illegally discriminatory. For example, the EEOC recently issued a new enforcement guidance making it clear that employers are not allowed to discriminate against employees in connection with their benefits plans.[85]

THE EEOC ENFORCEMENT PROCESS

Processing a Charge

What happens if a person decides to file an EEOC complaint? There are several steps involved.[86] Under CRA 1991, the charge itself must generally be filed within two years after the alleged unlawful practice took place. This charge must be filed in writing and under oath, by (or on behalf of) either the person claiming to be aggrieved or a member of the EEOC who has reasonable cause to believe that a violation occurred. In practice, though, a person's charge to the EEOC is often first deferred to the relevant state or local regulatory agency; if the latter waives jurisdiction or cannot obtain a satisfactory solution to the charge, it is referred back to the EEOC.

After a charge has been filed (or the state or local deferral period has ended), the EEOC has 10 days to serve notice of the charge on the employer. The EEOC then investigates the charge to determine whether there is reasonable cause to believe it is true; it is expected to make this determination within 120 days. If no reasonable cause is found, the EEOC must dismiss the charge, in which case the person who filed the charge has 90 days to file a suit on his or her own behalf. If reasonable cause for the charge is found, the EEOC must attempt to conciliate. If this conciliation is not satisfactory, the EEOC may bring a civil suit in a federal district court or issue a notice of right to sue to the person who filed the charge. Figure 2.2 summarizes important questions an employer should ask after receiving notice from the EEOC that a bias complaint has been filed.

Today, the EEOC refers about 10% of its charges to a voluntary mediation mechanism. If the plaintiff agrees to mediation, the employer is asked to participate. A mediation session usually lasts up to four hours. If no agreement is reached or one of the parties rejects participation, the charge is then processed through the EEOC's usual mechanisms.[87] The new mediation program seems to be successful. Since its implementation, about 11,600 private sector charges have been resolved through the program; charging parties have obtained more than $150 million through the program. Nine out of ten participants say they would participate again.[88]

Faced with an offer to mediate, three responses are generally possible: agree to mediate the charge; make a settlement offer without participating in mediation; or prepare a "position statement" for the EEOC. If the employer does not mediate or make an offer, the position statement is required. It should include information relating to the company's business and the charging party's position; a description of any rules or policies and procedures that are applicable; and the chronology of the offense that led to the adverse action.[89]

1. To what protected group does the worker belong? Is the employee protected by more than one statute?

2. Would the action complained of have been taken if the worker were not a member of a protected group? Is the action having an adverse impact on other members of a protected group?

3. Is the employee's charge of discrimination subject to attack because it was not filed on time, according to the applicable law?

4. In the case of a sexual harassment claim, are there offensive posters or calendars on display in the workplace?

5. Do the employees' personnel records demonstrate discriminatory treatment in the form of unjustified warnings and reprimands?

6. In reviewing the nature of the action complained of, can it be characterized as disparate impact or disparate treatment? Can it be characterized as an individual complaint or a class action?

7. What are the company's probable defenses and rebuttal?

8. Who are the decision makers involved in the employment action, and what would be their effectiveness as potential witnesses?

9. What are the prospects for a settlement of the case that would be satisfactory to all involved?

FIGURE 2.2 Questions to Ask When an Employer Receives Notice That a Bias Complaint Has Been Filed

Source: Reprinted with permission from *Fair Employment Practices Summary of Latest Developments*, January 7, 1988, p. 3. Copyright © 1988 by The Bureau of National Affairs, Inc. (800-372-1033) <http://www.bna.com>.

How to Respond to Employment Discrimination Charges

There are several things to keep in mind when confronted by a charge of illegal employment discrimination; some of the more important can be summarized as follows:[90]

1. Be methodical. One expert notes that when you get official correspondence from the EEOC, "Odds are you won't be opening a love letter." Therefore, proceed methodically: Is the charge signed and dated and notarized by the person who filed it? Was it filed within the time allowed? Does the charge name the proper employer? Is it filed against a company that is subject to federal antidiscrimination statutes (for instance, only companies with 15 or more employees are subject to Title VII and the ADA). Company records and persons with first-hand knowledge of the facts then should be scoured.[91]

2. Remember that EEOC investigators are not judges and aren't empowered to act as courts; they cannot make findings of discrimination on their own but can merely make recommendations. If the EEOC eventually determines that an employer may be in violation of a law, its only recourse is to file a suit or issue a notice of right to sue to the person who filed the charge.

3. Some experts advise meeting with the employee who made the complaint to determine all relevant issues. For example, ask What happened? Who was involved? When did the incident take place? Was the employee's ability to work affected? Were there any witnesses? Then prepare a written statement summarizing the complaints, facts, dates, and issues involved and request that the employee sign and date this.[92]

4. Give the EEOC a position statement based on your own investigation of the matter. According to one management attorney, employers' position statements should contain words to the effect that "We understand that a charge of discrimination has been filed against this establishment and this statement is to inform the agency that the company has a policy against discrimination and would not discriminate in the manner charged in the complaint." The statement should be supported by some statistical analysis of the workforce, copies of any documents that support the employer's position, or an explanation of any legitimate business justification for the employment decision that is the subject of the complaint.[93]

5. Ensure that there is information in the EEOC's file demonstrating lack of merit of the charge; often the best way to do that is not by answering the EEOC's questionnaire but by providing a detailed statement describing the firm's defense in its best and most persuasive light.

6. Limit the information supplied as narrowly as possible to only those issues raised in the charge itself. For example, if the charge only alleges sex discrimination, the firm should not respond unwittingly to the EEOC's request for a breakdown of employees by age and sex. Releasing too much information invites more probing by the EEOC, says one expert.[94]

7. Seek as much information as possible about the charging party's claim in order to ensure that you understand the claim and its ramifications.

8. Prepare for the EEOC's *fact-finding conferences*, which are supposed to be informal meetings held early in the investigatory process aimed at defining issues and determining whether there is a basis for negotiation. According to one expert, however, the EEOC's emphasis is often on settlement. Its investigators therefore use the conferences to find weak spots in each party's respective position so that they can use this information as leverage to push for a settlement. Therefore, thoroughly prepare witnesses who are going to testify at a fact-finding conference, especially supervisors, because their statements can be considered admissions against the employer's interest.

Mandatory Arbitration of Employment Discrimination Claims

Given the fact that even winning a discrimination lawsuit can cost an employer more than $100,000 in attorneys' fees and defense costs, it's not surprising that more employers are switching to compulsory mandatory arbitration.[95] For example, after a long and expensive equal employment lawsuit, Rockwell International implemented a grievance procedure that provides for binding arbitration at the last step. Initially, Rockwell's 970 executives had to sign a mutual agreement to arbitrate employment disputes as a condition of participation in an executive stock plan. The program (called, as is traditional, an *alternative dispute resolution*, or ADR, program) was later extended to cover all nonunion employees at some locations. New hires at Rockwell must also sign the agreement to arbitrate as a condition of employment, and current employees must sign it to be promoted or transferred.[96] ADR plans appear to be becoming more popular, although the EEOC has reasserted its long-standing opposition to such mandatory arbitration of workplace bias claims.[97]

DIVERSITY MANAGEMENT AND AFFIRMATIVE ACTION PROGRAMS

To some extent the goals of equitable and fair treatment driving equal employment legislation are being overtaken by demographic changes and market globalization. Today, as we've seen, white males no longer dominate the labor force, and women and minorities will represent the lion's share of labor force growth over the foreseeable future. Furthermore, globalization of markets increasingly requires employers to hire minority members with the cultural and language skills to deal with customers abroad. As a result, companies today are increasingly striving for racial, ethnic, and sexual workforce balance, "not because of legal imperatives, but as a matter of enlightened economic self-interest."[98] At least one study suggests that cultural diversity contributes to improved productivity, return on equity, and market performance.[99]

Although there's no unanimity about what *diversity* means, there's considerable agreement about the components of diversity. For example, in one study a majority of the respondents listed race, sex, culture, national origin, handicap, age, and religion as diversity components. In other words, these comprise the demographic building blocks that represent diversity at work and that people often think of when asked what employers mean by diversity.[100]

Managing Diversity

Managing diversity means maximizing diversity's potential advantages while minimizing the potential barriers—such as prejudices and bias—that can undermine the functioning of a diverse workforce. In practice, *diversity management* involves both compulsory and voluntary management actions. There are (as we've seen in this chapter) many legally mandated actions employers must take to minimize discrimination at work.

However, although such compulsory actions can reduce the more blatant diversity barriers, blending a diverse workforce into a close-knit and thriving community also requires employers to take other steps. Based on his review of research studies, one diversity expert concluded that five sets of voluntary organizational activities are at the heart of any diversity management program. These can be summarized as follows:

> *Provide strong leadership.*   Companies that have exemplary reputations in managing diversity are typically led by chief executives who champion the cause of diversity. Leadership in this case means, for instance, taking a strong stand on the need for change and becoming a role model for the behaviors required for the change.
>
> *Research: Assess the situation.*   The company must assess the current state of affairs with respect to diversity management. One study found that the most common tools for measuring diversity include equal employment hiring and retention metrics, employee attitude surveys, management and employee evaluations, and focus groups.[101]
>
> *Provide diversity training and education.*   One expert says that "the most commonly utilized starting point for . . . managing diversity is some type of employee education program."[102] (Yet some argue that generalized diversity training is actually backfiring, for instance, by diminishing participants' attention to racial relations.)[103]
>
> *Change culture and management systems.*   Ideally, education programs should be combined with other concrete steps aimed at changing the organization's culture and management systems. For example, the performance appraisal procedure might be changed to emphasize that supervisors will henceforth be appraised based partly on their success in reducing intergroup conflicts.
>
> *Evaluate the diversity management program.*   For example, do the employee attitude surveys now indicate any improvement in employees' attitudes toward diversity?

Boosting Workforce Diversity

Employers use various means to increase workforce diversity. Many companies, such as Baxter Healthcare Corporation, start by adopting strong company policies advocating the benefits of a culturally, racially, and sexually diverse workforce: "Baxter International believes that a multi-cultural employee population is essential to the company's leadership in healthcare around the world." Baxter then publicizes this philosophy throughout the company.

Next, Baxter takes concrete steps to foster diversity at work. These steps include evaluating diversity program efforts, recruiting minority members to the board of directors, and interacting with representative minority groups and networks. Diversity training is another concrete activity. It aims at sensitizing all employees to the need to value differences, build self-esteem, and generally create a more smoothly functioning and hospitable environment for the firm's diverse workforce.

An IBM diversity program for women, begun in 1995, includes an extensive part-time program that lets IBM employees and executives, mostly women, work as permanent part-time employees; departmental diversity meetings conducted and attended by managers; and the organizing of special networking and mentoring groups for women.[104] Similarly, AT&T helps employees form in-house groups with others of a similar race, ethnicity, gender, or other common interest.[105]

Some employers have also attempted to better manage diversity through voluntary affirmative action programs, which means employers make an extra effort to hire and promote those in protected (such as female or minority) groups. This is in contrast to the involuntary affirmative action programs a number of courts have imposed on some employers since enactment of the 1964 Civil Rights Act.

Although laudable in many respects, affirmative action can have several adverse consequences. For one thing, voluntary affirmative action programs may now conflict with sections of the Civil Rights Act of 1991.[106] Two experts have written that "read literally, this new statutory restriction appears to bar employers from giving any consideration whatsoever to an individual's status as a racial or ethnic minority or as a woman when making an employment decision."[107]

At the present time, this does not seem to be much of a problem, as long as employers emphasize the external recruitment and internal development of better-qualified minority and female employees, "while basing employment decisions on legitimate criteria."[108] However, with CRA 1991, employers have to take care that in achieving the desired goal of workforce diversity they do not inadvertently, "step over the line of permissible diversity management into the realm of unlawful affirmative action (i.e., reverse discrimination)."[109]

Affirmative action may also backfire on both the beneficiaries and nonbeneficiaries of the program. For example, nonbeneficiaries may have adverse reactions to the program and feel that the program has resulted in them being treated unfairly.[110] Even the beneficiary may be adversely affected: For example, a perception that an individual has benefited from affirmative action–based preferential selection resulted in unfavorable self-evaluations in several studies.[111] However, such voluntary programs are often advisable.

Equal Employment Opportunity Versus Affirmative Action

Equal employment opportunity aims to ensure that anyone, regardless of race, color, disability, sex, religion, national origin, or age has an equal chance for a job based on his or her qualifications.

Affirmative action goes beyond equal employment opportunity by requiring the employer to make an extra effort to hire and promote those in a protected group. Affirmative action thus includes specific actions (in recruitment, hiring, promotions, and compensation) that are designed to eliminate the present effects of past discrimination. According to the EEOC, an affirmative action program should result in "measurable, yearly improvements in hiring, training, and promotion of minorities and females" in all parts of the organization.

Steps in an Affirmative Action Program

According to the EEOC, in an affirmative action program the employer ideally takes eight steps:

1. Issues a written equal employment policy indicating that it is an equal employment opportunity employer, as well as a statement indicating the employer's commitment to affirmative action.

2. Appoints a top official with responsibility and authority to direct and implement the program.
3. Publicizes the equal employment policy and affirmative action commitment.
4. Surveys present minority and female employment by department and job classification to determine locations where affirmative action programs are especially desirable. (Today, reporting race for EEOC purposes is more complex. Employers now [through fall 2002] have five choices for reporting race: American Indian/Alaska native; Asian/Pacific Islander; black; white; and Hispanic/Latino. Employees considering themselves multiracial are unable to report their combined backgrounds. New government regulations will require reporting on five modified single race categories: white; black/African American; Asian; native Hawaiian/Pacific Islander; and American Indian/Alaska native. There will also be four multiple race combinations: black/African American and white; Asian and white; American Indian/Alaska native and white; American Indian/Alaska native and black/African American; as well as several others.)[112]
5. Develops goals and timetables to improve utilization of minorities, males, and females in each area where utilization has been identified.
6. Develops and implements specific programs to achieve these goals. According to the EEOC, this is the heart of the affirmative action program. Here the employer has to review its entire personnel management system (including recruitment, selection, promotion, compensation, and disciplining) to identify barriers to equal employment opportunity and to make needed changes.
7. Establishes an internal audit and reporting system to monitor and evaluate progress in each aspect of the program.
8. Develops support for the affirmative action program, both inside the company (among supervisors, for instance) and outside the company in the community.[113]

Affirmative Action: Two Basic Strategies

When designing an affirmative action program, the employer can pursue either of two basic strategies—the good faith effort strategy or the quota strategy—each of which has risks.[114] The **good faith effort strategy** emphasizes identifying and eliminating the obstacles to hiring and promoting women and minorities on the assumption that eliminating these obstacles will result in increased utilization of women and minorities. The **quota strategy**, on the other hand, mandates bottom-line results by instituting hiring and promotion restrictions.

REVIEW

Summary

1. Legislation barring discrimination is not new. For example, the Fifth Amendment to the U.S. Constitution (ratified in 1791) states that no person shall be deprived of life, liberty, or property without due process of law.
2. Legislation barring employment discrimination includes Title VII of the 1964 Civil Rights Act (as amended), which bars discrimination because of race, color, religion, sex, or national origin; various executive orders; federal guidelines (covering procedures for validating employee selection tools, etc.); the Equal Pay Act of 1963; and the Age Discrimination in Employment Act of 1967. In addition, various Court decisions (such as

Griggs v. *Duke Power Company*) and state and local laws bar various aspects of discrimination.

3. The EEOC was created by Title VII of the Civil Rights Act. It is empowered to try conciliating discrimination complaints, but if this fails, the EEOC has the power to go directly to court to enforce the law.

4. The Civil Rights Act of 1991 had the effect of revising several Supreme Court equal employment decisions and "rolling back the clock." For example, it placed the burden of proof back on employers and held that a nondiscriminatory reason was insufficient to let an employer avoid liability for an action that also had a discriminatory motive.

5. The Americans with Disabilities Act prohibits employment discrimination against the disabled. Specifically, qualified persons cannot be discriminated against if the firm can make reasonable accommodations without undue hardship on the business.

6. A person who believes he or she has been discriminated against by a personnel procedure or decision must prove either that he or she was subjected to unlawful disparate treatment (intentional discrimination) or that the procedure in question has a disparate impact (unintentional discrimination) on members of his or her protected class. Once a prima facie case of disparate treatment is established, an employer must produce evidence that its decision was based on legitimate nondiscriminatory reasons. If the employer does that, the person claiming discrimination must prove that the employer's reasons are only a pretext for letting the company discriminate. Once a prima facie case of disparate impact has been established, the employer must produce evidence that the allegedly discriminatory practice or procedure is job related and is based on a substantial business reason.

7. An employer should avoid various specific discriminatory human resource management practices:

   a. *In recruitment.* An employer usually should not rely on word-of-mouth advertising or give false or misleading information to minority group members. Also (usually), an employer should not specify the desired sex in advertising or in any way suggest that applicants might be discriminated against.

   b. *In selection.* An employer should avoid using any educational or other requirements where (1) it can be shown that minority-group members are less likely to possess the qualification and (2) such requirement is also not job related. Tests that disproportionately screen out minorities and women and that are not job related are deemed unlawful. Remember that you can use various tests and standards, but must prove that they are job related or show that they are not used to discriminate against protected groups.

8. In practice, a person's charge to the EEOC is often first referred to a local agency. When it proceeds, and if it finds reasonable cause to believe that discrimination occurred, the EEOC has 30 days to try to work out a conciliation. Important points for the employer to remember include (1) EEOC investigators can only make recommendations, (2) you cannot be compelled to submit documents without a court order, and (3) you may limit the information you do submit. Also, make sure you clearly document your position (as the employer).

9. An employer can use three basic defenses in the event of a discriminatory practice allegation. One is *business necessity.* Attempts to show that tests or other selection standards are valid is one example of this defense. Bona fide occupational qualification is the second defense. This is applied when, for example, religion, national origin, or sex is a bona fide requirement of the job (such as for actors or actresses). A third is that the decision was made on the basis of legitimate nondiscriminatory reasons (such as poor performance) having nothing to do with the prohibited discrimination alleged.

10. Eight steps in an affirmative action program (based on suggestions from the EEOC) are (1) issue a written equal employment policy, (2) appoint a top official, (3) publicize policy, (4) survey present minority and female employment, (5) develop goals and timetables, (6) develop and implement specific programs to achieve goals, (7) establish an internal audit and reporting system, and (8) develop support of in-house and community programs.

11. Recruitment is one of the first activities to which EEOC laws and procedures are applied. We turn to this in the following chapter.

Key Terms

Title VII of the 1964 Civil Rights Act
Equal Employment Opportunity Commission (EEOC)
affirmative action
Office of Federal Contract Compliance Programs (OFCCP)
Equal Pay Act of 1963
Age Discrimination in Employment Act (ADEA) of 1967
Vocational Rehabilitation Act of 1973

Vietnam Era Veterans' Readjustment Act of 1974
Pregnancy Discrimination Act (PDA)
federal agency guidelines
sexual harassment
Federal Violence Against Women Act of 1994
Griggs v. *Duke Power Company*
protected class
Albemarle Paper Company v. *Moody*

Wards Cove Packing Company v. *Atonio*
Civil Rights Act of 1991 (CRA 1991)
Americans with Disabilities Act (ADA)
adverse impact
bona fide occupational qualification (BFOQ)
business necessity
good faith effort strategy
quota strategy

Discussion Questions and Exercises

1. What is Title VII? What does it say?

2. What important precedents were set by the *Griggs* v. *Duke Power Company* case? the *Albemarle* v. *Moody* case?

3. What is adverse impact? How can it be proven?

4. Assume that you are a supervisor on an assembly line; you are responsible for hiring subordinates, supervising them, and recommending them for promotion. Compile a list of discriminatory management practices you should avoid.

5. Explain the defenses and exceptions to discriminatory practice allegations.

6. What is the difference between affirmative action and equal employment opportunity? Explain how you would set up an affirmative action program.

APPLICATION EXERCISES

Case Incident: A Case of Racial Discrimination?

John Peters (not his real name) was a 44-year-old cardiologist on the staff of a teaching hospital in a large city in the southeastern United States. Happily married with two teenage children, he had served with distinction for many years at this same hospital, and in fact served his residency there after graduating from Columbia University's medical school.

Alana Anderson (not her real name) was an attractive African American registered nurse on the staff at the same hospital with Peters. Unmarried and without children, she lived in a hospital-owned apartment on the hospital grounds and diligently devoted almost all her time to her work at the hospital or to taking additional coursework to further improve her already excellent nursing skills.

The hospital's chief administrator, Gary Chapman, took enormous pride in what he called the extraordinary professionalism of the doctors, nurses, and other staff members at his hospital. Although he took a number of rudimentary steps to guard against blatant violations of equal employment opportunity laws, he believed that most of the professionals on his staff were so highly trained and committed to the highest professional standards that "they would always do the right thing," as he put it.

Chapman was therefore upset to receive a phone call from Peters, informing him that Anderson had (in Peters's eyes) "developed an unwholesome personal attraction" to him and was bombarding the doctor with Valentine's Day cards, affectionate personal notes, and phone calls—often to the doctor's home. Concerned about hospital decorum and the possibility that Peters was being sexually harassed, Chapman met privately with Anderson, explained that Peters was very uncomfortable with the personal attention she was showing to him, and asked that she please not continue to exhibit her show of affection for the doctor.

Chapman assumed that the matter was over. Several weeks later, when Anderson resigned her position at the hospital, Chapman didn't think much of it. He was therefore shocked and dismayed to receive a registered letter from a local attorney, informing him that both the hospital and Peters and Chapman personally were being sued by Anderson for racial discrimination: Her claim was that Chapman, in their private meeting, had told her, "We don't think it's right for people of different races to pursue each other romantically at this hospital." According to the lawyer, his preliminary research had unearthed several other alleged incidents at the hospital that apparently supported the idea that racial discrimination at the hospital was widespread.

Questions

1. What do you think of the way Chapman handled the accusations from Peters and his conversation with Anderson? How would you have handled them?

2. Do you think Peters had the basis for a sexual harassment claim against Anderson? Why or why not?

3. What would you do now if you were Chapman to avoid further incidents of this type?

Experiential Exercise: Too Informal?

Dan Jones had run his textile plant in a midsize southern town for many years without a whiff of trouble with the EEOC. He did not take formal steps to avoid making EEO-type mistakes; just the opposite. In fact, a professor from a local college had once told him to be more careful about how applicants were recruited and screened and employees were treated. However, Jones's philosophy was "if it ain't broke, don't fix it," and because he'd never had any complaints, he assumed that his screening process wasn't "broke."

For many years Jones had no problems. If he needed a new employee, he simply asked his current employees (most of whom were Hispanic) if they had any friends who were looking for jobs. Sometimes, he would also ask the local state employment office to list the open jobs and send over some candidates. He then had his sewing supervisor and plant manager (both also Hispanic) interview the applicants. No tests or other background checks were carried out, in part, said Jones, because, "most of these applicants are friends and relatives of my current employees, and they wouldn't send me any lemons."

Now Jones is being served with a formal notice from the county's Equal Rights

Commission. It seems that of the 20 or so non-Hispanic applicants sent to Jones's firm last year from the state employment office, none had received a job offer. In fact, Jones's supervisor had not even returned the follow-up card to the employment office to verify that each applicant had shown up and been interviewed. Jones was starting to wonder if his HR process was too informal.

Purpose: The purpose of this exercise is to provide practice in analyzing and applying knowledge of equal opportunity legislation to a realistic problem.

Required Understanding: Be thoroughly familiar with the material presented in this chapter. In addition, read "Too Informal?" the case on which this experiential exercise is based.

How to Set up the Exercise/Instructions:

1. Divide the class into groups of four or five students.
2. Each group should develop answers to the following questions:
   a. How could the EEOC prove *adverse impact?*
   b. Cite specific discriminatory personnel practices at Dan Jones's company.
   c. How could Jones's company defend itself against the allegations of discriminatory practice?
3. If time permits, a spokesperson from each group can present his or her group's findings. Would it make sense for this company to try to defend itself against the discrimination allegations?

TAKE IT TO THE WEB

For Internet exercises, updates to chapter material, and more, visit the Dessler Web site at

www.prenhall.com/dessler

ENDNOTES

1. Bureau of National Affairs, "$65 Million Sex Bias Settlement," *Fair Employment Practices* (October 2, 1997): 120.
2. "Smith Barney Issues Settlement Offers to Resolve 2,000 Sex Harassment Claims," *BNA Fair Employment Practices* (December 9, 1999): 147.
3. "California Bakery Workers Awarded $131 Million on Race Bias Claims," *BNA Fair Employment Practices* (August 17, 2000): 99.
4. "Coca-Cola Agrees to Settle Race Bias Suit; Proceeds Expected to Be Shared by 2,000," *BNA Fair Employment Practices* (June 22, 2000): 75.
5. "Federal Government Settles for $508 Million Bias Case Involving U.S. Information Agency," *BNA Fair Employment Practices* (March 30, 2000): 39.
6. "You'll Be Hearing from My Lawyer," *The Economist* (June 21, 1997): 67.
7. "Employee Lawsuits Spur New Insurance Coverage," *BNA Bulletin to Management* (June 6, 1997): 177.
8. James Higgins, "A Manager's Guide to the Equal Employment Opportunity Laws," *Personnel Journal* 55, no. 8 (August 1976): 406.

9. The Equal Employment Opportunity Act of 1972, Subcommittee on Labor or the Committee of Labor and Public Welfare, United States Senate, March 1972, p. 3. In general, it is not discrimination but unfair discrimination against a person merely because of that person's race, age, sex, national origin, or religion that is forbidden by federal statutes. In the federal government's *Uniform Employee Selection Guidelines, unfair* discrimination is defined as follows: "unfairness is demonstrated through a showing that members of a particular interest group perform better or poorer on the job than their scores on the selection procedure (test, etc.) would indicate through comparison with how members of the other groups performed." For a discussion of the meaning of fairness, see James Ledvinka, "The Statistical Definition of Fairness in the Federal Selection Guidelines and Its Implications for Minority Employment," *Personnel Psychology* 32 (August 1979): 551–62. In summary, a selection device (such as a test) may discriminate—for example, between low and high performers. However, unfair discrimination—discrimination that is based solely on the person's race, age, sex, national origin, or religion—is illegal.

10. A growing issue today is whether homosexuals are due equal protection from discrimination. Initially, attempts to assert that discrimination based on sexual orientation was illegal were unsuccessful, and even the EEOC was unsympathetic. However, a relevant case (*Watkins* v. *U.S. Army*, F.2d 1428, 1429, 9th Cir. 1988) involving an army sergeant forced to resign after 14 years, notable service may possibly open the door to successful suits by identifying homosexuals as a "suspect class that deserves special protection against discrimination." Sabrina Wrenn, "Gay Rights and Workplace Discrimination," *Personnel Journal* 67, no. 10 (October 1988): 94; "Proposed Bill Would Ban Workplace Discrimination Based on Sexual Orientation," *HR Focus* (October 1994): 1, 8.

11. "EEOC Reached Record Monetary Benefits, Continued Cutting Inventory of Last Year," *BNA Fair Employment Practices* (February 3, 2000): 15.

12. "OFCCP Lists Egregious Bias Cases," *BNA Fair Employment Practices* (November 28, 1996): 139.

13. Bureau of National Affairs, *Fair Employment Practices* (October 8, 1992): 117.

14. Note that under The Vocational Rehabilitation act, the law strictly speaking applied only to a particular "program" of the employer. In March 1988 congress passed the Civil Rights Restoration Act of 1987, overturning this interpretation. Now, with few exceptions, any institution, organization, corporation, state agency, or municipality using federal funding in any of its programs must abide by the section of the act prohibiting discriminating against handicapped individuals. See Bureau of National Affairs, "Federal Law Mandates Affirmative Action for Handicapped," *Fair Employment Practices* (March 30, 1989): 42.

15. Howard J. Anderson and Michael D. Levin-Epstein, *Primer of Equal Employment Opportunity*, 2nd ed. (Washington, DC: Bureau of National Affairs, 1982), pp. 5–7; and Commerce Clearing House, "Federal Contractors Must File VETS-100 by March 31," *Ideas and Trends* (February 23, 1988): 32.

16. Ann Harriman, *Women/Men Management* (New York: Praeger, 1985), pp. 66–68.

17. Commerce Clearing House, "Pregnancy Leave," *Ideas and Trends* (January 23, 1987): 10.

18. Bureau of National Affairs, "High Court Upholds Pregnancy Law," *Fair Employment Practices* (January 22, 1987): 7; Betty Sonthard Murphy, Wayne E. Barlow, and D. Diane Hatch, "Manager's Newsfront: U.S. Supreme Court Approves Preferential Treatment for Pregnancy," *Personnel Journal* 66, no. 3 (March 1987): 18.

19. Thomas Dhanens, "Implications of the New EEOC Guidelines," *Personnel* 56 (September/October): 32–39.

20. Bureau of National Affairs, "First Two Chapters of Long-Awaited Manual Released by OFCCP," *Fair Employment Practices* (January 5, 1989): 6.

21. Lawrence S. Kleiman and Robert Faley, "The Applications of Professional and Legal Guidelines for Court Decisions Involving Criterion-Related Validity: A Review and Analysis," *Personnel Psychology* 38, no. 4 (winter 1985): 803–33.

22. Oscar A. Ornati and Margaret J. Eisen, "Are Your Complying with EEOC's New Rules on National Origin Discrimination?" *Personnel* 58 (March/April 1981): 12–20; Paul S. Greenlaw and John P. Kohn, "National Origin Discrimination and the New EEOC Guidelines," *Personnel Journal* 60, no. 8 (August 1981): 634–36.

23. Barbara Berish Brown, "Guidance and Regs from EEOC, OFCCP, and INS," *Employment Relations Today* (spring 1992): 81–86; Morgan Hodgson and Ronald Cooper, "EEOC Issues Proposed Guidelines and Guidance Memorandum," *Employment Relations Today* (winter 1993/1994): 455–59; "EEOC Issues Disability Guidance," *BNA Fair Employment Practices* (March 23, 1995): 31.

24. 29 CFR 1625.2(a) quoted in Paul Greenlaw and John Kohl, "Age Discrimination and Employment Guidelines," *Personnel Journal* 61, no. 3 (March 1982): 224–28.

25. Patricia Linenberger and Timothy Keaveny, "Sexual Harassment: The Employer's Legal Obligations," *Personnel* 58 (November/December 1981): 60–68.

26. Larry Drake and Rachel Moskowitz, "Your Rights in the Workplace," *Occupational Outlook Quarterly* (summer 1997): 19–20.

27. *Mattison* v. *Click Corp. of America*, DC Epa#97-cv-2736, 1/27/98; discussed in "Preventing Sexual Harassment: Helpful Advice and Another Reason," *BNA Fair Employment Practices* (February 19, 1998): 21.

28. Mary Rowe, "Dealing with Sexual Harassment," *Harvard Business Review* 61 (May/June 1981): 42–46.

29. Edward Felsenthal, "Justice's Ruling Further Defines Sex Harassment," *Wall Street Journal* (March 5, 1998): B1, B5.

30. Linda Greenhouse, "Court Spells Out Rules for Finding Sexual Harassment," *New York Times* (June 27, 1998): A1–A10.

31. Robert H. Faley, "Sexual Harassment: Critical Review of Legal Cases with General Principles and Preventive Measures," *Personnel Psychology* 35, no. 3 (autumn 1982): 590–91; Bureau of National Affairs, "In Terms of Sexual Harassment, What Makes an Environment 'Hostile'?" *Fair Employment Practices* (June 1988): 78.

32. Linenberger and Keaveny, "Sexual Harassment," p. 64.

33. Felsenthal, "Justice's Ruling Further Defines Sexual Harassment," p. B5.

34. See the discussion in "Examining Unwelcome Conduct in a Sexual Harassment Claim," *BNA Fair Employment Practices* (October 19, 1995): 124.

35. *Ibid.*, p. 124.

36. Commerce Clearing House, *Sexual Harassment Manual*, p. 8.

37. Louise Fitzgerald et al., "Antecedents and Consequences of Sexual Harassment in Organizations: A Test of an Integrated Model," *Journal of Applied Psychology* 82, no. 4 (1997): 577–89.

38. "New EEOC Guidance Explains Standards of Liability for Harassment by Supervisors," *BNA Fair Employment Practices* (June 24, 1999): 75.

39. "Adequate Response Bars Liability," *BNA Fair Employment Practices* (June 26, 1997): 74.

40. Federick L. Sullivan, "Sexual Harassment: The Supreme Court Ruling," *Personnel* 65, no. 12 (December 1986): 42–44. Also see the following for additional information on sexual harassment: Jonathan S. Monat and Angel Gomez, "Decisional Standards Used by

Arbitrators in Sexual Harassment Cases," *Labor Law Journal* 37, no. 10 (October 1986): 712–18; George M. Sullivan and William H. Nowlin, "Critical New Aspects of Sexual Harassment Law," *Labor Law Journal* 37, no. 9 (September 1986): 617–23. See also Gillian Flynn, "A Pioneer Program Nurtures a Harassment Free Workplace," *Workforce* (October 1997): 38–43.

41. *Griggs* v. *Duke Power Company*, 3FEP Cases 175.

42. James Ledvinka, *Federal Regulation of Personnel and Human Resource Management* (Boston: Kent, 1982), p. 41.

43. IOFEP cases 1181.

44. James Ledvinka and Lyle Schoenfeldt, "Legal Development in Employment Testing: Albemarle and Beyond," *Personnel Psychology* 31, no. 1 (spring 1978): 1–13. It should be noted that in its Albemarle opinion, the court made one important modification regarding the EEOC guidelines. The guidelines required that employers using tests that screened out disproportionate numbers of minorities or women had to validate those tests—prove that they did in fact predict performance on the job—and further had to prove that there was no other alternative screening device the employer could use that did not screen out disproportionate numbers of minorities and women. This second requirement proved a virtually impossible burden for employers. Up through the *Griggs* decision, it was not enough to just validate the test; instead, the employer also had to show that some other tests or screening tools were not available that were also valid but that did not screen out a disproportionate numbers of minorities or women. In the *Albemarle* case, the Court held that the burden of proof was no longer on the employer to show that there was no suitable alternative screening device available. Instead, the burden for that was now on the charging party (the person allegedly discriminated against) to show that a suitable alternative is available. Ledvinka and Schoenfeldt, "Legal Development," p. 4; Gary Lubben, Dwayne Thompson, and Charles Klasson, "Performance Appraisal: The Legal Implications of Title VII," *Personnel* (May/June 1980): 11–21.

45. See Milton Zall, "What to Expect from the Civil Rights Act," *Personnel Journal* 71, no. 3 (March 1992): 46–50.

46. Commerce Clearing House, "House and Senate Pass Civil Rights Compromise by Wide Margin," *Ideas and Trends in Personnel* (November 13, 1991): 179.

47. *Ibid.*, p. 182.

48. Mark Kobata, "The Civil Rights Act of 1991," *Personnel Journal* (March 1992): 48.

49. Karen Simpkins and Rochelle Kaplan, "Fair Play for Disabled Persons: Responsibilities Under the Americans with Disabilities Act," *Journal of Career Planning and Employment* 51, no. 2 (January 1991): 41.

50. Elliot H. Shaller and Dean Rosen, "A Guide to the EEOC's Final Regulations on the Americans with Disabilities Act," *Employee Relations* 17, no. 3 (winter 1991–1992): 408.

51. *Ibid.*, p. 409.

52. Patricia Feltes, Robert Robinson, and Ross Fink, "American Female Expatriates and the Civil Rights Act of 1991: Balancing Legal and Business Interests," *Business Horizons* (March/April 1993): 82–85.

53. *Ibid.*, p. 84.

54. Title VII does not apply to foreign operations not owned or controlled by a U.S. employer, however.

55. Based on Gregory Baxter, "Over There: Enforcing the 1991 Civil Rights Act Abroad," *Employee Relations Law Journal* 19, no. 2 (autumn 1993): 257–66.

56. *Ibid.*, p. 265.

57. *Ibid.*, p. 265.

58. "No Sitting for Store Greeter," *BNA Fair Employment Practices* (December 14, 1995): 150.

59. "Blind Bartender Not Qualified for Job, Court Says in Dismissing Americans with Disabilities Act Claim," *BNA Fair Employment Practices* (February 4, 1999): 17.

60. "Differing Views: Punctuality as Essential Job Function," *BNA Fair Employment Practices* (April 27, 2000): 56.

61. "Sleepy Poor Performer Seeks ADA Protection," *BNA Bulletin to Management* (January 14, 1999): 14.

62. "Tips for Employers with Asymptomatic HIV-Positive Employees," *BNA Fair Employment Practices* (November 27, 1997): 141.

63. "Odds Against Getting Even Are Long in ADA Cases," *BNA Bulletin to Management* (August 20, 2000): 229.

64. "Determining Employers' Responsibilities Under ADA," *BNA Fair Employment Practices* (May 16, 1996): 57.

65. *Ibid.*, p. 57.

66. "Mitigating Measures and ADA," *BNA Fair Employment Practices* (September 2, 1999): 108.

67. Timothy Bland, "The Supreme Court Focuses on the ADA," *HRMagazine* (September 1999): 42–46. See also James Hall and Diane Hatch, "Supreme Court Decisions Require ADA Revision," *Workforce* (August 1999): 60–66.

68. James Ledvinka and Robert Gatewood, "EEO Issues with Preemployment Inquiries," *Personnel Administrator* 22, no. 2 (February 1977): 22–26.

69. Based on Bureau of National Affairs, "A Wrap-up of State Legislation: 1988 Anti-bias Laws Focus on AIDS," *Fair Employment Practices* (January 5, 1988): 3–4.

70. John Klinefelter and James Thompkins, "Adverse Impact in Employment Selection," *Public Personnel Management* (May/June 1976): 199–204.

71. "The Eleventh Circuit Explains Disparate Impact, Disparate Treatment," *BNA Fair Employment Practices* (August 17, 2000): 102.

72. International Association of Official Human Rights Agencies, *Principles of Employment Discrimination Law* (Washington, D.C.); James M. Higgins, "A Manager's Guide to the Equal Opportunity Laws," *Personnel* 55 (August 1976); James Ledvinka, *Federal Regulation of Personnel and Human Resource Management.*

73. *Usery* v. *Tamiami Trail Tours*, 12FEP cases 1233.

74. Anderson and Levin-Epstein, *Primer of Equal Employment Opportunity*, pp. 13–14.

75. *U.S.* v. *Bethlehem Steel Company*, 3FEP cases 589.

76. *Robinson* v. *Lorillard Corporation*, 3FEP cases 653.

77. *Spurlock* v. *United Airlines*, 5FEP cases 17.

78. Ledvinka and Gatewood, "EEO Issues with Preemployment Inquiries," pp. 22–26.

79. Anderson and Levin-Epstein, *Primer of Equal Opportunity*, p. 28.

80. "Many Well-Intentioned HR Policies Hold Legal Headaches, Consultant Says," *BNA Bulletin to Management* (February 17, 2000): 47.

81. Mark Roehling, "Weight-Based Discrimination in Employment: Psychological and Legal Aspects," *Personnel Psychology* 52 (1999): 969–1016.

82. "American Airlines, Worldwide Flight Sued by EEOC Over Questioning of Applicants," *BNA Fair Employment Practices* (October 12, 2000): 125.

83. Richard Connors, "Law at Work," lawatwork.com/news/applicat.html.

84. This is based on Anderson and Levin-Epstein, *Primer of Equal Opportunity*, pp. 93–97.

85. "EEOC Issues New Enforcement Guidance on Discrimination in Employee Benefits," *BNA Fair Employment Practices* (October 12, 2000): 123.

86. Even during President Reagan's administration—often viewed as a not particularly supportive period for equal rights enforcement in the United States—an EEOC press release dated June 13, 1988, says it filed 527 court actions during fiscal year 1987, "setting an agency record for legal activity and maintaining its high level of enforcement on behalf of persons discriminated against in the work place." The release continues: "A record high 430 lawsuits were filed on the merits of discrimination charges in fiscal 1987, topping the previous record of 427 direct suits and interventions filed in fiscal 1986. Cases filed under Title VII of the Civil Rights Act totaled 69 and 12 filings, respectively. Twenty-nine cases were filed concurrently under Title VII and ADEA or Title VII and EPA. Agency investigative subpoena enforcement actions totaled 97, slightly below the 99 filed in fiscal 1986." Furthermore, in fiscal 1987, "The commission resolved more cases of discrimination through litigation than ever before: 460 as compared to 386 in fiscal 1986, the previous record number of resolutions. Direct suits and interventions accounted for 357 of the resolutions and there were 103 subpoena enforcement actions." EEOC news release dated June 13, 1988, and titled "EEOC Continues Record Enforcement Pace in Fiscal Year 1987." Quoted in Commerce Clearing House, *Ideas and Trends* (June 28, 1988): 101–102.

87. "EEOC's New Nationwide Mediation Plan Offers Option of Informal Settlements," *BNA Fair Employment Practices* (February 18, 1999): 21.

88. "Independent Report Shows High Satisfaction for Participants," *BNA Fair Employment Practices* (October 12, 2000): 127.

89. Timothy Bland, "Sealed Without a Kiss," *HRMagazine* (October 2000): 85–92.

90. Robert H. Sheahan, "Responding to Employment Discrimination Charges," *Personnel Journal* 60, no. 3 (March 1981): 217–20; Wayne Baham, "Learn to Deal with Agency Investigations," *Personnel Journal* 67, no. 9 (September 1988): 104–107.

91. Timothy Bland, "Sealed Without a Kiss," *op cit.*, pp. 85–92.

92. "Conducting Effective Investigations of Employee Bias Complaints," *BNA Fair Employment Practices* (July 13, 1995): 81.

93. Based on Commerce Clearing House, *Ideas and Trends* (January 23, 1987): 14–15.

94. "Tips for Employers on Dealing with EEOC Investigations," *BNA Fair Employment Practices* (October 31, 1996): 130.

95. "Preventing Costly Employment Discrimination Lawsuits," *BNA Fair Employment Practices* (September 9, 1994): 105.

96. David Nye, "When the Fired Fight Back," *Across-the-Board* (June 1995): 31–34.

97. "EEOC Opposes Mandatory Arbitration," *BNA Fair Employment Practices* (July 24, 1997): 85.

98. James Coil, III, and Charles Rice, "Managing Work-Force Diversity in the 90s: The Impact of the Civil Rights Act of 1991," *Employee Relations Law Journal* 18, no. 4 (spring 1993): 547–65. See also Stephanie Mehta, "What Minority Employees Really Want," *Fortune* (July 10, 2000): 81–188.

99. Orlando Richard, "Racial Diversity, Business Strategy, and Firm Performance: A Resource Based View," *Academy of Management Journal* 43, no. 2 (2000): 164–77.

100. Michael Carrell and Everett Mann, "Defining Work-Force Diversity in Public Sector Organizations," *Public Personnel Management* 24, no. 1 (spring 1995): 99–111.

101. Patricia Digh, "Creating a New Balance Sheet: The Need for Better Diversity Metrics," *Mosaics*, Society for Human Resource Management (September/October 1999): 1.

102. Taylor Cox, Jr., *Cultural Diversity in Organizations: Theory, Research and Practice* (San Francisco: Berrett-Koehler, 1993), p. 236.

103. Robert Grossman, "Is Diversity Working?" *HRMagazine* (March 2000): 47–50.

104. "Three Winning Ways to Promote Executive Diversity," *BNA Bulletin to Management* (January 27, 2000): 31.

105. Phaedra Brotherton, "Employee Networks Help Advance of Diversity Efforts," *Mosaics*, Society for Human Resource Management (July/August 2000): 1.

106. Coil and Rice, "Managing Work-Force Diversity in the 90s," p. 548.

107. *Ibid.*, p. 560.

108. *Ibid.*, pp. 562–63.

109. *Ibid.*, p. 563.

110. Madeline Heilman, Winston McCullough, and David Gilbert, "The Other Side of Affirmative Action: Reactions of Nonbeneficiaries to Sex-Based Preferential Selection," *Journal of Applied Psychology* 81, no. 4 (1996): 346–57.

111. *Ibid.*, p. 346.

112. Frank Jossi, "Reporting Race," *HRMagazine* (September 2000): 87–94.

113. U.S. Equal Employment Opportunity Commission, *Affirmative Action and Equal Employment* (Washington, DC: January 1974): Antonio Handler Chayes, "Make Your Equal Opportunity Program Court Proof," *Harvard Business Review* (September 1974): 81–89. See also David Kravitz and Steven Klineberg, "Reactions to Two Versions of Affirmative-Action Among Whites, Blacks, and Hispanics," *Journal of Applied Psychology* 85, no. 4 (2000): 597–611.

114. Based on Kenneth Marino, "Conducting an Internal Compliance Review of Affirmative Action," *Personnel* 59 (March/April 1980): 24–34.

Personnel Planning and Recruitment

When you finish studying this chapter, you should be able to:

■ *Describe* the basic methods of collecting job analysis information.

■ *Conduct* a job analysis.

■ *Explain* the process of forecasting personnel requirements.

■ *Compare* eight methods for recruiting job candidates.

■ *Explain* how to use application forms to predict job performance.

INTRODUCTION

Cisco Systems, Inc. has a problem that most companies just dream about: The San Jose, California–based company is growing so fast that it's adding about 6,000 jobs per year, so rounding up enough applicants is quite a "problem," if you can call it that. Management's solution? Among other things, an employment opportunities Web site listing "hot jobs—job descriptions for hard to fill positions," and "Cisco culture—A look at Cisco worklife."[1]

WHAT IS JOB ANALYSIS?

Job Analysis Defined

Organizations consist of jobs that have to be staffed. **Job analysis** is the procedure through which you determine the duties of these jobs and the characteristics of the people who should be hired for them.[2] The analysis produces information on the job's requirements; this information is then used for developing **job descriptions** (what the job entails) and **job specifications** (what kind of people to hire for the job).

A supervisor or HR specialist normally does the job analysis,[3] perhaps using a questionnaire like the one in Figure 3.1. The information collected includes, for example, information on the work activities performed (such as cleaning, selling, teaching, or painting), and information about such matters as physical working conditions and work schedule.

Job analysis information is the basis for several interrelated HR management activities. For example, information regarding the job's duties may be the basis for creating training programs, and information about the human characteristics required to do the job are used to decide what sort of people to recruit and hire. Job analysis therefore plays a central role in HR management. This fact is acknowledged by the U.S. Federal Agencies Uniform Guidelines on Employee Selection, "which stipulate that job analysis is a crucial step in validating all major personnel activities."[4]

Job Analysis and Equal Employment Opportunity   Job analysis therefore plays a central role in equal employment compliance. We discussed EEO issues in Chapter 2. Employers must be able to show that their screening tools and appraisals are related to performance on the job in question. To do this, of course, requires knowing what the job entails—which in turn requires a competent job analysis.

Methods of Collecting Job Analysis Information

In practice, job analysis data is usually collected from multiple "subject matter experts" (mostly job incumbents), using questionnaires and interviews. Data from these employees (say, HR assistants) from different departments is then averaged to determine how much time a typical employee spends on each of several specific tasks (such as interviewing).

However, employees, even with the same job title but working in different departments, may experience very different pressures and constraints. Adding up and simply averaging the amount of time that, say, HR assistants need to devote to "interviewing candidates" could therefore lead to misleading results where there are actually differences in job demands among departments. It's therefore important to understand the departmental context of the job; don't assume that the way someone with a particular job title spends his or her time is necessarily the same from department to department.[5]

Various specific techniques are used to do a job analysis; in other words, to collect information on the duties, responsibilities, and activities of the job. Some of the more popular techniques are discussed in the following sections.

Interviews   Interviews are popular for collecting job analysis data: They may involve *individual interviews* with each employee; *group interviews* with groups of

JOB QUESTIONNAIRE
KANE MANUFACTURING COMPANY

NAME_____   JOB TITLE_____

DEPARTMENT_____   JOB NUMBER_____

SUPERVISOR'S NAME_____   SUPERVISOR'S TITLE_____

1. *SUMMARY OF DUTIES:* State in your own words briefly your main duties. If you are responsible for filling out reports/records, also complete Section 8.
_____
_____

2. *SPECIAL QUALIFICATIONS:* List any licenses, permits, certifications, etc. required to perform duties assigned to your position.
_____
_____

3. *EQUIPMENT:* List any equipment, machines, or tools (e.g., typewriter, calculator, motor vehicles, lathes, fork lifts, drill presses, etc.) you normally operate as a part of your position's duties.

         MACHINE   *AVERAGE NO. HOURS PER WEEK*
_____
_____
_____

4. *REGULAR DUTIES:* In general terms, describe duties you regularly perform. Please list these duties in descending order of importance and percent of time spent on them per month. List as many duties as possible and attach additional sheets, if necessary.
_____
_____
_____

5. *CONTACTS:* Does your job require any contacts with other department personnel, other departments, outside companies or agencies? If yes, please define the duties requiring contacts and how often.
_____
_____

6. *SUPERVISION:* Does your position have supervisory responsibilities? ( ) Yes ( ) No. If yes, please fill out a Supplemental Position Description Questionnaire for Supervisors and attach it to this form. If you have responsibility for the work of others but do not directly supervise them, please explain.
_____
_____

7. *DECISION MAKING:* Please explain the decisions you make while performing the regular duties of your job.
_____
_____
_____

FIGURE 3.1 Job Analysis Questionnaire for Developing Job Descriptions

Source: From *Job Evaluation: Wage and Salary Administration* by Douglas Bartley. Reprinted by permission of the author.

(a) What would be the probable result of your making (a) poor judgment(s) or decision(s), or (b) improper actions?

_____

_____

8. *RESPONSIBILITY FOR RECORDS:* List the reports and files you are required to prepare or maintain. State, in general, for whom each report is intended.

(a)   *REPORT*   *INTENDED FOR*

_____

_____

_____

(b)   *FILES MAINTAINED*

_____

_____

9. *FREQUENCY OF SUPERVISION:* How frequently must you confer with your supervisor or other personnel in making decisions or in determining the proper course of action to be taken?

( ) Frequently   ( ) Occasionally   ( ) Seldom   ( ) Never

10. *WORKING CONDITIONS:* Please describe the conditions under which you work—inside, outside, air conditioned area, etc. Be sure to list any disagreeable or unusual working conditions.

_____

_____

11. *JOB REQUIREMENTS:* Please indicate the minimum requirements you believe are necessary to perform satisfactorily in your position.

(a) Education:
Minimum schooling _____
Number of years _____
Specialization or major_____

(b) Experience:
Type _____
Number of years _____

(c) Special training:

           TYPE   *NUMBER OF YEARS*

_____

_____

(d) Special Skills:
Typing: _____ w.p.m.   Shorthand _____ w.p.m.
Other: _____

12. *ADDITIONAL INFORMATION:* Please provide additional information, not included in any of the previous items, which you feel would be important in a description of your position.

_____

_____

_____

EMPLOYEE'S SIGNATURE _____ DATE: _____

FIGURE 3.1 (continued)

employees having the same job; and *supervisor interviews* with one or more supervisors who are thoroughly knowledgeable about the job being analyzed. Typical interview questions might include: What is the job being performed? What are the major duties of your position? What exactly do you do? and What activities do you participate in?

Interviews are probably the most widely used method for determining a job's duties and responsibilities, and their wide use reflects their advantages. Most important, interviewing allows the worker to report activities and behavior that might not otherwise come to light. For example, important activities that occur only occasionally, or informal communication (between, say, a production supervisor and the sales manager) that would not be obvious from the organization chart, could be unearthed by a skilled interviewer.

Interviewing's major problem is distortion of information, whether due to outright falsification or honest misunderstandings.[6] A job analysis is often used as a prelude to changing a job's pay rate. Employees, therefore, sometimes legitimately view them as efficiency evaluations that may affect their pay. Employees thus tend to exaggerate certain responsibilities and minimize others. Obtaining valid information can thus be a slow process.

Questionnaires   Employees can also be asked to fill out questionnaires to describe their job-related duties and responsibilities. It is, first, important to decide how structured the questionnaire should be and what questions to include. Some questionnaires are very structured checklists. Each employee is presented with an inventory of perhaps hundreds of specific duties or tasks (such as "change and splice wire"). Each is asked to indicate whether he or she performs each task and, if so, how much time is normally spent on each. At the other extreme, the questionnaire can be open-ended and simply ask the employee to "describe the major duties of your job." In practice, the best questionnaire often falls between these two extremes. As illustrated in Figure 3.1, a typical job analysis questionnaire might have several open-ended questions (such as "state your main job duties") as well as structured questions (concerning, for instance, previous experience required).

Observation   Direct observation is especially useful when jobs consist mainly of observable physical activity. Jobs such as janitor, assembly-line worker, and accounting clerk are examples. On the other hand, observation is usually not appropriate when the job entails a lot of unmeasurable mental activity (lawyer, design engineer). Nor is it useful if the employee engages in important activities that might occur only occasionally, such as a nurse who handles emergencies.

Participant Diary/Logs   Another approach is to ask workers to keep a diary/log or list of what they do during the day. For every activity the employee engages in, he or she records the activity (along with the time) in a log. This can produce a very complete picture of the job, especially when supplemented with subsequent interviews with the worker and his or her supervisor. The employee might, of course, try to exaggerate some activities and underplay others. However, the detailed, chronological nature of the log tends to mediate against this.

Other Job Analysis Methods   You may encounter several other job analysis methods. For example, the U.S. Civil Service Commission has a job analysis technique used for providing a standardized procedure for comparing and classifying jobs. Information here is compiled on a *job analysis record sheet.* Identifying information (such as job title) and a brief summary of the job are listed first. Next the job's specific tasks are listed in order of importance. Then, for each task, the analyst specifies such things as the knowledge required (for example, the facts or principles the worker must be acquainted with to do his or her job); skills required (for example, the skills needed to operate machines or vehicles); and abilities required (for example, mathematical, reasoning, problem solving, or interpersonal abilities).

Position analysis questionnaire   The *position analysis questionnaire (PAQ)* is a very structured job analysis questionnaire.[7] The PAQ is filled in by a job analyst, a person who should be acquainted with the particular job to be analyzed. The PAQ contains 194 items, each of which (such as "written materials") represents a basic element that may or may not play an important role in the job. The job analyst decides whether each item plays a role on the job and, if so, to what extent. In Figure 3.2, for example, "written materials" received a rating of 4, indicating that written materials (such as books, reports, and office notes) play a considerable role in this job.

The advantage of the PAQ is that it provides a quantitative score or profile of any job in terms of how that job rates on five basic job traits such as "having decision-making/communications/social responsibilities." The PAQ lets you assign a single quantitative score or value to each job. You can therefore use the PAQ results to compare jobs relative to one another; this information can then be used to assign pay levels for each job.

Department of Labor procedure   The U.S. Department of Labor (DOL) procedure also aims to provide a standardized method by which different jobs can be quantitatively rated, classified, and compared. The heart of this analysis is a rating of each job in terms of an employee's specific functions with respect to *data, people,* and *things.* As illustrated in Table 3.1, a set of basic activities called *worker functions* describes what a worker can do with respect to data, people, and things. With respect to *data,* for instance, the basic functions include synthesizing, coordinating, and copying. Note also that each worker function has been assigned an importance level. Thus, "coordinating" is 1, and "copying" is 5. If you were analyzing the job of a receptionist/clerk, for example, you might label the job 5, 6, 7, which would represent copying data, speaking-signaling people, and handling things.

Writing Job Descriptions

The job analysis should provide the basis for writing a job description. A job description is a written statement of *what* the jobholder does, *how* he or she does it, and under *what conditions* the job is performed. This information is in turn used to write a job specification that lists the knowledge, abilities, and skills needed to perform the job satisfactorily. An example of a job description is presented in Figure 3.3. As is usual, it contains several types of information.

Job Identification   As in Figure 3.3, the job identification section contains the job title, which specifies the title of the job, such as supervisor of data processing operations, sales manager, or inventory control clerk.[8]

INFORMATION INPUT

1 INFORMATION INPUT

1.1 Sources of Job Information

Rate each of the following items in terms of the extent to which it is used by the worker as a source of information in performing his job.

	Extent of Use (U)
NA	Does not apply
1	Nominal/very infrequent
2	Occasional
3	Moderate
4	Considerable
5	Very substantial

1.1.1 Visual Sources of Job Information

1 | 4   Written materials (books, reports, office notes, articles, job instructions, signs, etc.)

2 | 2   Quantitative materials (materials which deal with quantities or amounts, such as graphs, accounts, specifications, tables of numbers, etc.)

3 | 1   Pictorial materials (pictures or picturelike materials used as *sources* of information, for example, drawings, blueprints, diagrams, maps, tracings, photographic films, x-ray films, TV pictures, etc.)

4 | 1   Patterns/related devices (templates, stencils, patterns, etc., used as *sources* of information when observed during use; do *not* include here materials described in item 3 above)

5 | 2   Visual displays (dials, gauges, signal lights, radarscopes, speedometers, clocks, etc.)

6 | 5   Measuring devices (rulers, calipers, tire pressure gauges, scales, thickness gauges, pipettes, thermometers, protractors, etc., used to obtain visual information about physical measurements; do *not* include here devices described in item 5 above)

7 | 4   Mechanical devices (tools, equipment, machinery, and other mechanical devices which are *sources* of information when *observed* during use or operation)

8 | 3   Materials in process (parts, materials, objects, etc., which are *sources* of information when being modified, worked on, or otherwise processed, such as bread dough being mixed, workpiece being turned in a lathe, fabric being cut, shoe being resoled, etc.)

9 | 4   Materials *not* in process (parts, materials, objects, etc., not in the process of being changed or modified, which are *sources* of information when being inspected, handled, packaged, distributed, or selected, etc., such as items or materials in inventory, storage, or distribution channels, items being inspected, etc.)

10 | 3   Features of nature (landscapes, fields, geological samples, vegetation, cloud formations, and other features of nature which are observed or inspected to provide information)

11 | 2   Man-made features of environment (structures, buildings, dams, highways, bridges, docks, railroads, and other "man-made" or altered aspects of the indoor or outdoor environment which are *observed* or *inspected* to provide job information; do not consider equipment, machines, etc., that an individual uses in his work, as covered by item 7)

FIGURE 3.2   Portions of a Completed Page from the Position Analysis Questionnaire

Note: This exhibits 11 of the "information input" questions or elements. Other PAQ pages contain questions regarding mental processes, work output, relationships with others, job context, and other job characteristics.

Source: From *Position Analysis Questionnaire* by E. J. McCormick, P. R. Jeanneret, and R. D. Mecham. Copyright © 1989 by Purdue Research Foundation, West Lafayette, Indiana 47907. Reprinted by permission.

TABLE 3.1 Basic Department of Labor Worker Functions

	Data	People	Things
Basic Activities	0 Synthesizing 1 Coordinating 2 Analyzing 3 Compiling 4 Computing 5 Copying 6 Comparing	0 Mentoring 1 Negotiating 2 Instructing 3 Supervising 4 Diverting 5 Persuading 6 Speaking—signaling 7 Serving 8 Taking instructions —helping	0 Setting up 1 Precision working 2 Operating—controlling 3 Driving—operating 4 Manipulating 5 Tending 6 Feeding—offbearing 7 Handling

Note: Determine employee's job "score" on data, people, and things by observing his or her job and determining, for each of the three categories, which of the basic functions illustrates the person's job. "0" is high, "6," "8," and "7"s are lows in each column.

Job Summary The job summary should describe the general nature of the job, listing only its major functions or activities.

Relationships The relationships statement shows the jobholder's relationships with others inside and outside the organization, and might look like this for a human resource manager:[9]

> *Reports to:* Vice-president of employee relations.
>
> *Supervises:* Human resource clerk, test administrator, labor relations director, and one secretary.
>
> *Works with:* All department managers and executive management.
>
> *Outside the company:* Employment agencies, executive recruiting firms, union representatives, state and federal employment offices, and various vendors.[10]

Responsibilities and Duties This section is the heart of the job description, and presents a detailed list of the job's responsibilities and duties. As in Figure 3.3, each of the job's major duties should be listed separately and described in a few sentences. In the figure, for instance, the duty "selects, trains, and develops subordinate personnel" is further defined as follows: "develops spirit of cooperation and understanding," "ensures that work group members receive specialized training as necessary," and "directs training involving teaching, demonstrating, and/or advising."

The Department of Labor's *Dictionary of Occupational Titles* can be used to itemize the job's duties and responsibilities. An example is shown in Figure 3.4: The dictionary lists a human resource manager's specific duties and responsibilities, including "plans and carries out policies relating to all phases of personnel activity," "recruits, interviews, and selects employees to fill vacant positions," and "conducts wage survey within labor market to determine competitive wage rate."

The *Dictionary of Occupational Titles* is being replaced as a source of occupational information by the U.S. Department of Labor's *Occupational Information Network,* or

SAMPLE JOB DESCRIPTION

Supervisor of Data Processing Operations	*Exempt*	012.168
Job Title	Status	Job Code

July 3, 1997	*Olympia, Inc.–Main Office*
Date	Plant/Division
	Information
Arthur Allen	*Data Processing–Systems*
Written By	Department/Section
Juanita Montgomery	*12* *736*
Approved By	Grade/Level Points
Manager of Information Systems	*14,800–Mid 17,760–20,720*
Title of Immediate Supervisor	Pay Range

SUMMARY

Directs the operation of all data processing, data control, and data preparation requirements.

JOB DUTIES*

1. Follows broadly based directives.
   (a) Operates independently.
   (b) Informs Manager of Information Systems of activities through weekly, monthly, and/or quarterly schedules.
2. Selects, trains, and develops subordinate personnel.
   (a) Develops spirit of cooperation and understanding among work group members.
   (b) Ensures that work group members receive specialized training as necessary in the proper functioning or execution of machines, equipment, systems, procedures, processes, and/or methods.
   (c) Directs training involving teaching, demonstrating, and/or advising users in productive work methods and effective communications with data processing.
3. Reads and analyzes wide variety of instructional and training information.
   (a) Applies latest concepts and ideas to changing organizational requirements.
   (b) Assists in developing and/or updating manuals, procedures, specifications, etc., relative to organizational requirements and needs.
   (c) Assists in the preparation of specifications and related evaluations of supporting software and hardware.
4. Plans, directs, and controls a wide variety of operational assignments by 5 to 7 subordinates; works closely with other managers, specialists, and technicians within Information Systems as well as with managers in other departments with data needs and with vendors.
   (a) Receives, interprets, develops, and distributes directives ranging from the very simple to the highly complex and technological in nature.
   (b) Establishes and implements annual budget for department.
5. Interacts and communicates with people representing a wide variety of units and organizations.
   (a) Communicates both personally and impersonally, through oral or written directives and memoranda, with all involved parties.
   (b) Attends local meetings of professional organizations in the field of data processing.

*This section should also include description of uncomfortable, dirty, or dangerous assignments.

FIGURE 3.3   Sample Job Description

Source: From *Compensation Management in a Knowledge-Based World,* 7th ed., by Richard I. Henderson. Copyright © 1997. Adapted by permission of Prentice-Hall, Inc., Upper Saddle River, NJ.

166.117–018 MANAGER, PERSONNEL (profess. & kin.) alternate titles: manager, human resources

Plans and carries out policies relating to all phases of personnel activity: Recruits, interviews, and selects employees to fill vacant positions. Plans and conducts new employee orientation to foster positive attitude toward company goals. Keeps record of insurance coverage, pension plan, and personnel transactions, such as hires, promotions, transfers, and terminations. Investigates accidents and prepares reports for insurance carrier. Conducts wage survey within labor market to determine competitive wage rate. Prepares budget of personnel operations. Meets with shop stewards and supervisors to resolve grievances. Writes separation notices for employees separating with cause and conducts exit interviews to determine reasons behind separations. Prepares reports and recommends procedures to reduce absenteeism and turnover. Represents company at personnel-related hearings and investigations. Contracts with outside suppliers to provide employee services, such as canteen, transportation, or relocation service. May prepare budget of personnel operations, using computer terminal. May administer manual and dexterity tests to applicants. May supervise clerical workers. May keep records of hired employee characteristics for governmental reporting purposes. May negotiate collective bargaining agreement with BUSINESS REPRESENTATIVE, LABOR UNION (profess & kin.) 187.167–018. *GOE: 11.05.02 STRENGTH: S GED: R5 M5 L5 SVP: 8 DLU: 88*

FIGURE 3.4 "Personnel Manager" description from *Dictionary of Occupational Titles.* (Superintendent of Documents, Government Printing Office, Washington, D.C., 20402-9325.)

O*NET (www.doleta.gov/programs/onet). As of today, O*NET contains data adapted from preexisting sources such as the *Dictionary of Occupational Titles.* However, it is growing fast, and adding new data about jobs in today's increasingly information-based economy. Built-in software allows users to see the most important characteristics of an occupation, as well as the training, experience, and education and knowledge that are required to do the job well.[11]

Authority This section defines the limits of the jobholder's authority. For example, the jobholder might have authority to approve purchase requests up to $5,000, grant time off or leaves of absence, discipline department personnel, recommend salary increases, and interview and hire new employees.[12]

Standards of Performance Some job descriptions also contain a standards-of-performance section, which states the standards the employee is expected to achieve in each of the job description's main duties and responsibilities.

Working Conditions and Physical Environment The job description also lists the general working conditions involved in the job. These might include noise level, hazardous conditions, heat, and other conditions.

Writing Job Descriptions That Comply with the ADA As explained in Chapter 2, the Americans with Disabilities Act (ADA) does not require employers to have job descriptions. However, almost all ADA lawsuits revolve around the question, What are the essential functions of the job? Without a job description listing these functions, it is difficult to convince a court that the functions were in fact essential to the job.[13] The corollary is that the essential functions can't just be listed on the description, but should also be clearly identified as "essential."[14] *Essential job functions* are those job duties that employees must be able to perform, with or without reasonable accommodation.[15]

Using the Internet Most employers probably still write their own job descriptions, but more are using the Internet. JobDescription.com illustrates why. The process is simple. First find the desired job title. That leads you to a generic job description for the position. Then use the wizard to customize the description. For example, choose from a number of possible desirable competencies and experience levels.

Writing Job Specifications

The job specification uses the job description to answer the question, What human traits and experience are required to do this job well?[16] It shows what kind of person to recruit and for what qualities that person should be tested. The job specification may be a separate section on the job description or a separate document entirely; often it is presented on the back of the job description.

Writing job specifications for trained employees is relatively straightforward. For example, suppose you want to fill a position for a trained bookkeeper (or trained counselor or programmer). In cases like these your job specifications might focus mostly on traits such as length of previous service, quality of relevant training, and previous job performance. Thus, it's usually not too difficult to determine the human requirements for placing already trained people on a job.

But the problems are more complex when you're seeking to fill jobs with untrained people (probably with the intention of training them on the job). Here you need to specify qualities such as physical traits, personality, interests, or sensory skills that imply some potential for performing the job or for having the ability to be trained for the job. For example, suppose the job requires detailed manipulation on a circuit board assembly line. You might want to ensure that the person scores high on a test of finger dexterity. Your goal, in other words, is to identify those personal traits—or human requirements—that predict which candidate would do well on the job and which would not. Identifying these human requirements for a job is accomplished either through a subjective, judgmental approach or through statistical analysis.

Common sense needs to be applied when compiling a list of the job's human requirements. Certainly job-specific human traits such as manual dexterity and educational level are important. However, it's important not to ignore the fact that there are also work behaviors such as industriousness, thoroughness, good attendance, and honesty that seem to apply to almost any job one could think of, but might not normally be unearthed through a job analysis.[17]

Job Analysis in a "Jobless" World

A *job* is generally defined as a set of closely related activities carried out for pay, but over the past few years the concept of *job* has been changing quite dramatically. As one observer recently put it:

> The modern world is on the verge of another huge leap in creativity and productivity, but the job is not going to be part of tomorrow's economic reality. There still is and will always be enormous amounts of work to do, but it is not going to be contained in the familiar envelopes we call jobs. In fact, many organizations are today well along the path toward being "de-jobbed."[18]

"De-jobbing" is a product of the changes taking place in business today. Organizations need to grapple with several forces: accelerating product and technological change, globalized competition, deregulation, political instability, demographic changes, and trends toward a service society and the information age. Forces like these have changed the playing field on which firms compete. Specifically, rapid change has dramatically increased the need for firms to be responsive, flexible, and capable of competing in a global marketplace.

The organizational changes firms have made to foster competitiveness have helped to blur the meaning of *job* as a set of well-defined and clearly delineated responsibilities. The following is a sampling of how two of these changes have contributed to this blurring.

Flatter Organizations   Instead of pyramid-shaped organizations with seven or more management layers, flat organizations with just three or four levels are becoming more prevalent. As the remaining managers are left with more people reporting to them, they can supervise them less; the jobs of subordinates thus end up bigger in terms of both breadth and depth of responsibilities.

Work Teams   Work itself is increasingly organized around teams and processes rather than around specialized functions. For example, at Chesebrough-Ponds USA, a subsidiary of Unilever United States, Inc., a traditional pyramidal organization was replaced with multiskilled, cross-functional, and self-directed teams that now run the plant's four product areas.[19] In an organization like this, employees' jobs change daily; the effort to avoid having employees view their jobs as a limited and specific set of responsibilities is intentional.

The Future of Job Descriptions   Most firms today continue to utilize job descriptions and to rely on jobs as traditionally defined. However, it's clear that more and more firms are moving toward new organizational configurations, ones built around jobs that are broad and that may change every day. Some feel that "job descriptions, although they include the ubiquitous phrase, 'and all other duties as assigned,' are still relatively rigid and limiting."[20] Another writer has said, "In such a situation people no longer take their cues from a job description or a supervisor's instructions. Signals come from the changing demands of the project. Workers learn to focus their individual efforts and collective resources on the work that needs doing, changing as that changes. Managers lose their 'jobs,' too."[21]

THE RECRUITMENT AND SELECTION PROCESS

Employers use job analysis and job descriptions for several things—for example, as the basis for developing training programs or for determining how much to pay for various jobs. But the most familiar use for job descriptions is probably as the basis for deciding what types of people to recruit and then select for the company's jobs.

The recruiting and selecting process can be viewed as a series of steps, as follows:

1. Do workforce planning and forecasting to determine the positions to be filled.
2. Build a pool of candidates for these jobs by recruiting internal or external candidates.
3. Have the applicants fill out application forms and perhaps undergo an initial screening interview.

4. Utilize various selection techniques such as tests, background investigations, and physical exams to identify viable job candidates.
5. Send one or more viable job candidates to the supervisor responsible for the job.
6. Have the candidate(s) go through one or more selection interviews with the supervisor and other relevant parties for the purpose of finally determining to which candidate(s) an offer should be made.

Recruiting is the subject of the remainder of this chapter. Chapter 4 then focuses on employee selection techniques including tests, background checks, and physical exams.

WORKFORCE PLANNING AND FORECASTING

Workforce (or employment) planning is the process of formulating plans to fill the employer's future openings, based on projecting (1) the positions that are expected to be open and (2) whether these will be filled by inside or outside candidates. Therefore, it refers to planning to fill any or all of the firm's future positions, from maintenance clerk to CEO. Most firms use the term *succession planning* to refer to the process of planning how the company's most important top executive positions will be filled.

Like any good plans, employment plans are built on premises—basic assumptions about the future. The purpose of *forecasting* is to develop these basic premises. If you are planning for employment requirements, you'll usually need three sets of forecasts: one for personnel needs, one for the supply of inside candidates, and one for the supply of outside candidates.

How to Forecast Personnel Needs

There are several ways to predict future employment needs.[22] For example, **trend analysis** involves studying your firm's employment levels over the past five years or so to predict future needs. Thus, you might compute the number of employees in your firm at the end of each of the past five years, or perhaps the number in each subgroup (such as salespeople, production people, secretarial, and administrative) at the end of each of those years. The purpose is to identify employment trends you think might continue into the future.

Another approach, **ratio analysis,** means making forecasts based on the ratio between some causal factor (such as sales volume) and the number of employees required (for instance, number of salespeople). For example, suppose you find that a salesperson traditionally generates $500,000 in sales. Then, if the sales revenue-to-salespeople ratio remains the same, you would require six new salespeople next year (each of whom produces an extra $500,000 in sales) to produce the desired extra $3 million in sales.

Managerial judgment always plays a big role in employment planning. It's rare that any historical trend, ratio, or relationship will continue unchanged into the future. Judgment is thus required to adjust the forecast based on factors you believe will change in the future. Important factors that may influence your forecast include, for instance: decisions to upgrade the quality of products or services or enter into new markets; technological and administrative changes resulting in increased productivity; and the financial resources you plan to have available.

Forecasting the Supply of Inside Candidates

The preceding forecast provides only half the staffing equation, by answering the question, How many employees will we need? Next, *supply*—both internal and external candidates—must be forecast.

A qualifications inventory can facilitate forecasting the supply of internal candidates. **Qualifications inventories** contain summary data such as each current employee's performance record, educational background, and promotability, compiled either manually or in a computerized system. **Personnel replacement charts** (see Figure 3.5) show the present performance and promotability for each potential replacement for important positions. As an alternative, you can develop a *position replacement card* for each position, showing possible replacements as well as present performance, promotion potential, and training required by each possible candidate.

Computerized Information Systems   Qualifications inventories on hundreds or thousands of employees cannot be adequately maintained manually. Many firms computerize this information, and a number of packaged systems are available for accomplishing this task.[23]

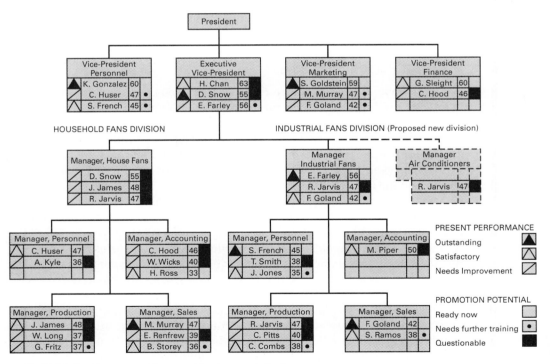

FIGURE 3.5 Management Personnel Replacement Chart

In one such system, employees fill out a 12-page booklet in which they describe their background and experience. All this information is stored on disk. When a manager needs a qualified person to fill a position, he or she describes the position (for instance, in terms of the education and skills it entails) and then enters this information into the computer. After scanning its bank of possible candidates, the program presents the manager with a computer printout of qualified candidates.

Internal Sources of Candidates

Although *recruiting* may bring to mind employment agencies and classified ads, filling open jobs with current employees is often an employer's best source of recruits. To be effective, this approach requires using job posting, personnel records, and skill banks.[24] **Job posting** means posting the open job and listing its attributes, such as qualifications, supervisor, working schedule, and pay rate (as in Figure 3.6). Some union contracts require such postings to ensure that union members get first choice of better positions. Yet posting is also good practice in nonunion firms, if it facilitates the transfer and promotion of qualified inside candidates. *Personnel records* are also useful here. An examination of personnel records (including application forms) may uncover employees who are working in jobs below their educational or skill levels. It may also reveal persons who have potential for further training or those who already have the right background for the open jobs in question. Computerized skills banks (as discussed previously) can help ensure that qualified inside candidates are identified and considered for the openings.

Succession Planning   Forecasting the availability of inside candidates is particularly important in succession planning. In a nutshell, succession planning refers to the plans a company makes to fill its most important executive positions. In practice, the process often involves a fairly complicated and integrated series of steps. For example, potential successors for top management might be routed through the top jobs at several key divisions as well as overseas, and might then be sent through the Harvard Business School's Advanced Management Program. As a result, a more comprehensive definition of succession planning is that it is "the process of ensuring a suitable supply of successors for current and future key jobs arising from business strategy, so that the careers of individuals can be planned and managed to optimize the organization's needs and the individuals' aspirations."[25] Succession planning includes these activities:

Analysis of the demand for managers and professionals by company level, function, and skill.

Audit of existing executives and projection of likely future supply from internal and external sources.

Planning of individual career paths based on objective estimates of future needs and drawing on reliable performance appraisals and assessments of potential.

Career counseling undertaken in the context of a realistic understanding of the future needs of the firm, as well as those of the individual.

Accelerated promotions, with development targeted against the future needs of the business.

NO._____

POSTED: _____
CLOSING: _____

_____

There is a full-time position available for a _____ in the
_____ Department. This position is/is not open to outside
candidates.

PAY SCALE

Minimum	Midpoint	Maximum
$_____	$_____	$_____

or
SALARIED
DUTIES
See attached job description.

REQUIRED SKILLS AND ABILITIES
(Must possess all the following skills and abilities to be considered for this
position.)
1. Demonstrated successful performance at past/present positions including:
   - ability to perform tasks in a complete and accurate manner
   - demonstrated timeliness and follow-through on duties and assignments
   - ability to work well with other people
   - ability to communicate effectively
   - reliability and good attendance
   - good organizational skills
   - problem solving attitude and approach
   - positive work attitude: enthusiastic, confident, outgoing, helpful,
     committed
2.

DESIRED SKILLS AND ABILITIES
(These skills and abilities will make a candidate more competitive.)

Application procedure FOR EMPLOYEES is as follows:

1. Apply by phoning _____, on ext. ____, by 3:00 p.m.
   _____

2. Ensure that a completed Internal Job Application and up-to-date
   resume/application is delivered to _____ by the same
   date.

Applicants will be pre-screened according to the above qualifications.
Selection will be made by the _____ .
   is an equal opportunity employer.
0255M/1

FIGURE 3.6 Job Posting Form

Source: Reprinted with permission from *Recruiting and Selection Procedures,* Personnel Policies Forum
Survey, no. 146 (May 1988): 35. Copyright © 1988 by The Bureau of National Affairs, Inc. (800-372-1033)
<http://www.bna.com>.

Performance-related training and development to prepare individuals for future roles as well as current responsibilities.

Planned strategic recruitment not only to fill short-term needs but also to provide people for development to meet future needs.

The actual activities by which openings are filled.[26]

Forecasting the Supply of Outside Candidates

If there are not enough inside candidates to fill anticipated openings, employers focus next on projecting supplies of outside candidates—those not currently employed by your organization. This may require forecasting general economic conditions, local market conditions, and occupational market conditions.

The first step is to forecast general economic conditions and, for instance, the expected prevailing rate of unemployment. Usually, the lower the rate of unemployment, the lower the labor supply and the more difficult it is to recruit personnel.

Local labor market conditions are also important. For example, the growth of computer and semiconductor companies resulted in relatively low unemployment in cities such as Seattle, quite aside from general economic conditions in the country.

Finally, you may want to forecast the availability of potential job candidates in specific occupations (engineers, drill press operators, accountants, and so on) for which you will be recruiting. Recently, for instance, there has been an undersupply of computer systems specialists.

RECRUITING JOB CANDIDATES

Once you have been authorized to fill a position, the next step is to develop an applicant pool, probably using internal recruiting (discussed above) and one or more outside recruitment sources. Recruiting is important because the more applicants you have, the more selective you can be in your hiring.

Effective recruiting is increasingly important today, for several reasons. First, the U.S. unemployment rate has generally declined in most recent years; this led some experts to refer to the current recruiting situation as one of "evaporated employee sources."[27] Related to this, many believe that today's Generation X employees (those born between 1963 and 1981) are less inclined to build long-term employment relationships than were their predecessors; finding the right inducements for attracting and hiring them may thus be trickier than in previous years.[28] Various tools are available.

Advertising as a Source of Candidates

To use help wanted ads successfully, you need to address two issues: the media to be used and the ad's construction. The selection of the best medium—be it your local paper, the *Wall Street Journal*, or a technical journal—depends on the type of positions for which you're recruiting. Your local newspaper is usually the best source of blue-collar help, clerical employees, and lower-level administrative employees. For specialized employees, you can advertise in trade and professional journals such as the

American Psychologist, Sales Management, Chemical Engineering, and *Electronic News.* In publications such as *Travel Trade, Women's Wear Daily, American Banker, Hospital Administration,* and the *Chronicle of Higher Education,* you would most likely place your ads for professionals such as bankers, hospital administrators, or educators. One drawback to such trade paper advertising is the long lead time that is often required; there may be a month or more between insertion of the ad and publication of the journal or specialized paper, for instance. Yet ads remain good sources, and ads such as Figure 3.7 continue to appear.

Help wanted ads in papers such as the *Wall Street Journal* can be good sources of middle- or senior-management personnel. For instance, the *Wall Street Journal* has several regional editions so that the entire country or the appropriate geographic area can be targeted for coverage.

Employment Agencies as a Source of Candidates

There are three basic types of employment agencies: (1) those operated by federal, state, or local governments; (2) those associated with nonprofit organizations; and (3) privately owned agencies.[29]

Public state employment service agencies exist in every state. They are aided and coordinated by the U.S. Department of Labor, which also maintains a nationwide computerized job bank to which all state employment offices are connected. Public agencies are a major source of blue-collar and often white-collar workers.

Today, these agencies' usefulness is on the rise. Beyond just filling jobs, for instance, counselors will visit an employer's work site, review the employer's job requirements, and even assist the employer in writing job descriptions. And some states, like Illinois and Wisconsin, are turning their local state employment service agencies into "one-stop" shops. Under this concept, say managers from Illinois' Department of Employment Security, "employers and jobseekers now access, under a single roof, a broader array of employment security, workforce-development, and business-support programs. Services available to employers include recruitment services, tax credit information, employee training programs and access to the latest local and national labor market information."[30]

Other employment agencies are associated with nonprofit organizations. For example, most professional and technical societies have units that help their members find jobs. Similarly, many public welfare agencies try to place people who are in special categories, such as those who are physically disabled or who are war veterans.

Private employment agencies are important sources of clerical, white-collar, and managerial personnel. Such agencies charge a fee for each applicant they place. These fees are usually set by state law and are posted in their offices. Whether the employer or the candidate pays the fee is mostly determined by market conditions. However, the trend has been toward "fee-paid jobs," in which the employer pays the fees.

Some specific reasons you might want to turn to an agency include the following:

- Your firm does not have its own HR department and is not geared to do recruiting and screening.
- Your firm has found it difficult in the past to generate a pool of qualified applicants.
- A particular opening must be filled quickly.
- There is a perceived need to attract a greater number of minority or female applicants.

REGIONAL VICE PRESIDENT

SALES & MARKETING

A progressive, half-billion dollar company with operations in 42 states, Millbrook offers breakthrough career potential for a seasoned sales professional whose creativity, drive, and dedication to value-added services match our own.

The selected candidate will oversee all aspects of sales and sales strategy in the assigned region and report directly to the Sr. Vice President for Sales & Marketing. Primary responsibilities include developing and executing regional business strategy, making sales calls on current and prospective customers, and managing, coaching and developing Account Managers. The qualified candidate will be a high-energy, results-oriented coach/leader with top-notch oral and written communication skills. College degree in business management or related field preferable and at least 5 years' sales experience and 2 to 3 years in a managerial capacity. Also essential is the willingness to travel up to three nights per week.

Millbrook offers fully competitive compensation and a comprehensive benefits package. For prompt, confidential consideration, please forward resume and salary history to: Human Resources Dept., Millbrook Distribution Center, P.O. Box 35, Leicester, MA 01524; Fax: (508) 892-3265. E-mail: susan.kornacki@millbrookds.com

We are an equal opportunity employer M/F/D/V.

FIGURE 3.7 Managerial Help Wanted Ad
Source: Courtesy of Millbrook Distribution Services.

■ The recruitment effort is aimed at reaching individuals who are currently employed and who might feel more comfortable dealing with employment agencies than with competing companies.

On the other hand, employment agencies are no panacea. For example, the employment agency's screening may let poor applicants bypass the preliminary stages of your own selection process.[31] Unqualified applicants may thus go directly to the supervisors responsible for the hiring, who may in turn naïvely hire them.

Temporary Workers Many employers today are supplementing their permanent employee base by hiring contingent or temporary workers, often through the services of temporary help agencies. Also defined as *part-time* or *just-in-time* workers, the contingent workforce is big and growing and is broadly defined as workers who don't have permanent jobs.[32]

Contingent staffing owes its growing popularity to several things. First, corporate downsizing seems to be driving up the number of temporary workers firms employ. For example, although Du Pont says it has cut its workforce by 47,000 in the past few years, it also estimates that only 70% of those workers actually stopped working for the company: "The remaining 30%—about 14,000 workers—returned as vendors or contractors."[33] Historically, employers have also used "temps" to fill in for the days or weeks that permanent employees were out sick or on vacation. Today's desire for ever-higher productivity also contributes to temp workers' growing popularity. In general, as one expert puts it, "Productivity is measured in terms of output per hour paid for," and "if employees are paid only when they're working, as contingent workers are, overall productivity increases."[34] Contingent workers also usually aren't paid any benefits, which is another saving for the employer.

Some firms today employ so many temporary workers that they hire temporary agencies to manage their temporary workforces. New York–based MasterCard, for instance, has a temporary workforce of 200 to 400 workers on any given day, and retained Manpower, Inc., a large temporary staffing agency, to coordinate the hiring, training, and paperwork of temporary workers. In such a situation, the temporary employment agency may even assign on-site supervisors to the employer to manage the duties involved in managing the temporary employees.[35] Some temp agencies are even opening in shopping malls. Olsten Staffing Services, for instance, has opened centers in six locations to offer mall tenants assistance in areas such as job postings, temporary employment, candidate screening and interviewing, background checks, reliability and integrity testing, and training.[36]

The contingent workforce is no longer limited to clerical or maintenance staff: In one recent year, almost 100,000 people found temporary work in engineering, science, or management support occupations, for instance.[37] In fact, growing numbers of firms use temporary workers as short-term chief financial officers, or even chief executive officers: It's estimated that 60% of the total U.S. temporary payroll is nonclerical and includes "CEOs, human resources directors, computer systems analysts, accountants, doctors, and nurses."[38]

Executive Recruiters as a Source of Candidates

Executive recruiters (also called *headhunters*) are special employment agencies retained by employers to seek out top-management talent for their clients. They fill jobs in the $50,000 and up category, although $70,000 is often the lower limit. The percentage of your firm's positions filled by these services might be small. However, these jobs include the most crucial executive and technical positions. For executive positions, headhunters may be your *only* source. Their fees are always paid by the employer.

Headhunting firms can be useful. They have many contacts and are especially adept at contacting qualified candidates who are employed and not actively looking to change jobs. They can also keep your firm's name confidential until late into the search process. The recruiter can save top management time by doing the preliminary work of advertising for the position and screening what could turn out to be hundreds of applicants. The recruiter's fee might actually turn out to be insignificant compared to the cost of the executive time saved.

But there are some pitfalls. As an employer, it is essential for you to explain completely what sort of candidate is required and why. Some recruiters are also more salespeople than professionals. They may be more interested in persuading you to hire a candidate than in finding one who will do the job you want. Recruiters also claim that what their clients say or think they want is often not really what they need. Therefore, be prepared for some in-depth dissecting of your request. Also make sure to meet the person who will be handling your search, and nail down exactly what the charges will be.[39]

Two trends—technology and specialization—are changing the executive search business. Top firms traditionally took up to seven months to complete a big search, much of that time spent shuffling chores between headhunters and researchers who need to dig up the initial "long list" of candidates; this often took too long in today's fast-moving environment.[40] Most of these firms are therefore establishing Internet-linked computerized databases, the aim of which, according to one senior recruiter, is "to create a long list by pushing a button."[41] Recruiter Korn/Ferry launched a net Internet service called Futurestep to draw more managerial applicants into its files; in turn, it has teamed up with the *Wall Street Journal,* which runs a career Web site of its own.[42]

As a job candidate, keep several things in mind when dealing with executive search firms. Most of these firms pay little heed to unsolicited résumés, preferring instead to find out their own candidates. Some firms have also been known to present an unpromising candidate to a client simply to make their other one or two proposed candidates look better. Some eager clients may also jump the gun, checking your references and undermining your present position prematurely. Also remember that executive recruiters and their clients are usually more impressed with candidates who are obviously "not looking" for a job, and that overeagerness to take a job can be a candidate's downfall.[43]

College Recruiting and Interns as a Source of Candidates

Many promotable candidates are originally hired through college recruiting. Such recruiting is thus an important source of management trainees, as well as of professional and technical employees.

There are two main problems with on-campus recruiting. First, it is relatively expensive and time consuming for the recruiters. Schedules must be set well in advance, company brochures printed, records of interviews kept, and much recruiting time spent on campus. Second, recruiters themselves are sometimes ineffective. Some recruiters are unprepared, show little interest in candidates, and act superior. Many recruiters also don't effectively screen their student candidates. For example, students' physical attractiveness often outweighs other more valid traits and skills.[44] Some recruiters also tend to assign females to "female type" jobs and males to "male type" jobs.[45] Such findings underscore the need to train recruiters before sending them to a campus.[46]

Campus recruiters should have two goals. The main goal is screening, which means determining whether a candidate is worthy of further consideration. Exactly which traits you look for depend on your specific recruiting needs. However, the checklist presented in Figure 3.8 is typical. Traits to assess include motivation, communication skills, education, appearance, and attitude.[47]

Although the main goal is to find and screen good candidates, the other aim is to attract them to your firm. A sincere and informal attitude, respect for the applicant, and prompt follow-up letters can help you to sell the employer to the interviewee.

Job seekers should know that recruiters are usually coy when it comes to revealing the full amount they're willing to pay. For example, one researcher found that nine out of ten recruiters say they do not reveal during hiring interviews the full amount they're willing to pay to hire good employees for the job. Thus, there's often more flexibility at the top than applicants may realize.[48]

Internships   Many college students get their jobs through college internships, a recruiting approach that has grown dramatically in recent years. Today, it's estimated that almost three-quarters of all college students take part in an internship before they graduate, compared to 1 in 36 in 1980, for instance.[49]

Internships can be win–win situations for both students and employers. For students, an internship may mean being able to hone business skills, check out potential employers, and learn more about their likes (and dislikes) when it comes to choosing careers. Employers can use the interns to make useful contributions while they're being evaluated as possible full-time employees.

Referrals and Walk-ins as a Source of Candidates

Employee referrals campaigns are another option: Announcements of openings and requests for referrals are made on the organization's bulletin and posted on wall boards; prizes may be offered for referrals that culminate in hirings.

Employee referral programs have their pros and cons. Current employees can and usually do provide accurate information about the job applicants they are referring, especially because they're often putting their reputations on the line by recommending them.[50] The new employees may also come with a more realistic picture of what working in the firm is really like after speaking with their friends who are currently employed there. Referral programs may also result in higher-quality candidates, insofar as employees are reluctant to refer less qualified candidates. But the success of the campaign depends a lot on your employees' morale.[51] And the campaign can backfire if an employee's referral is rejected and the employee becomes dissatisfied. Using referrals exclusively may also turn out to be discriminatory if most of your current employees (and their referrals) are male or white.

Employee referral programs are increasingly popular. Of the firms responding to one survey, 40% said they use an employee referral system and hire about 15% of their employees through such referrals. A cash award for referring candidates who are hired is the most common referral incentive. Large firms reportedly spent about

CAMPUS INTERVIEW REPORT

Name _____ Anticipated Graduation Date _____

Current Address _____
If different than placement form

Position Applied For _____
_____

If Applicable (Use Comment Section if necessary)

     Drivers License   Yes _____ No _____

     Any special considerations affecting your availability for relocation?
_____
_____

     Are you willing to travel? _____ If so, what % of time _____
_____

EVALUATION	Outstanding	Above Average	Average	Below Average
Education: Courses relevant to job? Does performance in class indicate good potential for work?	_____	_____	_____	_____
Appearance: Was applicant neat and dressed appropriately?	_____	_____	_____	_____
Communication Skills: Was applicant mentally alert? Did he or she express ideas clearly?	_____	_____	_____	_____
Motivation: Does applicant have high energy level? Are his or her interests compatible with job?	_____	_____	_____	_____
Attitude: Did applicant appear to be pleasant, people-oriented?	_____	_____	_____	_____

COMMENTS: (Use back of sheet if necessary)

_____
_____
_____

Given Application   Yes _____ No _____ Received Transcript Release Authorization _____

Recommendations   Invite _____ Reject _____

Interviewed by: _____ Date: _____

Campus _____

FIGURE 3.8 Campus Applicant Interview Review

Source: From *Handbook of Personnel Forms, Records, and Reports* by Joseph J. Famularo. Copyright © 1982 McGraw-Hill Book Company. Reprinted by permission of The McGraw-Hill Companies.

$34,000 annually on their referral programs (including cash payments for candidates), medium companies spent about $17,000, and small ones with fewer than 500 employees spent about $3,600. The cost per hire, however, was uniformly low: Average per hire expenses were only $388, far below the cost of an employment service.[52] Even fast-moving companies like the Internet firm DoubleClick rely heavily on employee referral programs. For example, the company's internal referrals were up to 43% in the first quarter of 2000.[53]

Particularly for hourly workers, *walk-ins*—direct applications made at your office—are a major source of applicants, and can even be encouraged by posting "for hire" signs on your property. All walk-ins should be treated courteously and diplomatically, for the sake of both the employer's community reputation and the applicant's self-esteem. Many employers thus give every walk-in a brief interview with someone in the HR office, even if it is only to get information on the applicant in case a position should open in the future. Good business practice also requires that all letters of inquiry from applicants be answered promptly and courteously.

Former Employees

It is increasingly common to welcome back employees who previously left "for greener pastures." For example, many former employees are finding that the life of a start-up entrepreneur is not all they'd hoped it would be. Hiring executives like Troy Todd of EDS in Plano, Texas, says his company rehired over 500 such "boomerang" employees in January to July 2000. And with more and more dot-com firms facing tough times recently, more and more employers are reportedly "sniffing around" these beleaguered firms to find employees that want to return to the bricks-and-mortar world.[54]

Recruiting on the Internet

A large and growing proportion of employers use the Internet as a recruiting tool. The percentage of *Fortune* 500 companies recruiting via the Internet jumped from 10% in 1997 to 75% in 2000. For example, www.gepowercareers.com (part of General Electric's basic Web site) not only provides useful information about working for the company, but includes numerous useful job seeker aids, such as separate category buttons titled "experienced professionals," "entry-level," and "military officer."[55] Not surprisingly, computer-related positions were the jobs most commonly filled through Internet postings (accounting for 59% of the workers hired).

Employers are using Internet recruiting in a variety of ways. One Boston-based recruiting firm posts job descriptions on its Web page.[56] NEC Electronics, Inc., Unisys Corp., and LSI Logicorp have all posted Internet-based "cyber fairs" to recruit for applicants.[57] As mentioned earlier in the chapter, Cisco Systems, Inc. has a Web site with a Cisco Employment Opportunities page, which offers links to such things as hot jobs—job descriptions for hard to fill positions; Cisco culture—a look at Cisco work life; Cisco College—internships and mentoring program information; and jobs—job listings.[58] Using a corporate Web site to attract surfers to job opportunities requires making it easy to access that information. Thus, 71% of the Standard & Poor's 500 companies make employment information just one click away from their home pages.[59]

Employers list several advantages of using Internet recruiting. First, it is cost effective: Newspapers may charge employers from $50 to $100 to several thousand dollars for print ads; job listings on the Internet may cost as little as $10 each, one expert points out.[60] The newspaper ad might also have a life span of perhaps 10 days, whereas the Internet ad may keep attracting applications for 30 days or more.[61] Internet recruiting can also be more timely: Responses to electronic job listings may come the day the ad is posted, whereas responses to newspaper want ads can take a week to reach an employer (although inserting a fax-response number can provide timely responses, too). Employers increasingly use Internet support tools such as Recruiter Toolbox of Oakbrook Terrace, Illinois, to help them develop online ads that have highly developed prescreening tests to further automate the recruiting process.[62]

Some firms have been phenomenally successful using Internet recruiting. For example, when Boeing Company had to hire 13,000 employees fast, it opened its recruiting Web site: Only 200 résumés were received the first month, but within three months 19,000 résumés had arrived, and in six months, 50,000.[63]

Yet some employers cite just such a flood of responses as a possible downside of Internet recruiting. The problem is that the relative ease of responding to Internet ads may encourage unqualified job seekers to apply; furthermore, the nature of the Internet is that applications may arrive from geographic areas that are unrealistically far away. On the whole, though, more applicants are usually better than fewer, and more companies are using their computers to scan, digitize, and process applicant résumés automatically.[64] More firms are also installing applicant tracking systems to support their on- and offline recruiting efforts. Well-known applicant tracking systems (such as recruitsoft.com and Itrack-IT solutions) help employers keep track of their applicants. They also help the employers perform searches (such as by skill or college degree) and to match candidates with positions. Systems like these also help employers compile reports, such as "EEO applicant summary," and "applicants by reject reason."[65]

Employers can also use a variety of job search Web sites, such as monster.com. A sample list of recruiting Web sites is presented in Figure 3.9.[66] Also see the *HR in Practice* box.

Some online recruiting Web sites are hedging their bets by getting into the bricks-and-mortar recruiting business. For example, hotjobs.com set up a separate division called WorkWorld; this brings prospective employees face to face with employers at one day job fairs. These give both the employer and employee a chance to get a sense of each other that you might not get online, says hotjobs' CEO.[67]

Recruiting a More Diverse Workforce

Recruiting a diverse workforce is not just socially responsible, it's a necessity. As noted earlier, the composition of the U.S. workforce is changing dramatically: The white labor force is projected to increase less than 15%, whereas the black labor force is expected to grow by nearly 29% and the Hispanic labor force by more than 74% by the end of 2005. Women will account for about 64% of the net increase in the labor force in these years. Related to this, about two-thirds of all single mothers are in the labor force today, as are almost 45% of mothers with children under three.

America's Job Bank   www.ajb.dni.us
On this site candidates can search for jobs by occupation, location, education and experience levels, and salary. Those with a military background can search for civilian jobs that match their areas of expertise. Employers can cull a pool of nearly two million job seekers.

CareerBuilder   www.careerbuilder.com
CareerBuilder, which recently merged with careerpath.com, offers information about career advancement and workplace trends, including tips and news for students and recent grads. Users can search more than 50 leading job sites that are part of the CareerBuilder network, with access to more than three million job postings.

CareerIndex.com   www.careerindex.com
This lets you search several recruiting sites simultaneously. For example, you can choose from Monster.com and CareerWeb.com and others. You can find both U.S. and international jobs here, as well as post your résumé and test your skills.

CareerMosaic   www.careermosaic.com
CareerMosaic offers insider profiles on such companies as Microsoft and Canon. Job seekers can search for openings by geographical area, job description, or company name. CareerMosaic has links to more than a dozen countries in North America, Europe, and the Pacific Rim.

CareerShop.com   www.careershop.com
In addition to providing easy searchers for job seekers and a pool of nearly 300,000 résumés for employers, CareerShop offers a marketplace for freelancers and employers, guidance for employers on human resources issues, and myriad counseling services.

ComputerJobs.com   www.computerjobs.com
ComputerJobs.com is the leading information technology employment site, with job opportunities organized by specific skills and regional markets. As part of its virtual recruiting service for employers, ComputerJobs.com will do online behavioral testing and credit checks of candidates.

FIGURE 3.9   Sample List of Recruiting Web Sites

Therefore, smart employers have to actively recruit a more diverse workforce. This means taking special steps to recruit older workers, minorities, and women.

Older Workers as a Source of Candidates   More employers are looking to older workers as a source of recruits, for several reasons. For one thing, because of buyouts and early retirements, many workers have retired early and are ready and willing to reenter the job market.[68] Furthermore, over the next 10 or 15 years the number of annual retirees will double to approximately 4 million, and, according to a demographer, "there will be, I guarantee it, many millions of boomers who will have to work beyond age 65 because they simply haven't saved enough money to retire."[69] (A recent survey by the American Association of Retired Persons concluded that about 80% of the baby boomers expect to work after retirement.[70]) Furthermore, fewer 18- to 25-year-olds are entering the workforce.[71]

Dice.com   www.dice.com
This is the first place to look for many IT professionals. This site lists over 150,000 job openings, both permanent and contractual.

Employment911.com   www.employment911.com
Another Meta-site: It can speed your search by quickly scanning its own listings and those of 35 other sites.

JobOptions   www.joboptions.com
Contemplating a move? On the JobOptions site users can compute comparable salaries for different cities based on housing and other factors, and they can search by job classification, location, and qualifications. Employers can search more than 250,000 résumés.

Jobs.com   www.jobs.com
Get the inside scoop on working for major companies with Jobs.com's Testify section. Jobs.com offers free software that simplifies the process of writing and delivering a résumé via the Internet. The site features interactive career fairs (with chat and video Webcasts) with employers.

JobTrak.com   www.jobtrak.com
Jobtrak.com is the largest site for college students and alumni. It has partnerships with more than 1,000 university career centers, MBA programs, and alumni associations. Students can receive advice from college counselors, contact alumni, and learn to negotiate a salary package.

Monster.com   www.monster.com
The big daddy of job boards, with three million résumés, Monster.com has "communities" for students, techies, and the self-employed. Users can create a career management account, where they can store up to five résumés, track applications, and receive news tailored to their interests.

FIGURE 3.9   (continued)

Is it practical in terms of productivity to keep older workers? The answer seems to be yes.[72] Age-related changes in physical ability, cognitive performance, and personality have little effect on a worker's output except in the most physically demanding tasks.[73] Similarly, creative and intellectual achievements do not decline with age, and absenteeism drops as age increases. Older workers also usually display more company loyalty than youthful workers, tend to be more satisfied with their jobs and supervision, and can be trained or retrained as effectively as anyone.

Recruiting and attracting older workers involves any or all of the sources described earlier (advertising, employment agencies, and so forth), but with one big difference. Recruiting and attracting older workers generally requires a comprehensive HR retiree effort before the recruiting begins, in part because older workers can be hard to find.[74] The aim is to make the company an attractive place in which the older worker can work. For example:

■ *Develop flexible work options.* For example, at Wrigley Company, workers over 65 can progressively shorten their work schedules; another company uses "minishifts" to accommodate those interested in working less than full time.[75]

Online Recruiting

Online recruiting Web sites like monster.com represent just the tip of the iceberg for employers seeking good résumés. For example, one online recruiter points out that "while monster and its competitors have about 5 million unique résumés in their databases, you can find double or triple that number on the open Internet." These résumés are hidden away at the Web sites of virtual communities such as GeoCities and Tripod, and at the Web sites of archived newsgroup postings and several message boards.

Suppose, for example, you want to find résumés of programmers in Florida who are comfortable on the UNIX platform. On GeoCities, go to www.GeoCities.com and in the text field under "explore our neighborhoods," type:

resume *and* programmer *and* UNIX *and* Florida. Then, click "search" and start reviewing résumés.

You can get even better results on sites like Angelfire or Tripod. These allow you to use Boolean operators (such as *and, or, not,* and *near*), and even to focus specifically on telephone area codes for your search. So, for your programmer search, on Angelfire, type:

resume *and* programmer *and* UNIX *and* (Florida *near* 305 or 954). Then click the "go get it" button for personal Web sites and résumés—possible candidates.

Source: Glenn Gutmacher, "Secrets of Online Recruiter's Exposed!" *Workforce* (October 2000): 44–50.

- *Create or redesign suitable jobs.* At Xerox, unionized hourly workers over 55 with 15 years of service and those over 50 with 20 years of service can bid on jobs at lower stress and lower pay levels if they so desire.
- *Offer flexible benefit plans.* For example, older employees often put more emphasis on longer vacations or on continued accrual of pension credits than do younger workers.

Recruiting Single Parents   About two-thirds of all single parents are in the workforce today, and this group thus represents an important source of candidates.

Formulating an intelligent program for attracting single parents should begin with understanding the considerable problems that they often encounter in balancing work and family life.[76] In one recent survey, working single parents (the majority are single mothers) stated that their work responsibilities interfered significantly with their family life. They described as a no-win situation the challenge of having to do a good job at work and being a good parent, and many expressed disappointment at feeling like failures in both endeavors.

The respondents generally viewed themselves as having "less support, less personal time, more stress and greater difficulty balancing job and home life" than other working parents.[77] However, most were hesitant to dwell on their single-parent status at work for fear that such a disclosure would affect their jobs adversely. Thirty-five percent of the single mothers reported feeling that it was more difficult for them to achieve a proper work–family balance, compared with 10% of the dual-earner mothers.[78]

Given such concerns, the first step in attracting (and keeping) single parents is to make the workplace as user friendly for single mothers as practical. Organizing regular, ongoing support groups and other forums at which single parents can share their concerns is a good way to provide the support that may be otherwise lacking. Furthermore, although many firms have instituted programs aimed at becoming more family friendly, they may not be extensive enough, particularly for single parents. For example, *flextime* programs provide employees some flexibility (such as one-hour windows at the beginning or end of the day) around which to build their workdays. The problem is that "for some single mothers, this flexibility can help but it may not be sufficient to really make a difference in their ability to juggle work and family schedules."[79] In addition to providing increased flexibility, employers can and should train their supervisors to have an increased awareness of and sensitivity to the sorts of challenges single parents face. As two researchers concluded:

> Very often, the relationships which the single mother has with her supervisor and coworkers is a significant factor influencing whether the single-parent employee perceives the work environment to be supportive.[80]

Single parents reentering the workforce can turn to various agencies for support. For example, *displaced homemakers*—individuals who reenter the workforce after a long period out of the workforce, or who are forced to work due to hardship—can call the Displaced Homemakers Network (202-628-6767) for advice on obtaining training and placement.[81] Women entering or reentering the workforce can also call *Women Work! The National Network for Women's Employment* (1-800-235-2732) in Washington, D.C., for referrals to local training programs and information about financial aid options, child support, and health insurance.

Recruiting Minorities and Women   The same prescriptions that apply to recruiting single parents apply to recruiting minorities and women. In other words, employers have to formulate comprehensive plans for attracting minorities and women, plans that may include reevaluating personnel policies, developing flexible work options, redesigning jobs, and offering flexible benefit plans.

An employer can do many specific things to become more attractive to minorities. To the extent that many minority applicants may not meet the educational or experience standards for a job, many companies (including Aetna Life & Casualty) offer remedial training in basic arithmetic and writing.[82] Diversity data banks or nonspecialized minority-focused recruiting publications are another option. For example, Hispan Data provides recruiters at companies such as McDonald's access to a computerized data bank; it costs a candidate $5.00 to be included.[83] Checking with your own minority employees can also be useful. In one study, about 32% of job seekers of Hispanic origin cited "check with friends or relatives" as a strategy when looking for jobs.[84]

Welfare-to-Work   Employers are also implementing various "welfare-to-work" programs for attracting and assimilating as new employees former welfare recipients. In 1996, President Clinton signed the Personal Responsibility and Welfare Reconciliation Act, an act that prompted many employers to implement these types of programs. (The act required 25% of people receiving welfare assistance to be either working or involved in a work-training program by September 30, 1997, with the percentage rising each year to 50% by September 30, 2002.)[85]

Global Issues in HR

The Global Talent Search

As companies expand across national borders, they must increasingly tap overseas recruiting sources.[86] For example, Gillette International has an international graduate training program aimed at identifying and developing foreign nationals. Gillette subsidiaries overseas hire outstanding business students from top local universities. These foreign nationals are then trained for 6 months at the Gillette facility in their home countries. Some are selected to then spend 18 months being trained at the firm's Boston headquarters in areas such as finance and marketing. Those who pass muster are offered entry-level management positions at Gillette facilities in their home countries.

Coca-Cola also actively recruits foreign nationals. In addition to recruiting students abroad, it looks for foreign students studying in well-known international business programs such as those at the University of South Carolina, UCLA, and the American Graduate School of International Management in Arizona.

Global recruiting isn't a one-way street, by the way—in other words, you're not just looking for local talent to send abroad, but possibly for talent from abroad that you can bring here. For example, many U.S. companies are reportedly looking in the United Kingdom, Germany, and Western Europe for high-tech employees to fill jobs that are going begging in the United States.[87] New technology can be very useful in that regard. For example, the Internet, fax, and videoconferencing can make the recruiting process easier by enabling you to place ads more easily and then do at least your initial screening while the candidate is still abroad.[88]

Increasingly today, when employers hire "global" employees, they're not just hiring employees who will be sent to work abroad. Although it's true that for many corporations "international recruitment is synonymous with expatriate selection,"[89] HR professionals recognize today that with business increasingly being multinational, "every employee needs to have a certain level of global awareness."[90]

As a result, many employers want their recruiters to look for evidence of global awareness early in the interview process. For example, at the U.S. headquarters of Tetra PAK, Inc., the personnel manager reportedly looks for expatriate potential every time she makes a hire: "We don't often go out and search for someone to go abroad next year . . . but when we recruit, we always look for candidates who have global potential. We're interested in people who eventually could relocate internationally and handle that adjustment well."[91] International experience (including internships and considerable travel abroad) as well as language proficiency are two of the things employers such as these often look for.

The key to welfare-to-work program's success seems to be the employer's pre-training assimilation and socialization program, during which participants receive counseling and basic skills training spread over several weeks.[92] For example, Marriott International has hired 600 welfare recipients under its Pathways to Independence program. The heart of the program is a six-week preemployment training program teaching work and life skills designed to rebuild workers' self-esteem and instill positive attitudes about work.[93] Programs such as Marriott's have reportedly been successful; for instance, 77% of the welfare recipients hired by the company are reportedly still employed there.[94] On the other hand, other companies report difficulty in hiring and assimilating people off welfare, in part because they sometimes lack basic work skills such as reporting for work on time, working in teams, and "taking orders without losing their temper."[95]

DEVELOPING AND USING APPLICATION FORMS

Purpose of Application Forms

Once you have a pool of applicants, the selection process can begin, and for most employers the **application form** is the first step in this process. (Some firms first require a brief, prescreening interview.) The application form is a good way to quickly collect verifiable and therefore fairly accurate historical data from the candidate. It usually includes information about such areas as education, prior work history, and hobbies.

A filled-in form provides four types of information.[96] First, you can make judgments on substantive matters, such as "Does the applicant have the education and experience to do the job?". Second, you can draw conclusions about the applicant's previous progress and growth, a trait that is especially important for management candidates. Third, you can draw tentative conclusions regarding the applicant's stability based on previous work record. (However, you have to be careful not to assume that an unusual number of job changes necessarily reflects on the applicant's ability; for example, the person's two most recent employers may have had to lay off large numbers of employees.) Fourth, you may be able to use the data in the application to predict which candidates will succeed on the job and which will not (a point to which we return later in the chapter).

In practice, most organizations need several application forms. For technical and managerial personnel, for example, the form may require detailed answers to questions concerning such areas as the applicant's education. The form for hourly factory workers might focus on such areas as the tools and equipment the applicant has used.

Equal Opportunity and Application Forms

Employers should carefully review their application forms to ensure that they comply with equal employment laws. Questions concerning race, religion, age, sex, or national origin are generally not illegal per se under federal laws, but are illegal under certain state laws. However, they are viewed with disfavor by the EEOC, and the burden of proof will always be on the employer to prove that the potentially discriminatory items are both related to success or failure on the job and not unfairly discriminatory.

Figure 3.10 presents the approach one employer—Chapman Academy—uses to collect application form information. Several things are worth noting on this application. The Employment History section requests detailed information on each prior

EMPLOYMENT APPLICATION

As an equal opportunity employer, the firm does not discriminate in hiring or in terms and conditions of employment because of an individual's race, creed, color, sex, age, religion, disability or natural origin. The firm only hires individuals authorized for employment in the United States.

Position Applying for: _____

Schedule Desired:
( ) Full time   ( ) Temporary
( ) Part time

_____ / _____ / _____
Date of Application

PERSONAL INFORMATION

Last Name	First Name	Middle Name	Are you authorized for employment in the U.S.? ( ) Yes ( ) No
Present Street Address	City	State	Zip	How long have you lived there? Yrs. Mo.
Previous Street Address	City	State	Zip	How long did you live there? Yrs. Mo.
Home Phone Number	Social Security Number	If you are under 18 years of age, state your age:	

EDUCATION

Type of School	Name and Location of School	Degree/Area of Study	Number of Years Attended	Graduated (Check One) Yes / No
HIGH SCHOOL	Name City State			Yes ☐ No ☐
JUNIOR COLLEGE	Name City State			Yes ☐ No ☐
COLLEGE	Name City State			Yes ☐ No ☐
GRADUATE SCHOOL	Name City State			Yes ☐ No ☐
OTHER	Name City State			Yes ☐ No ☐

ACADEMIC AND PROFESSIONAL ACTIVITIES AND ACHIEVEMENTS

Academic and Professional Activities and Achievements, Awards, Publications or Technical-Professional Societies. Indicate type or name. Exclude organizations which indicate race, creed, color, sex, age, religion, handicap or national origin of its members.	Date Awarded

SKILLS

Skills applicable to position applied for

PERSON TO CONTACT IN CASE OF EMERGENCY

This information is to facilitate contact in the event of an emergency and is not used in the selection process.

Full Name	Address	Phone	Relationship to you?
Place of Employment	Address	Phone	

15-10.22227 Rev. 5/92

GC 7520

FIGURE 3.10   Chapman Academy Application Form

EMPLOYMENT HISTORY

List employment starting with your most recent position. Account for any time during this period that you were unemployed by stating the nature of your activities. If you have less than four places of employment, include personal references to be contacted. May we contact your present employer?
( ) Yes ( ) No

DATES	NAME AND ADDRESS OF EMPLOYER	POSITION HELD AND SUPERVISOR	LIST MAJOR DUTIES	WAGES	REASON FOR LEAVING
FROM: / MO. YR. TO: / MO. YR.	NAME / ADDRESS / PHONE	YOUR JOB TITLE / SUPERVISOR		STARTING / FINAL	
FROM: / MO. YR. TO: / MO. YR.	NAME / ADDRESS / PHONE	YOUR JOB TITLE / SUPERVISOR		STARTING / FINAL	
FROM: / MO. YR. TO: / MO. YR.	NAME / ADDRESS / PHONE	YOUR JOB TITLE / SUPERVISOR		STARTING / FINAL	
FROM: / MO. YR. TO: / MO. YR.	NAME / ADDRESS / PHONE	YOUR JOB TITLE / SUPERVISOR		STARTING / FINAL	

MISCELLANEOUS

Is there any additional information involving a change of your name or assumed name that will permit us to check your work record? If yes, please explain.

Have you ever been employed by The Firm or any of its divisions or subsidiaries before?   ☐ Yes   ☐ No

If yes, Please indicate: | When | Where | Position

List Names of Friends or Relatives now employed by The Firm.

Have you ever been convicted of a crime?   ☐ Yes   ☐ No   If yes, please explain:

PLEASE READ THIS STATEMENT CAREFULLY

I hereby affirm that the information given by me on this application for employment is complete and accurate. I understand that any falsification or omission will be immediate grounds for dismissal. I authorize a thorough investigation to be made in connection with this application concerning my character general reputation, employment and education background, and criminal record, whichever may be applicable. I understand what this investigation may include and I hereby authorize the release of documents, and personal interviews with third parties, such as prior employers, family members, business associates, financial sources, friends, neighbors or others with whom I am acquainted. I further understand that I have the right to make a written request within a reasonable period of time for a complete and accurate disclosure of the nature and scope of the investigation.

It is understood that, as a condition of initial or continued employment, I agree to submit to such lawful examinations, medical, substance abuse, or other, as may be required by the company. The company will pay the reasonable cost of any such examination which may be required.

If I am hired, I agree that my employment and compensation can be terminated with or without cause and without notice, at any time, at the option of the firm or myself. I understand that no store manager or other representative of the firm other than a Vice-President, and in writing, has the authority to enter into any agreement for employment for any specified period of time, or to make any agreement contrary to the foregoing.

I have read and affirm as my own the above statements.

_____   _____
Signature   Date

APPLICANTS IN THE STATE OF MARYLAND ONLY

Under Maryland law an employer may not require or demand any applicant for employment or prospective employment or any employee to submit to or take a polygraph, lie detector or similar test or examination as a condition of employment or continued employment. Any employer who violates this provision is guilty of a misdemeanor and subject to a fine not to exceed $100.

_____   _____
Signature   Date

APPLICANTS IN THE STATE OF MASSACHUSETTS ONLY

It is unlawful in Massachusetts to require or administer a lie detector test as a condition of employment or continued employment. An employer who violates this law shall be subject to criminal penalties and civil liability.

_____   _____
Signature   Date

FIGURE 3.10   (continued)

employer, including job title, duties, name of supervisor, and whether the employment was involuntarily terminated. Also note that in signing the application, the applicant certifies his or her understanding of several things: that falsified statements may be cause for dismissal; that investigation of credit, employment, and driving records is authorized; that a medical examination may be required; that drug screening tests may be required; and that employment is for no definite period of time.

Mandatory Dispute Resolution   Although the EEOC is generally opposed to the idea, more employers are requiring applicants to sign *mandatory alternative dispute resolution forms* as part of the application process. For example, the employment application package for Circuit City requires applicants to agree to arbitrate certain legal disputes related to their application for employment or employment with the company (including, for instance, those relating to the Age Discrimination in Employment Act); Circuit City will not consider the application unless this agreement is signed.[97]

While mandatory arbitration is on the rise, it is also under attack.[98] Courts, federal agencies, and even the organizations providing arbitrators are increasingly concerned that too many employees' rights are stripped away by mandatory binding arbitration (*voluntary* arbitration is not under attack). In fact, in 1997, a Maryland federal court ruled that Circuit City, Inc. could not force its arbitration program on a job applicant in a case there. In an indication of where the matter is probably heading, many companies that supply arbitrators are refusing to do so unless the employers have ADR policies that are fair to the aggrieved employees (for instance, in terms of giving them an equal right to representation and factual investigation).[99]

REVIEW

Summary

1. Developing an organization structure results in jobs that have to be staffed. Job analysis is the procedure through which you find out (1) what the job entails and (2) what kinds of people should be hired for the job. It involves six steps: (1) Determine the use of the job analysis information, (2) collect background information, (3) select the positions to be analyzed, (4) collect job analysis data, (5) review information with participants, and (6) develop a job description and job specification.

2. The job description should portray the work of the position so well that the duties are clear without reference to other job descriptions. Always ask yourself Will the new employee understand the job if he or she reads the job description?

3. The job specification supplements the job description to answer the question What human traits and experience are necessary to do this job well? It tells what kind of person to recruit and for what qualities that person should be tested. Job specifications are usually based on the educated guesses of managers; however, a more accurate statistical approach to developing job specifications can also be used.

4. De-jobbing is ultimately a product of the rapid changes taking place in business today. As firms try to speed decision making by taking steps such as reengineering, individual jobs are becoming broader and much less specialized. Increasingly, firms don't want employees to feel limited by a specific set of responsibilities such as those listed in a job description. As a

result, more employees are deemphasizing detailed job descriptions, often substituting brief job summaries, perhaps combined with summaries of the skills required for the position.

5. Developing personnel plans requires three forecasts: one for personnel requirements, one for the supply of outside candidates, and one for the supply of inside candidates. To predict the need for personnel, first project the demand for the product or service. Next project the volume of production required to meet these estimates. Finally, relate personnel needs to these production estimates.

6. Once personnel needs are projected, the next step is to build up a pool of qualified applicants. We discussed several sources of candidates, including internal sources (or promotion from within), advertising, employment agencies, executive recruiters, college recruiting, the Internet, and referrals and walk-ins. Remember that it is unlawful to discriminate against any individual with respect to employment because of race, color, religion, sex, national origin, or age (unless these are bona fide occupational qualifications).

7. Once you have a pool of applicants, the work of selecting the best can begin. We turn to employee selection in the following chapter.

Key Terms

job analysis	trend analysis	personnel replacement charts
job description	ratio analysis	job posting
job specification	qualifications inventories	application form

Discussion Questions and Exercises

1. What items are typically included in a job description? What items are not shown?

2. What is job analysis? How can you make use of the information it provides?

3. We discussed several methods for collecting job analysis data. Compare these methods, explain what each is useful for, and list the pros and cons of each.

4. Explain how you would conduct a job analysis.

5. Working individually or in groups, obtain copies of job descriptions for clerical positions at the college or university you attend or the firm where you work. What types of information do they contain? Do they give you enough information to explain what the job involves and how to do it? How would you improve the descriptions?

6. Compare five sources of job candidates.

7. What types of information can an application form provide?

8. Working individually or in groups, bring to class several classified and display ads from this Sunday's help wanted ads. Analyze the effectiveness of these ads using the suggestions discussed in this chapter.

9. Working individually or in groups, obtain a recent copy of the *Monthly Labor Review* or *Occupational Outlook Quarterly*, both published by the U.S. Bureau of Labor Statistics. Based on information in either of these publications, develop a forecast for the next five years of occupational market conditions for various occupations such as accountant, nurse, and engineer.

10. Working individually or in groups, visit your local office of your state employment agency. Come back to class prepared to discuss the following questions: What types of jobs seemed to be available through this agency, predominantly? To what extent do you think this particular agency would be a good source of professional, technical, and/or managerial applicants? What sort of paperwork are applicants to the state agency

required to complete before their applications are processed by the agency? What other opinions did you form about the state agency?

11. Working individually or in groups, review help wanted ads placed over the past few Sundays by local employment agencies. Do some employment agencies seem to specialize in some types of jobs? If you were an HR manager seeking a relationship with an employment agency for each of the following types of jobs, which local agencies would you turn to first, based on their help wanted ad history: engineers, secretaries, data processing clerks, accountants, and factory workers?

APPLICATION EXERCISES

Case Incident: Hurricane Bonnie

In August 1998 Hurricane Bonnie hit North Carolina and the Optima Air Filter Company. Many employees' homes were devastated, and the firm found that it had to hire almost three completely new crews, one for each of its shifts. The problem was that the "old-timers" had known their jobs so well that no one had ever bothered to draw up job descriptions for them. When about 30 new employees began taking their posts, there was general confusion about what they should do and how they should do it.

The hurricane quickly became old news to the firm's out-of-state customers who wanted filters, not excuses. Phil Mann, the firm's president, was at his wits' end. He had about 30 new employees, 10 old-timers, and his original factory supervisor, Maybelline. He decided to meet with Linda Lowe, a consultant from the local university's business school, who immediately had the old-timers fill out a job questionnaire that listed all their duties. Arguments ensued almost at once because both Phil and Maybelline thought the old-timers were exaggerating to make themselves look more important, and the old-timers insisted that the list faithfully reflected their duties. Meanwhile, the customers clamored for their filters.

Questions

1. Should Phil and Linda ignore the old-timers' protests and write up the job descriptions as they see fit? Why? Why not? How would you go about resolving the differences?

2. How would you have conducted the job analysis?

Case Incident: A Tight Labor Market for Cleaners

While most of the publicity about "tight" labor markets usually revolves around systems engineers, Web site designers, and chemical engineers, some of the tightest markets are often found in some surprising places. For example, if you were to ask Jennifer Carter, the head of her family's six-store chain of dry-cleaning stores, what the main problem was in running their firm, the answer would be quick and short: hiring good people. The typical dry-cleaning store is heavily dependent on hiring good managers, cleaner-spotters, and pressers. Employees generally have no more than a high school education (many have less), and the market is very competitive. Over a typical weekend, literally dozens of want ads for cleaner-spotters or pressers can be found in area newspapers. These people are generally paid about $8 an hour, and they change jobs frequently.

Why so much difficulty finding good help? The work is hot and uncomfortable; the hours are often long; the pay is often the same or less than the typical applicant could earn working in an air-conditioned environment, and the fringe benefits are usually nonexistent, unless you count getting your clothes cleaned for free.

Complicating the problem is the fact that Jennifer and other cleaners are usually faced with the continuing task of recruiting and hiring qualified workers out of a pool of individuals that are almost nomadic in their propensity to move around. The turnover in her stores and the stores of many of their competitors is often 400% per year. The problem, Jennifer says, is maddening: "On the one hand, the quality of our service depends on the skills of the cleaner-spotters, pressers, and counter staff. People come to us for our ability to return their clothes to them spotless and crisply pressed. On the other hand, profit margins are thin and we've got to keep our stores running, so I'm happy just to be able to round up enough live applicants to be able to keep my stores fully manned."

Questions

1. Provide a detailed list of recommendations concerning how Jennifer should go about increasing the number of acceptable job applicants, so that her company need no longer hire just about anyone who walks in the door. Specifically, your recommendations should include:

   a. Completely worded classified ads

   b. Recommendations concerning any other recruiting strategies you would suggest they use

2. What practical suggestions could you make that might help reduce turnover and make the stores an attractive place in which to work, thereby reducing recruiting problems?

Experiential Exercise

Purpose: The purpose of this exercise is to give you experience in developing a job description, by developing one for your instructor.

Required Understanding: You should understand the mechanics of job analysis and be thoroughly familiar with the job analysis questionnaire (Figure 3.1) and with finding job descriptions on the Internet.

How to Set up the Exercise/Instructions: Set up groups of four to six students for this exercise. As in all exercises in this book, the groups should be separated and should not converse with each other. Half the groups in the class will develop the job description using the job analysis questionnaire, and the other half of the groups will develop it using an Internet source such as www.JobDescription.com. Each student should review the questionnaire or format (as appropriate) before joining his or her group.

1. Each group should do a job analysis of the instructor's job; half the groups (to repeat) will use the job analysis questionnaire for this purpose, and half will use the one from the Internet Web site.

2. Based on this information, each group will develop its own job description and job specification for the instructor.

3. Next, each group should choose a partner group, one that developed the job description and job specification using the alternate method. (A group that used the job analysis questionnaire should be paired with a group that used the Internet.)

4. Finally, within each of these new combined groups, compare and criticize each of the two sets of job descriptions and job specifications. Did each job analysis method provide different types of information? Which seems superior? Does one seem more advantageous for some types of jobs than others?

TAKE IT TO THE WEB

 For Internet exercises, updates to chapter material, and more, visit the Dessler Web site at

www.prenhall.com/dessler

ENDNOTES

1. Gillian Flynn, "Cisco Turns the Internet Inside (and) Out," *Personnel Journal* (October 1996): 28–34.

2. For a good discussion of job analysis, see James Clifford, "Job Analysis: Why Do It, and How Should It Be Done?" *Public Personnel Management* 23, no. 2 (summer 1994): 321–40.

3. Ernest J. McCormick, "Job and Task Analysis," in Marvin D. Dunnette (ed.), *Handbook of Industrial and Organizational Psychology* (Chicago: Rand McNally, 1976), pp. 651–96.

4. The quote is from James Clifford, "Manage Work Better to Better Manage Human Resources: A Comparative Study of Two Approaches to Job Analysis," *Public Personnel Management* (spring 1996): 89–102.

5. Michael K. Lindel et al., "Relationship Between Organizational Context and Job Analysis Task Ratings," *Journal of Applied Psychology* 83, no. 5 (1998): 769–76.

6. Wayne Cascio, *Applied Psychology in Personnel Management* (Reston, VA: Reston, 1978), p. 140.

7. Note that the PAQ (and other quantitative techniques) can also be used for job evaluation, which is explained in Chapter 7.

8. James Evened, "How to Write a Good Job Description," *Supervisory Management* (April 1981): 14–19.

9. *Ibid.*, p. 16.

10. *Ibid.*, p. 17.

11. Matthew Mariani, "Replaced with a Database: O*NET Replaces the *Dictionary of Occupational Titles*," *Occupational Outlook Quarterly* (spring 1999): 3–9.

12. *Ibid.*, p. 18.

13. Deborah Kearney, *Reasonable Accommodations: Job Descriptions in the Age of ADA, OSHA, and Workers Comp* (New York: Van Nostrand Reinhold, 1994), p. 9.

14. *Ibid.*

15. Michael Esposito, "There's More to Writing Job Descriptions Than Complying with the ADA," *Employee Relations Today* (autumn 1992): 279.

16. The remainder of this section, except as noted, is based on Ernest J. McCormick and Joseph Tiffin, *Industrial Psychology* (Englewood Cliffs, NJ: Prentice Hall, 1974), pp. 56–61.

17. Steven Hunt, "Generic Work Behavior: An Investigation into the Dimensions of Entry-Level, Hourly Job Performance," *Personnel Psychology* 49 (1996): 51–83.

18. William Bridges, "The End of the Job," *Fortune* (September 19, 1994): 64.

19. William H. Miller, "Chesebrough-Ponds at a Glance," *Industry Week* (October 19, 1992): 14–15. For an interesting discussion of the need to move from an "it's not my job" mentality from the point of view of an employee, see Kathy Shaw, "It's Not in My Job Description," *CMA Magazine* (June 1994): 42.

20. Sharon Leonard, "The Demise of Job Descriptions," *HRMagazine* (August 2000): 184.

21. Bridges, "The End of the Job," p. 68.

22. Richard B. Frantzreb, "Human Resource Planning: Forecasting Manpower Needs," *Personnel Journal* 60, no. 11 (November 1981): 850–57. See also John Gridley, "Who Will Be There When? Forecast the Easy Way," *Personnel Journal* 65 (May 1986): 50–58.

23. For a discussion of skill inventories, see, for example, John Lawrie, "Skill Inventories: Pack for the Future," *Personnel Journal* (March 1987): 127–30; John Lawrie, "Skill Inventories: A Developmental Process," *Personnel Journal* (October 1987): 108–10.

24. Arthur R. Pell, *Recruiting and Selecting Personnel* (New York: Regents, 1969), pp. 10–12.

25. This is a modification of a definition found in Peter Wallum, "A Broader View of Succession Planning," *Personnel Management* (September 1993): 45.

26. *Ibid.*, pp. 43–44.

27. Shari Caudron, "Low Unemployment Is Causing a Staffing Draught," *Personnel Journal* (November 1996): 59–67.

28. "Tight Labor Markets Bring New Paradigm," *BNA Bulletin to Management* (October 23, 1997): 344.

29. Pell, *Recruiting and Selecting Personnel*, pp. 34–42.

30. Lynn Doherty and E. Norman Sims, "Quick, Easy Recruitment Help—From a State?" *Workforce* (May 1998): 36.

31. *Ibid.*, p. 40.

32. Allison Thompson, "The Contingent Work Force," *Occupational Outlook Quarterly* (spring 1995): 45.

33. Amy Kover, "Manufacturing's Hidden Asset: Temp Workers," *Fortune* (November 10, 1997): 28–29.

34. One Bureau of Labor Statistics study suggests that temporary employees produce the equivalent of two or more hours of work per day more than their permanent counterparts. For a discussion, see Shari Caudron, "Contingent Workforce Spurs HR Planning," *Personnel Journal* (July 1994): 54.

35. "Temps Get a Boss of Their Own," *BNA Bulletin to Management* (November 7, 1996): 360.

36. "The Newest Shop in the Mall: An Employment Center," *BNA Bulletin to Management* (May 14, 1998): 145.

37. *Ibid.*, p. 47.

38. Brenda Paik Sunoo, "From Santa to CEO—Temps Play All Rolls," *Personnel Journal* (April 1996): 34–44.

39. John Wareham, *Secrets of a Corporate Headhunter* (New York: Playboy Press, 1981), pp. 213–25.

40. "Search and Destroy," *The Economist* (June 27, 1998): 63.

41. *Ibid.*

42. *Ibid.*

43. Allen J. Cox, *Confessions of a Corporate Headhunter* (New York: Trident Press, 1973).

44. Robert Dipboye, Howard Fronkin, and Ken Wiback, "Relative Importance of Applicant Sex, Attractiveness, and Scholastic Standing in Evaluation of Job Applicant Resumes," *Journal of Applied Psychology* 61 (1975): 39–48. See also Laura M. Graves, "College Recruitment: Removing the Personal Bias from Selection Decisions," *Personnel* (March 1989): 48–52.

45. Dipboye, et al., *op. cit.*, pp. 39–48. See also "A Measure of the HR Recruitment Function: The 1994 College Relations and Recruitment Survey," *Journal of Career Planning and Employment* 53, no. 3 (spring 1995): 37–48.

46. See, "College Recruiting," in *Personnel*, May/June 1980. For a study of how applicant sex can impact recruiters' evaluations, see, for example, Laura Graves and Gary Powell, "The

Affect of Sex Similarity on Recruiters' Evaluations of Actual Applicants: A Test of the Similarity-Attraction Paradigm," *Personnel Psychology* 48, no. 1 (spring 1995): 85–98.

47. See, for example, Richard Becker, "Ten Common Mistakes in College Recruiting—Or How to Try Without Really Succeeding," *Personnel* 52, no. 2 (March/April 1975): 19–28. See also Sara Rynes and John Boudreau, "College Recruiting in Large Organizations: Practice, Evaluation, and Research Implications," *Personnel Psychology* 39 (winter 1986): 729–57.

48. "In Negotiating Game, Most Recruiters Hold Back, Knowing Few Candidates Hold Out for Better Offer," *BNA Bulletin to Management* (2000): 291.

49. "Internships Provide Workplace Snapshot," *BNA Bulletin to Management* (May 22, 1997): 168.

50. "Employee Referrals Improve Hiring," *BNA Bulletin to Management* (March 13, 1997): 88.

51. *Ibid.*, p. 13.

52. The study on employment referrals was published by Bernard Hodes Advertising, Dept. 100, 555 Madison Avenue, New York, NY 10022. See also Allan Halcrow, "Employees Are Your Best Recruiters," *Personnel Journal* (November 1988): 43–49. See also Andy Bargerstock and Hank Engel, "Six Ways to Boost Employee Referral Programs," *HRMagazine* 39, no. 12 (December 1994): 72ff.

53. Charlene Solomon, "The Creative Approach to Staffing," *Workforce*, p. 76.

54. Carol Vinzant, "They Want You Back," *Fortune* (October 2, 2000): 271–72.

55. Michelle Neely Martinez, "Get Job Seekers to Come to You," *HRMagazine* (August 2000): 45–52.

56. Elaine Appleton, "Recruiting on the Internet," *Datamation* (August 1995): 39.

57. Julia King, "Job Networking," *Enterprise Networking* (January 26, 1995).

58. Flynn, "Cisco Turns the Internet Inside (and) Out," pp. 28–34.

59. "Does Your Company's Website Click with Job Seekers?" *Workforce* (August 2000): 26.

60. "Internet Recruiting Holds Promise," *BNA Bulletin to Management* (July 17, 1997): 232.

61. *Ibid.*

62. "Online Filtering of Applicants Let Key Skills Shine Through," *BNA Bulletin to Management* (June 29, 2000): 206.

63. "Internet Recruiting Takes Off," *BNA Bulletin to Management* (February 20, 1997): 64.

64. Laura Romei, "Human Resource Management Systems Keep Computers Humming," *Managing Office Technology* (November 1994): 45.

65. Jim Meade, "Where Did They Go?" *HRMagazine* (September 2000): 81–84.

66. *Fortune*, Tech Guide (2000): 102. See also Joanne Charles, "Finding a Job on the Web," *Black Enterprise* (March 2000): 90; and "Browse, Click, Career: Online Sites for Job Recruiting and Searching are Blooming on the Web," *Fortune* (December 1, 2000): 223.

67. Tyler Maroney, "Web Recruiting is Find, But We Like a Job Fair," *Fortune* (March 20, 2000): 236.

68. "Retirees Increasingly Reentering the Workforce," *BNA Bulletin to Management* (January 16, 1997): 17.

69. Diane Cyr, "Lost and Found—Retired Employees," *Personnel Journal* (November 1996): 41.

70. Dayton Fandray, "Gray Matters," *Workforce* (July 2000): 28.

71. Harold E. Johnson, "Older Workers Help Meet Employment Needs," *Personnel Journal* (May 1988): 100–105.

72. Glenn McEvoy and Wayne Cascio, "Cumulative Evidence of the Relationship Between

Employee Age and Job Performance," *Journal of Applied Psychology* 74, no. 1 (February 1989): 11–17.

73. Goddard, "How to Harness America's Gray Power," p. 33.

74. "Older Workers Valued but Hard to Find, Employers Say," *BNA Bulletin to Management* (April 30, 1998): 129–34.

75. For this and other examples here, see Goddard, "How to Harness America's Gray Power."

76. Unless otherwise noted, this section is based on Judity Casey and Marcie Pitt-Catsouphes, "Employed Single Mothers: Balancing Job and Home Life," *Employee Assistance Quarterly* 9, no. 3/4 (1994): 37–53.

77. *Ibid.*, p. 44.

78. *Ibid.*, p. 45.

79. *Ibid.*, p. 48.

80. *Ibid.*, p. 48.

81. See Robert W. Wendover, "Smart Hiring," *B & E Review* (July/September 1990): 6–15.

82. Elizabeth Blacharczyk, "Recruiters Challenged by Economy, Shortages," *HR News* (February 1990): B4. Diversity management programs may also make a firm more attractive to job candidates. See, for example, Margaret Williams and Talya Bauer, "The Effect of Managing Diversity Policy on Organizational Attractiveness," *Group & Organization Management* 19, no. 3 (September 1994): 295–308.

83. Jennifer Koch, "Finding Qualified Hispanic Candidates," *Recruitment Today* 3, no. 2 (spring 1990): 35.

84. This compares with 21.5% for black job seekers and 23.9% for white job seekers. Michelle Harrison Ports, "Trends in Job Search Methods, 1990–92," *Monthly Labor Review* (October 1993): 64.

85. Bill Leonard, "Welfare Reform: A New Deal for HR," *HRMagazine* (March 1997): 78–86.

86. This is based on Jennifer Laabs, "The Global Talent Search," *Personnel Journal* (August 1991): 38–42.

87. Jennifer Laabs, "Recruiting in the Global Village," *Workforce* (spring 1998): 30–33.

88. *Ibid.*

89. Shannon Peters Talbott, "Building a Global Workforce Starts with Recruitment," *Personnel Journal* (March 1996): 9–11.

90. *Ibid.*, p. 10.

91. *Ibid.*, p. 11.

92. Herbert Greenberg, "A Hidden Source of Talent," *HRMagazine* (March 1997): 88–91.

93. "Welfare-to-Work: No Easy Chore," *BNA Bulletin to Management* (February 13, 1997): 56.

94. *Ibid.*, p. 56.

95. *Ibid.*, p. 56.

96. Pell, *Recruiting and Selecting Personnel*, pp. 96–98. See also Wayne Cascio, "Accuracy of Verifiable Biographical Information Blank Responses," *Journal of Applied Psychology* 60 (December 1975) for a discussion of accuracy of bio data.

97. Circuit City Stores, Inc., Employment Packet, January 1997.

98. De'Ann Weimer and Stephanie Anderson Forest, "Forced into Arbitration? Not Anymore," *Business Week* (March 16, 1998): 66, 68.

99. *Ibid.*, p. 66.

Testing and Selecting Employees

When you finish studying this chapter, you should be able to:

■ *Define* basic testing concepts, including validity and reliability.

■ *Discuss* at least four basic types of personnel tests.

■ *Explain* the pros and cons of background investigations, reference checks, and preemployment information services.

■ *Explain* the factors and problems that can undermine an interview's usefulness, and techniques for eliminating them.

INTRODUCTION

It was one of those small news reports in the corner of your morning paper, but it certainly wasn't small to the families of the people involved. The employer thought he had done a good job screening job candidates, but it turned out that the reference letter from one applicant's former employer was totally inaccurate. The former employer had provided the departing employee with a letter of recommendation that stated his departure was not related to job performance, although it was: The man's former employer had provided the letter so the employee would not become angry with the employer over his firing. But violent he was: Just after being fired by his new employer—for absenteeism—he returned to that company and shot a former supervisor, the HR director, and three other people, before taking his own life.[1]

THE BASICS OF TESTING AND SELECTING EMPLOYEES

With a pool of completed applications, your next step is to select the best person for the job. This usually means whittling down the applicant pool by using the screening tools explained in this chapter, including tests, background and reference checks, and interviews.

Why Careful Selection Is Important

Selecting the right employees is important for three main reasons. First, your own performance always depends in part on your subordinates. Employees with the right skills and attributes will do a better job for you and the company. Employees without these skills or who are abrasive or obstructionist won't perform effectively, and your own performance and the firm's will suffer. The time to screen out such undesirables is before they are in the door, not after.

Effective screening is also important because it's costly to recruit and hire employees. Hiring and training even a clerk can cost $5,000 or more in fees and supervisory time. The total cost of hiring a manager could easily be 10 times as high, after search fees, interviewing time, reference checking, and travel and moving expenses are tallied.

Legal Implications and Negligent Hiring Careful selection is also important because of the legal implications of incompetent selection. For one thing (as we saw in Chapter 2), EEO legislation and court decisions require you to systematically evaluate your selection procedure's effectiveness to ensure that you're not unfairly discriminating against any protected group. Furthermore, courts are increasingly finding employers liable when employees with criminal records or other problems use their access to customers' homes or other similar opportunities to commit crimes. Hiring workers with such backgrounds without proper safeguards is called *negligent hiring.*[2]

Validity

A test is a sample of a person's behavior, but some tests more clearly reflect the behavior being sampled than do others. A typing test, for instance, clearly corresponds to some on-the-job behavior—typing. At the other extreme, there may be no apparent relationship between the items on the test and the behavior. For example, in the Thematic Apperception Test illustrated in Figure 4.1 the person is asked to explain how he or she interprets the blurred picture. That interpretation is then used to draw conclusions about the person's personality and behavior. In such tests, it is harder to "prove" that the tests are measuring what they are purported to measure—that they are *valid.*

Test validity answers the question: "Does this test measure what it's supposed to measure?"[3] Stated differently, "validity refers to the confidence one has in the meaning attached to the scores."[4] With respect to employee selection tests, the term *validity* often refers to evidence that the test is job related, in other words that performance on the test is a *valid predictor* of subsequent performance on the job. A selection test must be valid because, without proof of its validity, there is no logical or legally permissible reason to continue using it to screen job applicants.

FIGURE 4.1 Sample Picture from Thematic Apperception Test

Source: Reprinted by permission of the publisher from Henry A. Murray. *Thematic Apperception Test*, Cambridge, MA: Harvard University Press, Copyright © 1943 by the President and Fellows of Harvard College, © 1971 by Henry A. Murray.

In employment testing, there are two main ways to demonstrate a test's validity: **criterion validity** and **content validity**. Demonstrating criterion validity means demonstrating that those who do well on the test also do well on the job, and that those who do poorly on the test do poorly on the job. In psychological measurement, a predictor is the measurement (in this case, the test score) that you are trying to relate to a criterion, such as performance on the job: In criterion validity, the two should be closely related. The term *criterion validity* comes from that terminology.

The content validity of a test is demonstrated by showing that the test constitutes a fair sample of the content of a job. A typing test used to hire a typist is an example. If the content of the typing test is a representative sample of the typist's job, then the test is probably content valid.

Reliability

Reliability is a test's second important characteristic and refers to its consistency. It is "the consistency of scores obtained by the same person when retested with the identical tests or with an equivalent form of a test."[5] A test's reliability is very important: If a person scored 90 on an intelligence test on Monday and 130 when retested on Tuesday, you probably wouldn't have much faith in the test.

There are several ways to estimate a test's consistency or reliability. You could administer the same test to the same people at two different points in time, comparing their test scores at time two with their scores at time one; this would be a retest estimate. Or your could administer a test and then administer what experts believe to be an equivalent test at a later date; this would be an equivalent-form estimate. The SAT is an example of the latter.

A test's internal consistency is another measure of its reliability. For example, suppose you have 10 items on a test of vocational interest, which are supposed to measure in various ways the person's interest in working outdoors. You administer the test and then statistically analyze the degree to which responses to these items vary together. This would provide a measure of the internal reliability of the test and is referred to as an internal comparison estimate. Internal consistency is one reason you often find questions that apparently are repetitive on some test questionnaires.

How to Validate a Test

What makes a test such as the Graduate Record Examination (GRE) useful for college admissions directors? What makes a mechanical comprehension test useful for managers trying to hire machinists?

The answer to both questions is usually that people's scores on these tests have been shown to be predictive of how people perform. Thus, other things equal, students who score high on the GRE also do better in graduate school. Applicants who score higher on a mechanical comprehension test perform better as machinists.

Strictly speaking, an employer should be fairly sure that scores on the tests are related in a predictable way to performance on the job before using that test to screen employees. In other words, it is important that you validate the test before using it. This is done by ensuring that test scores are a good predictor of some criterion such as job performance. In other words, you should demonstrate the test's criterion validity. This validation process usually requires the expertise of an industrial psychologist, and is summarized in Figure 4.2.

Ethical and Legal Questions in Testing

Equal Employment Opportunity Aspects of Testing   We've seen that various federal and state laws bar discrimination on the basis of race, color, age, religion, sex, disability, and national origin. With respect to testing, these laws boil down to two things: (1) You must be able to prove that your tests were related to success or failure on the job; and (2) you must prove that your tests don't unfairly discriminate against either minority or nonminority subgroups. If confronted by a discrimination charge, the burden of proof rests with you; you are presumed guilty until proven innocent and must demonstrate the validity and selection fairness of the allegedly discriminatory test or item.

You can't avoid EEO laws by not using tests, by the way. EEO guidelines and laws apply to any and all screening or selection devices, including interviews, applications, and references. In other words, the same burden of proving job relatedness falls on interviews and other techniques (including performance appraisals) that falls on tests.

Individual Rights of Test Takers and Test Security   Test takers have various privacy and information rights. Under the American Psychological Association's standard for educational and psychology tests, for example, they have the right to the confidentiality of the test results and the right to informed consent regarding the use of these results. They have the right to expect that only people qualified to interpret the scores will have access to them or that sufficient information will accompany the scores to ensure their appropriate interpretation. They have the right to expect that the test is secure; no person taking the test should have prior information concerning the questions or answers.

Using Tests as Supplements   Do not use tests as your only selection technique; instead, use them to supplement other techniques such as interviews and back-

Step 1: Analyze the Job. First, analyze the job and write job descriptions and job specifications. Specify the human traits and skills you believe are required for adequate job performance. For example, must an applicant be aggressive? Must the person be able to assemble small, detailed components? These requirements become your predictors. They are the human traits and skills you believe to be predictive of success on the job.

In this first step, you must also define what you mean by "success on the job" because it is this success for which you want predictors. The standards of success are called *criteria*. You could focus on production-related criteria (quantity, quality, and so on), personnel data (absenteeism, length of service, and so on), or judgments (of worker performance by persons such as supervisors). For an assembler's job, predictors for which to test applicants might include manual dexterity and patience. Criteria that you would hope to predict with your test might then include quantity produced per hour and number of rejects produced per hour.

Step 2: Choose the Tests. Next, choose tests that you think measure the attributes (predictors) important for job success. This choice is usually based on experience, previous research, and best guesses, and you usually won't start off with just one test. Instead, you choose several tests, combining them into a test battery aimed at measuring a variety of possible predictors, such as aggressiveness, extroversion, and numeric ability.

Step 3: Administer Tests. Administer the selected test(s) to employees. Predictive validation is the most dependable way to validate a test. The test is administered to applicants before they are hired. Then these applicants are hired using only existing selection techniques, not the results of the new test you are developing. After they have been on the job for some time, you measure their performance and compare it to their performance on the earlier test. You can then determine whether their performance on the test could have been used to predict their subsequent job performance.

Step 4: Relate Test Scores and Criteria. Next, determine whether there is a significant relationship between scores (the predictor) and performance (the criterion). The usual way to do this is to determine the statistical relationship between scores on the test and performance through correlation analysis, which shows the degree of statistical relationship.

Step 5: Cross-Validate and Revalidate. Before putting the test into use, you may want to check it by cross-validating, by again performing steps 3 and 4 on a new sample of employees. At a minimum, an expert should validate the test periodically.

FIGURE 4.2 How to Validate a Test

ground checks. Tests are not infallible. Even in the best cases, the test score usually accounts for only about 25% of the variation in the measure of performance. In addition, tests are often better at telling you which candidates will fail than which will succeed.

USING TESTS AT WORK

While widely used, testing has actually fallen off a bit in the past year or so. For example, 47% of the respondents in one survey required employees to take drug tests in 2000, down from 70% in 1996. About one-third of the respondents required some form of psychological measurement in 2000, about the same as in 1999, but down from 52% in 1998.[6]

Tests have long been used to predict behavior and performance, and they can be effective. For example, researchers recently administered an aggression question-naire to high school hockey players prior to the season. Preseason aggressiveness as measured by the questionnaire predicted the amount of minutes they subsequently spent in the penalty box for penalties such as fighting, slashing, and tripping.[7]

Want to see what such tests are like? Try the short test in Figure 4.3 to see how prone you might be to on-the-job accidents.

How Are Tests Used at Work?

Tests are used to measure a wide range of candidate attributes, including cognitive (mental) abilities, motor and physical abilities, personality and interests, and achievement.

CHECK YES OR NO   YES   NO

1. You like a lot of excitement in your life.

2. An employee who takes it easy at work is cheating on the employer.

3. You are a cautious person.

4. In the past three years you have found yourself in a shouting match at school or work.

5. You like to drive fast just for fun.

Analysis: According to John Kamp, an industrial psychologist, applicants who answered no, yes, yes, no, no to questions 1, 2, 3, 4, and 5 are statistically likely to be absent less often, to have fewer on-the-job injuries, and, if the job involves driving, to have fewer on-the-job driving accidents. Actual scores on the test are based on answers to 130 questions.

FIGURE 4.3 Sample Selection Test
Source: Courtesy of NYT Permissions.

Tests of Cognitive Abilities Employers often want to assess a candidate's cognitive or mental abilities. For example, you may be interested in determining whether a supervisory candidate has the intelligence to do the paperwork required of the job or whether a bookkeeper candidate has the required numeric aptitude.

Intelligence tests, such as IQ tests, are tests of general intellectual abilities. They measure not a single intelligence trait, but rather a range of abilities, including memory, vocabulary, verbal fluency, and numeric ability. Today, intelligence is often measured with individually administered tests such as the Stanford-Binet or the Wechsler test. Other IQ tests such as the Wonderlic can be administered to groups of people.

There are also measures of specific mental abilities. Tests in this category are often called aptitude tests because they aim to measure the applicant's aptitudes for the job in question. For example, consider the Test of Mechanical Comprehension illustrated in Figure 4.4. It tests the applicant's understanding of basic mechanical principles. It may therefore reflect a person's aptitude for jobs—such as engineer—that require mechanical comprehension.

Tests of Motor and Physical Abilities There are many motor or physical abilities you might want to measure, such as finger dexterity, strength, manual dexterity,

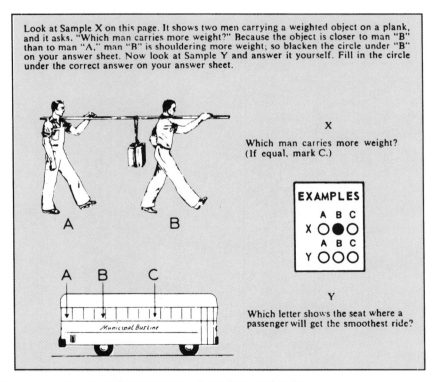

FIGURE 4.4 Two Problems from the Test of Mechanical Comprehension

Source: From the Bennett Mechanical Comprehension Test. Copyright © 1942, 1967–1970, 1980 by The Psychological Corporation. Reproduced by permission. All rights reserved. "Bennett Mechanical Comprehension Test" and "BMCT" are registered trademarks of The Psychological Corporation.

and reaction time (for instance, for machine operators or police candidates). The Stromberg Dexterity Test is one example. It measures the speed and accuracy of simple judgment as well as the speed of finger, hand, and arm movements.

Measuring Personality and Interests A person's mental and physical abilities are seldom enough to explain his or her job performance. Other factors, such as motivation and interpersonal skills, are important, too. Personality and interests inventories are sometimes used as predictors of such intangibles.

Personality tests measure basic aspects of an applicant's personality, such as introversion, stability, and motivation. Many of these tests are projective, meaning that an ambiguous stimulus such as an inkblot or clouded picture is presented to the person taking the test and he or she is then asked to interpret or react to it. Because the pictures are ambiguous, the person's interpretation must come from within. He or she supposedly projects into the picture his or her own emotional attitudes about life. Thus, a security-oriented person might describe the woman in Figure 4.1 as "Me worrying about my mother worrying about what I'll do if I lose my job."

Personality tests—particularly the projective type—are the most difficult to evaluate and use. An expert must analyze the test taker's interpretations and reactions and infer from them his or her personality. The usefulness of such tests for selection then assumes that you find a relationship between a measurable personality trait (such as introversion) and success on the job.

The difficulties notwithstanding, studies confirm that personality tests can help companies hire more effective workers. Industrial psychologists often emphasize the "big five" personality dimensions as they apply to personnel testing: extroversion, emotional stability, agreeableness, conscientiousness, and openness to experience.[8] One study focused on the extent to which these five personality dimensions predicted performance (for instance, in terms of job and training proficiency) for professionals, police officers, managers, sales workers, and skilled/semi-skilled workers. Conscientiousness showed a consistent relationship with all job performance criteria for all the occupations. Extroversion was a valid predictor of performance for managers and sales employees—two of the occupations involving the most social interaction. Openness to experience and extroversion predicted training proficiency for all occupations.[9]

There are many other examples. The responsibility, socialization, and self-control scales of the California Psychological Inventory were used to successfully predict dysfunctional job behaviors among law-enforcement officers.[10] Emotional stability, extroversion, and agreeableness were found to be negatively related to whether expatriates of multinational companies want to leave their assignments early.[11] Employee theft is another aspect of employee behavior that has proven amenable to employee testing.[12]

Because they are personal in nature, personality tests should always be used with caution, particularly where the focus is on aberrant behavior. Rejected candidates may (validly) claim that the results are false, or that they violate the Americans with Disabilities Act or employees' privacy.[13]

Interest inventories compare one's interests with those of people in various occupations. Thus, if a person takes the Strong-Campbell Interest Inventory, he or she receives a report comparing his or her interests to those of people already in occupations such as accounting, engineering, management, and medical technology.

Achievement Tests   An achievement test is basically a measure of what a person has learned. Most of the tests you take in school are thus achievement tests. They measure your job knowledge in areas such as economics, marketing, or personnel. In addition to job knowledge, achievement tests can measure the applicants' abilities; a typing test is one example.[14]

Computerized Testing   Computerized tests are increasingly replacing conventional paper-and-pencil and manual tests. For example, a computerized testing procedure was developed for the selection of clerical personnel in a large manufacturing company.[15] In this case, eight test components were constructed to represent actual work performed by secretarial personnel, such as maintaining and developing databases and spreadsheets, answering the telephone and filing, and handling travel arrangements. For example, for the word processing test, applicants were given three minutes (monitored by the computer) to type as much of a letter as possible; the computer recorded and corrected the manuscript.[16]

Management Assessment Centers

In a **management assessment center**, management candidates are asked to take tests and to make decisions in simulated situations, and to be scored on their performance. The time at the assessment center is usually two or three days and involves 10 to 12 management candidates performing realistic management tasks (such as making presentations) under the observation of expert appraisers. The center may be a plain conference room, but often it is a special room with a one-way mirror to facilitate unobtrusive observations. Examples of the simulated but realistic exercises included in a typical assessment center are as follows:

- *The in-basket*. In this exercise, the candidate is faced with an accumulation of reports, memos, notes of incoming phone calls, letters, and other materials collected in the in-basket of the simulated job he or she is to take over. The candidate is asked to take appropriate action on each of these materials.
- *The leaderless group discussion*. A leaderless group is given a discussion question and told to arrive at a group decision. The raters then evaluate each group member's interpersonal skills, acceptance by the group, leadership ability, and individual influence.
- *Individual presentations*. A participant's communication skills and persuasiveness are evaluated by having the person make an oral presentation on an assigned topic.

Most studies suggest that assessment centers are useful for predicting success in management jobs.[17] On the other hand, the cost of organizing and running such a center can be quite high. Some, therefore, suggest that a straightforward review of the participants' personnel files can often do as good a job as assessment center evaluations of predicting which participants would succeed.[18]

An analysis of more than 200 assessment centers produced the following snapshot of typical assessment center practices: Supervisor recommendations play a big role in who is invited to participate; center candidates typically get little information about the assessment center before it begins; the multiple exercises are usually observed by line or staff managers who serve as assessors; assessors typically attend comprehensive training programs before serving in a center; self- or peer evaluations rarely influence candidate ratings; candidates generally get about a hour's worth of oral feedback and a written report following the center; promotion is the most popular purpose for which assessment centers are administered; in-basket and leaderless group exercises are among the assessment tools used most often.[19]

INTERVIEWING PROSPECTIVE EMPLOYEES

Although not all companies use tests or assessment centers, it would be very unusual for a manager not to interview a prospective employee; interviewing is thus an indispensable management tool. An **interview** is a procedure designed to solicit information from a person's oral responses to oral inquiries; a *selection interview*, which we'll focus on in this chapter, is "a selection procedure designed to predict future job performance on the basis of applicants' oral responses to oral inquiries."[20]

Types of Selection Interviews

As you probably know from your own experience, there are several types of selection interviews. For example, there are nonstructured and structured interviews. In the former, you ask questions as they come to mind, and there is generally no set format to follow. In a more structured or directive interview, such as the one illustrated in Figure 4.5, the questions and perhaps even acceptable responses are specified in advance and the responses may be rated for appropriateness of content.

Structured interviews are generally more valid. With structured interviews all applicants are generally asked all required questions by all the interviewers with whom they meet. This can build consistency and fairness into the process. Structured interviews can also help inexperienced interviewers to ask questions and conduct useful interviews. On the other hand, structured interviews don't always leave the flexibility to pursue points of interest as they develop.

Interviews can also be classified according to the type of questions they contain. In situational interviews, your questions focus on the candidate's ability to project what his or her behavior would be in a given situation.[21] For example, you might ask a candidate for a supervisory position how he or she would respond to a subordinate coming to work late three days in a row. A behavioral interview is another type of interview: Interviewees are asked how they behaved in the past in some situation. For example, the interviewer might ask, "Did you ever have a situation in which a subordinate came in late? If so, how did you handle the situation?"

Interviews can also be classified based on how they are administered. For example, most interviews are administered one on one; two people meet alone and one interviews the other by seeking oral responses to oral inquiries. Most selection processes are also sequential. In a sequential interview the applicant is interviewed by several persons in sequence before a selection decision is made. In a panel interview the candidate is interviewed simultaneously by a group (or panel) of interviewers, rather than sequentially.

Some interviews are done entirely by phone. These interviews can actually be more accurate than face-to-face ones for judging an applicant's conscientiousness, intelligence, and interpersonal skills. Since neither side has to worry about things like clothing or handshakes, the telephone interviews may let both focus more on substantive answers. Or perhaps candidates—somewhat surprised by unexpected calls from the recruiter—simply give more spontaneous answers.[22]

CANDIDATE RECORD

NAP 100 (10/77)

CANDIDATE NUMBER | NAME (LAST NAME FIRST) | COLLEGE NAME | COLLEGE CODE

I U 921
(1-7)   (8-27)   (28-30)

INTERVIEWER NUMBER

0
(33-40)
INTERVIEWER NAME

SOURCE(41)
Campus ☐C
Walk-In ☐W
Intern ☐I
Agency ☐A

RACE (42)
White ☐W
Black ☐B
Asian ☐A
Hispanic ☐H
Native Am. ☐NA

SEX (43)
Male ☐M
Female ☐F
Init.
Cont.
Date
(46-51)

DEGREE (53)
Bachelors ☐B
Masters ☐M
Law ☐L
Majors

AVERAGE
(A = 4.0)
Overall (54-55)
Acctg (56-57)

CLASS STANDING
(58-59)
Top 10% ☐10
Top 25% ☐25
Top Half ☐50
Bottom Half ☐75

CAMPUS INTERVIEW EVALUATIONS

ATTITUDE – MOTIVATION – GOALS

POOR ☐   AVERAGE ☐   GOOD ☐   OUTSTANDING ☐
(POSITIVE, COOPERATIVE, ENERGETIC, MOTIVATED, SUCCESSFUL, GOAL-ORIENTED)
COMMENTS:

COMMUNICATIONS SKILLS-PERSONALITY-SALES ABILITY

POOR ☐   AVERAGE ☐   GOOD ☐   OUTSTANDING ☐
(ARTICULATE, LISTENS, ENTHUSIASTIC, LIKEABLE, POISED, TACTFUL, ACCEPTED, CONVINCING)
COMMENTS:

EXECUTIVE PRESENCE – DEAL WITH TOP PEOPLE

POOR ☐   AVERAGE ☐   GOOD ☐   OUTSTANDING ☐
(IMPRESSIVE, STANDS OUT, A WINNER, REMEMBERED, LEVELHEADED, AT EASE, AWARE)
COMMENTS:

INTELLECTUAL ABILITIES

POOR ☐   AVERAGE ☐   GOOD ☐   OUTSTANDING ☐
(INSIGHTFUL, CREATIVE, CURIOUS, IMAGINATIVE, UNDERSTANDS, REASONS, INTELLIGENT, SCHOLARLY)
COMMENTS:

JUDGMENT – DECISION MAKING ABILITY

POOR ☐   AVERAGE ☐   GOOD ☐   OUTSTANDING ☐
(MATURE, SEASONED, INDEPENDENT, COMMON SENSE, CERTAIN, DETERMINED, LOGICAL)
COMMENTS:

LEADERSHIP

POOR ☐   AVERAGE ☐   GOOD ☐   OUTSTANDING ☐
(SELF-CONFIDENT, TAKES CHARGE, EFFECTIVE, RESPECTED, MANAGEMENT MINDED, GRASPS AUTHORITY)
COMMENTS:

CAMPUS INTERVIEW SUMMARY

INVITE (Circle)
YES   NO
DATE AVAILABLE

AREA OF INTEREST (Circle)
AUDIT   TAX
MCS   ABC
OTHER

SEMESTER HRS.
Acct'g.
Audit
Tax

OFFICES PREFERRED:
No. 1
No. 2
No. 3

SUMMARY COMMENTS:

FIGURE 4.5 Structured Interview Form for College Applicants

How Useful Are Interviews?

While interviews are used by virtually all employers, the statistical evidence regarding their validity is quite mixed. Much of the early research gave selection interviews low marks for reliability and validity.[23] However, recent studies indicate that the key to an interview's usefulness is the manner in which it is administered. Specifically, the following conclusions are warranted based on one study of interview validity:

- With respect to predicting job performance, situational interviews yield a higher mean (average) validity than do behavioral interviews.
- Structured interviews, regardless of content, are more valid than unstructured interviews for predicting job performance.
- Both when they are structured and when they are unstructured, individual interviews are more valid than are panel interviews, in which multiple interviewers provide ratings in one setting.[24]

In summary, structured situational interviews (in which you ask the candidates what they would do in a particular situation) conducted one on one seem to be the most useful for predicting job performance. However, whether you are an effective interviewer depends in part on avoiding common interviewing mistakes, a subject to which we now turn.

How to Avoid Common Interviewing Mistakes

Several common interviewing mistakes can undermine an interview's usefulness. Some of these common mistakes—and suggestions for avoiding them—are described in this section.

Snap Judgments   One of the most consistent findings is that interviewers tend to jump to conclusions—make snap judgments—about candidates during the first few minutes of the interview. In fact, this often occurs even before the interview begins, based on test scores or résumé data.[25]

For interviewees, such findings underscore why it's important to start off on the right foot with the interviewer. Interviewers usually make up their minds about you during the first few minutes of the interview, and prolonging the interview past this point usually adds little to change their decisions. From the interviewer's point of view, the findings underscore the importance of consciously delaying a decision and keeping an open mind until the interview is over.

Negative Emphasis   Jumping to conclusions is especially troublesome given the fact that interviewers also tend to have a consistent negative bias. They are generally more influenced by unfavorable than favorable information about the candidate. Furthermore, their impressions are much more likely to change from favorable to unfavorable than from unfavorable to favorable. Often, in fact, interviews are mostly searches for negative information.

What are the implications? As an interviewer, remember to keep an open mind and consciously work against being preoccupied with negative feedback. As an interviewee, remember the old saying that "You only have one chance to make a first impression." If you start off with a poor initial impression, you'll find it almost impossible to overcome that first, bad impression during the interview.

Not Knowing the Job   Interviewers who don't know precisely what the job entails and what sort of candidate is best suited for it usually make decisions based on incorrect stereotypes about what makes a good applicant. They then erroneously match interviewees against these incorrect stereotypes. Studies therefore indicate that more job knowledge on the part of interviewers translates into better interviews.[26] Interviewers should know as much as possible about the nature of the position for which they're interviewing, and about the human requirements (e.g., interpersonal skills, job knowledge) that the job requires.

Pressure to Hire   Being under pressure to hire undermines an interview's usefulness. In one study a group of managers were told to assume that they were behind in their recruiting quota. A second group was told that they were ahead of their quota. Those behind evaluated the same recruits much more highly than did those ahead.[27]

Candidate Order (Contrast) Error   Candidate order (or contrast) error means that the order in which you see applicants affects how you rate them. In one study, managers were asked to evaluate a candidate who was "just average" after first evaluating several "unfavorable" candidates. The average candidate was evaluated more favorably than he might otherwise have been, because in contrast to the unfavorable candidates the average one looked better than he actually was.[28]

Influence of Nonverbal Behavior   Not just what the candidate says but how he or she looks and behaves can influence the interviewer's ratings. For example, studies have shown that applicants who demonstrate greater amounts of eye contact, head moving, smiling, and other similar nonverbal behaviors are rated higher. In fact, such nonverbal behaviors often account for more than 80% of the applicant's rating.[29] In one study of 99 graduating college seniors, the interviewee's personality, particularly his or her apparent level of extroversion, had a pronounced influence on whether or not he or she received follow-up interviews and job offers. In part, this seems to be because "interviewers draw inferences about the applicant's personality based on the applicant's behavior during the interview."[30]

In one recent study, interviewers listened to audio interviews and watched video interviews. Vocal cues (such as the interviewee's pitch, speech rates, and pauses) and visual cues (such as physical attractiveness, smile, and body orientation) correlated with the evaluator's judgments of whether or not the interviewees could be liked and trusted, and were credible.[31]

An applicant's attractiveness and sex also play a role.[32] In general, for instance, studies of attractiveness find that individuals ascribe more favorable traits and more successful life outcomes to attractive people.[33] A gender study reportedly found that "even when female managers exhibited the same career advancing behaviors as male managers, they still earned less money and were offered fewer career-progressing transfer opportunities."[34] In one recent study, subjects were asked to evaluate candidates for promotability based on photographs: Men were perceived to be more suitable for hire and more likely to advance to a next executive level than were equally qualified women, and more attractive candidates, especially men, were preferred over less attractive ones.[35] Yet another study suggested that in some cases more attractive women may actually be less likely to be offered managerial positions than are less attractive women, possibly because the interviewers erroneously equate attractiveness with femininity and femininity with nonmanagerial jobs.[36]

Race also plays a role. One study examined racial differences in ratings of black and white interviewees' when the interviewees appeared before three interview panels: panels in which the racial composition was primarily black (75% black, 25% white), racially balanced (50% black, 50% white), and primarily white (75% white,

25% black).[37] On the primarily black panels, black and white raters judged black and white candidates similarly. On the other hand, in the primarily white panels or in those in which black and white interviewers were equally represented, white candidates were rated higher by white interviewers, and black candidates were rated higher by black interviewers.

The structure of the interview influences the extent to which race plays a role. One review of 31 prior studies, for instance, concluded that structured interviews produced less of a difference between minority and white interviewees on average than did unstructured interviews.[38] Findings such as these suggest several implications for interviewers. With respect to nonverbal behavior (such as eye contact), one implication is that otherwise inferior candidates who are trained to "act right" in interviews are often appraised more highly than are more competent applicants without the right nonverbal interviewing skills. Interviewers should thus work hard to look beyond the behavior to who the person is and what he or she is saying. Second, demographic and physical attributes, such as attractiveness, sex, or race, may influence your decisions as an interviewer. Because such attributes are generally irrelevant to job performance, interviewers should anticipate the potential impact of such biases and guard against letting them influence their ratings.

Guidelines for Conducting an Interview

You can generally conduct the interview more effectively if you follow the guidelines outlined in this section.

Plan the Interview   Begin by reviewing the candidate's application and résumé, and note any areas that are vague or that may indicate strengths or weaknesses. Review the job specification and plan to start the interview with a clear picture of the traits of an ideal candidate. In one study, about 39% of the 191 respondents said interviewers were unprepared or unfocused.[39]

If possible, use a structured form. Interviews based on structured guides such as those in Figure 4.5 usually result in the best interviews.[40] At a minimum, you should write out your questions prior to the interview.

The interview should take place in a private room where telephone calls are not accepted and interruptions can be minimized.

Also, plan to delay your decision. Plan on keeping a record of the interview, and review this record after the interview. Make your decision then.[41]

Establish Rapport   The main reason for the interview is to find out about the applicant. To do this, start by putting the person at ease. Greet the candidate and start the interview by asking a noncontroversial question, perhaps about the weather or the traffic conditions that day. As a rule, all applicants—even unsolicited drop-ins—should receive friendly, courteous treatment, not only on humanitarian grounds but because your reputation is on the line.

With technical, programming-type jobs, don't assume you'll spend a lot of time talking about "fuzzy" topics like career goals and teamwork in job interviews. One writer describes having six hours of intense job interviews with six separate interviewers at Microsoft, only to be handed off to a final interviewer who asked him to write programming code, but never introduced himself.[42]

Do's and Don'ts of Interview Questions

- **Don't** ask questions that can be answered "yes" or "no."
- **Don't** put words in the applicant's mouth or telegraph the desired answer, for instance, by nodding or smiling when the right answer is given.
- **Don't** interrogate the applicant as if the person is a criminal, and don't be patronizing, sarcastic, or inattentive.
- **Don't** monopolize the interview by rambling, nor let the applicant dominate the interview so you can't ask all your questions.
- **Do** ask open-ended questions.
- **Do** listen to the candidate to encourage him or her to express thoughts fully.
- **Do** draw out the applicant's opinions and feelings by repeating the person's last comment as a question (for example, "You didn't like your last job?").
- **Do** ask for examples.[43] For instance, if the candidate lists specific strengths or weaknesses, follow up with "What are specific examples that demonstrate each of your strengths?"

Be aware of the applicant's status. For example, if you are interviewing someone who is unemployed, he or she may be exceptionally nervous and you may want to take additional steps to relax the person.[44]

Ask Questions Try to follow your structured interview guide or the questions you wrote out ahead of time. A menu of questions to choose from (such as "What best qualifies you for the available position?") is presented in Figure 4.6.

One way to get more candid answers is to make it clear you're going to conduct reference checks. Ask, "If I were to arrange for an interview with your boss, and if the boss were very candid with me, what's your best guess as to what he or she would say are your strengths, weaker points, and overall performance?"[45]

Some do's and don'ts for asking questions are summarized in the *HR in Practice* box.

Close the Interview Toward the close of the interview, leave time to answer any questions the candidate may have and, if appropriate, to advocate your firm to the candidate.

Try to end all interviews on a positive note. The applicant should be told whether there is an interest and, if so, what the next step will be. Similarly, rejections should be made diplomatically (for instance, with a statement such as, "Although your background is impressive, there are other candidates whose experience is closer to our requirements"). If the applicant is still being considered but a decision can't be reached at once, say this. If your policy is to inform candidates of their status in writing, do so within a few days of the interview.

Review the Interview After the candidate leaves, review your interview notes, fill in the structured interview guide (if this was not done during the interview), and review the interview while it's fresh in your mind.

1. Did you bring a résumé?
2. What salary do you expect to receive?
3. What was your salary in your last job?
4. Why do you want to change jobs or why did you leave your last job?
5. What do you identify as your most significant accomplishment in your last job?
6. How many hours do you normally work per week?
7. What did you like and dislike about your last job?
8. How did you get along with your superiors and subordinates?
9. Can you be demanding of your subordinates?
10. How would you evaluate the company you were with last?
11. What were its competitive strengths and weaknesses?
12. What best qualifies you for the available position?
13. How long will it take you to start making a significant contribution?
14. How do you feel about our company—its size, industry, and competitive position?
15. What interests you most about the available position?
16. How would you structure this job or organize your department?
17. What control or financial data would you want and why?
18. How would you establish your primary inside and outside lines of communication?
19. What would you like to tell me about yourself?
20. Were you a good student?
21. Have you kept up in your field? How?
22. What do you do in your spare time?
23. What are your career goals for the next five years?
24. What are your greatest strengths and weaknesses?
25. What is your job potential?
26. What steps are you taking to help achieve your goals?
27. Do you want to own your own business?
28. How long will you stay with us?
29. What did your father do? Your mother?
30. What do your brothers and sisters do?
31. Have you ever worked on a group project and, if so, what role did you play?
32. Do you participate in civic affairs?
33. What professional associations do you belong to?
34. What is your credit standing?
35. What are your personal likes and dislikes?
36. How do you spend a typical day?
37. Would you describe your family as a close one?
38. How aggressive are you?
39. What motivates you to work?
40. Is money a strong incentive for you?
41. Do you prefer line or staff work?
42. Would you rather work alone or in a team?
43. What do you look for when hiring people?
44. Have you ever fired anyone?
45. Can you get along with union members and their leaders?
46. What do you think of the current economic and political situation?
47. How will government policy affect our industry or your job?
48. Will you sign a noncompete agreement or employment contract?
49. Why should we hire you?
50. Do you want the job?

FIGURE 4.6 Interview Questions to Expect

Source: Reprinted from *Jobsearch: The Complete Manual for Job Seekers.* Copyright © 1990 H. Lee Rust. Reprinted by permission of AMACOM, a division of American Management Association International, New York, NY. All rights reserved. http://www.amanet.org.

Would Your Company Pick You to Be an International Executive?

With many firms going global these days, there's a high likelihood you'll be interviewed for an assignment that involves some time abroad. What do companies look for when trying to identify international executives, and do you think you might have what it takes? If you'd like to know, read on.

A recent study by behavioral scientists at the University of Southern California provides some insights into these questions. The behavioral scientists studied 838 lower-, middle-, and senior-level managers from six international firms and 21 countries, focusing particularly on the manager's personal characteristics. Specifically, the researchers studied the extent to which personal characteristics such as "sensitivity to cultural differences" could be used to distinguish between managers who had high potential as international executives and those whose potential was not so high.

Fourteen personal characteristics successfully distinguished the managers identified by their companies as high potential from those identified as not high potential in 72% of the cases. To get an initial, tentative impression of how you would rate, review the 14 characteristics (along with some items), which are listed in Figure 4.7. For each, indicate (by placing a number in the space provided) whether you strongly agree (number 7), strong disagree (number 1), or fall somewhere in between.

Generally speaking, the higher you score on these 14 characteristics, the more likely it is that you might have been identified as a high-potential international executive in this study.[46] The average would be about 50.

USING OTHER SELECTION TECHNIQUES

Background Investigations and Reference Checks

Most employers try to check the background and references of job applicants, and there are two key reasons for doing so: to verify the accuracy of factual information previously provided by the applicant, and to uncover damaging background information such as criminal records and suspended drivers' licenses.[47] The most commonly verified background areas are legal eligibility for employment (to comply with immigration laws), dates of prior employment, military service (including discharge status), education, and identification (including date of birth and address).[48]

The information collected takes many forms. Most employers at least try to verify an applicant's current position and salary with his or her current employer by phone (assuming that doing so was cleared with the candidate). Others call the applicant's current and previous supervisors to try to discover more about the person's motivation, technical competence, and ability to work with others. Some employers get background reports from commercial credit rating companies; these can provide

SCALE	SAMPLE ITEM
Sensitive to Cultural Differences	When working with people from other cultures, works hard to understand their perspectives.
Business Knowledge	Has a solid understanding of our products and services.
Courage to Take a Stand	Is willing to take a stand on issues.
Brings Out the Best in People	Has a special talent for dealing with people.
Acts with Integrity	Can be depended on to tell the truth regardless of circumstances.
Is Insightful	Is good at identifying the most important part of a complex problem or issue.
Is Committed to Success	Clearly demonstrates commitment to seeing the organization succeed.
Takes Risks	Takes personal as well as business risks.
Uses Feedback	Has changed as a result of feedback.
Is Culturally Adventurous	Enjoys the challenge of working in countries other than his/her own.
Seeks Opportunities to Learn	Takes advantage of opportunities to do new things.
Is Open to Criticism	Appears brittle—as if criticism might cause him/her to break*
Seeks Feedback	Pursues feedback even when others are reluctant to give it.
Is Flexible	Doesn't get so invested in things that he/she cannot change when something doesn't work.

*Reverse scored.

FIGURE 4.7 Traits Distinguishing Successful International Executives

Source: From "Early Identification of International Executive Potential" by Gretchen Spreitzer, Morgan McCall, Jr. and Joan Mahoney, *Journal of Applied Psychology* 82, no. 1 (February 1997). Copyright © 1997 by the American Psychological Association. Adapted with permission.

information about an applicant's credit standing, indebtedness, reputation, character, and lifestyle.

The phenomenon of youth gangs infiltrating corporate America provides one of many examples of why employers should carefully check references.[49] The FBI estimates that more than 400,000 gang members live and work in 700 cities nationwide, and some say this number is just the tip of the iceberg.[50] One expert contends that gangs

> are impacting our companies by setting up shop for extortion and drug sales. Members increasingly cloak their illicit activity behind the legitimacy of the workplace. And . . . many also seek health benefits to cover huge medical bills that can result from gang related shootings and other activities.[51]

Even relatively sophisticated companies fall prey to gang member employees, in part because they haven't conducted proper background and reference checks. In

Chicago, for instance, a major pharmaceutical firm discovered that it had hired gang members in mail delivery and computer repair: The gang members were stealing close to a million dollars per year in computer parts and then using the mail department to ship them to a nearby computer store they owned.[52]

Reference Check Effectiveness   Handled correctly, background checks are an inexpensive and straightforward way of verifying factual information (such as current and previous job titles) about applicants. However, reference checking can also backfire. For one thing, it is not easy for the reference to prove that the bad reference he or she gave an applicant was warranted. The rejected applicant thus has various legal remedies, including suing the reference for defamation of character, a fact that can understandably inhibit former employers and supervisors from giving candid references.[53] In one case, for instance, a man was awarded $56,000 after being turned down for a job because, among other things, he was called a "character" by a former employer.

It is not just the fear of legal reprisal that can lead to a useless or misleading reference. Many supervisors don't want to diminish a former employee's chances for a job; others might rather give an incompetent employee good reviews if it will get rid of him or her. Even when checking references via the phone, therefore, you have to be careful to ask the right questions, and to judge whether the reference's answers are evasive and, if so, why.

Making Reference Checks More Productive   You can do at least two things to make your reference checking more productive. First, use a structured form as in Figure 4.8. The form helps ensure that you don't overlook important questions. Second, use the references offered by the applicant as merely a source for other references who may know of the applicant's performance. Thus, you might ask each of the applicant's references, "Could you please give me the name of another person who might be familiar with the applicant's performance?" In that way, you begin getting information from references who may be more objective because they weren't referred directly by the applicant. Some experts suggest contacting at least two superiors, two peers, and two subordinates from each job previously held by the candidate to form a reliable picture of the candidate.[54] Also, ask open-ended questions, such as "How much structure does the applicant need in his or her work?" in order to get the references to talk more about the candidate.[55]

Companies fielding requests for references should ensure that only authorized managers give them. Employees have taken legal action for defamatory references. There are even companies that, for a small fee, will call former employers on behalf of former employees who believe they're getting bad references from their former employers. One supervisor, describing a former city employee, reportedly "used swear words, said he was incompetent and said that he almost brought the city down on its knees."[56] Some suggested reference checking questions are summarized in Figure 4.9.

Using Preemployment Information Services   Computer databases have made it easier to check background information about candidates. As a result, preemployment information services that use databases to accumulate mounds of information about matters such as workers' compensation histories, credit histories, and conviction records have proliferated. Employers are increasingly turning to these information services to make better selection decisions.

TELEPHONE OR PERSONAL INTERVIEW

☐ FORMER EMPLOYER
☐ CHARACTER REFERENCE

COMPANY _____ ADDRESS _____ PHONE _____

NAME OF PERSON
CONTACTED _____ POSITION
OR TITLE _____

1. I WISH TO VERIFY SOME FACTS GIVEN BY
   (MISS, MRS., MS.)
   MR.
   WHO IS APPLYING FOR EMPLOYMENT WITH OUR FIRM.
   WHAT WERE THE DATES OF HIS/HER EMPLOYMENT BY
   YOUR COMPANY? _____ FROM ___ 19__ TO ___ 19__

2. WHAT WAS THE NATURE OF HIS/HER JOB? AT START _____

   AT LEAVING _____

3. HE/SHE STATES THAT HE/SHE WAS EARNING $ PER
   WHEN HE/SHE LEFT. IS THAT CORRECT? YES ___ NO ___ $ ___

4. WHAT DID HIS/HER SUPERIORS THINK OF HIM/HER? _____

   WHAT DID HIS/HER SUBORDINATES THINK OF HIM/HER? _____

5. DID HE/SHE HAVE SUPERVISORY RESPONSIBILITY? YES ___ NO ___

   (IF YES) HOW DID HE/SHE CARRY IT OUT? _____

6. HOW HARD DID HE/SHE WORK? _____

7. HOW DID HE/SHE GET ALONG WITH OTHERS? _____

8. HOW WAS HIS/HER ATTENDANCE RECORD? PUNCTUALITY? _____

9. WHAT WERE HIS/HER REASONS FOR LEAVING? _____

10. WOULD YOU REHIRE HIM/HER? (IF NO) WHY? YES ___ NO ___

11. DID HE/SHE HAVE ANY DOMESTIC, FINANCIAL OR
    PERSONAL TROUBLE WHICH INTERFERED WITH
    HIS/HER WORK? YES ___ NO ___

12. DID HE/SHE DRINK OR GAMBLE TO EXCESS? YES ___ NO ___

13. WHAT ARE HIS/HER STRONG POINTS? _____

14. WHAT ARE HIS/HER WEAK POINTS? _____

REMARKS: _____

FIGURE 4.8 Telephone or Personal Interview Form

Source: Adapted by permission of the publisher from *Book of Employment Forms*, American Management Association.

Just the facts
What were the candidate's dates
of employment?
What was the candidate's title?
What were the candidate's general responsibilities?
What is your relationship to the candidate (peer, subordinate, superior)?
How long have you known the candidate?

On the job
How would you describe the overall quality of the candidate's work?
Can you give me some examples?
(For superiors) What areas of performance did you have to work on?
What would you say are the candidate's strengths?
What would you say are the candidate's weaknesses?
How would you compare the candidate's work to the work of others who
performed the same job?
What kind of environment did the candidate work in?
How much of a contribution do you think the candidate made to your
company or department?
How would you describe the candidate's ability to communicate?
How does the candidate handle pressure/deadlines?
How well does the candidate get along with co-workers?
How well does the candidate get along with managers?
How well does the candidate supervise others? Can you give me your
impressions of his/her management style? Describe the candidate's
success in motivating subordinates.
How does the candidate handle conflict situations?
Based on the candidate's performance with your company, do you
think he/she would be good in the type of position we're considering
him/her for?
What motivates the candidate? How ambitious is he/she?

The bottom line
Why did the candidate leave your company?
Would you rehire this person?
Would you recommend this candidate for this type of position?
What type of work is the candidate ideally suited for?
Were there any serious problems with the candidate that we need to be
aware of before making a hiring decision?
Do you have any additional information to share with us about the
candidate?

FIGURE 4.9 Reference Checking Questions
Source: Carolyn Hirschman, "The Whole Truth," *HRMagazine*, June 2000, p. 88.

Although they are valuable, such services must be used with caution. Perhaps most importantly (as discussed in Chapter 2), various equal employment laws discourage or prohibit the use of such information in employee screening. For example, under the Americans with Disabilities Act, employers are prohibited from making preemployment inquiries into the existence, nature, or severity of a disability; this generally includes inquiries into a candidate's previous workers' compensation claims.

Honesty Testing

Polygraph Tests   The polygraph (or "lie detector") machine is a device that measures physiological changes such as increased perspiration. The assumption is that such changes reflect changes in the emotional stress that accompanies lying. The usual procedure is for an applicant or current employee to be attached to the machine with painless electronic probes. He or she is then asked a series of neutral questions by the polygraph expert. Once the person's emotional reactions to giving truthful answers to neutral questions has been ascertained, questions such as "Have you ever taken anything without paying for it?" can be asked. In theory, the expert can determine with some accuracy whether the applicant is lying.

Complaints about offensiveness as well as grave doubts about the polygraph's accuracy culminated in the Employee Polygraph Protection Act being signed into law in 1988. With few exceptions, the law prohibits most employers from conducting polygraph examinations of all applicants and most employees. Even in the case of ongoing investigations of theft, the employer's right to use polygraphs is quite limited under the act.[57]

Paper-and-Pencil Honesty Tests   The virtual elimination of the polygraph as a screening device has triggered a burgeoning market for other types of honesty testing devices. Paper-and-pencil honesty tests are psychological tests designed to predict job applicants' proneness to dishonesty and other forms of counterproductivity.[58] Most of these tests measure attitudes regarding things such as tolerance of others who steal, acceptance of rationalizations for theft, and admission of theft-related activities.

Although concerns were initially raised by psychologists concerning the proliferation of paper-and-pencil honesty tests, several recent studies support the validity of these selection tools.[59] One study focused on 111 employees hired by a major retail convenience store chain to work at convenience store or gas station outlet counters.[60] "Shrinkage" was estimated to equal 3% of sales, and internal theft was believed to account for much of this. The researchers found that scores on an honesty test successfully predicted theft in this study, as measured by termination for theft. One large-scale review of the use of such tests for measuring honesty, integrity, conscientiousness, dependability, trustworthiness, and reliability recently concluded that the "pattern of findings" regarding the usefulness of such tests "continues to be consistently positive."[61]

In practice, detecting dishonest candidates involves not just paper-and-pencil tests but a comprehensive screening procedure including reference checking and interviews. One expert suggests the steps presented in the following *HR in Practice* feature.

Graphology

The use of graphology (handwriting analysis) is based on the assumption that the writer's basic personality traits will be expressed in his or her handwriting. Handwriting analysis thus has some resemblance to projective personality tests.

Although some writers estimate that more than 1,000 U.S. companies use handwriting analysis to assess applicants for certain strategic positions, the validity of handwriting analysis is questionable, to say the least.[63] In general, the evidence suggests that graphology does not predict job performance.[64]

Physical Examinations

Physical examinations are often the next step in the selection process, and there are several reasons for requiring them. Such exams can be used to confirm that the applicant qualifies for the physical requirements of the position and to discover any medical limitations that should be taken into account in placing the applicant. The examination can, of course, also detect communicable diseases that may be unknown to the applicant. Under the ADA, a person with a disability can't be rejected for the job if he or she is otherwise qualified and if the person could perform the essential job functions with reasonable accommodation. According to the ADA, a medical exam is permitted during the period between the job offer and commencement of work, but only if such exams are standard practice for all applications for that job category.[65]

Drug Screening

Drug abuse is a serious problem at work.[66] The U.S. Chamber of Commerce estimates that employee drug and alcohol use costs U.S. employers more than $60 billion each year in reduced productivity, increased accidents, increased sick benefits, and higher workers' compensation claims.[67]

Employers are therefore increasingly conducting drug tests. The most common practice is to test new applicants just before they are formally hired. Many firms also test current employees when there is reason to believe an employee has been using drugs after a work accident, or in the presence of obvious behavioral symptoms, or in the face of chronic lateness or high absenteeism. Some firms routinely administer drug tests on a random or periodic basis, whereas others require drug tests when an employee is transferred or promoted to a new position.[68] Virtually all (96%) employers that conduct such tests use urine sampling.[69] Unfortunately, drug testing in general doesn't always correlate very closely with actual impairment levels.[70] Although Breathalyzers and blood tests for alcohol such as those given at the roadside to inebriated drivers correlate closely with impairment levels, urine and blood tests for other drugs only indicate whether the drug residues are present: They cannot measure impairment or, for that matter, habituation or addiction.[71]

Drug testing therefore raises several issues. Without strong evidence linking blood or urine drug levels to impairment, some argue that drug testing violates citizens' rights to privacy and due process and that the procedures themselves are degrading and intrusive. Others argue that one's use of drugs during leisure hours might be identified through workplace drug testing but have little or no relevance to the job itself.[72] Furthermore, as one attorney writes, "It is not uncommon for employees to claim that drug tests violate their rights to privacy under common law or, in some states, a state statutory or constitutional provision."[73]

Several federal laws also have direct relevance for workplace drug testing. For example, under the ADA, a former drug user (one who no longer uses illegal drugs and successfully completed or is participating in a rehabilitation program) would probably be considered a qualified applicant with a disability.[74] U.S. Department of Transportation workplace regulations require firms with more than 50 eligible employees in transportation industries to now conduct alcohol testing on workers with sensitive or safety-related jobs. These include mass-transit workers, air traffic controllers, train crews, and school bus drivers.[75]

What should you do when a candidate tests positive? Most companies do not hire such candidates, and a few immediately fire current employees whose test results are positive.[76] However, current employees have more legal recourse if dismissed and must therefore be told the reason for their dismissal if they are dismissed for a positive drug test.[77] But, particularly where safety-sensitive jobs are concerned, courts appear to side with employers. In one recent case, for instance, the U.S. Court of

Appeals for the First Circuit (which includes Maine, Massachusetts, New Hampshire, Rhode Island, and Puerto Rico) ruled that Exxon acted properly in firing a truck driver who failed a drug test. Exxon Corporation's drug-free workplace program included random testing of employees in safety-sensitive jobs. In this case, the employee drove a tractor trailer carrying 12,000 gallons of flammable motor fuel and tested positive for cocaine; Exxon discharged him. The union representing the employee challenged the firing, an arbitrator reduced the penalty to a two-month suspension, and the appeals court reversed the arbitrator's decision and ruled that the employer acted properly in firing the truck driver, given the safety-sensitiveness of the job.[78]

Complying with the Immigration Law

Under the Immigration Reform and Control Act of 1986, people hired in the United States must prove that they are eligible to be employed in the United States. A person does not have to be a U.S. citizen to be employed under this act. However, employers should ask a candidate who is about to be hired whether he or she is a U.S. citizen or an alien lawfully authorized to work in the United States.

There are two basic ways prospective employees can show their eligibility for employment. One is to show a document such as a U.S. passport or alien registration card with photograph that proves both identity and employment eligibility. However, many prospective employees do not have either of these documents. Therefore, the other way to verify employment eligibility is to see a document that proves the person's identity, along with a separate document showing the person's employment eligibility, such as a work permit.

Employers cannot and should not use the I-9 Employment Eligibility Verification form required to document eligibility to discriminate in any way based on race or country of national origin. For example, the requirement to verify eligibility does not provide any basis to reject an applicant just because he or she is a foreigner, or not a U.S. citizen, or an alien residing in the United States, as long as that person can prove his or her identity and employment eligibility.

REVIEW

Summary

1. In this chapter we discuss several techniques for screening and selecting job candidates: The first is testing.

2. Test validity answers the question What does this test measure? Criterion validity means demonstrating that those who do well on the test do well on the job. Content validity is demonstrated by showing that the test constitutes a fair sample of the content of the job.

3. As used by psychologists, the term *reliability* always means consistency. One way to measure reliability is to administer the same (or equivalent) tests to the same people at two different points in time. Or you could focus on internal consistency, comparing the responses to roughly equivalent items on the same test.

4. There are many types of personnel tests in use, including intelligence tests, tests of physical skills, tests of achievement, aptitude tests, interest inventories, and personality tests.

5. Under equal rights legislation, an employer may have to be able to prove that his or her tests are predictive of success or failure on the job. This usually requires a predictive validation study, although other means of validation are often acceptable.

6. Management assessment centers are a screening device that expose applicants to a series of real-life exercises. Performance is observed and assessed by experts, who then check their assessments by observing the participants when they are back at their jobs. Examples of such real-life exercises include a simulated business game, an in-basket exercise, and group discussions.

7. Several factors and problems can undermine the usefulness of an interview: making premature decisions, letting unfavorable information predominate, not knowing the requirements of the job, being under pressure to hire, not allowing for the candidate-order effect, and nonverbal behavior.

8. The five steps in the interview include plan, establish rapport, question the candidate, close the interview, and review the data.

9. Once you've selected and hired your new employees, they must be trained. We turn to training in the following chapter.

Key Terms

test validity	reliability	interview
criterion validity	management assessment	
content validity	center	

Discussion Questions and Exercises

1. Explain what is meant by *reliability* and *validity*. What is the difference between them? In what respects are they similar?

2. Write a short essay discussing some of the ethical and legal considerations in testing.

3. Working individually or in groups, contact the publisher of a standardized test such as the SAT and obtain written information regarding the test's validity and reliability. Present a short report in class discussing what the test is supposed to measure and the degree to which you think the test does what it is supposed to do, based on the reported validity and reliability scores.

4. Give some examples of how interest inventories could be used to improve employee selection. In doing so, suggest several examples of occupational interests that you believe might predict success in various occupations, including college professor, accountant, and computer programmer.

5. Why is it important to conduct preemployment background investigations? How would you go about doing so?

6. For what sorts of jobs do you think computerized interviews are most appropriate? Why?

7. Give a short presentation titled "How to Be Effective as an Interviewer."

8. Briefly discuss and give examples of at least five common interviewing mistakes. What recommendations would you give for avoiding these interviewing mistakes?

APPLICATION EXERCISES

Case Incident: The Tough Screener

Everyone who knows Mark Rosen knows he is a very tough owner when it comes to screening applicants for jobs in his firm. His company, located in a large northeastern city, provides financial planning advice to wealthy clients and sells insurance and sets up pension plans for individuals and businesses. His firm's clients range from professionals such as doctors and lawyers to business owners, who are fairly sophisticated in financial matters and very busy people. They expect accurate advice provided in a clear and expeditious manner. It is safe to say that Rosen's firm can be no better than its financial advisors.

Rosen has always been described as somewhat autocratic. The need to be very selective in whom he hires has led him to be extraordinarily careful about how he screens his job applicants. Some of his methods are probably beyond reproach. For example, he requires every applicant to provide a list of names and phone numbers for at least five people he or she worked with at each previous employer to be used as references. The resulting reference check is time consuming but effective.

On the other hand, given legislation including the Civil Rights Act of 1991 and the ADA, some of his other "tough screening" methods could be problematic. For example, Rosen requires that all applicants take a purported honesty test, which he found in the catalog of an office supply store. He also believes it is extremely important to check every viable applicant's credit history and workers' compensation history in order to screen out what he refers to as "potential undesirables." Unknown to his applicants, he runs a credit check on each of them and also retains the services of a firm that checks workers' compensation and driving violation histories.

Questions

1. What specific legal problems do you think Rosen might run into as a result of his firm's current screening methods? What steps would you suggest he take to eliminate these problems?

2. Given what you know about Rosen's business, write a two-page proposal describing an employee testing and selection program that you would recommend for his firm. Say a few words about the sorts of tests, if any, you would recommend and the application blank questions you would ask, as well as other methods, including drug screening and reference checking.

Experiential Exercise

Purpose: The purposes of this exercise are:
1. To give you practice in developing a structured interview form
2. To give you practice in using this form

Required Understanding: The reader should be familiar with the interviewing problems discussed, and with the example of the structured interview form presented in Figure 4.5.

How to Set Up the Exercise/Instructions:

1. Set up groups of four or five students. One student will be the interviewee, and the other students in the group will develop the structured interview form and, as a group, interview the interviewee.

2. Instructions for the *interviewee*: Please do not read the exercise beyond this point (you can leave the room for a few minutes).

3. Instructions for the *interviewers*: You are an assistant plant manager who has to interview a candidate for data processing supervisor in about an hour. Each of you knows you'd do best to use a structured interview form to guide the interview, so you're now meeting for about half an hour to develop such a form, based in part of the job description presented in Figure 3.3 (p. 69). (*Hint:* Start by listing the most relevant abilities and then rate these in importance on a five-point scale. Then use the high-rated abilities on your interview form.)

4. As soon as you have completed your structured interview form, call in your interviewee and explain that he or she is a candidate for the job and that you (to whom the candidate will report if hired) the plant manager, and perhaps one or more programmers will interview him as a group. You may tell the interviewee what his or her job summary calls form.

Next, interview the candidate, with each interviewer separately keeping notes on his or her own copy of the group's structured interview form. Each interviewer can take turns asking questions.

After the interview, discuss the following questions in the group. Based on each interviewer's notes, how similar were your perceptions of the candidate's responses? Did you all agree on the candidate's potential for the job? Did the candidate ask good questions of his or her interviewers? Did any of the interviewers find themselves jumping to conclusions about the candidate?

TAKE IT TO THE WEB

For Internet exercises, updates to chapter material, and more, visit the Dessler Web site at

www.prenhall.com/dessler

ENDNOTES

1. "Employer Sued for Not Disclosing Worker's Past," *BNA Bulletin to Management* (September 7, 1995): 281.

2. See, for example, Ann Marie Ryan and Marja Lasek, "Negligent Hiring and Defamation: Areas of Liability Related to Pre-employment Inquiries," *Personnel Psychology* 44, no. 2 (summer 1991): 293–319.

3. Leona Tyler, *Tests and Measurements* (Englewood Cliffs, NJ: Prentice Hall, 1971), p. 25.

4. Robert M. Guion, "Changing Views for Personnel Selection Research," *Personnel Psychology* 40, no. 2 (summer 1987): 199–213.

5. Anne Anastasi, *Psychological Patterns* (New York: Macmillan, 1968), reprinted in W. Clay Hamner and Frank Schmidt, *Contemporary Problems in Personnel* (Chicago: St. Clair Press, 1974): 102–109.

6. "Workers Find Employment Less of a Test as the Use of Medical, Psych Exams Subsides," *BNA Bulletin to Management* (August 24, 2000): 265–66.

7. Brad Bushman and Gary Wells, "Trait Aggressiveness and Hockey Penalties: Predicting Hot Tempers on the Ice," *Journal of Applied Psychology* 83, no. 6 (1998): 969–74.

8. See, for example, Douglas Cellar et al., "Comparison of Factor Structures and Criterion-Related Validity Coefficients for Two Measures of Personality Based on the Five Factor Model," *Journal of Applied Psychology* 81, no. 6 (1996): 694–704; and Jesus Salgado, "The

Five Factor Model of Personality and Job Performance in the European Community," *Journal of Applied Psychology* 82, no. 1 (1997): 30–43.

9. Murray Barrick and Michael Mount, "The Big Five Personality Dimensions and Job Performance: A Meta Analysis," *Personnel Psychology* 44, no. 1 (spring 1991): 1–26. See also Robert Schneider, Leatta Hough, and Marvin Dunnette, "Broad-Sided by Broad Traits: How to Sink Science in Five Dimensions or Less," *Journal of Organizational Behavior* 17, no. 6 (November 1996): 639–55.

10. Charles Sarchione et al., "Prediction of Dysfunctional Job Behaviors Among Law-Enforcement Officers," *Journal of Applied Psychology* 83, no. 6 (1998): 904–12.

11. Paula Caligiuri, "The Big Five Personality Characteristics as Predictors of Expatriate's Desire to Terminate the Assignment and Supervisor Rated Performance," *Personnel Psychology* 53 (2000): 67–68.

12. Brian Niehoff and Robert Paula, "Causes of Employee Theft and Strategies that HR Managers Can Use for Prevention," *Human Resource Management* 39, no. 1 (spring 2000): 51–64. See also Andrew Vinchur et al., "A Meta Analytic Review of Predictors of Job Performance for Salespeople," *Journal of Applied Psychology* 83, no. 4 (1998): 586–97. For a sample of the employment tests available, see, for example, "Introduction to 1999 Testing and the Employee Survey Matrix," *HRMagazine* (February 1999): 153–67.

13. "Can Testing Prevent Violence?" *Bulletin to Management* (November 28, 1996): 384.

14. Kathryn Tyler, "Put Applicants' Skills to the Test," *HRMagazine* (January 2000): 75–79.

15. Neal Schmitt et al., "Computer-Based Testing Applied to Selection of Secretarial Candidates," *Personnel Psychology* 46 (1991): 149–65.

16. Randall Overton et al., "The Pen-Based Computer as an Alternative Platform for Test Administration," *Personnel Psychology* 49 (1996): 455–64.

17. For example, see Ahron Tziner et al., "A Four Year Validation Study of an Assessment Center in a Financial Corporation," *Journal of Organizational Behavior* 14 (1993): 225–37.

18. Phillip Lowry, "Selection Methods: Comparison of Assessment Centers with Personnel Records' Evaluations," *Public Personnel Management* 23, no. 3 (fall 1994): 383–94.

19. Annette Spychalski et al., "A Survey of Assessment Center Practices in Organizations in the United States," *Personnel Psychology* 50 (1997): 83.

20. Michael McDaniel et al., "The Validity of Employment Interviews: A Comprehensive Review and Meta-Analysis," *Journal of Applied Psychology* 79, no. 4 (1994): 599.

21. *Ibid.*, p. 601. See also Steven Maurer, "The Potential of the Situational Interview: Existing Research and Unresolved Issues," *Human Resource Management Review* 7, no. 2 (summer 1997): 185–201.

22. "Phone Interviews Might Be the Most Telling, Study Finds," *BNA Bulletin to Management* (September 1998): 273.

23. See, for example, M. M. Harris, "Reconsidering the Employment Interview: A Review of Recent Literature and Suggestions for Future Research," *Personnel Psychology* 42 (1989): 691–726.

24. The validity discussion and these findings are based on McDaniel et al., "The Validity of Employment Interviews," pp. 607–10.

25. *Ibid.*, p. 608.

26. Don Langdale and Joseph Weitz, "Estimating the Influence of Job Information on Interviewer Agreement," *Journal of Applied Psychology* 57 (1973): 23–27.

27. R. E. Carlson, "Selection Interview Decisions: The Effects of Interviewer Experience, Relative Quota Situation, and Applicant Sample on Interview Decisions," *Personnel Psychology* 20 (1967): 259–80.

28. R. E. Carlson, "Effects of Applicant Sample on Ratings of Valid Information in an Employment Setting," *Journal of Applied Psychology* 54 (1970): 217–22.

29. See, for example, T. V. McGovern and H. E. Tinsley, "Interviewer Evaluations of Interviewees' Nonverbal Behavior," *Journal of Vocational Behavior* 13 (1978): 163–71. See also Scott Fleischmann, "The Messages of Body Language in Job Interviews," *Employee Relations* 18, no. 2 (summer 1991): 161–76.

30. David Caldwell and Jerry Burger, "Personality Characteristics of Job Applicants and Success in Screening Interviews," *Personnel Psychology* 51 (1998): 119–36.

31. Tim DeGroot and Stephen Motowidlo, "Why Visual and Vocal Interview Cues Can Affect Interviewer's Judgments and Predicted Job Performance," *Journal of Applied Psychology* (December 1999): 968–84.

32. See, for example, Madelaine Heilmann and Lewis Saruwatari, "When Beauty Is Beastly: The Effects of Appearance and Sex on Evaluation of Job Applicants for Managerial and Nonmanagerial Jobs," *Organizational Behavior and Human Performance* 23 (June 1979): 360–70; and Cynthia Marlowe, Sondra Schneider, and Carnot Nelson, "Gender and Attractiveness Biases in Hiring Decisions: Are More Experienced Managers Less Biased?" *Journal of Applied Psychology* 81, no. 1 (1996): 11–21.

33. Marlowe et al., "Gender and Attractiveness Biases in Hiring Decisions," p. 11.

34. *Ibid.*, p. 11.

35. *Ibid.*, p. 18.

36. Heilmann and Saruwatari, "When Beauty Is Beastly," pp. 360–72.

37. Amelia J. Prewett-Livingston et al., "Effects of Race on Interview Ratings in a Situational Panel Interview," *Journal of Applied Psychology* 81, no. 2 (1996): 178–86.

38. Alan Huffcutt and Philip Roth, "Racial Group Differences in Employment Interview Evaluations," *Journal of Applied Psychology* 83, no. 2 (1998): 179–89.

39. "The Tables Have Turned," *American Management Association International* (September 1998): 6.

40. Carlson, "Selection Interview Decisions," pp. 259–80.

41. William Tullar, Terry Mullins, and Share Caldwell, "Effects of Interview Length and Applicant Quality of Interview Decision Time," *Journal of Applied Psychology* 64 (December 1979): 669–74. See also Tracy McDonald and Milton Hakel, "Effects of Applicant Race, Sex, Suitability, and Answers on Interviewers Questioning Strategy on Ratings," *Personnel Psychology* 38, no. 2 (summer 1985): 321–34.

42. Ellen McCarty, "It's Not a Job Interview, It's a Subculture," *Fast Company* (August 2000): 46–50.

43. Panel Kaul, "Interviewing Is Your Business," *Association Management* (November 1992): 29. See also Nancy Woodward, "Asking for Salary Histories," *HRMagazine* (February 2000): 109–12. Gathering information about specific interview dimensions such as sociability, responsibility, and independence (as is often done with structured interviews) can improve interview accuracy, at least for more complicated jobs. See Yoza Ganzach et al., "Making Decisions from an Interview: Expert Measurement and Mechanical Combination," *Personnel Psychology* 53 (2000): 1–20; and Paul Falcone, "Five Questions," *HRMagazine* (February 2000): 129–35.

44. Edwin Walley, "Successful Interviewing Techniques," *The CPA Journal* (September 1993): 70.

45. "Looking to Hire the Very Best? Ask the Right Questions. Lots of Them," *Fortune* (June 21, 1999): 192–94.

46. Gretchen Spreitzer, Morgan McCall, Jr., and Joan Mahoney, "Early Identification of International Executive Potential," *Journal of Applied Psychology* 82, no. 1 (February 1997):

6–29. Copyright © 1997 by the American Psychological Association. Adapted with permission.

47. Seymour Adler, "Verifying a Job Candidate's Background: The State of Practice in a Vital Human Resources Activity," *Review of Business* 15, no. 2 (winter 1993): 3–8. See also James Burns, Jr., "Employment References: Is There a Better Way?" *Employee Relations Law Journal* 23, no. 2 (fall 1997): 157–68.

48. *Ibid.*, p. 6.

49. Based on Samuel Greengard, "Have Gangs Invaded Your Workplace?" *Personnel Journal* (February 1996): 47–57.

50. *Ibid.*, p. 47.

51. *Ibid.*, pp. 47–48.

52. *Ibid.*, p. 48.

53. For example, see Lawrence Dube, Jr., "Employment References and the Law," *Personnel Journal* 65, no. 2 (February 1986): 87–91. See also Mickey Veich, "Uncover the Resume Ruse," *Security Management* (October 1994): 75–76.

54. Howard Fischer, "Select the Right Executive," *Personnel Journal* (April 1989): 110–14.

55. "Getting Applicant Information Difficult but Still Necessary," *BNA Bulletin to Management* (February 5, 1999): 63.

56. "Undercover Callers Tipoff Job Seekers to Former Employers' Negative References," *BNA Bulletin to Management* (May 27, 1999): 161.

57. This is based on "When Can Workers Refuse Lie Detector Tests?" *BNA Bulletin to Management* (March 9, 1995): 73, and is based on the case *Lyle* v. *Mercy Hospital Anderson, DCS, Ohio*, 1995, 10 IER cases 401.

58. John Jones and William Terris, "Post-Polygraph Selection Techniques," *Recruitment Today* (May/June 1989): 25–31.

59. For a discussion of the earlier caveats see, for example, Kevin Murphy, "Detecting Infrequent Deception," *Journal of Applied Psychology* 72, no. 4 (November 1987): 611–14.

60. John Bernardin and Donna Cooke, "Validity of an Honesty Test in Predicting Theft Among Convenience Store Employees," *Academy of Management Journal* 36, no. 5 (1993): 1097–108.

61. Paul Sackett and James Wanek, "New Developments in the Use of Measures of Honesty, Integrity, Conscientiousness, Dependability, Trustworthiness, and Reliability for Personnel Selection," *Personnel Psychology* 49 (1996): 821.

62. These are based on Commerce Clearing House, *Ideas and Trends* (December 29, 1988): 222–23. See also Bureau of National Affairs, "Diving Integrity Through Interview," *Bulletin to Management* (June 4, 1987): 184.

63. See, for example, Gershon Ben-Shakhar, et al., "Can Graphology Predict Occupational Success? Two Empirical Studies and Some Methodological Ruminations," *Journal of Applied Psychology* 71, no. 4 (November 1986): 645–53.

64. Anthony Edwards, "An Experiment to Test the Discrimination Ability of Graphologists," *Personality and Individual Differences* B, no. 1 (January 1992): 69–74; George Langer, "Graphology in Personality Assessment: A Reliability and Validity Study," *Dissertation Abstracts International: Section B: The Sciences and Engineering* 54, no. 7-B (1994): 3856.

65. Mick Haus, "Pre-Employment Physicals and the ADA," *Safety and Health* (February 1992): 64–65.

66. Discussed in Scott MacDonald, Samantha Wells, and Richard Fry, "The Limitations of Drug Screening in the Workplace," *International Labor Review* 132, no. 1 (1993): 99.

67. Ian Miners et al., "Put Drug Detection to the Test," *Personnel Journal* 66, no. 8 (August 1987): 191–97.

68. MacDonald et al., "The Limitations of Drug Screening in the Workplace," p. 98.

69. Eric Greenberg, "Workplace Testing: Who's Testing Whom?" *Personnel* (May 1989): 39–45.

70. MacDonald et al., "The Limitations of Drug Screening in the Workplace," pp. 102–104.

71. *Ibid.*, p. 103.

72. *Ibid.*, pp. 105–106.

73. Ann O'Neill, "Legal Issues Presented by Hair Follicle Testing," *Employee Relations Today* (winter 1991–1992): 411–15.

74. *Ibid.*, p. 411.

75. Richard Lisko, "A Manager's Guide to Drug Testing," *Security Management* 38, no. 8 (August 1994): 92.

76. Eric Greenberg, "Workplace Testing: Results of a New AMA Survey," *Personnel* (April 1988): 40.

77. Michael McDaniel, "Does Pre-employment Drug Use Predict On-the-Job Suitability?" *Personnel Psychology* 41, no. 4 (winter 1988): 717–29.

78. *Exxon Corp. v. Esso Workers Union, Inc.*, CA1#96–2241, 7/8/97; discussed in *BNA Bulletin to Management* (August 7, 1997): 249.

Chapter 5

Training and Developing Employees

> ➤ Orienting Employees
> ➤ The Training Process
> ➤ Training Techniques
> ➤ Managerial Development and Training
> ➤ Evaluating the Training and
>   Development Effort

When you finish studying this chapter, you should be able to:

- ■ *Describe* the basic training process.

- ■ *Discuss* at least two techniques used for assessing training needs.

- ■ *Explain* the pros and cons of at least five training techniques.

- ■ *Explain* what management development is and why it is important.

- ■ *Describe* the main development techniques.

INTRODUCTION

Martin Starr, founder and president of Starr Valve Corp., had a problem. His company—which made sophisticated pollution-control valves used to control the gases and liquids leaving chemical plants—annually hired five or six newly minted chemical engineers to work on applications for customers. Increasingly, though, customers were complaining about slow service and poor engineering design, problems Starr attributed to inadequate training of his new engineers. How could he solve the problem? After employees have been recruited and hired, the next step is to orient and train them. This involves providing them with the information and skills they need to successfully perform their new jobs.

ORIENTING EMPLOYEES

Employee orientation provides new employees with the basic background information they need to perform their jobs satisfactorily, such as information about company rules. Orientation is one component of the employer's new-employee socialization process. Socialization is the ongoing process of instilling in all employees the prevailing attitudes, standards, values, and patterns of behavior that are expected by the organization and its departments.[1]

Orientation programs range from brief, informal introductions to lengthy, formal programs of a half a day or possibly more. In either, new employees are usually given handbooks that cover matters such as working hours, performance reviews, getting on the payroll, and vacations, as well as a tour of the facilities. Other information typically includes employee benefits, personnel policies, the employee's daily routine, company organization and operations, and safety measures and regulations.[2] (Because there is a possibility that courts will find that your employee handbook's contents represent a contract with the employee, disclaimers should be included: They should make it clear that statements of company policies, benefits, and regulations do not constitute the terms and conditions of an employment contract, either express or implied.)

A successful orientation should accomplish four main things: The new employee should feel welcome; he or she should understand the organization in a broad sense (its past, present, culture, and vision of the future), as well as key facts such as policies and procedures; the employee should be clear about what is expected in terms of work and behavior; and, hopefully, the person should begin the process of becoming socialized into the firm's traditional ways of acting and doing things.[3]

The first part of the orientation is usually performed by the HR specialist, who explains such matters as working hours and vacation. The employee is then introduced to his or her new supervisor. The latter continues the orientation by explaining the exact nature of the job, introducing the person to his or her new colleagues, and familiarizing the new employee with the workplace.

THE TRAINING PROCESS

Training refers to the methods used to give new or present employees the skills they need to perform their jobs.

Training's focus has broadened in the past few years. Training used to focus on teaching technical skills, such as training assemblers to solder wires or training teachers to make up lesson plans.[4] Today, training might also mean remedial-education training, because quality improvement programs assume that employees can produce charts and graphs, and analyze data.[5] Employees today may also reacquire team building, decision making, and communication skills training. And, as firms become more technologically advanced, employees require training in technological and computer skills (such as desktop publishing and computer-aided design and manufacturing).[6] All told, this shift from purely production-process training helps to explain why in one recent year an average production worker received 37 hours of training compared with only 31 hours in the previous year.[7]

The Five-Step Training and Development Process

Training and development programs can be visualized as consisting of five steps, as summarized in Figure 5.1.

Training Needs Analysis   The first step in training is to determine what training, if any, is required. Some call this the "skills gapping" process. Employers determine the skills each job requires, and the skills of the job's current or prospective employees. Training is then designed to eliminate the skills gap.[8] Assessing current employees' training needs usually involves *task analysis*—breaking the jobs into subtasks and teaching each to the new employee. Needs analysis for current employees is more complex: Is training the solution, or is performance down because the person's not motivated? Here *performance analysis* is required.

Task analysis is used for determining the new employees' training needs. Particularly with lower-echelon workers, it is common to hire inexperienced personnel and train them.[9] Your aim is to provide them with the skills and knowledge required for effective performance. How do you determine what skills and knowledge are required? Task analysis is a detailed study of the job to determine what specific skills—such as soldering (in the case of an assembly worker) or interviewing (in the case of a supervisor)—are required. The job description and job specification will provide useful information. They list the specific duties and skills required on the job and become the

---

1. **NEEDS ANALYSIS**
   - Identify specific job performance skills needed to improve performance and productivity.
   - Analyze the audience to ensure that the program will be suited to their specific levels of education, experience, and skills, as well as their attitudes and personal motivations.
   - Set training objectives.

2. **INSTRUCTIONAL DESIGN**
   - Gather instructional objectives, methods, media, description of and sequence of content, examples, exercises, and activities. Organize them into a curriculum.
   - Make sure all materials, such as video scripts, leaders' guides, and participants' workbooks, complement each other, are written clearly, and blend into unified training geared directly to the stated learning objectives.

3. **VALIDATION**
   - Introduce and validate the training before a representative audience. Base final revisions on pilot results to ensure program effectiveness.

4. **IMPLEMENTATION**
   - When applicable, boost success with a train-the-trainer workshop that focuses on presentation knowledge and skills in addition to training content.

FIGURE 5.1   The Five Steps in the Training and Development Process

Source: Adapted from *HRFocus*, April 1993. Copyright © 1993 American Management Association International. Reprinted by permission of American Management Association International, New York, NY. All rights reserved. http://www.amanet.org.

basic reference point in determining the training required for performing the job. Figure 5.2 summarizes methods for uncovering a job's training needs.

For current employees whose performance is deficient, task analysis is usually not enough: **Performance analysis** means verifying that there is a significant performance deficiency and determining whether that deficiency should be rectified through training or through some other means (such as transferring the employee or changing the compensation plan).

An employee's training needs can be identified in several ways. These include supervisor, peer, self-, and 360-degree performance reviews; job-related performance data (including productivity, absenteeism and tardiness, accidents, short-term sickness, grievances, waste, late deliveries, product quality, downtime, repairs, equipment utilization, and customer complaints); observation by supervisors or other specialists; interviews with the employee or his or her supervisor; tests of things like job knowledge, skills, and attendance; attitude surveys; individual employee daily diaries; devised situations such as role plays and case studies and other types of tests; assessment centers; and management by objective-type evaluations.[10] The first step is usually to appraise the employee's performance. Examples of specific performance deficiencies follow:

> "I expect each salesperson to make 10 new contracts per week, but John averages only 6."
>
> "Other plants our size average no more than two serious accidents per month; we're averaging five."

Distinguishing between *can't do* and *won't do* problems is the heart of performance analysis. First, determine whether it's a can't do problem and, if so, its specific causes: The employees don't know what to do or what your standards are; there are obstacles in the system such as lack of tools or supplies; job aids are needed, such as color-coded wires that show assemblers which wire goes where; poor selection results in hiring people who haven't the skills to do the job; or training is inadequate. On the other hand, it might be a won't do problem in which employees could do a good job if they wanted to. If this is the case, the reward system might have to be changed, perhaps by installing an incentive system.

Setting Training Objectives   After training needs have been uncovered, concrete, measurable training objectives should be set. Training, development, or (more generally) instructional objectives are defined as "a description of a performance you want learners to be able to exhibit before you consider them competent."[11] For example:

> Given a tool kit and a service manual, the technical representative will be able to adjust the registration (black line along paper edges) on this Xerox duplicator within 20 minutes according to the specifications stated in the manual.[12]

Objectives specify what the trainee should be able to accomplish after successfully completing the training program. They thus provide a focus for the efforts of both the trainee and the trainer and a benchmark for evaluating the success of the training program. A helpful tactic is to also create, for the trainee, a perceived training need, such as by illustrating with a filmed example what can go wrong if the training isn't taken seriously.[13]

Tools for Uncovering a Job's Training Needs

Sources for Obtaining Job Data	*Training Need Information*
1. Job Descriptions	Outlines the job's typical duties and responsibilities but is not meant to be all-inclusive. Helps define performance discrepancies.
2. Job Specifications or Task Analysis	List specified tasks required for each job. More specific than job descriptions. Specifications may extend to judgments of knowledge and skills required of job incumbents.
3. Performance Standards	Objectives of the tasks of job, and standards by which they are judged. This may include baseline data as well.
4. Perform the Job	Most effective way of determining specific tasks, but has serious limitations in higher level jobs because performance requirements typically have longer gaps between performance and resulting outcomes.
5. Observe Job-Work Sampling	Same as 4 above.
6. Review Literature Concerning the Job a. Research in other industries b. Professional journals c. Documents d. Government sources e. PhD theses	Possibly useful in comparison analyses of job structures, but far removed from either unique aspects of the job structure within any *specific* organization or specific performance requirements.
7. Ask Questions About the Job a. Of the job holder b. Of the supervisor c. Of higher management	Inputs from several viewpoints can often reveal training needs or training desires.
8. Training Committees or Conferences	Same as 7 above.
9. Analysis of Operating Problems a. Downtime reports b. Waste c. Repairs d. Late deliveries e. Quality control	Indications of task interference, environmental factors, etc.

FIGURE 5.2 Tools for Uncovering a Job's Training Needs.

Source: Adapted from P. Nick Blanchard and James Thacker, *Training: Systems, Strategies and Practices* (Upper Saddle River, NJ: Prentice-Hall, 1999), pp. 138–39.

TRAINING TECHNIQUES

After you have determined the employees' training needs, created a perceived need, and set training objectives, a training program can be designed and implemented. Popular training techniques are described in this section.

On-the-Job Training

There are several types of **on-the-job training (OJT)**. The most familiar is the coaching or understudy method. Here the employee is trained on the job by an experienced worker or the trainee's supervisor. At lower levels, trainees may acquire skills for, say, running a machine by observing the supervisor. But this technique is also widely used at top-management levels. The position of assistant is often used to train and develop the company's future top managers, for instance. Job rotation, in which an employee (usually a management trainee) moves from job to job at planned intervals, is another on-the-job technique. Special assignments similarly give lower-level executives firsthand experience in working on actual problems.

Apprenticeship Training

More employers are going "back to the future" by implementing apprenticeship training programs, an approach to training that began in the Middle Ages. Apprenticeship training is a structured process by which individuals become skilled workers through a combination of classroom instruction and on-the-job training. It is widely used to train individuals for many occupations, including electrician and plumber.[14]

Apprenticeship training involves having the learner/apprentice study under the tutelage of a master craftsman.[15] In Germany, for instance, students ages 15 to 18 often divide their time between classroom instruction in vocational schools and part-time work under the master craftsman. The apprenticeship lasts about three years and ends with a certification examination.

Several U.S. facilities of Siemens are successfully using such an approach. For example, the Siemens Stromberg-Carlson plant in Florida has apprenticeships for adults and high school students training for jobs as electronics technicians. Here, according to an observer,

> Adults work on the factory floor, receive classroom instruction at Seminole Community College, and also study at the plant's hands-on apprenticeship lab. Graduates receive Associates Degrees in telecommunications and electronics engineering. High school students spend two afternoons per week at the apprenticeship lab.[16]

Simulated Training

Simulated training is a technique in which trainees learn on the actual or simulated equipment they will use on the job but are actually trained off the job. Therefore, it aims to obtain the advantages of on-the-job training without actually putting the trainee on the job. Such training is a necessity when it is too costly or dangerous to train employees on the job. Putting new assembly-line workers right to work could slow production, for instance, and when safety is a concern—as with pilots—simulated training may be the only practical alternative.

Simulated training may just take place in a separate room with the equipment the trainees will actually be using on the job. (It is therefore sometimes called **vestibule training**.) However, it often involves the use of equipment simulators. In pilot training, for instance, the main advantages of flight simulators are:[17]

- *Safety.* Crews can practice hazardous flight maneuvers in a safe, controlled environment.
- *Learning efficiency.* The absence of the conflicting air traffic and radio chatter that exists in real flight situations allows for total concentration on the business of learning how to fly the craft.
- *Money.* The cost of using a flight simulator is only a fraction of the cost of flying an aircraft. This includes savings on maintenance costs, pilot cost, fuel cost, and the cost of not having the aircraft in regular service.

Audiovisual and Distance Learning Techniques

Audiovisual techniques such as films, closed-circuit television, audiotapes, and videotapes can be very effective and are widely used.[18] The Ford Motor Company uses films in its dealer training sessions to simulate sample reactions to various customer complaints, for example.

Teletraining   Firms today also use various forms of distance learning methods for training. Distance learning techniques include the familiar paper-and-pencil correspondence courses, as well as teletraining, videoconferencing, and Internet-based classes.[19]

For example, companies today are experimenting with teletraining, through which a trainer in a central location can train groups of employees at remote locations via television hookups.[20] For example, AMP Incorporated (which makes electrical and electronic connection devices) uses satellites to train its engineers and technicians at 165 sites in the United States and 27 other countries. To reduce costs for one training program, AMP supplied the program content. PBS affiliate WITF, Channel 33 of Harrisburg, Pennsylvania, supplied the equipment and expertise required to broadcast the training program to 5 AMP facilities in North America.[21] Macy's, a New York–based retailer, has established the Macy's Satellite Network, in part to provide training to the firm's 59,000 employees around the country.[22]

In a low-tech twist to televised teletraining, some firms are successfully using the telephone. For example, Cadillac has what it calls the Craftsman's League, which is a training, testing, and motivational program for Cadillac dealers' mechanics. Employees receive Cadillac materials and service manuals regarding factory-approved service procedures and ongoing technical changes. Then, four times per year, technicians must take a phone exam on any one of eight categories, including, for instance, paint repair and electrical and mechanical systems.[23]

Videoconference Distance Learning   Videoconferencing is an increasingly popular way to train employees who are geographically separated from each other—or from the trainer. It has been defined as "a means of joining two or more distant groups using a combination of audio and visual equipment."[24] Videoconferencing allows people in one location to communicate live with people in another city or country or with groups in several other cities.[25] The communication links are established by sending specially compressed audio and video signals over telephone lines or via satellite. Keypad systems allow for audience interactivity. For instance, in a program at Texas Instruments, the keypad system lets instructors determine immediately whether trainees are learning.[26]

Given that videoconferencing is by nature visual, interactive, and remote, there are several things to keep in mind before getting up in front of the camera. For example, because the training is remote, it's particularly important to prepare a training guide ahead of time, specifically a manual the learners can use to keep track of the points that the trainer is making. Several other hints are to avoid bright, flashy jewelry or heavily patterned clothing;[27] arrive at least 20 minutes before the session is to begin, and test all equipment you will be using.

Computer-Based Training

In computer-based training the trainee uses a computer-based system to interactively increase his or her knowledge or skills. Although simulated training doesn't necessarily have to rely on computerization, computer-based training almost always involves presenting trainees with computerized simulations, and using multimedia including videotapes to help the trainee learn how to do the job.[28]

Consider this example of computer-assisted training. At a major employer in the Pacific Northwest, CBT helps train interviewers to conduct correct and legally defensible interviews.[29] Trainees start with a computer screen that shows the "applicant's" employment application, as well as information about the job. The trainee then begins a simulated interview by typing in questions, which are answered by a videotaped model acting as the applicant and whose responses to a multitude of questions have been programmed into the computer. Some items require follow-up questions. As each question is answered, the trainee records his or her evaluation of the applicant's answer and makes a decision about the person's suitability for the position. At the end of the session the computer tells the trainee where he or she went wrong (perhaps in asking discriminatory questions, for instance) and offers further instructional material to correct these mistakes.

CBT programs can be very beneficial. Studies indicate that interactive technologies reduce learning time by an average of 50%.[30] They can also be very cost-effective once designed and produced: FedEx reportedly expects to save more than $100 million by using an interactive system for employee training.[31]

Training via CD-ROM and the Internet

Internet-based learning programs range from the simple to the complex. Roadmap is one example of the former, and is the brainchild of an undergraduate student at the University of Alabama.[32] The course is a bit like a correspondence course that lands in users' e-mail boxes, one new lesson a day for about four weeks. This program uses what's known as listserv software to simultaneously distribute the lessons to approximately 20,000 "trainees" per month. Trainees get to work through each new lesson; some lessons include assignments that send trainers to the outer reaches of the

Internet to practice what they've learned about using the Internet, and to retrieve information pertinent to the course. The creator of another Internet training program not only delivers courses to the e-mail recipient trainees but also assigns students to discussion groups, so participants "not only learn something, they'll probably meet some new people."[33]

Many firms already use their proprietary internal *Intranets*, to facilitate computer-based training. For example, Silicon Graphics transferred many of its training materials onto CD-ROMs. However, because not every desktop computer had a CD-ROM drive, many employees couldn't access the training programs. Silicon Graphics is therefore replacing the CD-ROM distribution method with distribution of training materials via its Intranet. "Now employees can access the programs whenever they want. Distribution costs are zero, and if the company wants to make a change to the program, it can do so at a central location."[34]

As a result of such benefits, technology-based learning is booming. Management Recruiters International (MRI) uses the firm's ConferView system (see Figure 5.3) to train hundreds of employees—each in their individual offices—simultaneously.[35] Instead of sending new rental sales agents to weeklong classroom-based training courses, Value Rent-a-Car now provides them with interactive, multimedia-based training programs utilizing CD-ROMs: These programs help the sales agents learn the car rental process by walking them through various procedures such as how to operate the rental computer system.[36] Polls suggest that such training technology will continue to grow in popularity. For example, one poll of 1,911 trainers found that almost 83% plan to increase their use of multimedia/CD-ROMs, 81% their use of the Internet, and 80% their use of computer-based training.[37]

FIGURE 5.3 Doug Donkin, an instructor for Management Recruiters International (MRI), uses the firms ConferView system to conduct MRI University training. ConferView is one type of videoconferencing technology that allows companies to train hundreds of employees simultaneously.

Source: Courtesy of Management Recruiters International, Inc.

Learning Portals

Many firms are using business portals today. Also called Enterprise Information Portals (EIPs) they are, like Yahoo!, Windows to the Internet, but also much more. Through its business portal, categories of a firm's employees—secretaries, engineers, salespeople, and so on—are able to access all the corporate applications they need to use, and "get the tools you need to analyze data inside and outside your company, and see the customized content you need, like industry news and competitive data."[38]

Training today is increasingly found and delivered through such portals. Business to consumer (B2C) portals such as fatbrain, learn.com, ScheduleEarth.com, and SmartPlanet aggregate training content for "free agent learners," individuals anywhere who want to upgrade their knowledge and skills on their own. Business to business (B2B) portals such as DigitalThink.com, Headlight.com, and click2learn.com target the business community. They contract with employers to deliver training options—often Web-based—to the firm's employees. Some B2Bs are "vortals," or vertical industry learning portals; they target specific industries with relevant offerings. For example, KnowledgePlanet.com contracted with a firm called VerticalNet to create learning portals for specific industries. Other firms are creating their own learning portals for employees and customers. Called business to employee (B2E), they let the company contract with specific training content providers, who offer their content to the firm's employees via the vortal.[39]

The technology of the learning portals puts "more and more information into everyone's hands." Instead of limiting training opportunities to teacher-led conventional classes or to periodic training sessions, training becomes available "24–7." Employees can learn at their own pace, when they want to.[40]

Training for Special Purposes

Training today does more than just prepare employees to perform their jobs effectively. Training for special purposes—dealing with AIDS and adjusting to diversity, for instance—is required too. A sampling of such special-purpose training programs follows.

Literacy Training Techniques Functional literacy—reading, writing, and arithmetic—is seriously lacking in the workplace. For example, a survey of 316 employers concluded that about 43% of all new hires required basic skill improvements, as did 37% of current employees.[41] This need reflects, in part, the changing nature of workers' jobs: Thus, today's emphasis on teamwork and quality requires employees to have a level of analytical skills that's impossible to attain without the ability to adequately read, write, and understand numbers.

Employers take various approaches to teaching literacy and other basic skills. The Life Skills program implemented at the Bellwood plant of Borg-Warner Automotive, Inc. is one example. Based on test scores, employee participants were chosen and placed in three classes of 15 students each. Two trainers were retained from a local training company. Each session was planned for a maximum of 200 hours. However, employees could leave when they reached a predetermined skill level, so that some were in the program for only 40 hours and others stayed the entire course.[42] Classes were held five days per week, two hours per day, with classes scheduled so that one hour was during the employee's personal time and the second was on company time. In this particular program, a sort of buddy system was used in which employees were paired so that they could help each other (for instance, someone good with decimals was paired with someone who was not). The students then helped each other through a series of timed exercises in math and reading.

Another simple approach is to have supervisors "teach" basic skills by giving employees writing and speaking exercises. After each exercise has been completed, the supervisor can provide personal feedback.[43] One way to do this is to convert materials used in the employees' jobs into instructional tools. For example, if an employee needs to use a manual to find out how to replace a certain machine part, he or she could be taught how to use an index to locate the relevant section.[44] Another approach is to bring in outside professionals such as teachers from a local high school or community college to institute, say, a remedial reading or writing program.[45] Having employees attend adult education or high school evening classes is another option.

Values Training   Many training programs today are aimed at educating employees about the firm's most cherished values and at convincing employees that these should be their values as well.

The orientation program at Saturn Corporation illustrates this. The first two days are devoted to discussions of benefits, safety and security, and the company's production process—just-in-time delivery, materials management, and so forth.[46] On the third and fourth days, the focus shifts to values. Each new employee gets a copy of Saturn's mission card. Trainees and trainer then go through each of the Saturn values listed on the card—teamwork, trust and respect for the individual, and quality, for example—to illustrate its meaning. Short, illustrated exercises are used. The new employees might be asked, "If you saw a team member do this, what would you do?" or "If you saw a team member 'living' this value, what would you see?"

Diversity Training   With an increasingly diverse workforce, more firms have implemented diversity training programs. As a personnel officer for one firm put it, "We're trying to create a better sensitivity among our supervisors about the issues and challenges women and minorities face in pursuing their careers."[47] Diversity training refers to techniques for creating better cross-cultural sensitivity among supervisors and nonsupervisors with the aim of creating more harmonious working relationships among a firm's employees.

Diversity training is no panacea, and a poorly conceived program can backfire. Potential negative outcomes include "the possibility of post-training participant discomfort, reinforcement of group stereotypes, perceived disenfranchisement or backlash by white males, and even lawsuits based on managers' exposure of stereotypical beliefs blurted out during 'awareness raising' sessions."[48]

Strictly speaking, it's probably more accurate to talk about diversity-oriented training programs than about "diversity training." According to one survey of HR directors, specific training programs aimed at offsetting problems associated with a diverse workforce included (from most used to least used) improving interpersonal skills; understanding/valuing cultural differences; improving technical skills; socializing into corporate culture; reducing stress; indoctrinating into U.S. work ethic;

mentoring; improving English proficiency; improving basic math skills; and improving bilingual skills for English-speaking employees.[49]

Training for Teamwork and Empowerment   Many firms today use work teams and employee empowerment to improve their effectiveness. Both the team approach and worker employment are components of what many firms call **worker involvement programs**. These programs aim to boost organizational effectiveness by getting employees to participate in the planning, organizing, and general managing of their jobs.

Employees must be trained to be good team members. For instance, Toyota devotes hours to training new employees to listen to each other and to cooperate. Throughout Toyota's training process, dedication to teamwork is stressed. For example, short exercises are used to illustrate examples of good and bad teamwork, and to mold new employees' attitudes regarding good teamwork.

Some firms use outdoor training such as Outward Bound programs to build teamwork.[50] Outdoor training usually involves taking a firm's management team out into rugged, mountainous terrain. There they learn team spirit and cooperation and the need to trust and rely on each other by overcoming physical obstacles. As one participant put it, "Every time I climbed over a rock, I needed someone's help."[51] An example of one activity is the trust fall, in which an employee has to slowly lean back and fall backward, perhaps from a height of 10 feet, into the waiting arms of 5 or 10 team members. The idea is to build trust, particularly in one's colleagues.[52]

MANAGERIAL DEVELOPMENT AND TRAINING

Management development is any attempt to improve managerial performance by imparting knowledge, changing attitudes, or increasing skills. It thus includes in-house programs such as courses, coaching, and rotational assignments, professional programs such as American Management Association seminars; and university programs such as executive MBA programs.[53] It is estimated that well over one million U.S. managers participate in management development programs yearly[54] for a cost to industry of several billion dollars per year.[55]

The ultimate aim of such development programs is, of course, to enhance the future performance of the organization itself. For this reason, the general management development process consists of assessing the company's needs (for instance, to fill future executive openings, or to make the firm more responsive), appraising the managers' performance, and then developing the managers themselves.

Globalization and increased competitiveness mean its more important today for leader development programs to be organizationally relevant and effective. There is, for instance, more emphasis on clarifying a program's business purpose and desired outcomes; linking the program more clearly to the company's missions; involving the top management team; specifying concrete competencies and knowledge, rather than just attitudes; and supplementing traditional development methods (such as lectures, case discussion groups, and simulations) with more realistic methods like action learning projects.[56] Several principles for designing leader development programs (such as "use practical, concrete content") are summarized in Figure 5.4.

- Use practical, concrete content, not academic or theoretical.
- Structure job-related activities rather than those irrelevant to the real work of the organization.
- Use involving, emotionally engaging, action-oriented learning methods and activities.
- Create ongoing activities and short (3- to 5-day) sessions, rather than long, one-time events.
- Focus on implementation skills instead of stopping at problem-solving and decision-making skills.
- Emphasize learning that can be immediately applied instead of distant applications.
- Generate accountability on the part of participants.
- Use the most respected, talented executives of the organization. Let them coach the aspiring leaders.
- Organize groups from the same organizational level. They'll be more comfortable and will face similar issues.

FIGURE 5.4   The New Leadership Development

Source: Jack Zenger, Dave Ulrich, and Norm Smallwood, "The New Leadership Development," *Training & Development* (March 2000): 26.

Development methods (many equally useful for nonmanagers as well) are described on the next few pages.

Managerial On-the-Job Training

On-the-job training is not just for nonmanagers: It is a popular manager development method, too. Important techniques include job rotation, the coaching/understudy approach, and action learning.

Job Rotation   **Job rotation** means moving management trainees from department to department to broaden their understanding of all parts of the business.[57] The trainee—often a recent college graduate—may spend several months in each department; this helps not only broaden his or her experience, but also discover the jobs he or she prefers. The person may be just an observer in each department, but more commonly becomes fully involved in its operations. The trainee thus learns the department's business by actually doing it, whether it involves sales, production, finance, or some other function.

Action Learning

Action learning gives managers time to work full time on projects, analyzing and solving problems in departments other than their own.[58] The trainees meet periodically within a four- or five-person project group to discuss their findings.

For example, several CIGNA International Property and Casualty Corporation managers spent four weeks in an action learning group.[59] The group was assigned the problem of analyzing the strategies of one of the insurance company's business units over the previous three years. Each of the four weeks was devoted to a different set of activities. In the first week, the group received training from business professors as well as a briefing from the division staff that had the business problem. In the second, they split into four teams and traveled the country interviewing about 100 of the division's employees, distributors, and customers on a one-to-one basis. In the third week, the group assimilated and analyzed the data, and in the fourth week, it formulated recommendations and wrote a 40-plus-page paper. The group presented its recommendations to the president and executive staff of the troubled division at the end of the fourth week and fielded questions from the executives.[60]

The Case Study Method

The **case study method** presents a trainee with a written description of an organizational problem. The person analyzes the case in private, diagnoses the problem, and presents his or her findings and solutions in a discussion with other trainees.[61] The case study method is aimed at giving trainees realistic experience in identifying and analyzing complex problems in an environment in which their progress can be subtly guided by a trained discussion leader. Through the class discussion of the case, trainees learn that there are usually many ways to approach and solve complex organizational problems. Trainees also learn that their solutions are often influenced by their own needs and values.

The case method ideally has five main features:[62] (1) the use of actual organizational problems; (2) the maximum possible involvement of participants in stating their views, inquiring into others' views, confronting different views, and making decisions; resulting in (3) a minimal degree of dependence on the faculty members; who, in turn, (4) hold the position that there are rarely any right or wrong answers, and that cases are incomplete and so is reality; and (5) who still strive to make the case method as engaging as possible through creation of appropriate levels of drama.[63]

Integrated case scenarios expand the case analysis concept by creating long-term, comprehensive case situations. For example, the FBI Academy recently created an integrated case scenario. It starts "with a concerned citizen's telephone call and ends 14 weeks later with a simulated trial. In between is the stuff of a genuine investigation, including a healthy sampling of what can go wrong in an actual criminal inquiry." To create such scenarios, scriptwriters (often just creative employees in the firm's training group) create scripts. The scripts include themes, background stories, detailed personal histories, and role-play instructions. In the case of the FBI, the scenarios are aimed at developing specific training skills, such as interviewing witnesses and analyzing crime scenes.[64]

Management Games

In computerized **management games**, trainees are divided into five- or six-person companies, each of which has to compete with the others in a simulated marketplace. Each company sets a goal (such as "maximum sales") and is told it can make several decisions. For example, the group may be allowed to decide how much to spend on advertising, how much to produce, how much inventory to maintain, and how many of which product to produce. Usually, the game compresses a two- or three-year period into days, weeks, or months. As in the real world, each company usually can't see what decisions the other firms have made, although these decisions do affect their own sales. For example, if a competitor decides to increase its advertising expenditures, that firm may end up increasing its sales at the expense of yours.[65]

Management games can be good development tools. People learn best by getting involved in the activity itself, and the games can be useful for gaining such involvement.

Outside Seminars

Many organizations offer seminars and conferences aimed at developing managers. The American Management Association (AMA), for instance, provides thousands of courses in areas such as general management, human resources, sales and marketing, and international management.

The courses cover topics such as how to sharpen business writing skills, strategic planning, and assertiveness training for managers.[66] Other organizations offering management development services include AMR International, Inc., the Conference Board, and Cornell University.

Many of these programs offer continuing education units (CEUs) for course completion. Earning CEUs provides a recognized measure of educational accomplishment, says the AMA, one that is today used by more than 1,000 colleges. CEUs generally can't be used to obtain degree-granting credit at most colleges or universities, but they provide a record of the fact that the trainee participated in and completed a conference or seminar.

University-Related Programs

Colleges and universities provide several types of management development activities. First, many schools provide continuing education programs in leadership, supervision, and the like. As with the AMA, these range from one- to four-day programs to executive development programs lasting one to four months.

Many also offer individual courses in areas such as business, management, and health care administration. Managers can take these as matriculated or nonmatriculated students to fill gaps in their backgrounds. Thus, a prospective division manager with a gap in experience with accounting controls might sign up for a two-course sequence in managerial accounting. Finally, schools offer degree programs such as the master of business administration.

Some companies have experimented with offering selected employees in-house degree programs in cooperation with colleges and universities. Many also offer a variety of in-house lectures and seminars by university staff. For example, Technicon, a high-tech medical instruments company, asked one university to offer an executive education program for its key middle managers. The coursework covered topics ranging from finance to executive communication.[67] Schools such as Duke University offer programs (like MBAs) online; some customize the programs for client companies.

Universities and corporations are also experimenting with videolinked classroom education. For example, the School of Business and Public Administration at California State University, Sacramento, and a Hewlett-Packard facility in Roseville, California,

Global Issues in HR

Executive Development in Global Companies

Selecting and developing executives to run the employer's overseas operations present management with a dilemma. One expert cites "an alarmingly high failure rate when executives are relocated overseas." This failure rate is usually caused by inappropriate selection and poor expatriate development.[68] Yet in an increasingly globalized economy, employers must develop managers for overseas assignments despite these difficulties.

A number of companies, including Dow and Ciba-Geigy, have developed and implemented international executive relocation programs that are successful. In addition to the general requirements for successful executive development programs previously listed, preparing and training executives for overseas assignments should also include the following considerations:

1. Choose for international assignments candidates whose educational backgrounds and experiences are appropriate for overseas assignments. For example, a person who has already accumulated a track record of successfully adapting to foreign cultures (perhaps through overseas college studies and summer internships) will more likely succeed as an international transferee.

2. Choose those whose personalities and family situations can withstand the cultural changes they will encounter in their new environments. When many of these executives fail, it's not because the individuals couldn't adapt but because their spouses or children were unhappy in the new foreign setting.

3. Brief candidates fully and clearly on all relocation policies. Transferees should be given a realistic preview of what the assignment will entail, including the company's policies regarding matters such as moving expenses and salary differentials.

4. Give executives and their families comprehensive training in their new country's culture and language.

5. Provide all relocating executives with a mentor to monitor their overseas careers and help them secure appropriate jobs with the company when they repatriate. (At Dow, for instance, this person is usually a high-level supervisor in the expatriate's functional area.) This helps to avoid the problem of having expatriates feel lost overseas, particularly in terms of career progress.

6. Establish a repatriation program that helps returning executives and their families readjust to their professional and personal lives in their home country. At Dow, for instance, the expatriate receives his or her new job assignment as much as a year before returning to the United States.[69]

are videolinked. A videolink allows for classroom learning on campuses with simultaneous broadcasting to other locations via telephone communication lines.

Some global issues in manager development are discussed in the *Global Issues in HR* box.

Behavior Modeling

Behavior modeling involves showing trainees the right, or *model,* way of doing something, letting each person practice the right way to do it, and providing feedback regarding each trainee's performance.[70] It has been used, for example, to train middle managers to better handle interpersonal situations such as performance problems and undesirable work habits.

The basic behavior modeling procedure is as follows:

1. *Modeling.* First, trainees watch films or videotapes that show model persons behaving effectively in a problem situation.
2. *Role-playing.* Next, the trainees are given roles to play in a simulated situation; here, they practice and rehearse the effective behaviors demonstrated by the models.
3. *Social reinforcement.* The trainer provides reinforcement in the form of praise and constructive feedback based on how the trainee performs in the role-playing situation.
4. *Transfer of training.* Finally, trainees are encouraged to apply their new skills when they are back on their jobs.

Studies suggest that behavior modeling can be very effective. For example, 160 novice computer users from the U.S. Naval Construction Battalion at Gulfport, Mississippi, were put through one of three types of computer training—behavioral modeling, self-paced study, or lecturing. The researchers concluded, "behavior modeling was clearly superior across all evaluation measures. Trainees in this condition learned more than other trainees, did best at demonstrating the skills taught in training in a hands-on test, and were most satisfied with the computer system four weeks after training."[71]

In-House Development Centers

Some employers have **in-house development centers**, which usually combine classroom learning (lectures and seminars, for instance) with other techniques such as assessment centers, in-basket exercises, and role playing to help develop employees and other managers. For example, *Fortune* magazine calls Crotonville, General Electric's Management Development Institute, the Harvard of corporate America. The firm's management development courses range from entry-level programs in manufacturing and sales to a course for English majors called "Everything You Always Wanted to Know About Finance."[72]

For many firms, their learning portals are becoming their virtual corporate universities. While firms such as General Electric have long had their own bricks-and-mortar corporate universities, learning portals let even smaller firms have their own corporate universities, on the Web. Bain & Company, a management consulting firm, has such a Web-based virtual university for its employees. It not only provides a means for conveniently coordinating all the company's training efforts, but also for delivering Web-based modules that cover topics from strategic management to mentoring.[73]

Many companies today try to avoid the "country club" atmospheres of earlier corporate universities. For example, at Boeing's Leadership Center, you won't find the golf course that often marks other such universities. And the training experience is described as "intense, but . . . one of the most useful intense experiences I've ever had."[74]

Organizational Development

Organizational development (OD) is aimed at changing the attitudes, values, and beliefs of employees so that the employees can identify and implement changes (such as reorganizations), usually with the aid of an outside change agent, or consultant.

Action research is the foundation of most OD interventions. It means gathering data about the organization and its operations and attitudes, with an eye toward solving a particular problem (for example, conflict between the sales and production departments); feeding back these data to the parties (employees) involved; and then having these parties team-plan solutions to the problems. In OD, the participants always get involved in gathering data about themselves and their organization, analyzing these data, and planning solutions based on these analyses.[75]

OD efforts include survey feedback, sensitivity training, and team building. **Survey feedback** uses questionnaires to survey employees' attitudes and provides feedback to department managers so that problems can be solved by the managers and employees. The results can be used to compare departments and to underscore dramatically the existence of some problem such as low morale, and serve as a basis for discussion among employees for developing alternative solutions. Employee attitude surveys have been used since at least the 1930s to assess and document employee morale.[76] Their continuing wide use reflects the fact, as several researchers recently concluded, that:

> There is validity in employee reports of their experiences and these reports can be very useful as diagnoses of the degree to which a new strategy is being implemented and the degree to which policies and practices are related to the achievement of strategic goals like customer satisfaction and customer attention.[77]

Sensitivity training aims to increase participants' insights into their behavior and the behavior of others by encouraging an open expression of feelings in the trainer-guided "T-group laboratory" (the "T" is for training).[78] Sensitivity training seeks to accomplish its aim of increasing interpersonal sensitivity by requiring frank, candid discussions in the T-group, discussions of participants' personal feelings, attitudes, and behavior. As a result, it is a controversial method surrounded by heated debate and is used much less today than in the past.[79]

Finally, **team building** refers to a group of OD techniques aimed at improving the effectiveness of teams at work. The typical team-building program begins with the consultant interviewing each of the group members prior to the group meeting, asking them what their problems are, how they think the group functions, and what obstacles are in the way of the group's performing better.[80] The consultant usually categorizes the interview or attitude survey data into themes and presents the themes to the group at the beginning of the meeting. They might include, for example, "Not enough time to get my job done," or "I can't get any cooperation around here." The group then ranks the themes by importance. The most important ones form the agenda for the meeting. The group examines and discusses the issues, examines the underlying causes of the problem, and begins work on a solution to the problems.

Building Learning Organizations

In a fast-changing world, the last thing a company needs is for new information—about competitors' actions, customers' preferences, or technological improvements—to be ignored or lost in a bureaucratic sinkhole. For years, for instance, General Motors seemed oblivious to the competitive and technological advances of its foreign competitors; it finally awoke when its board decided that too much market share had been lost. On the other hand, firms such as Microsoft and General Electric (GE) are traditionally quick on their feet, "adept at translating new knowledge into new ways of behaving."[81]

HR's Role in Building Learning Organizations Firms such as GE have successfully made the leap into rebuilding themselves as learning organizations. A **learning organization** "is an organization skilled at creating, acquiring, and transferring knowledge, and at modifying its behavior to reflect new knowledge and insights."[82]

Training can help develop such skills. At Xerox, for instance, employees are trained to analyze and display data on special simple statistical charts and to plan the actions they will take to solve the problem using special planning charts.[83] GE has programs for building the skills required to perform and evaluate experiments, such as how to use statistical methods and design experiments.[84]

Providing Employees with Lifelong Learning Employers can't build learning organizations just around managers. In today's empowered organizations, employers must also depend on first-line employees—the team members building the Saturn cars, or the Microsoft programmers—to recognize new opportunities, identify problems, and react quickly with analyses and recommendations. As a result, the need has arisen for encouraging lifelong learning, in other words, for providing extensive continuing training from basic remedial skills to advanced decision-making techniques throughout employees' careers.

One Canadian Honeywell manufacturing plant called its lifelong learning program the Honeywell Scarborough Learning for Life Initiative.[85] It was "a concerted effort to upgrade skill and education levels so that employees can meet workplace challenges with confidence."[86] It began with adult basic education. In partnership with the employees' union, the company offered courses in English as a second language, basic literacy, arithmetic, and computer literacy. Next the factory formed a partnership with a local community college. Honeywell provides in-house after-work college-level courses to all factory employees—hourly, professional, and managerial—giving them the opportunity to earn college diplomas and certificates.[87]

In addition, job-related training is provided for two hours every other week. Sessions focus on skills specifically important to the job, "such as the principles of just-in-time inventory systems, team effectiveness, interpersonal communication skills, conflict resolution, problem solving and dealing with a diverse workforce."[88]

Organizational Change

Today, intense international competition means companies have to change fast, perhaps changing their strategies to enter new businesses, or their organization charts, or their employees' attitudes and values.

Major organizational changes like these are never easy, but perhaps the hardest part of leading a change is overcoming the resistance to it. Individuals, groups, and even entire organizations may resist the change, perhaps because they are accustomed to the usual way of doing things; or because of perceived threats to their power and influence; or because of the fear of the unknown; or because of what the employee sees as a violation of the unwritten "personal compact" or agreement he or she has with the company (for instance, in terms of what the employer expects from the employee and vice versa).[89]

Lewin's Process for Overcoming Resistance Psychologist Kurt Lewin formulated a model of change to summarize what he believed was the basic process for implementing a change with minimal resistance. To Lewin, all behavior in organizations was a product of two kinds of forces: those striving to maintain the status quo and those pushing for change. Implementing change thus meant either reducing the forces for the status quo or building up the forces for change. Lewin's process consisted of three steps:

1. *Unfreezing*, which means reducing the forces that are striving to maintain the status quo, usually by presenting a provocative problem or event to get people to recognize the need for change and to search for new solutions.
2. *Moving*, which means developing new behaviors, values, and attitudes, sometimes through organizational structure changes and sometimes through the other management development techniques (such as team building).
3. Refreezing, which means building in the reinforcement to make sure the organization doesn't slide back into its former ways of doing things.

Of course, the devil is in the details, and actually finding the right techniques that will help you accomplish each of those three steps and then using them is the difficult part. A 10-step process for leading organizational change is summarized in the *HR in Practice* box.[90]

EVALUATING THE TRAINING AND DEVELOPMENT EFFORT

There are two basic issues to address when evaluating a training program. The first is the design of the evaluation study and, in particular, whether controlled experimentation will be used. The second is the training effect to be measured.

Controlled experimentation is the best method to use in evaluating a training program. In a controlled experiment, both a training group and a control group (which receives no training) are used. Data (for instance, on quantity of production or quality of soldered junctions) should be obtained both before and after the training effort in the group exposed to training and before and after a corresponding work period in the control group. In this way it is possible to determine the extent to which any change in performance in the training group resulted from the training itself rather than from some organizationwide change such as a raise in pay; we assume that the latter would have equally affected employees in both groups. This approach is feasible and is sometimes used.[91] In terms of current practices, however, one survey found that something less than half of the companies responding

A 10-Step Process for Leading Organizational Change

1. *Establish a sense of urgency.* For instance, create a crisis by exposing managers to major weaknesses relative to competitors.
2. *Mobilize commitment to change through joint diagnosis of business problems.* Next, create one or more task forces to diagnose the business problems. Such teams can produce a shared understanding of what can and must be improved and thereby mobilize the commitment of those who must actually implement the change.
3. *Create a guiding coalition.* No leader can accomplish any significant change alone. That's why most leaders create a guiding coalition of influential people who can be missionaries and implementers of change.
4. *Develop a shared vision*, a general statement of the organization's intended direction that evokes emotional feelings in organization members.
5. *Communicate the vision.* Use multiple forums, repetition, and leading by example to foster support for the new vision.
6. *Remove barriers to the change: Empower employees.* Accomplishing the change usually requires the assistance of the employees themselves, but sometimes this requires empowering them—in other words, removing barriers that stand in the way of their being able to actually assist in making the changes. For example, Sony's CEO removed the former studio executives and installed a new team when he set about fixing Sony's movie business.[92] Allied Signal's CEO Lawrence Bossidy put all of his 80,000 employees through quality training within two years.[93]
7. *Generate short-term wins.* Maintain employees' motivation to stay involved in the change by ensuring that they have short-term goals to achieve from which they will receive positive feedback.
8. *Consolidate gains and produce more change.* As momentum builds and changes are made, the leader has to guard against renewed complacency. To do this, the leader and guiding coalition can use the increased credibility that comes from short-term wins to change all the systems, structures, and policies that don't fit well with the company's new vision.
9. *Anchor the new ways of doing things in the company's culture.* Few organizational changes survive without a corresponding change in employees' shared values. For example, if you want to emphasize more openness, camaraderie, and customer service, you as a leader must get the organization's employees to share those values. Do this by issuing a core value statement and by "walking the talk," and by using signs, symbols, and ceremonies to reinforce the values you want your employees to share.
10. *Monitor progress and adjust the vision as required.* For example, regular surveys may be used to monitor customer and employee attitudes.

attempted to obtain before-and-after measures from trainees; the number of organizations using control groups was negligible.[94]

Training Effects to Measure

Four basic categories of training outcomes can be measured:

1. *Reaction.* First, evaluate trainees' reactions to the program. Did they like the program? Did they think it worthwhile?
2. *Learning.* Second, test the trainees to determine whether they learned the principles, skills, and facts they were supposed to learn.
3. *Behavior.* Next, ask whether the trainees' behavior on the job changed because of the training program. For example, are employees in the store's complaint department more courteous toward disgruntled customers than previously?
4. *Results.* Finally, but probably most importantly, ask What final results were achieved in terms of the training objectives previously set? Did the number of customer complaints about employees drop? Did the reject rate improve? Did scrappage cost decrease? Was turnover reduced?

REVIEW

Summary

1. The training process consists of five steps: needs analysis, instructional design, validation, implementation, and evaluation.
2. Vestibule training combines the advantages of on- and off-the-job training and is also called simulated training.
3. On-the-job training is a third basic training technique. It might take the form of the understudy method, job rotation, or special assignments and committees. Other training methods include: audiovisual techniques, lectures, computer-aided instruction, apprenticeship training, simulated training, CD-ROM- and Internet-based training, learning portals, and special-purpose training.
4. Management development is aimed at preparing employees for future jobs with the organization, or at solving organizationwide problems concerning, for instance, inadequate interdepartmental communication.
5. On-the-job experience is by far the most popular form of management development.
6. Managerial on-the-job training methods include job rotation, coaching, and action learning. Case studies, management games, outside seminars, university-related programs, behavior modeling, and in-house development centers are other methods.
7. Organizational development is an approach to instituting change in which employees themselves play a major role in the change process by providing data, by obtaining feedback on problems, and by team-planning solutions. There are several OD methods, including sensitivity training, team development, and survey feedback.
8. Overcoming employee resistance is a crucial aspect of implementing organizational change. The *HR in Practice* box summarizes the process.

Key Terms

employee orientation
training
task analysis
performance analysis
on-the-job training (OJT)
vestibule or simulated
training
worker involvement
programs

management
development
job rotation
action learning
case study method
management games
behavior modeling
in-house development
centers

organizational
development (OD)
survey feedback
sensitivity training
team building
learning organization
controlled
experimentation

Discussion Questions and Exercises

1. "A well-thought out orientation program is especially important for employees (such as recent graduates) who have had little or no work experience." Explain why you agree or disagree with this statement.

2. You're the supervisor of a group of employees whose task is to assemble tuning devices that go into radios. You find that quality is not what it should be and that many of your group's tuning devices have to be brought back and reworked; your own boss says, "You better start doing a better job of training your workers."

   a. What are some of the staffing factors that could be contributing to this problem?

   b. Explain how you would go about assessing whether it is in fact a training problem.

3. Explain how you would go about developing a lecture, say, on orientation and training.

4. John Santos is an undergraduate business student majoring in accounting. He has just failed the first accounting course, Accounting 101, and is understandably upset. Explain how you would use performance analysis to identify what, if any, are Santos's training needs.

5. What are some typical on-the-job training techniques? What do you think are some of the main drawbacks of relying on informal on-the-job training for helping new employees become accustomed to their jobs?

6. Experts argue that one reason for implementing special global training programs is the need to avoid lost business "due to cultural insensitivity." What sort of cultural insensitivity do you think is referred to and how might that translate into lost business? What sort of training program would you recommend to avoid such cultural insensitivity?

7. Do you think job rotation is a good method to use for developing management trainees? Why or why not?

8. Working individually or in groups, contact a provider of management development seminars such as the American Management Association. Obtain copies of the provider's recent listings of seminar offerings. At what levels of managers do they aim their seminar offerings? What seems to be the most popular type of development programs? Why do you think that's the case?

9. Working individually or in groups, use the definition of a learning organization found in this chapter to discuss whether you think the college you are currently attending is or is not a learning organization. On what do you base your conclusion?

APPLICATION EXERCISES

Case Incident: Reinventing the Wheel at Apex Door Company

Jim Delaney, president of Apex Door Company, has a problem. No matter how often he tells his employees how to do their jobs, they invariably "decide to do things their way," as he puts it, and arguments ensue between Delaney, the employee, and the employee's supervisor. One example is in the door-design department; the designers are expected to work with the architects to design doors that meet the specifications. Although it's not "rocket science," as Delaney puts it, the designers often make mistakes—such as designing in too much steel—a problem that can cost Apex tens of thousands of wasted dollars, especially considering the number of doors in, say, a 30-story office tower.

The order processing department is another example. Although Jim has a specific, detailed way he wants each order written up, most of the order clerks don't understand how to use the multipage order form, and they improvise when it comes to a question such as whether to classify a customer as "industrial" or "commercial."

The current training process is as follows. None of the jobs have training manuals per se, although several have somewhat out-of-date job descriptions. The training for new employees is all on the job: Usually, the person leaving the company trains the new person during the one- or two-week overlap period, but if there's no overlap, the new person is trained as well as possible by other employees who have occasionally filled in on the job in the past. The training is basically the same throughout the company—for machinists, secretaries, assemblers, and accounting clerks, for example.

Questions

1. What do you think of Apex's training process? Could it help to explain why employees "do things their way," and if so, how?

2. What role do job descriptions play in training?

3. Explain in detail what you would do to improve the training process at Apex. Make sure to provide specific suggestions.

Experiential Exercise

Purpose: The purpose of this exercise is to give you practice in developing a training program.

Required Understanding: You should be thoroughly familiar with the training methods discussed in this chapter, including computer-based training, vestibule training, and on-the-job training. Because you'll be developing a training program for directory assistance operators, you should read the following description of a directory assistance operator's duties:

> *Customers contact directory assistance operators to obtain the telephone numbers of persons whose numbers are not yet listed, whose listings have changed, or whose numbers are unknown to the customer. These operators check the requested number via a computerized video display, which then transmits the numbers to the customer. If more than one number is requested, the operator reports the first number, and the system then transmits the second to the caller. A number must be found quickly so that the customer is not kept waiting. It is often necessary to check various spellings of the same name because customers frequently give incorrect spellings.*

Next, imagine that you are the supervisor of about 10 directory assistance operators in a small regional phone company that has no formal training program for new operators. Because you get one or two new operators every few months, you think it would raise efficiency for you to develop a new directory assistance operator's training program for your own use in your department. Consider what such a program would consist of before proceeding to your assigned group.

How to Set Up the Exercise/Instructions: Divide the class into groups of four or five students. In keeping with the procedure discussed for setting up a training program, your group should, at a minimum, go through the following steps:

1. List the duties and responsibilities of the job (of directory assistance operator) using the description provided.

2. List some assumed standards of work performance for the job.

3. Within your group, develop some assumptions about what parts of the job give new employees the most trouble (you'd normally be able to do this based on your experience as the operators' supervisor).

4. Determine what kind of training is needed to overcome these differences.

5. Develop a new directory assistance operator's training package that provides two things. First, provide a one-page outline showing the type(s) of training each new operator in your unit will go through. (For example, you might indicate that the first two hours on the job will involve the new operator observing existing operators), four hours of lectures, etc.) Second, in this package, expand on exactly what each training technique will involve. For example, if you are going to use computer-based training, show the steps to be included; if you're going to use lectures, provide an outline of what you'll discuss.

If time permits, a spokesperson from each group can put his or her group's training program outline on the board, and the class can discuss the relative merits of each group's proposal.

TAKE IT TO THE WEB

 For Internet exercises, updates to chapter material, and more, visit the Dessler Web site at

www.prenhall.com/dessler

ENDNOTES

1. For a good discussion of socialization see, for example, George Chao et al., "Organizational Socialization: Its Content and Consequences," *Journal of Applied Psychology* 79, no. 5 (1994): 730–43; and Blake Ashforth and Alan Saks, "Socialization Tactics: Longitudinal Effects on Newcomer Adjustment," *Academy of Management Journal* 39, no. 1 (1996): 149–78.

2. Joseph Famularo, *Handbook of Modern Personnel Administration* (New York: McGraw-Hill, 1972), pp. 23.7–23.8. See also Ronald Smith, "Employee Orientation: Ten Steps to Success," *Personnel Journal* 63, no. 12 (December 1984): 46–49.

3. Sabrina Hicks, "Successful Orientation Programs," *Training & Development* (April 2000): 59. See also Howard Klein and Natasha Weaver, "The Effectiveness of an Organizational Level Orientation Program in the Socialization of New Hires," *Personnel Psychology* 53 (2000): 47–66.

4. See, for example, Carolyn Wiley, "Training for the 90s: How Leading Companies Focus

on Quality Improvement, Technological Change, and Customer Service," *Employment Relations Today* (spring 1993): 80.

5. *Ibid.,* pp. 81–82.

6. Harley Frazis, Diane Herz, and Michael Horrigan, "Employer-Provided Training: Results from a New Survey," *Monthly Labor Review* (May 1995): 3–17.

7. Wiley "Training for the 90s," p. 82. See also "Employee Training: Practices in 1995," *BNA Bulletin to Management* (November 2, 1995): 352; and "Employee Training," *BNA Bulletin to Management* (January 23, 1997): 28–29.

8. Marcia Jones, "Use Your Head When Identifying Skills Gaps," *Workforce* (March 2000): 118.

9. E. J. McCormick and J. Tiffin, *Industrial Psychology* (Englewood Cliffs, NJ: Prentice Hall, 1974), p. 245. See also James C. Georges, "The Hard Realities of Soft Skills Training," *Personnel Journal* 68, no. 4 (April 1989): 40–45; Robert H. Buckham, "Applying Role Analysis in the Workplace," *Personnel* 64, no. 2 (February 1987): 63–65; and J. Kevin Ford and Raymond Noe, "Self-Assessed Training Needs: The Effects of Attitudes Towards Training, Management Level, and Function," *Personnel Psychology* 40, no. 1 (spring 1987): 39–54.

10. P. Nick Blanchard and James Thacker, *Effective Training: Systems, Strategies, and Practices* (Upper Saddle River, NJ: Prentice Hall, 1999), pp. 154–56.

11. Richard Camp et al., *Toward a More Organizationally Effective Training Strategy and Practice* (Englewood Cliffs, NJ: Prentice Hall, 1986), p. 100.

12. J. P. Cicero, "Behavioral Objectives for Technical Training Systems," *Training and Development Journal* 28 (1973): 14–17. See also Larry D. Hales, "Training: A Product of Business Planning," *Training and Development Journal* 40, no. 7 (July 1986): 87–92; and Pamela Prewitt, "Army Job Standard vs. Training Standard," *Training and Development Journal* 51, no. 9 (September 1997): 52–53.

13. Erica Gordon Sorohan, "We Do; Therefore, We Learn," *Training & Development* (October 1993): 47–55; and Melvin LeBlanc, "Learning Objectives Key to Quality Safety," *Occupational Hazards* (January 1994): 127–28. See also, Kimberly A. Smith-Jentsch et al., "Can Pre-Training Experiences Explain Individual Differences in Learning?" *Journal of Applied Psychology* 81, no. 1 (1996): 110–116.

14. Frazis et al., "Employer-Provided Training: Results from a New Survey," p. 4.

15. "German Training Model Imported," *BNA Bulletin to Management* (December 19, 1996): 408.

16. *Ibid.*

17. Kenneth Wexley and Gary Latham, *Developing and Training Human Resources in Organizations* (Glenview, IL: Scott Foresman, 1981), p. 141. See also Raymond Wlozkowski, "Simulation," *Training and Development Journal* 39, no. 6 (June 1985): 38–43.

18. Wexley and Latham, *Developing and Training Human Resources in Organizations*, pp. 131–33. See also Teri O. Grady and Mike Matthews, "Video . . . Through the Eyes of the Trainee," *Training* 24, no. 7 (July 1987): 57–62. For a description of the use of computer-based multimedia training, see Erica Schroeder, "Training Takes Off, Using Multimedia," *PC Week* (August 29, 1994): 33–34.

19. Michael Blotzer, "Distance Learning," *Occupational Hazards* (March 2000): 53–54.

20. Mary Boone and Susan Schulman, "Teletraining: A High-Tech Alternative," *Personnel* 62, no. 5 (May 1985): 4–9. See also Ron Zemke, "The Rediscovery of Video Teleconferencing," *Training* 23, no. 9 (September 1986): 28–36; and Paul Munger, "High-Tech Training Delivery Methods: When to Use Them," *Training and Development Journal* 51, no. 1 (January 1997): 46–47.

21. Joseph Giusti, David Baker, and Peter Braybash, "Satellites Dish Out Global Training," *Personnel Journal* (June 1991): 80–84.

22. "Macy's Goes 'On Air' to Inform Employees," *BNA Bulletin to Management* (May 15, 1997): 160.

23. "Cadillac Offers a Top-of-the-Line Training Program," *Personnel Journal* (February 1996): 25.

24. Michael Emery and Margaret Schubert, "A Trainer's Guide to Videoconferencing," *Training* (June 1993): 60. See also Mark Van Buren, "Learning Technologies: Can They or Can't They?" *Training & Development* (April 2000): 62.

25. *Ibid.*, p. 60.

26. "Employer to Learn the Benefits of Distance Learning," *BNA Bulletin to Management* (April 25, 1996): 130.

27. These are based on or quoted from Emery and Schubert, "A Trainer's Guide to Videoconferencing," p. 61.

28. See, for example, Tim Falconer, "No More Pencils, No More Books!" *Canadian Banker* (March/April 1994): 21–25.

29. Ralph E. Ganger, "Training: Computer-Based Training Works," *Personnel Journal* 73, no. 11 (November 1994): 51–52. See also Anat Arkin, "Computing: The Future Means of Training?" *Personnel Management* 26, no. 8 (August 1994): 36–40.

30. These are summarized in Rockley Miller, "New Training Looms," *Hotel and Motel Management* (April 4, 1994): 26, 30.

31. *Ibid.*, p. 26.

32. Bob Filipczak, "Trainers on the Net," *Training* (December 1994): 42–51.

33. *Ibid.*, p. 50.

34. Larry Stevens, "The Intranet: Your Newest Training Tool?" *Personnel Journal* (July 1996): 27–31.

35. Shari Caudron, "Your Learning Technology Primer," *Personnel Journal* (June 1996): 120–36.

36. *Ibid.*, p. 130.

37. *Ibid.*, p. 122.

38. David Kirkpatrick, "The Portal of the Future? Your Boss Will Run It," *Fortune* (August 2, 1999): 222–27.

39. Tom Barron, "A Portrait of Learning Portals," http://www.learningcircuits.com/may2000/barron.html.

40. Eileen Garger, "Goodbye Training, Hello Learning," *Workforce* (November 1999): 35–42.

41. "Skill Deficiencies Pose Increasing Problems," *BNA Bulletin to Management* (October 26, 1995): 337–38.

42. Valerie Frazee, "Workers Learn to Walk So They Can Run," *Personnel Journal* (May 1996): 115–20.

43. *Ibid.*, p. 24.

44. *BNA Bulletin to Management* (December 17, 1987): 408.

45. Stephen Dolainski, "Partnering with the (School) Board," *Workforce* (May 1997): 28–37.

46. Adapted from Gary Dessler, *Winning Commitment* (New York: McGraw-Hill, 1993), Chapter 7.

47. See Joyce Santora, "Kinney Shoes Steps Into Diversity," *Personnel Journal* (September 1991): 74.

48. Sara Rynes and Benson Rosen, "What Makes Diversity Programs Work?" *HRMagazine* (October 1994): 64. See also Thomas Diamante and Leo Giglio, "Managing a Diverse

Workforce: Training as a Cultural Intervention Strategy," *Leadership & Organization Development Journal* 15, no. 2 (1994): 13–17.

49. Willie Hopkins, Karen Sterkel-Powell, and Shirley Hopkins, "Training Priorities for a Diverse Workforce," *Public Personnel Management* 23, no. 3 (fall 1994): 433.

50. Based on Jennifer Laabs, "Team Training Goes Outdoors," *Personnel Journal* (June 1991): 56–63.

51. *Ibid.*, p. 56. See also Shari Caudron, "Teamwork Takes Work," *Personnel Journal* (February 1994): 41–49.

52. Heidi Campbell, "Adventures in Teamland," *Personnel Journal* (May 1996): 56–62.

53. Lester A. Digman, "Management Development: Needs and Practices," *Personnel* 57 (July/August 1980): 45–57. See also James Cureton, Alfred Newton, and Dennis Tesolowski, "Finding Out What Managers Need," *Training and Development Journal* 40, no. 5 (May 1986): 106–107. Results of a 10-year survey show an increasingly important role for executive development in building and revitalizing corporate competitiveness. See Albert Vicere, Maria Taylor, and Virginia Freeman, "Executive Development in Major Corporations: A Ten-Year Study," *Journal of Management Development* 13, no. 1 (1994): 4–22.

54. William Kearney, "Management Development Programs Can Pay Off," *Business Horizons* 18 (April 1975): 81–88. See also Michael Hitt et al., "Human Capital and Strategic Competitiveness in the 1990s," *Journal of Management Development* 13, no. 1 (1994): 35–46.

55. According to a survey by Digman, the median percentage of executives receiving training during a typical year was 23%; middle managers, 38%; and first-line supervisors, 20%. See also Vicere et al., "Executive Development in Major Corporations."

56. Jack Zenger, Dave Ulrich, and Norm Smallwood, "The New Leadership Development," *Training & Development* (March 2000): 22–27.

57. Dale Yoder et al., *Handbook of Personnel Management and Labor Relations* (New York: McGraw-Hill, 1958), pp. 10–27; for a review, see William Rothwell, H. C. Kazanas, and Darla Haines, "Issues and Practices in Management Job Rotation Programs as Perceived by HRD Professionals," *Performance Improvement Quarterly* 5, no. 1 (1992): 49–69.

58. Based on Nancy Fox, "Action Learning Comes to Industry," *Harvard Business Review* 56 (September/October 1977): 158–68.

59. Based on Paul Froiland, "Action Learning: Taming Real Problems in Real Time," *Training* (January 1994): 27–34. See also Gillian Cribbs, "Back in Fashion—Yet Again. Action Learning: The Perennial Attraction of Action Learning Is That Its Objective Is to Help Resolve Real-Life Situations," *The Financial Times* (May 23, 2000): 6.

60. For several other examples of action learning, see Barry Smith, "Building Managers from the Inside Out—Developing Managers Through Competency-Based Action Learning," *Journal of Management Development* 12, no. 1 (1993): 43–48; Thomas Downham, James Noel, and Albert Prendergast, "Executive Development," *Human Resource Management* 31, nos. 1 and 2 (spring/summer 1992): 95–107. See also Michael Gregory, "Accrediting Work-Based Learning: Action Learning, a Model for Empowerment," *Journal of Management Development* 13, no. 4 (1994): 41–52. Louise Keys, "Action Learning: Executive Development of Choice for the 1990s," *Journal of Management Development* 13, no. 8 (1994): 50–56. See also Allison Rossett, "Action Learning in Action: Transforming Problems and People for World-Class Organizational Learning," *Personnel Psychology* (winter 1999): 1100.

61. Wexley and Latham, *Developing and Training Human Resources in Organizations*, p. 193.

62. Chris Argyris, "Some Limitations of the Case Method: Experiences in a Management Development Program," *Academy of Management Review* 5, no. 2 (1980): 291–28. For a discussion of the advantages of case studies over traditional methods, see, for example,

Eugene Andrews and James Noel, "Adding Life to the Case Study," *Training and Development Journal* 40, no. 2 (February 1986): 28–33. See also Gerald F. Smith, "Experience Is the Best Teacher: Avoiding the Pitfalls of Methodolotry," *National Productivity Review* (summer 1999): 57-5.

63. David Rogers, *Business Policy and Planning* (Englewood Cliffs, NJ: Prentice Hall, 1977), pp. 532–33. See also Barra Cinneide, "The Role and Effectiveness of Case Studies: Student Performance in Case Study vs. 'Theory' Examinations," *Journal of European Industrial Training* (January 1997): 3-11.

64. Chris Whitcomb, "Scenario-Based Training at the FBI," *Training & Development* (June 1999): 42–46.

65. For a discussion of management games and also other noncomputerized training and development simulations, see Charlene Marmer Solomon, "Simulation Training Builds Teams Through Experience," *Personnel Journal* (June 1993): 100–105; Kim Slack, "Training for the Real Thing," *Training and Development* (May 1993): 79–89; and Bruce Lierman, "How to Develop a Training Simulation," *Training and Development* (February 1994): 50–52. Training games aren't limited to the computer-aided variety. See, for example, "Stop Playing Games," *Training & Development* (February 1999): 29–36.

66. Mona Pintkowski, "Evaluating the Seminar Marketplace," *Training and Development Journal* 40, no. 1 (January 1986): 74–77.

67. Lawrence G. Bridwell and Alvin B. Marcus, "Back to School—A High-Tech Company Sent Its Managers to Business School—to Learn 'People' Skills," *Personnel Administrator* 32, no. 3 (March 1987): 86–91.

68. Paul Blocklyn, "Developing the International Executive," *Personnel* (March 1989): 44–47. See also T. S. Chan, "Developing International Managers: A Partnership Approach," *Journal of Management Development* 13, no. 3 (1994): 38–46.

69. This section based on Blocklyn. See also "Developing Global Executives," *BNA Bulletin to Management* 44, no. 10 (March 11, 1993): 73–74. See also D. Bradford Neary and Don O'Grady, "The Role of Training in Developing Global Leaders: A Case Study at TRW, Inc.," *Human Resource Management* 39, nos. 2 and 3 (summer/fall 2000): 185–93.

70. This section based on Allen Kraut, "Developing Managerial Skill via Modeling Techniques: Some Positive Research Findings—a Symposium," *Personnel Psychology* 29, no. 3 (autumn 1976): 325–61. See also Steven Simon and Jon Werner, "Computer Training Through Behavioral Modelling, Self Paced and Instructional Approaches: A Field Experiment," *Journal of Applied Psychology* 81, no. 6 (1996): 648–59.

71. *Ibid.*, p. 655.

72. Thomas Stewart, "How GE Keeps Those Ideas Coming," *Fortune* (August 12, 1991): 43.

73. Russell Gerbman, "Corporate Universities 101," *HRMagazine* (February 2000): 101–106.

74. Carolyn Cole, "Boeing U," *Workforce* (October 2000): 63–68.

75. Mark Frohman, Marshall Sashkin, and Michael Kavanagh, "Action Research as Applied to Organization Development," *Organization and Administrative Science* 7 (spring/summer 1976): 129–42; Paul Shelbar, "The Seven Deadly Sins of Employee Attitude Surveys," *Personnel* 66, no. 6 (June 1989): 66–71. See also George Gallup, "A Surge in Surveys," *Personnel Journal* 67, no. 8 (August 1988): 42–43.

76. Benjamin Schneider, Steven Ashworth, A. Catherine Higgs, and Linda Carr, "Design, Validity, and Use of Strategically Focused Employee Attitude Surveys," *Personnel Psychology* 49 (1996): 695–705.

77. *Ibid.*, p. 74.

78. Based on J. P. Campbell and M. D. Dunnette, "Effectiveness of T-Group Experiences in Managerial Training and Development," *Psychological Bulletin* 7 (1968): 73–104. See also

Paul Sachdev, "Cultural Sensitivity Training Through Experiential Learning: A Participatory Demonstration Field Education Project," *International Social Work* 40, no. 1 (January 1997): 7–25.

79. John Kimberly and Warren Nielson, "Organization Development and Change in Organizational Performance," *Administrative Science Quarterly* 20, no. 2 (June 1975): Peter Smith, "Controlled Studies of the Outcome of Sensitivity Training," *Psychological Bulletin* 82 (1976): 597–622. See also Michael Blum and James Wall, Jr., "HRM: Managing Conflicts in the Firm," *Business Horizons* 40, no. 3 (May 1997): pp. 84–87.

80. Wendell French and Cecil Bell, Jr., *Organization Development* (Englewood Cliffs, NJ: Prentice Hall, 1978). See also David M. Zakeski, "Reliable Assessments of Organizations," *Personnel Journal* 67, no. 12 (December 1988): 42–44.

81. David A. Garvin, "Building a Learning Organization," *Business Credit* (January 1994): 20.

82. David A. Garvin, "Building a Learning Organization," *Harvard Business Review* (July/August 1993): 80.

83. Garvin, "Building a Learning Organization," *Business Credit*, p. 21.

84. *Ibid.*, p. 21.

85. Based on Norman Nopper, "Reinventing the Factory with Lifelong Learning," *Training* (May 1993): 55–57.

86. *Ibid.*, p. 56.

87. *Ibid.*, p. 56.

88. *Ibid.*, p. 64. For another example, see Kevin Kelly and Peter Burrows, "Motorola: Training for the Millennium," *Business Week* (March 28, 1994): 158–60; and "Some Nuts and Bolts of Lifelong Learning," *Training* (March 1994): 30.

89. Paul Strebel, "Why Do Employees Resist Change?" *Harvard Business Review* (May/June 1996): 86–92.

90. The 10 steps are based on Michael Beer et al., "Why Change Programs Don't Product Change," *Harvard Business Review* (November/December 1990): 158–66; Thomas Cumings and Christopher Worley, *Organization Development and Change* (Minneapolis: West Publishing Co., 1993); and John Kotter, *Leading Change* (Boston: Harvard Business School Press, 1966).

91. See, for example, Charlie Morrow, M. Quintin Jarrett, and Melvin Rupinski, "An Investigation of the Effect and Economic Utility of Corporate-Wide Training," *Personnel Psychology* 50 (1997): 91–119.

92. Kathryn Harris, "Mr. Sony Confronts Hollywood," *Fortune* (December 23, 1996): 36.

93. Noel Tichy and Ram Charan, "The CEO as Coach: An Interview with Allied Signal's Lawrence A. Bossidy," *Harvard Business Review* (March/April 1995): 77.

94. R. E. Catalano and D. L. Kirkpatrick, "Evaluating Training Programs—The State of the Art," *Training and Development Journal* 22, no. 5 (May 1968): 2–9. See also J. Kevin Ford and Steven Wroten, "Introducing New Methods for Conducting Training Evaluation and for Linking Training Evaluation to Program Redesign," *Personnel Psychology* 37, no. 4 (winter 1984): 651–66. See also Basil Paquet et al., "The Bottom Line," *Training and Development Journal* 41, no. 5 (May 1987): 27–33; Harold E. Fisher and Ronald Weinberg, "Make Training Accountable: Assess Its Impact," *Personnel Journal* 67, no. 1 (January 1988): 73–75; Timothy Baldwin and J. Kevin Ford, "Transfer of Training: A Review and Directions for Future Research," *Personnel Psychology* 41, no. 1 (spring 1988): 63–105; and Anthony Montebello and Maurine Haga, "To Justify Training, Test, Test Again," *Personnel Journal* 73, no. 1 (January 1994): 83–87; Pamela Kidder and Janice Rouiller, "Evaluating the Success of a Large-Scale Training Effort," *National Productivity Review* 16, no. 2 (1997): 79–89.

Chapter 6

Appraising Performance

➤ An Introduction to Appraising
  Performance
➤ Basic Appraisal Methods
➤ The Appraisal Feedback Interview
➤ Toward More Effective Appraisals

When you finish studying this chapter, you should be able to:

■ *Explain* the purpose of performance appraisal.

■ *Answer* the question Who should do the appraising?

■ *Discuss* the pros and cons of at least eight performance appraisal methods.

■ *Explain* how to conduct an appraisal feedback interview.

INTRODUCTION

The administrators at St. Luke's Hospital knew the employee-appraisal system needed to be streamlined. At St. Luke's, the appraisal procedure had evolved over the years to respond to the needs of various departments and to various federal, state, and health care industry standards. As a result, the size of the appraisal and supporting documents had grown to an average of 20 pages per employee: It was just too time consuming to do an appraisal, and the process had to be changed. But how?

AN INTRODUCTION TO APPRAISING PERFORMANCE

Performance appraisal may be defined as evaluating an employee's current or past performance relative to his or her performance standards. Although "appraising performance" usually brings to mind specific appraisal tools such as the classroom teaching appraisal form in Figure 6.1, the form itself is usually only part of the appraisal process. Appraising performance also assumes that performance standards have been set, and that you'll give the employee feedback to help him or her eliminate performance deficiencies or continue to perform above par.

Why Appraise Performance?

There are three main reasons bosses appraise their subordinates' performance. First, appraisals provide important input on which promotion and salary raise decisions can be made. Second, the appraisal lets the boss and subordinate develop a plan for correcting any deficiencies the appraisal might have unearthed, and to reinforce the things the subordinate does correctly. Finally, appraisals can serve a useful career-planning purpose by providing the opportunity to review the employee's career plans in light of his or her exhibited strengths and weaknesses.

Who Should Do the Appraising?

Appraisals by the immediate supervisor are still at the heart of most appraisal processes. Getting a supervisor's appraisal is relatively straightforward and also makes sense. The supervisor should be—and usually is—in the best position to observe and evaluate his or her subordinate's performance and is also responsible for that person's performance. Most appraisals—92% in one survey—are made by the employee's immediate supervisor. These appraisals are in turn reviewed by the supervisor's own supervisor in 74% of the respondents in this survey.[1]

Yet although widely used, supervisors' ratings are no panacea and sole reliance on them is not always advisable.[2] For example, an employee's supervisor may not understand or appreciate how such people as customers and colleagues who depend on the employee rate the person's performance, and it is not inconceivable that an immediate supervisor may be biased for or against the employee. One or more options are therefore sometimes used to obtain appraisal data.

Peer Appraisals With more firms using self-managing teams, appraisal of an employee by his or her peers—*peer appraisal*—is becoming more popular. At Digital Equipment Corporation, for example, an employee due for an annual appraisal chooses an appraisal chairperson. The latter then selects one supervisor and three peers to evaluate the employee's work.[3]

Research indicates that peer appraisals can be effective. One study involved undergraduates that placed into self-managing work groups. The researchers found that peer appraisals had "an immediate positive impact on [improving] perception of open communication, task motivation, social loafing, group viability, cohesion, and satisfaction."[4]

Evaluating Faculty for Promotion and Tenure

Classroom Teaching Appraisal by Students

Teacher_____ Course_____
Term _____ Academic Year_____

    Thoughtful student appraisal can help improve teaching effectiveness. This questionnaire is designed for that purpose, and your assistance is appreciated. Please do not sign your name.

    Use the back of this form for any further comments you might want to express; use numbers 10, 11, and 12 for any additional questions that you might like to add.

Directions: Rate your teacher on each item, giving the highest scores for exceptional performances and the lowest scores for very poor performances. Place in the blank space before each statement the rating that most closely expresses your view.

Excep- tional			Moder- ately Good			Very Poor	Don't Know
7	6	5	4	3	2	1	X

_____ 1. How do you rate the agreement between course objectives and lesson assignments?

_____ 2. How do you rate the planning, organization, and use of class periods?

_____ 3. Are the teaching methods and techniques employed by the teacher appropriate and effective?

_____ 4. How do you rate the competence of the instructor in the subject?

_____ 5. How do you rate the interest of the teacher in the subject?

_____ 6. Does the teacher stimulate and challenge you to think and to question?

_____ 7. Does he or she welcome differing points of view?

_____ 8. Does the teacher have a personal interest in helping you in and out of class?

_____ 9. How would you rate the fairness and effectiveness of the grading policies and procedures of the teacher?

_____ 10. _____

Faculty Evaluation Rating Forms

_____ 11. _____

_____ 12. _____

_____ 13. Considering all the above items, what is your over-all rating of this teacher?

_____ 14. How would you rate this teacher in comparison with all others you have had in the college or university?

FIGURE 6.1 Departmental Teaching Appraisal Form

Source: Reprinted with permission from *Evaluating Faculty for Promotion and Tenure* by Richard I. Miller, pp. 164–65. Copyright © 1987 Jossey-Bass, Inc., Publishers. All rights reserved.

Rating Committees Some companies use rating committees. A rating committee is usually composed of the employee's immediate supervisor and three or four other supervisors.

Using multiple raters can be advantageous. It can help cancel out problems such as bias on the part of individual raters. It can also provide a way to include in the appraisal the different facets of an employee's performance observed by different appraisers. This is probably why composite ratings tend to be more reliable, fair, and valid than those done by individual supervisors.[5]

Self-Ratings Employees' self-ratings of performance are also sometimes used, usually in conjunction with supervisors' ratings. The basic problem with self-ratings is that employees usually rate themselves higher than they are rated by supervisors or peers.[6] In one study it was found that when asked to rate their own job performances, 40% of employees in jobs of all types placed themselves in the top 10%, and virtually all remaining employees rated themselves at least in the top 50%. At least one recent study concluded that individuals do not necessarily always have such positive illusions about their own performance; however, in rating the performance of their groups, group members consistently assigned their group unrealistically high performance ratings in one study.[7]

Appraisal by Subordinates Some firms let subordinates evaluate their supervisors' performance, a process many call *upward feedback*.[8] Such feedback can help top managers diagnose management styles, identify potential people problems, and take corrective action with individual managers, as required. Firms such as FedEx use upward feedback to help improve supervisory performance; for example, if a supervisor scores low on the item "I feel free to tell my manager what I think," FedEx managers are trained to ask their groups questions such as "What do I do that makes you feel that I'm not interested?"

Anonymity can have a big impact on the usefulness of upward feedback. Managers who get feedback from subordinates who identify themselves view the upward feedback process more positively than do managers who get anonymous feedback; however, subordinates are more comfortable giving anonymous responses, and those who must identify themselves tend to give inflated ratings.[9]

Research supports the idea that upward feedback can improve a manager's performance. One study focused on 252 managers during five annual administrations of an upward feedback program. Managers who were initially "rated poor or moderate showed significant improvements in [their] upward feedback ratings over the five-year period . . ." Furthermore, managers who met with their subordinates to discuss their upward feedback improved more than the managers who did not.[10]

360-Degree Feedback With 360-degree feedback, performance information is collected all around an employee, from his or her supervisors, subordinates, peers, and internal or external customers; this approach is increasingly popular.[11] It is generally used for development rather than for pay raises. The usual process is to have various individuals complete appraisal surveys on an individual; computerized systems then compile all this feedback into individualized reports that are presented to the person being appraised. The person being appraised may then meet with his or her supervisor to develop a self-improvement plan.[12]

With multiple employees to appraise and multiple raters for each employee, 360-degree assessments can be paperwork nightmares. Several software programs are thus available. For example, Visual 360 from MindSolve Technologies of Gainesville, Florida, lets the rater log in, open a screen with a rating scale, and then rate the person along a series of competencies with ratings such as "top five percent."[13]

There are also several systems for accomplishing 360-degree assessments via the Internet. For example, in the Internet-based 360 system used at Farmington, Connecticut–based Otis Elevator Company, managers and others are evaluated by their peers, customers, teammates, supervisors, direct subordinates, suppliers, and themselves. All information submitted is encrypted; passwords are used to ensure that only authorized persons can access the actual Internet-based evaluations.[14]

BASIC APPRAISAL METHODS

The appraisal itself is usually conducted using one or more of the formal methods described in this section.

Graphic Rating Scale Method

A **graphic rating scale** lists a number of traits and a range of performance for each. As in Figure 6.2, it lists traits (such as quality and reliability) and a range of performance values (in this case from unsatisfactory to outstanding) for each trait. The supervisor rates each subordinate by circling or checking the score that best describes the subordinate's performance for each trait. The assigned scores for all traits are then totaled.

Alternation Ranking Method

Ranking employees from best to worst on a trait or traits is another popular appraisal method. Because it is usually easier to distinguish between the worst and best employees than to rank them, an **alternation ranking method** is useful. With this method a form like that in Figure 6.3 is used to indicate the employee who is highest on the trait being measured and also the one who is the lowest, alternating between highest and lowest until all employees to be rated have been addressed.

Paired Comparison Method

With the **paired comparison method**, every subordinate to be rated is paired with and compared to every other subordinate on each trait.

For example, suppose there are five employees to be rated. With this method, a chart such as that in Figure 6.4 shows all possible pairs of employees for each trait. Then for each trait, the supervisor indicates (with a plus or minus) who is the better employee of the pair. Next, the number of times an employee is rated better is added up. In Figure 6.4, employee Maria ranked highest (has the most plus marks) for quality of work, and Art ranked highest for the trait creativity.

Performance Appraisal Form

Employee Name _____ Title _____

Department _____ Employee Payroll Number _____

Reason for Review: ☐ Annual   ☐ Promotion   ☐ Unsatisfactory Performance

                        ☐ Merit   ☐ End Probation Period   ☐ Other _____

Date employee began present position _____/_____/_____

Date of last appraisal _____/_____/_____   Scheduled appraisal date _____/_____/_____

Instructions : Carefully evaluate employee's work performance in relation to current job requirements. Check rating box to indicate the employee's performance.

RATING DEFINITIONS

O–Outstanding–Performance is exceptional in all areas and is recognizable as being far superior to others.
V–Very Good–Results clearly exceed most position requirements. Performance is of high quality and is achieved on a consistent basis.
G–Good–Competent and dependable level of performance. Meets performance standards of the job.

I–Improvement Needed–Performance is deficient in certain areas. Improvement is necessary.
U–Unsatisfactory–Results are generally unacceptable and require immediate improvement. No merit increase should be granted to individuals with this rating.
N–Not Rated–Not applicable or too soon to rate.

PERFORMANCE DIMENSIONS	RATINGS:	O	V	G	I	U	N
1. Quality–The accuracy, thoroughness, and acceptability of work performed.							
2. Productivity–The quantity and efficiency of work produced in a specified period of time.							
3. Job Knowledge–The practical/technical skills and information used on the job.							
4. Reliability–The extent to which employee can be relied upon regarding task completion and follow up.							
5. Availability–The extent to which employee is punctual, observes prescribed work break/meal periods, and the overall attendance record.							
6. Independence–The extent of work performed with little or no supervision.							

FIGURE 6.2 Graphic Rating Scale

ALTERNATION RANKING SCALE

For the Trait: _____

For the trait you are measuring, list all the employees you want to rank. Put the highest-ranking employee's name on line 1. Put the lowest-ranking employee's name on line 20. Then list the next highest ranking on line 2, the next lowest ranking on line 19, and so on. Continue until all names are on the scale.

Highest-ranking employee

1. _____   11. _____
2. _____   12. _____
3. _____   13. _____
4. _____   14. _____
5. _____   15. _____
6. _____   16. _____
7. _____   17. _____
8. _____   18. _____
9. _____   19. _____
10. _____   20. _____

Lowest-ranking employee

FIGURE 6.3 Alternation Ranking Method

Forced Distribution Method

With the **forced distribution method**, predetermined percentages of subordinates are placed in performance categories. For example, as when a professor "grades on a curve," the supervisor may decide to distribute employees as follows:

> 15% high performers
>
> 20% high-average performers
>
> 30% average performers
>
> 20% low-average performers
>
> 15% low performers

Critical Incident Method

The **critical incident method** involves keeping a record of uncommonly good or undesirable examples of an employee's work-related behavior and reviewing it with the employee at predetermined times.

The critical incident method is often used to supplement a rating or ranking

FOR THE TRAIT "QUALITY OF WORK"					
Employee Rated:					
As Compared to:	A Art	B Maria	C Chuck	D Diane	E José
A Art		+	+	−	−
B Maria	−		−	−	−
C Chuck	−	+		+	−
D Diane	+	+	−		+
E José	+	+	+	−	

Maria Ranks Highest Here

FOR THE TRAIT "CREATIVITY"					
Employee Rated:					
As Compared to:	A Art	B Maria	C Chuck	D Diane	E José
A Art		−	−	−	−
B Maria	+		−	+	+
C Chuck	+	+		−	+
D Diane	+	−	+		−
E José	+	−	−	+	

Art Ranks Highest Here

FIGURE 6.4   Paired Comparison Method

Note: + means "better than," − means "worse than." For each chart, add up the number of +'s in each column to get the highest-ranked employee.

method. It ensures that the supervisor thinks about the subordinate's appraisal all during the year because the incidents must be accumulated; therefore, the rating does not just reflect the employee's most recent performance. Keeping a running list of critical incidents should also provide concrete examples of what specifically your subordinates can do to eliminate any performance deficiencies.

Behaviorally Anchored Rating Scales

A behaviorally anchored rating scale (BARS) is an appraisal method that combines the benefits of narrative critical incidents and quantitative ratings by anchoring a quantified scale with specific narrative examples of good and poor performance.

Figure 6.5 is an example that shows the behaviorally anchored rating scale for the trait "Salesmanship skills" used for armed forces recruiters. Note how the various performance levels are anchored with specific behavioral examples such as "When a prospect states an objection to being in the Navy, the recruiter ends the conversation. . . ."

The Management by Objectives Method

The **management by objectives (MBO)** method requires the manager to set specific measurable goals with each employee and then periodically discuss his or her progress toward these goals. The term *MBO* usually refers to an organizationwide goal-setting and appraisal program that consists of six steps:

Skillfully persuading prospects to join the navy; using navy benefits and opportunities effectively to sell the navy; closing skills; adapting selling techniques appropriately to different prospects; effectively overcoming objections to joining the navy.

9 ⊤

A prospect stated he wanted the nuclear power program or he would not sign up. When he did not qualify, the recruiter did not give up; instead, he talked the young man into electronics by emphasizing the technical training he would receive.

8 —

The recruiter treats objections to joining the navy seriously; he works hard to counter the objections with relevant, positive arguments for a navy career.

7 —

When talking to a high school senior, the recruiter mentions names of other seniors from that school who have already enlisted.

6 —

When an applicant qualifies for only one program, the recruiter tries to convey to the applicant that it is a desirable program.

5 —

When a prospect is deciding on which service to enlist in, the recruiter tries to sell the navy by describing navy life at sea and adventures in port.

4 —

During an interview, the recruiter said to the applicant, "I'll try to get you the school you want, but frankly it probably won't be open for another three months, so why don't you take your second choice and leave now."

3 —

The recruiter insisted on showing more brochures and films even though the applicant told him he wanted to sign up right now.

2 —

When a prospect states an objection to being in the navy, the recruiter ends the conversation because he thinks the prospect must not be interested.

1 ⊥

FIGURE 6.5 Behaviorally Anchored Rating Scale

Source: From "Behavior Based Rating Scales" by Walter C. Borman in *Performance Assessment: Methods & Applications* edited by Ronnald A. Berk. Reprinted by permission of the publisher.

1. *Set the organization's goals.* Establish an organizationwide plan for next year and set goals.
2. *Set departmental goals.* Department heads and their superiors jointly set goals for their departments.

3. *Discuss departmental goals.* Department heads discuss the department's goals with all subordinates in the department and ask them to develop their own individual goals; in other words, how can each employee contribute to the department's attaining its goals?

4. *Define expected results (set individual goals).* Department heads and their subordinates set short-term performance targets.

5. *Conduct performance reviews and measure the results.* Department heads compare the actual performance of each employee with expected results.

6. *Provide feedback.* Department heads hold periodic performance review meetings with subordinates to discuss and evaluate the subordinates' progress in achieving expected results.

Computerized and Web-Based Performance Appraisals

Several relatively inexpensive performance appraisal software programs are on the market.[15] These generally enable managers to log notes on their subordinates during the year, and then to rate employees on a series of computerized performance traits. The programs then generate written text to support each part of the appraisal.

For example, Employee Appraiser (developed by the Austin-Hayne Corporation, San Mateo, California) presents a menu of more than a dozen evaluation dimensions, including dependability, initiative, communication, decision making, leadership, judgment, and planning and productivity. Within each dimension are various performance factors, again presented in menu form. For example, under "Communication" are separate factors for writing, verbal communication, receptivity to feedback and criticism, listening skills, ability to focus on the desired results, keeping others informed, and openness.

When the user clicks on a performance factor, he or she is presented with a relatively sophisticated version of a graphic rating scale. However, instead of numbers, Employee Appraiser uses behaviorally anchored examples. For example, for verbal communication there are six choices, ranging from "presents ideas clearly" to "lacks structure." After the manager picks the phrase that most accurately describes the worker, Employee Appraiser generates sample text.

PerformanceNow, from KnowledgePoint of Petaluma, California, lets managers evaluate employees based on their competencies, goals, and development plans. Managers can choose from standard competencies such as "communications," or create their own. Clicking on the "rate" button in the dialog boxes then brings up ratings from 1 to 5.[16]

PeformancePro.net from the Exxceed Company of Chicago, Illinois, is an Internet-based performance review system. It helps the manager and his or her subordinates develop performance objectives for the employee, and to conduct the annual review.[17]

The Web site improvenow.com lets employees fill out a 60-question assessment online with or without their supervisor's approval, and then give the supervisor the team's feedback with an overall score.[18]

Electronic Performance Monitoring

With electronic performance monitoring (EPM), computer network technology is used to provide managers with access to their employees' computer terminals and telephones, thus "allowing managers to determine at any moment throughout the day the pace at which employees are working, their degree of accuracy, log-in and log-off times, and even the amount of time spent on bathroom breaks."[19] It appears that more than 10 million workers—more than 10% of the U.S. workforce—are subject to EPM.[20]

Research studies indicate that EPM can improve productivity under certain circumstances. For example, for more routine, less complex jobs, highly skilled and monitored subjects keyed in more data entries than did highly skilled unmonitored participants.[21] However, EPM can also backfire. In this same study, low-skilled but highly monitored participants did more poorly than did low-skilled, unmonitored participants. Empirical studies also provide strong evidence linking EPM with increased stress.[22]

THE APPRAISAL FEEDBACK INTERVIEW

An appraisal usually culminates in an **appraisal interview**, in which the supervisor and subordinate review the appraisal and make plans to remedy deficiencies and reinforce strengths. Interviews like these can be uncomfortable because few people like to receive—or give—negative feedback.[23] Adequate preparation and effective implementation are therefore essential.

Preparing for the Appraisal Interview

Adequate preparation involves three steps. First, give the subordinate at least a week's notice to review his or her work, read over his or her job description, analyze problems, and compile questions and comments. Next, study his or her job description, compare the employee's performance to his or her standards, and review the files of the person's previous appraisals. Finally, choose the right place for the interview and schedule enough time for it. The interview should be done in a private area where you won't be interrupted by phone calls or visitors. Find a mutually agreeable time for the interview and leave enough time—perhaps one-half hour for lower-level personnel such as clerical workers and maintenance staff, and an hour or so for management employees.

Conducting the Interview

There are several things to keep in mind when actually conducting appraisal interviews. First, the interview's main aim is to reinforce satisfactory performance or to diagnose and improve unsatisfactory performance. One way to help accomplish this is to be direct and specific. Talk in terms of objective work data, using examples such as absences, quality records, inspection reports, and tardiness. Second, get agreement before the subordinate leaves on how things will be improved and by when. An action plan showing steps and expected results (as in Figure 6.6) can be useful. Related to this, there are times when an employee's performance is so poor that a formal written warning is required. Such warnings should identify the standards under which the employee is judged, make it clear that the employee was aware of the standard, specify any violation of the standard, and show that the employee had an opportunity to correct his or her behavior.

```
                        ACTION PLAN


                                              Date: May 18, 2001



For: John, Assistant Plant Manager
Problem: Parts inventory too high
Objective: Reduce plant parts inventory by 10% in June


Action Steps                When          Expected Results
Determine average            6/2          Established a base from which to
   monthly parts inventory                   measure progress

Review ordering quantities   6/15         Identify overstock items
   and parts usage

Ship excess parts to         6/20         Clear stock space
   regional warehouse
   and scrap obsolete parts

Set new ordering quantities  6/25         Avoid future overstocking
   for all parts

Check records to measure     7/1          See how close we are to objective
   where we are now
```

FFIGURE 6.6   An Example of an Action Plan

The aim of the appraisal is often to get the employee to improve, and to that extent you should ensure that the process is fair. Letting the employee participate in the appraisal process by at least letting his or her opinions be heard is therefore essential.[24]

Supervisors may also have to deal with defensiveness. For example, when a person is accused of poor performance, the first reaction is usually denial. By denying the fault, the employee avoids having to question his or her own competence. Such defensiveness is normal. It is prudent not to attack the person's defenses (for instance, by trying to "explain someone to themselves" by saying things like, "You know the real reason you're using that excuse is that you can't bear to be blamed for anything"). Another tactic is to postpone action—for instance, by giving the person a five-minute breather to cool down after being informed of unsatisfactory performance.

TOWARD MORE EFFECTIVE APPRAISALS

Few of the manager's jobs are fraught with more peril than appraising subordinates' performance. Employees in general tend to be overly optimistic about what their ratings are, and also know that their raises, career progress, and peace of mind may hinge on how they are rated. This alone should make it somewhat difficult to rate performance; even more problematic, however, are the numerous structural problems (discussed below) that can cast doubt on just how fair the process is.

As a result, many experts argue that traditional appraisals may not work. They say that most performance appraisal systems neither motivate employees nor guide their development.[25] Furthermore, "they cause conflict between supervisors and subordinates and lead to dysfunctional behaviors."[26] One writer argues for an appraisal system that gives the employee a voice in the process, and that substitutes "continuous feedback in a timely and nonthreatening manner" for the once a year appraisals prevalent today.[27] Another found that replacing the firm's performance appraisal system with a more acceptable one boosted the employees' trust for top management.[28] It's clear that a problematic performance appraisal process may lead to employee disappointment and eventually employee disillusionment.[29]

Dealing with Common Appraisal Problems

Several chronic problems undermine appraisals and graphic rating scales in particular. Fortunately, as explained in this section, there are also ways to avoid or solve these problems.

Unclear Standards   The unclear standards appraisal problem means that an appraisal scale is too open to interpretation. As in Figure 6.7, the rating scale may seem objective, but would probably result in unfair appraisals because the traits and degree of merit are open to interpretation. For example, different supervisors would probably define "good" performance differently. The same is true of traits such as "quality of work." The best way to rectify this problem is to develop and include descriptive phrases that define each trait and degree of merit.

Halo Effect   The **halo effect** means that the rating of a subordinate on one trait (such as "gets along with others") influences the way the person is rated on other traits (such as "quantity of work"). Thus, an unfriendly employee might be rated unsatisfactory for all traits rather than just for the trait "gets along with others." Being aware of this problem is a major step toward avoiding it.

Central Tendency   The **central tendency** problem refers to a tendency to rate all employees about average. For example, if the rating scale ranges from 1 to 7, a supervisor may tend to avoid the highs (6 and 7) and lows (1 and 2) and rate most of his or her employees between 3 and 5. Such a restriction can distort the evaluations, mak-

	Excellent	*Good*	*Fair*	*Poor*
Quality of work				
Quantity of work				
Creativity				
Integrity				

Note: For example, what exactly is meant by "good," "quantity of work," and so forth?

FIGURE 6.7   A Graphic Rating Scale with Unclear Standards

ing them less useful for promotion, salary, and counseling purposes. Ranking employees instead of using a graphic rating scale can eliminate this problem because all employees must be ranked and thus can't all be rated average.

Leniency or Strictness   Conversely, some supervisors tend to rate all their subordinates consistently high or low, a problem referred to as the strictness/leniency problem. Again, one solution is to insist on ranking subordinates, because that forces the supervisor to distinguish between high and low performers.

The appraisal you do may, in fact, be less objective than you realize. One recent study focused on how personality influenced the peer evaluations students gave their peers. Raters who scored higher on "conscientiousness" tended to give their peers lower ratings; those scoring higher on "agreeableness" gave higher ratings.[30]

Bias   Bias refers to the tendency to let individual differences like age, race, and sex affect the appraisal ratings employees receive. A recent study illustrated how bias can influence the way one person appraises another. In this study researchers sought to determine the extent to which pregnancy is a source of bias in performance appraisals.[31] The results suggest that pregnant women may face additional workplace discrimination above and beyond any gender bias that may already exist against women in general. Despite having been exposed to otherwise identical behavior by the same female "employee," the student raters of this study "with a remarkably high degree of consistency" assigned lower performance ratings to pregnant women than to nonpregnant women.[32] Furthermore, men raters seemed more susceptible to negative influence than did women. One implication is that raters must be forewarned of such problems and trained to use objectivity in rating subordinates.

Legal Issues in Performance Appraisal[33]

The performance appraisal has to be legally defensible. In fact, since passage of Title VII, courts have often found that inadequate employee appraisal systems lay at the root of illegal discriminatory action (such as the failure to promote an otherwise qualified minority candidate).[34] A negative job appraisal may also constitute an adverse employment action under Title VII of the Equal Rights Act.[35] This being the case, you'll find recommendations in the *HR in Practice* box for ensuring the legal defensibility of an employer's performance appraisal system.[36]

TQM-Based Appraisals for Managing Performance

Total quality management (TQM) programs are companywide programs that integrate all functions and processes of the business such that all aspects of the business including design, planning, production, distribution, and field service become focused on maximizing customer satisfaction through continuous improvement.[37] Ironically, TQM proponents (including the late W. Edwards Deming) generally argue for eliminating performance appraisals.[38] They argue that the organization is a system of interrelated parts and that an employee's performance is more a function of factors such as training, communication, tools, and supervision than of his or her own motivation.

In fact, traditional appraisals often are useless or counterproductive. One recent study of appraisal reviews was conducted in Korea. Researchers concluded that even

HR in Practice

Making Sure Your Appraisals Are Defensible

Steps to take to ensure your appraisals are legally defensible include:

- Develop appraisal criteria from documented job analyses. Specifically, a formal job analysis should be conducted as a prerequisite for the development of valid performance appraisal criteria.
- Communicate performance standards to employees in writing.
- Base appraisals on separate evaluations of each of the job's performance dimensions. In particular, use of a single overall rating of performance or ranking of employees on a similar global standard is not acceptable to the courts.[39] Such systems are often characterized as vague by the courts. Courts generally require that separate ratings along each performance dimension be combined through some formal weighting system to yield a summary score.
- Include an employee appeals process. Employees should have the opportunity to review and make comments, written or verbal, about their appraisals before they become final and should have a formal appeals process through which to appeal their ratings.
- One appraiser should never have absolute authority to determine a personnel action. This is one reason why multiple-raters procedures are becoming more popular.
- Document all information bearing on a personnel decision in writing. Three experts assert that "without exception, courts condemn informal performance evaluation practices that eschew documentation."[40]
- Train supervisors in the use of the appraisal instruments. If formal rater training is not possible, at least provide raters with written instruction for using the rating scale for evaluating personnel.

when employees participated in the review discussion, and goals were clearly set and career issues discussed, few of the reviews had a positive impact on the employee's subsequent job performance.[41] (See also the *Global Issues in HR* box.)

This notwithstanding, it's not practical to eliminate appraisals. Managers still need some way to review subordinates' work-related behavior. Some suggest taking a "TQM-based approach" to performance appraisal. The characteristics of such a TQM-based performance system would include:

- An appraisal scale that contains relatively few performance categories and avoids a forced distribution.[42]
- Objective ways to measure results, avoiding subjective criteria such as teamwork and integrity.[43]
- A determination about whether any performance deficiency is a result of employee motivation, inadequate training, or factors such as poor supervision that are outside the employee's control.
- 360-degree feedback from a number of different sources, not just supervisors but internal and possibly external "customers" of the employee as well.[44]

Performance Appraisal of International Managers

Several factors complicate the task of appraising an expatriate's performance.[45] First, the question of who appraises the expatriate is a crucial issue. Obviously, local management must have some input into the appraisal, but the appraisals may then be distorted by cultural differences. Thus, a U.S. expatriate manager in India may be evaluated somewhat negatively by his host-country bosses who find his use of participative decision making inappropriate in their culture. On the other hand, home office managers may be so geographically distanced from the expatriate that they can't provide valid appraisals because they're not fully aware of the situation the manager faces. This can be problematic: The expatriate may be measured by objective criteria such as profits and market share, but local events such as political instability may undermine the manager's performance while remaining invisible to home-office staff.[46]

Two experts make five suggestions for improving the expatriate appraisal process:

1. Stipulate the assignment's difficulty level. For example, being an expatriate manager in China is generally considered more difficult than working in England, and the appraisal should take into account such difficulty-level differences.

2. Weight the evaluation more toward the on-site manager's appraisal than toward the home-site manager's distant perceptions of the employee's performance.

3. If, as is usually the case, the home-site manager does the written appraisal, have him or her ask a former expatriate from the same overseas location to provide background advice during the appraisal process. This can help ensure that unique local issues are considered during the appraisal process.

4. Modify the performance criteria normally used for that particular position to fit the overseas position and characteristics of that particular locale. For example, "maintaining positive labor relations" might be more important in Chile, where labor instability is more common, than it would be in the United States.

5. Attempt to give the expatriate manager credit for relevant insights into the functioning of the operation and specifically the interdependencies of the domestic and foreign operations. In other words, don't just appraise the expatriate manager in terms of quantifiable criteria such as profits or market share. His or her recommendations regarding how home office/foreign subsidiary communications might be enhanced and other useful insights should affect the appraisal, too.

- Adequate samples of work behavior—"regular observations of their staff members' work behaviors and performance."[47]
- An atmosphere of partnership and constructive advice.[48]
- A thorough analysis of key external and internal customers' needs and expectations on which to base performance appraisal standards. (For example, if accurately completing the sales slip is important for the accounting department, then the retail sales clerk should be appraised in part on this dimension.)

REVIEW

Summary

1. *Performance appraisal* may be defined as evaluating an employee's current or past performance relative to his or her performance standards.

2. Managers appraise their subordinates' performance to obtain input on which promotion and salary raise decisions can be made, to develop plans for correcting performance deficiencies, and for career planning purposes. Supervisory ratings are still at the heart of most appraisal processes.

3. The appraisal is generally conducted using one or more popular appraisal methods or tools. These include graphic rating scales, alternation ranking, paired comparison, forced distribution, critical incidents, behaviorally anchored rating scales, MBO, computerized performance appraisals, and electronic performance monitoring.

4. An appraisal typically culminates in an appraisal interview. Adequate preparation, including giving the subordinate notice, reviewing his or her job description and past performance, and choosing the right place for the interview and leaving enough time for it are essential. In conducting the interview, the aim is to reinforce satisfactory performance or to diagnose and improve unsatisfactory performance. A concrete analysis of objective work data and development of an action plan are therefore advisable. Employee defensiveness is normal and needs to be dealt with.

5. Many experts argue that traditional appraisals may actually backfire by causing conflict between supervisors and subordinates and leading to dysfunctional behaviors. The appraisal process can be improved, first, by eliminating chronic problems that often undermine appraisals and graphic rating scales in particular. These common problems include unclear standards, halo effect, central tendency, leniency or strictness, and bias.

6. Care should also be taken to ensure that the performance appraisal is legally defensible. For example, appraisal criteria should be based on documented job analyses, employees should receive performance standards in writing, and multiple performance dimensions should be rated.

7. Finally, some experts suggest taking a TQM-based approach to the performance appraisal. For example, avoid forced distribution methods, measure results objectively, determine the cause of the performance deficiency, use 360-degree feedback, and conduct a thorough analysis of key external and internal customers' needs and expectations on which to base performance appraisal standards.

Key Terms

graphic rating scale	forced distribution	appraisal interview
alternation ranking	method	halo effect
method	critical incident method	central tendency
paired comparison	management by	
method	objectives (MBO)	

Discussion Questions and Exercises

1. Discuss the pros and cons of at least four performance appraisal tools.

2. Working individually or in groups, develop a graphic rating scale for the following jobs: secretary, engineer, and directory assistance operator.

3. Working individually or in groups, evaluate the rating scale in Figure 6.1. Discuss ways to improve it.

4. Explain how you would use the alternation ranking method, the paired comparison method, and the forced distribution method.

5. Working individually or in groups, develop, over the period of a week, a set of critical incidents covering the classroom performance of one of your instructors.

6. Explain the problems to be avoided in appraising performance.

7. Discuss the pros and cons of using different potential raters to appraise an employee's performance.

8. Explain how to conduct an appraisal interview.

APPLICATION EXERCISES

Case Incident: Back with a Vengeance

Conducting an effective appraisal is always important. However, an appraisal can have life-and-death implications when you're dealing with unstable employees, particularly those who must be dismissed. An employee of a U.S. Postal Service station was recently terminated. The employee came back and shot and killed several managers who had been instrumental in the former employee's dismissal. It turned out this person had a history as a troublemaker and that many clues regarding his unstable nature over many years had been ignored.

Questions

1. Could a company with an effective appraisal process have missed so many signals of instability over several years? Why or why not?

2. What safeguards would you build into your appraisal process to avoid missing such potentially tragic signs of instability and danger?

3. What would you do if confronted during an appraisal interview by someone who began making threats regarding his or her use of firearms?

Experiential Exercise

Purpose: The purpose of this exercise is to give you practice in developing and using a performance appraisal form.

Required Understanding: You are going to develop a performance appraisal form for an instructor and should therefore be thoroughly familiar with the discussion of performance appraisals in this chapter.

How to Set Up the Exercise/Instructions: Divide the class into groups of four or five students.

1. First, based on what you now know about performance appraisal, do you think Figure 6.1 is an effective scale for appraising instructors? Why? Why not?

2. Next, your group should develop its own tool for appraising the performance of an instructor. Decide which of the appraisal tools (graphic rating scales, alternation ranking, and so on) you are going to use and then design the instrument itself.

3. Next, have a spokesperson from each group put his or her group's appraisal tool on the board. How similar are the tools? Do they all measure about the same factors? Which fac-

tor appears most often? Which do you think is the most effective tool on the board? Can you think of any way of combining the best points of several of the tools into a new performance appraisal tool?

TAKE IT TO THE WEB

 For Internet exercises, updates to chapter material, and more, visit the Dessler Web site at

www.prenhall.com/dessler

ENDNOTES

1. Allan Locher and Kenneth Teel, "Appraisal Trends," *Personnel Journal* (September 1988): 139–45. The survey included 324 responding companies.
2. For a discussion, see Keki Bhote, "Boss Performance Appraisal. A Metric Whose Time Has Gone," *Employment Relations Today* 21, no. 1 (spring 1994): 1–9.
3. Carol Norman and Robert Zawacki, "Team Appraisals—Team Approach," *Personnel Journal* (September 1991): 101–103.
4. Vanessa Druskat and Steven Wolf, "Effects and Timing of Developmental Peer Appraisals in Self-Managing Workgroups,"*Journal of Applied Psychology* 84, no. 1 (1999): 58–74.
5. Robert Libby and Robert Blashfield, "Performance of a Composite as a Function of the Number of Judges," *Organizational Behavior and Human Performance* 21 (April 1978): 121–29; M. M. Harris and J. Schaubroeck, "A Meta-Analysis of Self-Supervisor, Self-Peer, and Peer-Supervisor Ratings," *Personnel Psychology* 41 (1988): 43–62.
6. See, for example, John Lawrie, "Your Performance: Appraise It Yourself!" *Personnel* 66, no. 1 (January 1989): 21–33.
7. Forest Jourden and Chip Heath, "The Evaluation Gap in Performance Perceptions: Illusory Perceptions of Groups and Individuals," *Journal of Applied Psychology* 81, no. 4 (August 1996): 369–79.
8. Manuel London and Arthur Wohlers, "Agreement Between Subordinate and Self-Ratings in Upward Feedback," *Personnel Psychology* 44 (1991): 375–90; Robert McGarvey and Scott Smith, "When Workers Rate the Boss," *Training Magazine* (March 1993). See also, Todd Maurer et al., "Peer and Subordinate Performance Appraisal Measurement Equivalents," *Journal of Applied Psychology* 83, no. 5 (1998): 693–702.
9. David Antonioni, "The Effects of Feedback Accountability on Upward Appraisal Ratings," *Personnel Psychology* 47 (1994): 349–55.
10. Alan Walker and James Smither, "A Five-Year Study of Upward Feedback: What Managers Do With Their Results Matters," *Personnel Psychology* 52 (1999): 393–423.
11. Kenneth Nowack, "360-Degree Feedback: The Whole Story," *Training and Development* (January 1993): p. 69; and Matthew Budman, "The Rating Game," *Across-the-Board* 31, no. 2 (February 1994): 35–38. See also "360-Degree Feedback on the Rise Survey Finds," *BNA Bulletin to Management* (January 23, 1997): 31.
12. For further discussion on this technique, see, for example, Manuel London and James Smither, "Can Multi-Source Feedback Change Perceptions of Goal Accomplishment, Self-Evaluations, and Performance-Related Outcomes? Theory Based Applications and Directions for Research," *Personnel Psychology* 48, no. 4 (winter 1995): 803–39.

13. Jim Meade, "Visual 360: A Performance Appraisal System That's 'Fun'," *HRMagazine* (July 1999): 118–19.

14. G. Douglas Huet-Cox, "Get the Most from 360-Degree Feedback: Put It on the Internet," *HRMagazine* (May 1999): 92–102. See also Keith Morical, "A Product Review: 360 Assessment," *Training & Development* (April 1999): 43–53.

15. See, for example, Edward Baig, "So You Hate Rating Your Workers?" *Business Week* (August 22, 1994): 14.

16. Jim Meade, "Automated Performance Appraisal for the LAN and the Net," *HRMagazine* (October 1998): 42–43.

17. Gary Meyer, "Performance Reviews Made Easy, Paperless," *HRMagazine* (October 2000): 181–84.

18. Ann Harrington, "Workers of the World, Rate Your Boss!," *Fortune* 16 (2000): 340–42.

19. John Aiello and Kathryn Kolb, "Electronic Performance Monitoring and Social Context: Impact on Productivity and Stress," *Journal of Applied Psychology* 80, no. 3 (1995): 339.

20. *Stories of Mistrust and Manipulation: The Electronic Monitoring of the American Workforce* (Cleveland, Ohio, 9 to 5, Working Women Education Fund: 1990).

21. Aiello and Kolb, "Electronic Performance Monitoring and Social Context," pp. 339–53.

22. See, for example, John Aiello and Y. Shao, "Computerized Performance Monitoring: Effect of Monitoring Salients and Level, Task Difficulty and Climate, Feedback and Goal Setting." Paper presented at the Seventh Conference of the Society for Industrial and Organizational Psychology, Montreal, Quebec, Canada, May 1992.

23. Donald Fedor and Charles Parsons, "What Is Effective Performance Feedback?" in Gerald Ferris and M. Ronald Buckley, *Human Resources Management*, 3rd ed. (Upper Saddle River, NJ: Prentice Hall, 1996): 265–70.

24. Brian Cawley et al., "Participation in the Performance Appraisal Process and Employee Reactions: A Meta-Analytic Review of Field Investigations," *Journal of Applied Psychology* 83, no. 4 (1998): 615–33.

25. Edward Lawler III, "Performance Management: The Next Generation," *Compensation and Benefits Review* (May/June 1994): 16. See also Chockalingam Visweswaran, Denisones and Frank Schmidt, "Comparative Analysis of the Reliability of Job Performance Ratings," *Journal of Applied Psychology* 81, no. 5 (1996): 557–74.

26. *Ibid.*, p. 16.

27. Bob Nelson, "Are Performance Appraisals Obsolete?", *Compensation and Benefits Review* (May/June 2000): 39–42.

28. Roger Mayer and James Davis, "The Effect of the Performance Appraisal System on Trust For Management: A Field Causal Experiment," *Journal of Applied Psychology* 84, no.1 (1998): 123–36.

29. Ted Turnasella, "Dagwood Bumstead, Will You Ever Get That Raise?" *Compensation and Benefits Review* (September/October 1995): 25–27. See also Andrew Solmonson and Charles Lance, "Examination of the Relationship Between True Halo and Halo Error in Performance Ratings," *Journal of Applied Psychology* 82, no. 5 (1997): 665–74.

30. H. John Bernardin et al., "Conscientiousness and Agreeableness as Predictors of Rating Leniency," *Journal of Applied Psychology* 85, no. 2 (2000): 232–34.

31. Jane Halpert, Midge Wilson, and Julia Hickman, "Pregnancy as a Source of Bias in Performance Appraisals," *Journal of Organizational Behavior* 14 (1993): 649–63. See also Michael Mount et al., "Rater-Ratee Rate Efforts in Developmental Performance Ratings of Managers," *Personnel Psychology* 50 (1997): 51–69.

32. *Ibid.*, p. 655.

33. For further discussion on this technique, see, for example, London and Smither, "Can Multi-Source Feedback Change Perceptions of Goal Accomplishment, Self-Evaluations, and Performance-Related Outcomes?" pp. 803–39.

34. See, for example, David Martin and Kathryn Bartol, "The Legal Ramifications of Performance Appraisal: An Update," *Employee Relations Law Journal* 17, no. 12 (August 1991): 257–86.

35. "Is a Negative Job Evaluation an Adverse Employment Action?", *BNA Fair Employment Practices* (September 2000): 115.

36. Based on James Austin, Peter Villanova, and Hugh Hindman, "Legal Requirements and Technical Guidelines Involved in Implementing Performance Appraisal Systems," in Ferris and Buckley, *Human Resources Management*, pp. 271–88.

37. See, for example, Joel E. Ross, *Total Quality Management: Text, Cases, and Readings* (Delray Beach, FL: Saint Lucie Press, 1993), p. 1.

38. See, for example, Greg Boudreaux, "Response: What TQM Says About Performance Appraisal," *Compensation and Benefits Review* (May/June 1994): 20–24.

39. Mushin Lee and Byoungho Son, "The Effects of Appraisal Review Content on Employees' Reactions and Performance," *International Journal of Human Resource Management* 1 (February 1998): 283.

40. *Ibid.*, pp. 208–214.

41. *Ibid.*, p. 282.

42. Lawler, "Performance Management," p. 17.

43. M. Michael Markowich, "Response: We Can Make Performance Appraisels Work," *Compensation and Benefits Review* (May/June 1995): 26.

44. David Antonioni, "Improve the Management Process Before Discontinuing Performance Appraisals," *Compensation and Benefits Review* (May/June 1994): 30.

45. Except as noted, this is based on Gary Addou and Mark Mendenhall, "Expatriate Performance Appraisal: Problems and Solutions," in Mark Mendenhall and Gary Addou, *International Human Resource Management* (Boston: PWS-Kent Publishing Co., 1991), p. 30.

46. *Ibid.*, p. 366. See also Maddy Janssens, "Evaluating International Managers' Performance: Parent Company Standards as Control Mechanisms," *International Journal of Human Resource Management* 5, no. 4 (December 1994): 30.

47. *Ibid.*, pp. 364–74.

48. *Ibid.*, p. 853–73.

Compensating Employees

When you finish studying this chapter, you should be able to:

■ *Explain* each of the five basic steps in establishing pay rates.

■ *Discuss* four basic factors determining pay rates.

■ *Compare* and *contrast* piecework and team or group incentive plans.

■ *List* and *describe* each of the basic benefits most employers might be expected to offer.

INTRODUCTION

On the verge of purchasing family-held auto parts maker Fel-Pro, Inc., Federal-Mogul Corporation chair Richard Snell faced a big problem: Employees of Fel-Pro traditionally had access to extraordinary benefits, including a company-owned summer camp for children of its employees, and $3,500 in annual scholarships for employees' children's college education.[1] The problem for Snell was that although Fel-Pro's benefits were consistent with its values and strategies, they might not be with those of his own Federal-Mogul Corporation. He wondered how to address the problem.

WHAT DETERMINES HOW MUCH YOU PAY?

In most companies, four basic factors help determine the nature of what people are paid: legal, union, policy, and equity factors. We'll look at each in turn.

Some Important Compensation Laws

First, numerous laws stipulate what employers can or must pay in terms of minimum wages, overtime rates, and benefits. Some of these laws are outlined in this section.[2]

1931 Davis-Bacon Act   The **Davis-Bacon Act** provides for the Secretary of Labor to set wage rates for laborers and mechanics employed by contractors working for the federal government.

1936 Walsh-Healey Public Contract Act   The **Walsh-Healey Public Contract Act** sets basic labor standards for employees working on any government contract that amounts to more than $10,000. The law contains minimum wage, maximum hour, and safety and health provisions.

1938 Fair Labor Standards Act   The **Fair Labor Standards Act**, originally passed in 1938 and since amended many times, contains minimum wage, maximum hours, overtime pay, equal pay, record-keeping, and child labor provisions covering the majority of U.S. workers—virtually all those engaged in the production and/or sale of goods for interstate and foreign commerce.

One important provision governs overtime pay. It states that overtime must be paid at a rate of at least one and a half times normal pay for any hours worked over 40 in a workweek.

The act also sets a minimum wage. (The minimum wage in 2001 was $5.15 for the majority of those covered by the act, although a number of states have set their own minimum hourly rates above the federally mandated minimums.[3]) The act also contains child labor provisions, which prohibit employing minors between 16 and 18 years of age in hazardous occupations such as mining and carefully restricts employment of those under 16.

Some employees are *exempt* from the act or certain provisions of the act, and particularly from the act's overtime provisions. Whether an employee is exempt or nonexempt depends on the responsibilities, duties, and salary of the job. However, bona fide executive, administrative, and professional employees (such as architects) are generally exempt from the minimum wage and overtime requirements of the act.[4]

Violating provisions of this act can be problematic. For example, several years ago a federal judge ordered the owners of a Colorado beef processing plant to pay nearly $2 million in back wages to 5,071 employees because the firm violated the Fair Labor Standards Act by not paying those employees "time-and-a-half" their regular rate of pay for hours worked in excess of 40 per week and for not keeping required records.[5] Trying to evade the letter of the law by claiming that employees who are doing, say, computer programming are not employees at all but "independent contractors" (who are more like consultants than employees) can backfire, too.[6]

1963 Equal Pay Act The **Equal Pay Act**, an amendment to the Fair Labor Standards Act, states that employees of one sex may not be paid wages at a rate lower than that paid to employees of the opposite sex for doing roughly equivalent work. Specifically, if the work requires equal skills, effort, and responsibility and is performed under similar working conditions, employees of both sexes must receive equal pay unless the differences in pay are based on a seniority system, a merit system, the quantity or quality of production, or any factor other than sex.

1964 Civil Rights Act Title VII of the **Civil Rights Act** makes it an unlawful practice for an employer to discriminate against any individual with respect to hiring, compensation, terms, conditions, or privileges of employment because of race, color, religion, sex, or national origin.

Other Discrimination Laws Various other discrimination laws have an important influence on compensation decisions. For example, the Age Discrimination in Employment Act prohibits age discrimination against employees who are 40 years of age and older in all aspects of employment, including compensation.[7] The Americans with Disabilities Act similarly prohibits discrimination against qualified persons with disabilities in all aspects of employment, including compensation. The Family and Medical Leave Act entitles eligible employees, both men and women, to take up to 12 weeks of unpaid, job-protected leave for the birth of a child or for the care of a child, spouse, or parent. Employers that are federal government contractors or subcontractors are required by various executive orders not to discriminate and to take affirmative action in various areas of employment, including compensation.

How Unions Influence Compensation Decisions

Union-related issues also influence pay plan design. The National Labor Relations Act (NLRA) of 1935 (also called the Wagner Act) granted employees the right to organize, to bargain collectively, and to engage in concerted activities for the purpose of collective bargaining or other mutual aid or protection. Historically, the wage rate has been the main issue in collective bargaining. However, other pay-related issues including time off with pay, income security (for those in industries with periodic layoffs), cost-of-living adjustment, and various benefits such as health care are also important.[8]

Compensation Policies

An employer's compensation policies or guidelines also influence the wages and benefits it pays. One consideration is whether you want to be a leader or a follower regarding pay. For example, a hospital might have a policy of starting nurses at a wage at least 20% above the prevailing market wage. Other important policies include the basis for salary increases, promotion and demotion policies, and overtime pay policy.[9] From a practical point of view, locality plays a role in compensation policies, too. For example, a job that pays $36,831 annually in New York might pay about $31,773 in California and $25,640 in Florida because of geography-based cost of living and other differentials.[10]

Equity and Its Impact on Pay Rates

Equity, specifically the need for external equity and internal equity, is a crucial factor in determining pay rates. Externally, pay must compare favorably with rates in other companies, or an employer will find it hard to attract and retain qualified employees. Pay must also be equitable internally: Each employee should view his or her pay as equitable given other employees' pay in the organization.

In practice, setting pay rates while ensuring external and internal equity usually includes five steps:

1. Conduct a salary survey of what other employers are paying for comparable jobs (to help ensure external equity).
2. Determine the worth of each job in your organization through job evaluation (to ensure internal equity).
3. Group similar jobs into pay grades.
4. Price each pay grade by using wage curves.
5. Fine-tune pay rates.

Each of these steps is explained in the following section.

HOW EMPLOYERS ESTABLISH PAY RATES

Step 1: Conduct the Salary Survey

Salary surveys, also called compensation surveys—formal or informal surveys of what other employers are paying for similar jobs—play a central role in pricing jobs. Virtually every employer therefore conducts such surveys for pricing one or more jobs.[11]

Employers use salary surveys in three ways. They are used to price benchmark jobs that are used to anchor the employer's pay scale, and around which other jobs are then slotted based on their relative worth to the firm. (*Job evaluation,* explained next, is the technique used to determine the relative worth of each job.) Second, 20% or more of an employer's positions are usually priced directly in the marketplace (rather than relative to the firm's benchmark jobs) based on a formal or informal survey of what comparable firms are paying for comparable jobs. Finally, surveys also collect data on benefits such as insurance, sick leave, and vacation time and thus provide a basis on which to make decisions regarding employee benefits.

Finding salary data and negotiating raises are not as mysterious as they used to be, thanks to the Internet. Figure 7.1 summarizes some popular salary survey Web sites. The Bureau of Labor Statistics recently organized its various pay surveys into a new National Compensation Survey, and began publishing this information on the Web. The Internet site is *http://stats.bls.gov.*

Step 2: Determine the Worth of Each Job: Job Evaluation

Purpose of Job Evaluation   **Job evaluation** is a formal and systematic comparison of jobs to determine the worth of one job relative to another. The basic job evaluation procedure is to compare the content of jobs in relation to one another, for example, in terms of their effort, responsibility, and skills. Suppose you know (based

Some pay-data Web sites:

SPONSOR	INTERNET ADDRESS	WHAT IT PROVIDES	DOWNSIDE
Salary.com	Salary.com	Salary by job and zip code, plus job and description.	Based on national averages adjusted by geographical differences.
Wageweb	www.wageweb.com	Average salaries for more than 150 clerical, professional, and managerial jobs.	Charges $100 for breakdowns by industry, geography, etc.
Exec-U-Net	www.execunet.com	Salary, bonus, and options for about 650 management posts.	Charges an initial $125 for job details.
PinPoint Salary Service	members.aol.com/payraises	Individualized pay analyses, based on title, experience, desired industry, etc.	First job analysis costs $95.
Furturestep*	www.futurestep.com	Pay analyses for people eligible for managerial posts paying $50,000 to $200,000 a year.	Participants automatically subject to queries from Korn/Ferry recruiters.

* An alliance between recruiters Korn/Ferry International and *The Wall Street Journal*.

Source: *WSJ reports*

FIGURE 7.1   Some Pay-Data Web Sites

Source: Adapted from Joann S. Lublin, "Web Transforms Art of Negotiating Raises," *Wall Street Journal* (September 22, 1998): B1.

on your salary survey and compensation policies) how to price key benchmark jobs and can use job evaluation to determine the relative worth of all the other jobs in your firm relative to these key jobs. Then you are well on your way to being able to equitably price all the jobs in your organization.

Compensable Factors   There are two basic approaches to comparing the worth of several jobs. First, you could take an intuitive approach. You might decide that one job is more important than another and not dig any deeper into why in terms of specific job-related factors.

As an alternative, you could compare the jobs based on certain basic factors they have in common. In compensation management, these basic factors are called **compensable factors**. They are the factors that determine your definition of job content, establish how the jobs compare to each other, and set the compensation paid for each job. For example, the Equal Pay Act focuses on four compensable factors: skills, effort, responsibility, and working conditions. As another example, the job evaluation method popularized by Hay Associates focuses on three compensable factors: know-how, problem solving, and accountability.

Job Evaluation Methods   The simplest job evaluation method ranks each job relative to all other jobs, usually based on some overall factor such as job difficulty. There are several steps in this job **ranking method**, as summarized in the *HR in Practice* box. *Job classification* is another simple, widely used method in which jobs are categorized into groups based on their similarity in terms of compensable factors such as skills and responsibility. The groups are called *classes* if they contain similar jobs, or *grades* if they contain jobs that are similar in difficulty but otherwise different. Thus, in the federal government's pay grade system, a press secretary and a fire chief might both be graded GS-10 (GS stands for General Schedule). On the other hand, in its job class system, the State of Florida might classify all secretary IIs in one class, all maintenance engineers in another, and so forth.

The *point method* is a more quantitative job evaluation technique. It involves identifying several compensable factors, each having several degrees, as well as the degree to which each of these factors is present in the job. Thus, assume that there are five degrees of responsibility an employer's jobs could contain. Assume that a different number of points is assigned to each degree of each factor. Then, when the evaluation committee determines the degree to which each compensable factor (such as responsibility) is present in the job, the corresponding points for each factor can be added to arrive at a total point value for the job. The result is a quantitative point rating for each job.

Step 3: Group Similar Jobs into Pay Grades

Once a job evaluation method has been used to determine the relative worth of each job, the committee can turn to the task of assigning pay rates to each job; it usually first groups jobs into pay grades. A pay grade comprises jobs of approximately equal difficulty or importance as determined by job evaluation. If the point method was used, the pay grade would consist of jobs falling within a range of points. If the ranking plan were used, the grade would consist of all jobs that fall within two or three ranks. If the classification system were used, then the jobs are already categorized into classes or grades. Ten to 16 grades per job cluster (or logical grouping such as factory jobs, clerical jobs, etc.) are common.

Step 4: Price Each Pay Grade—Wage Curves

The next step is to assign average pay rates to each of the pay grades. (Of course, if you choose not to slot jobs into pay grades, an individual pay rate has to be assigned to each individual job.) Assigning pay rates to each pay grade (or to each job) is usually accomplished with the help of a **wage curve**, which shows the average pay rates currently being paid for jobs in each pay grade, relative to the points or rankings assigned to each job or grade by the job evaluation. An example of a wage curve is presented in Figure 7.2. The purpose of the wage curve is to show the relationship between (1) the value of the job as determined by one of the job evaluation methods and (2) the current average pay rates for the grades. The wage line then becomes the target for wages or salary rates for the jobs in each pay grade.

Step 5: Develop Rate Ranges

Finally, most employers do not just pay one rate for all jobs in a particular pay grade. Instead, they develop rate ranges for each grade so that there might, for instance, be 10 levels or steps and 10 corresponding pay rates within each pay grade. They may then fine-tune pay rates to account for any unique circumstances.

Ranking Method of Job Evaluation

1. *Obtain job information.* Job analysis is the first step. Job descriptions for each job are prepared and these are usually the basis on which the rankings are made. (Sometimes job specifications also are prepared, but the job ranking method usually ranks jobs according to the whole job rather than a number of compensable factors. Therefore, job specifications—which provide an indication of the demands of the job in terms of problem solving, decision making, and skills, for instance—are not as necessary with this method as they are for other job evaluation methods.)

2. *Select raters and jobs to be rated.* It is often not practical to make a single ranking of all jobs in an organization. The more usual procedure is to rank jobs by department or in clusters (such as factory workers and clerical workers). This eliminates the need for having to compare directly, say, factory jobs and clerical jobs.

3. *Select compensable factors.* In the ranking method, it is common to use just one factor (such as job difficulty) and to rank jobs on the basis of the whole job. Regardless of the number of factors you choose, it's advisable to explain the definition of the factor(s) to the evaluators carefully so that they evaluate the jobs consistently.

4. *Rank jobs.* Next the jobs are ranked. The simplest way is to give each rater a set of index cards, each of which contains a brief description of a job. These cards are then ranked from lowest to highest. Some managers use an alternation ranking method for making the procedure more accurate; they use the cards to first choose the highest and the lowest, and then the next highest and next lowest, and so forth until all the cards have been ranked. Because it is usually easier to choose extremes, this approach facilitates the ranking procedure. A job ranking is illustrated in Table 7.1. Jobs in this small health facility are ranked from maid up to office manager. The corresponding pay scales are shown on the right.

5. *Combine ratings.* Usually several raters rank the jobs independently. Then the rating committee (or employer) can average the rankings.

TABLE 7.1   **Job Ranking by Olympia Health Care**

Ranking Order	Annual Pay Scale
1. Office manager	$28,000
2. Chief nurse	27,500
3. Bookkeeper	19,000
4. Nurse	17,500
5. Cook	16,000
6. Nurse's aide	13,500
7. Maid	10,500

After ranking, it becomes possible to slot additional jobs between those already ranked and to assign appropriate wage rate.

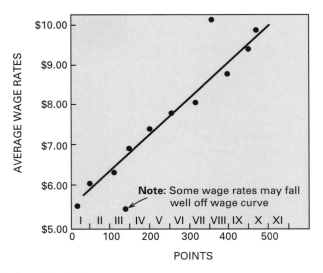

FIGURE 7.2 Plotting a Wage Curve

Note: The average pay rate for jobs in each grade (Grade I, Grade II, Grade III, etc.) are plotted, and the wage curve fitted to the resulting points.

Pricing Managerial and Professional Jobs

For managerial and professional jobs, job evaluation provides only a partial answer to the question of how to pay these employees. Managerial and professional jobs tend to emphasize nonquantifiable factors such as judgment and problem solving more than do production and clerical jobs. There is also more of a tendency to pay managers and professionals based on their performance, on what competitors are paying, or on what they can do, rather than on the basis of intrinsic job demands such as working conditions.

For a company's top executives, the compensation plan generally consists of four main components: base salary, short-term incentives, long-term incentives, and executive benefits and perks.[12] Base salary includes the obvious fixed compensation paid regularly, as well as, often, guaranteed bonuses such as "10 percent of pay at the end of the fourth fiscal quarter, regardless of whether the company makes a profit." Short-term incentives are usually paid in cash or stock for achieving short-term goals, such as year-to-year increases in sales revenue. Long-term incentives include such things as stock options: These generally give the executive the right to purchase stock at a specific price for a specific period of time, and are aimed at encouraging the executive to take actions that will drive up the price of the company's stock. Finally, special executive benefits and perks might include supplemental executive retirement plans, supplemental life insurance, and health insurance without a deductible or coinsurance.

Supplemental retirement plans head a list of executive perks, with about 60% of the companies offering them in one recent survey. Other popular executive perks include leased automobiles (57%), automobile allowance (45%), mobile phones (45%), free medical examinations (44%), financial counseling (39%), country club membership (33%), and first-class airline seating (30%).[13]

Executive compensation is obviously complicated by the variety of options and incentives it typically entails, so employers must be particularly aware of the tax and securities law implications of their executive compensation decisions.[14]

CURRENT TRENDS IN COMPENSATION

Several trends are important in determining how employees are paid. They are discussed in this section.

Competency–Skill-Based Pay

With competency- or skill-based pay, an employee is paid for the range, depth, and types of skills and knowledge he or she is capable of using rather than for the job currently held.[15] Competencies are "demonstrable characteristics of the person, including knowledge, skills, and behaviors, that enable performance."[16]

Why pay employees based on the skill levels they achieve, rather than based on the jobs they're assigned to? For example, why pay an accounting clerk II who has achieved a certain mastery of accounting techniques the same as (or more than) someone who is an accounting clerk IV? Because it fosters flexibility. With more companies organizing around teams, "jobs" themselves are becoming something of an anachronism because employees are often expected to easily rotate among jobs. And, indeed, the "jobs" themselves are becoming splintered as groups of individuals work interchangeably on projects together, as members of teams. Competency–skill-based pay can also help support an employer's new strategy; for example, consider Sony's strategic emphasis on miniaturization and precision manufacturing. It suggests that some Sony employees should be rewarded, not just based on the jobs they're assigned to, but on their level of accomplishment in these two strategically important areas.

Basing pay on skills or competencies rather than on the job can be easier said than done.[17] However, it's estimated that more than 50% of *Fortune* 1000 firms use some form of skill-based pay.[18] One major aerospace firm uses skill-based pay by having all exempt employees negotiate "learning contracts" with their supervisors. The employees then receive pay increases for meeting learning (skills-improvement) objectives.[19]

Skill-based pay programs generally contain four main components: (1) a system that defines specific skills, and a process for determining the person's pay based on his or her skill competencies; (2) a training system that lets employees seek and acquire skills; (3) a formal competency testing system; and (4) a work design that lets employees move among jobs to permit work assignment flexibility. A study of one such skill-based pay program concluded that it had resulted in 58% greater productivity, 16% lower labor cost per part, and an 82% reduction in scrap, versus a comparison facility.[20]

Broadbanding

Another trend today is for employers to collapse their salary grades and ranges from 10 or more down to 3 to 5, each of which then contains a relatively wide range of jobs and salary levels, a process called *broadbanding*. Thus, for example, instead of having 10 salary grades, each of which contains a salary range of $15,000, the firm might collapse the 10 grades into 3 broadbands, each with a set of jobs such that the difference between the lowest- and highest-paid jobs might be $40,000 or more. Companies broadband for several reasons, most often to support broader business, organizational, and strategic changes. For example, one British company cited a major delayering and downsizing as one rationale for broadbanding its pay plan.[21]

Broadbanding's greatest advantage is that it injects greater flexibility into employee compensation.[22] Broadbanding is especially sensible where firms flatten their hierarchies and organize around self-managing teams. The new, broad salary bands can encompass both supervisors and subordinates, and also facilitate moving employees slightly up or down in job level without accompanying raises or pay cuts. For example, "the employee who needs to spend time in a lower-level job to develop a certain skill set can receive higher-than-usual pay for the work, a circumstance considered impossible under traditional pay systems."[23] Yet, as a practical matter, one recent survey of 783 employers found that only about 15% were using broadbanding.[24]

The "New Pay"

Competency–skill-based pay and broadbanding are two examples of what experts today call "the new pay," an issue that is becoming increasingly important.

By *new pay compensation*, experts generally mean using a combination of traditional and nontraditional compensation elements (for instance, salary, merit increases, skill-based pay) to enable the organization to better achieve its objectives and implement its strategies.[25] For example, competency–skill-based pay can be used to focus employees' attention on raising their skill levels in the competencies that the company's strategy now emphasizes; broadbanding can help the company bring its pay plan into alignment with a reduced number of levels in the chain of command. Another new pay element is *variable pay*, in which a lump sum payment is awarded for meeting or exceeding one's goals, but does not become part of the employee's base pay. Thus, a product development team may get a one-time year-end award for accomplishing its objectives; or salespeople may receive special year-end bonuses for achieving customer satisfaction targets. One expert predicts three main compensation trends in the years ahead: more emphasis on rewarding individuals for their skills, knowledge, and competencies; more emphasis on performance-based variable pay and stock; and more emphasis on giving individuals a choice in the rewards they receive.[26] Most pay plans today—at least at larger firms—already integrate base pay, pay-for-performance, and options and benefits. Dow Chemical's total compensation package includes: *base pay* (which is based on a survey of a list of leading benchmark companies); *variable pay* (also called the Performance Award Program), an annual incentive plan based on three measures—company performance, business or functional performance, and individual team performance; *stock and long-term incentive plans*; and *benefits*.[27] (See the *Global Issues in HR* box.)

Compensating Expatriate Employees

The annual cost of sending a U.S. expatriate manager from the United States to Europe varies widely according to the host country. For example, it is estimated that the annual cost of keeping a U.S. expatriate in France might average $193,000, whereas in neighboring Germany the cost would be $246,000.[28] Such wide discrepancies raise the issue of how multinational firms should compensate overseas employees. The issue is particularly important because of the growing need to staff overseas operations and because of the frequency with which managers and professionals are moved from country to country. Two basic international compensation policies are popular: home-based and host-based policies.[29]

Under a home-based salary plan, an international transferee's base salary reflects his or her home country's salary structure. Additional allowances are then tacked on for cost-of-living differences and housing and schooling costs, for instance. This is a reasonable approach for short-term assignments and avoids the problem of having to change the employee's base salary every time he or she moves. However, it can result in some difficulty at the host office if, say, employees from several different countries assigned to the same host office are all being paid different base salaries for performing essentially the same tasks.

In the host-based plan, the base salary for the international transferee is tied to the host country's salary structure. In other words, the manager from New York who is sent to France would have his or her base salary changed to the prevailing base salary for that position in France rather than keep his or her New York base salary. Of course, cost-of-living, housing, schooling, and other allowances are tacked on here as well. This approach can keep all employees in a host country office paid similarly, but might cause some consternation to the New York manager, who might, for instance, see his or her base salary plummet with a transfer to Bangladesh.

The Issue of Comparable Worth

Should women who are performing jobs equal to men's or just comparable to men's be paid the same as men? This is the basic issue in **comparable worth**. Equal pay legislation in the United States and other industrialized countries has triggered a debate over whether *equal* or *comparable* should be the standard for comparison when comparing men's and women's jobs.[30] For years, equal was the standard in the United States, although comparable was and is used in Canada and many European countries.[31] As a result of court rulings, though, some comparable worth has become more important in the United States.[32]

Comparable worth refers to the requirement to pay equal wages for jobs of comparable (rather than strictly equal) value to the employer. In a limited sense, this may just mean jobs that are at least quite similar, such as assemblers on one line versus assemblers on a different assembly line. In its broadest sense, though, comparable worth includes comparing quite dissimilar jobs, such as nurses to fire truck mechanics to secretaries to electricians;[33] the assumption is that although the jobs are not the same, they are comparable in terms of compensable factors such as skill and responsibility.

Compensation Plans for Dot-Com Companies

Compensation practices we've discussed to this point can't all be applied across the board to dot-com companies. In traditional firms, for instance, jobs are generally slotted into grades based on market rates and internal equity. But in the dot-com world, "competitive salaries for these positions gyrate too rapidly for any corporate compensation structure to keep up with the changes . . ." For example, with the pay for Web designers and programmers jumping (often wildly) from month to month, hiring and keeping good employees is futile if the compensation plan isn't flexible. Furthermore, people aren't always hired for specific positions in fast-moving dot-com firms: "That's why the most successful dot-com companies don't hire people to fill in positions—they hire the best people possible and find jobs for them."[34]

Dot-com compensation plans therefore tend to be relatively flexible. They "link hiring pay to competitive practice for that position, based on real-time external research (not surveys that are out of date before they are published)"; they make salary adjustments based on the value created by the employee; and "they don't wait to the end of the year to adjust salaries—they reinforce value creation by giving raises when the individual has made himself or herself more valuable."[35]

On the other hand, dot-com employees want more than good pay. This is illustrated in Figure 7.3. In addition to competitive compensation and benefits, for instance, dot-com employees expect an entrepreneurial work environment and numerous skill development opportunities.[36]

INCENTIVE PLANS

Today many employees don't just earn a salary or hourly wage: They also earn some type of incentive. There are several types of **incentive plans**.[37] For example, individual incentive programs give income over and above base salary to individual employees who meet a specific individual performance standard.[38] *Variable pay* refers to group pay plans that tie payments to productivity or to some other measure of the firm's profitability; the payment in this case does not become a continuing part of the person's base salary. Several incentive plan examples follow.

Piecework Plans

Piecework is the oldest incentive plan and still the most commonly used. Earnings are tied directly to what the worker produces: The person is paid a piece rate for each unit he or she produces. Thus, if Tom Smith gets $0.40 apiece for stamping out door jambs, then he would make $40 for stamping out 100 a day and $80 for stamping out 200.

Research conducted by PricewaterhouseCoopers indicates that dot-com employees have specific expectations for their employers. These expectations fall into three categories: culture, rewards, and opportunity.

Cultural Expectations
Entrepreneurial work environment
High visibility within the organization
Respect for work–life balance

Rewards Expectations
Competitive compensation and benefits
Recognition for unique contributions
A piece of the action

Career Opportunity Expectations
Skill development opportunities
Active career mentoring
Flexibility in career pathing

FIGURE 7.3 Dot-Com Employees: What Do They Want?

Source: Paul Platten and Carl Weinberg, "Shattering the Myths About Dot.com Employee Pay," *Compensation and Benefits Review* (January/February 2000): 26.

Team or Group Incentive Plans

Sometimes, companies want to pay groups or teams (rather than individuals) on an incentive basis. There are several ways to do so.[39] One increasingly prevalent approach is to tie team performance to the company's strategic goals. One company, for instance, wanted to create a pay plan that was driven by strategy and to help do this by paying teams for results. The company set up a pool of money such that if the company reached 100 percent of its goal, the employees would share in about 5 percent of this. That 5 percent pool was then divided by the number of employees, to arrive at the value of a share. Each work team then received two goals, and if the team achieved both of its goals, each employee would earn one share (in addition to his or her base pay). Employees on teams that reached only one goal would earn one-half share. Those on teams reaching neither goal earned no shares. The results of this new plan—in terms of changing employee attitudes and focusing teams on strategic goals—was reportedly extraordinary.[40]

There are several reasons to use team or group incentive plans. Sometimes several jobs are interrelated, as they are on project teams, where one worker's performance reflects not just his or her own effort but that of co-workers as well; in this case team incentives make sense.

A group incentive plan's main disadvantage is that each worker's rewards are not based just on his or her own efforts. If the person does not see his or her effort translating directly into proportional rewards, a group plan may be less effective than an individual plan.

Incentives for Managers and Executives

Most employers give their managers incentives because of the role managers play in determining divisional and corporate profitability.[41] Surveys indicate, for instance, that over 90 percent of large companies pay managers and executives annual ("short-term") bonuses,[42] whereas about 70 percent of small firms have such plans,[43] in keeping with current trends to tie pay to stockholder value. Similarly, long-term incentive plans (such as stock options), which are intended to motivate and reward management for the corporation's long-term growth and prosperity, are used by most U.S. firms.[44] About 69% of companies in one survey had short-term incentives, although nearly a third of those said they didn't consider them effective in boosting employee performance.[45]

The size of the bonus is usually greater for top-level executives. Thus, an executive earning $250,000 in salary may be able to earn another 80 percent of his or her salary as a bonus, whereas a manager in the same firm earning $80,000 can earn only another 30 percent. Similarly, a supervisor might be able to earn up to 15 percent of his or her base salary in bonuses.

The stock option is a popular incentive. A **stock option** is the right to purchase a specific number of shares of company stock at a specific price during a period of time; the executive thus hopes to profit by exercising his or her option to buy the shares in the future but at today's price. Stock price is affected by the firm's profitability and growth, and because the executive can affect these factors, the stock option can be an incentive.

More firms today are tying top managers' incentives to *economic value*, rather than profits. For incentive purposes, economic value (as compared with traditional accounting profits) puts more emphasis on controlled factors like the net cash the company generates and on how well the firm uses its assets. This approach assumes that the managers who play a direct role in managing the firms' major business entities can have a big influence on economic value drivers like expenses, net operating capital, manufacturing cost, and inventories. It also assumes they should be rewarded based on their ability to boost the company's economic value, by managing these components.[46]

Incentives for Salespeople

Most companies pay their salespeople a combination of salary and commissions, usually with a sizable salary component. One compensation expert recently used a 70% base salary/30% incentive mix as an example that both cushioned the downside risk from the salesperson's point of view and limited the risk that the upside rewards would get out of hand from the firm's point of view.[47]

Sales quotas aren't set in stone, and setting effective quotas is an art. Questions to ask include: Are quotas communicated to the sales force within one month of the start of the period? Does the sales force know explicitly how their quotas are set? Do you combine bottom-up information (like account forecasts) with top-down requirements (like the company business plan)? Does 60 to 70% of the sale force generally hit their quota? Do high performers hit their targets consistently? Do low performers show improvement over time? Are quotas stable through the performance period? Are returns and debookings reasonably low? And, has your firm generally avoided compensation-related lawsuits?[48]

Experts have traditionally suggested "locking in" quotas and incentive plans, on the assumption that frequent changes undermine salesperson motivation and morale. But in today's fast-changing industrial scene, such inflexibility is usually not advisable. One expert says "Now that the product life cycles are often in the six-month to six-week range, the traditional approaches to most sales plans cannot accommodate the pace. . . . The sales organization and its emphasis must become more flexible than its been." The sales compensation plan and its quotas therefore tend to be reviewed more often today.[49]

Merit Pay as an Incentive

Merit pay, or a **merit raise**, is any salary increase that is awarded to an employee based on his or her individual performance. It is different from a bonus in that it becomes part of the employee's base salary, whereas a bonus is a one-time payment. Although the term *merit pay* can apply to the incentive raises given to any employees—exempt or nonexempt, office or factory, management or nonmanagement—the term is more often used with respect to white-collar employees and particularly professional, office, and clerical employees. Merit increases have been averaging about 4% recently.[50]

Merit pay has both advocates and detractors and is the subject of much debate.[51] Advocates argue that only rewards such as those that are tied directly to performance can motivate improved performance. On the other hand, merit pay detractors present good reasons why merit pay can backfire. One is that it undermines just the sort of teamwork that most companies want to cultivate today; another is that the usefulness of merit pay depends on the validity of the performance appraisal system because if the appraisals are viewed as unfair, so too will be the merit pay based on them.[52] Another problem is that almost every employee thinks he or she is an above-average performer; being paid a below-average merit increase can thus be demoralizing.[53]

Profit-Sharing Plans

In a **profit-sharing plan**, most employees receive a share of the company's annual profits. Research on the effectiveness of such plans is sketchy. In one survey, about half of the companies believed that their profit-sharing plans had been beneficial,[54] but the benefits were not necessarily just higher performance or motivation. Instead the plans may increase each worker's sense of commitment, participation, and partnership. They may thus reduce turnover and encourage employee thrift. Although there are many such plans, cash plans are the most popular; in these a percentage profits (usually 15% to 20%) is distributed as profit shares at regular intervals.

Employee Stock Ownership Plan

More and more companies are offering stock options as incentives to an everwidening circle of employees; IBM recently tripled the number of employees eligible for such options, for instance. About 35% of 400 U.S.-based companies recently surveyed provided stock options to both exempt and nonexempt employees.[55] One way to do this is through employee stock ownership plans. Under the most basic form of

employee stock ownership plan (ESOP), a corporation contributes shares of its own stock—or cash to be used to purchase such stock—to a trust established to purchase shares of the firm's stock for employees.[56] These contributions are generally made annually in proportion to total employee compensation, with a limit of 15 percent of compensation. The trust holds the stock in individual employee accounts and distributes it to employees upon retirement or other separation from service (assuming that the employee has worked long enough to earn ownership of the stock).

Employee stock ownership plans have several advantages. For example, the corporation receives a tax deduction equal to the fair market value of the shares that are transferred to the trustee. Corporations can also claim an income tax deduction for dividends paid on ESOP-owned stock.[57] Employees are not taxed until they receive a distribution from the trust, usually at retirement, when their tax rate is reduced. And the **Employee Retirement Income Security Act (ERISA)** allows a firm to borrow against employee stock held in trust and then repay the loan in pretax rather than after-tax dollars, which is another tax incentive for using such plans.[58] Research also suggests that ESOPs encourage employees to develop a sense of ownership in and commitment to the firm and are related to improved firm performance.[59]

Scanlon Plan

The **Scanlon plan** is aimed at synchronizing the company's goals with those of the employees: In other words, to ensure that by pursuing his or her own goals, the employee pursues the employer's goals as well. The Scanlon plan is an incentive plan developed in 1937 by Joseph Scanlon, a United Steel Workers Union official,[60] and is remarkably progressive considering that it was developed long ago: It is one of several gainsharing plans, the aim of which are to encourage improved employee productivity by sharing resulting financial gains with employees.

Scanlon plans today have five basic features.[61] The first is the *philosophy of cooperation* on which it is based. This philosophy assumes that managers and workers should rid themselves of the "us" and "them" attitudes that normally inhibit employees from developing a sense of ownership in the company. It substitutes instead a climate in which everyone cooperates because he or she understands that economic rewards are contingent on honest cooperation.

A second feature of a Scanlon plan is *identity,* which means that to focus employee involvement, the company's mission or purpose must be clearly articulated and employees must fundamentally understand how the business operates in terms of customers, prices, and costs, for instance. *Competence* is a third basic feature. The plan today, say three experts, "explicitly recognizes that a Scanlon plan demands a high level of competence from employees at all levels."[62]

The fourth feature is the *involvement system,*[63] which takes the form of two levels of committees—the departmental level of the executive level. Employees present productivity-improving suggestions to the appropriate departmental-level committees, which transmit the valuable ones to the executive-level committee. The latter then decides whether to implement the suggestions.

The fifth element of the plan is the *sharing of benefits formula*. Basically, the Scanlon plan assumes that employees should share directly in any extra profits resulting from their cost-cutting suggestions. For example, if a suggestion is implemented and successful, all employees might share in 75 percent of the savings.

The Scanlon plan is an early version of what today is called a **gain-sharing plan**, an incentive plan that engages all or most employees in a common effort to achieve a company's productivity objectives; any resulting incremental cost-savings gains are shared among employees and the company.[64] In addition to the Scanlon plan, other popular types of gain-sharing plans include the Rucker and Improshare plans.

At-Risk Pay Plans

The basic characteristic of an at-risk pay plan is that some portion of the employee's base salary is at risk. In the DuPont Company's plan, for instance, the employee's at-risk pay is a maximum of 6%. This means that each employee's base pay will be 94% of his or her counterpart's salary in other (non–at-risk) DuPont departments.[65] If the department achieves its goals, the employees get their full pay; if it exceeds its goals, they receive a bonus exceeding the 6%.

EMPLOYEE BENEFITS

Benefits represent an important part of just about every employee's pay; they can be defined as all the indirect financial payments an employee receives for continuing his or her employment with the company.[66] Benefits include such things as time off with pay, health and life insurance, and child care facilities.

Providing and administering benefits represents an increasingly expensive task. After almost a decade of the little or no growth, private sector employers' benefit costs jumped 3.5% recently, possibly indicating a return to the days when such costs were rising rapidly.[67] Benefits as a percentage of payroll are about 41%. That translates to around $15,000 in total annual benefits per employee, or close to $7.00 per payroll hour.

There are many benefits and various ways to classify them. In the remainder of this section we will classify benefits as pay for time not worked, insurance benefits, retirement benefits, and employee services.

Pay for Time Not Worked

Supplemental Pay Benefits   Supplemental pay benefits, or pay for time not worked, are typically one of an employer's most expensive benefits because of all the time off that employees receive. Common time-off-with-pay periods include holidays, vacations, jury duty, bereavement leave, military duty, sick leave, sabbatical leave, maternity leave, and unemployment insurance payments for laid-off or terminated employees.

Unemployment Insurance   All states have unemployment insurance or compensation acts, which provide for weekly benefits if a person is unable to work through some fault other than his or her own. The benefits derive from an unemployment tax on employers that can range from 0.1% to 5% of taxable payroll in most states. States each have their own unemployment laws, which follow federal guidelines. An organization's unemployment tax reflects its experience with personnel terminations.

Unemployment benefits are not meant for all dismissed employees, only those terminated through no fault of their own. Thus, strictly speaking, a worker fired for chronic lateness has no legitimate claim to benefits. But in practice many managers take a lackadaisical attitude toward protecting their employers against unwarranted claims. Therefore, employers spend thousands of dollars more per year on unemployment taxes than would be necessary if they protected themselves—for instance, by keeping careful records of lateness and absences, and by warning employees whose performance is inadequate.

Vacations and Holidays   The average number of annual vacation days varies around the world. For example, compared with the average 10-day U.S. vacation, vacation allowances vary from 6 days in Mexico to 10 days in Japan, 25 in Sweden, 25 in France, and 33 in Denmark. (On the other hand, Denmark, France, and several other European countries also have a six-day work week!)[68]

In the United States, the number of paid holidays similarly varies considerably from employer to employer, from a minimum of about 5 to 13 or more. The most common paid holidays include New Year's Day, Memorial Day, Independence Day, Labor Day, Thanksgiving Day, and Christmas Day. Other common holidays include Martin Luther King Jr. Day, Good Friday, President's Day, Veteran's Day, the Friday after Thanksgiving, the day before Christmas, and the day before New Year's Day.[69]

Sick Leave   Sick leave provides pay to employees when they are out of work because of illness. Most sick leave policies grant full pay for a specified number of permissible sick days, usually up to about 12 per year. The sick days are often accumulated at the rate of approximately one day per month of service.

Sick leave pay causes consternation for many employers. The problem is that although many employees use their sick days only when they are legitimately sick, others (in the eyes of some employers) take advantage of sick leave by using it as if it's extra vacation time, whether they are sick or not.

Employers have tried several tactics to eliminate or reduce this problem. Some now buy back unused sick leave at the end of the year by paying their employees a daily equivalent pay for each sick leave day not used. The drawback is that the policy can encourage legitimately sick employees to come to work despite their illness.[70] Others have experimented with holding monthly lotteries in which only employees with perfect attendance are able to participate; those who participate are eligible to win a cash prize. Still others aggressively investigate all unplanned absences, for instance, by calling the absent employees at their homes when they are taking sick days.

Sick leave policy is governed to some extent by the Family and Medical Leave Act of 1993. Among its provisions, the law stipulates that:

1. Private employers of 50 or more employees must provide eligible employees up to 12 weeks of unpaid leave for their own serious illness, the birth or adoption of a child, or the care of a seriously ill child, spouse, or parent.
2. Employers may require employees to take any unused paid sick leave or annual leave as part of the 12-week leave provided in the law.
3. Employees taking leave are entitled to receive health benefits while they are on unpaid leave under the same terms and conditions as when they were on the job.
4. Employers must guarantee employees the right to return to their previous or equivalent position with no loss of benefits at the end of the leave; however, the law provides a limited exception from this provision to certain highly paid employees.

Severance Pay   Some employers provide **severance pay**—a one-time separation payment—when terminating an employee. The payment may range from three or four days' wages to one or more years' salary. Other firms provide "bridge" severance pay by keeping employees (especially managers) on the payroll for several months, until they have found new jobs.

Such payments make sense on several grounds. It is a humanitarian gesture as well as good public relations. In addition, most managers expect employees to give them at least one or two weeks' notice if they plan to quit; it is therefore appropriate (and in some states mandatory) to provide at least one pay period's severance pay if an employee is terminated. Such payments can also be used to reduce the possibility that a terminated employee will retaliate, for instance, by suing.

Plant closings and downsizings have put thousands of employees out of work, often with little or no notice or severance pay. Many states have been attempting to fight such closings, and a Supreme Court ruling (*Fort Halifax Packing Co. v. Coyne*) paved the way for states to cushion the economic impact of such closings. The Court ruled that states may force employers to provide severance pay to workers who lose their jobs because of plant closings. The Worker Adjustment and Retraining ("plant closing") Act of 1989 requires covered employers to give employees 60 days' written notice of plant closures or mass layoffs.

Insurance Benefits

Workers' Compensation   **Workers' compensation** laws[71] are aimed at providing sure, prompt income and medical benefits to work-related accident victims or their dependents, regardless of fault.[72] Every state has its own workers' compensation law, and some states even offer their own insurance programs. However, most require employers to purchase workers' compensation insurance through private state-approved insurance companies.

Workers' compensation benefits can be either monetary or medical. In the event of a worker's death or disablement, the person or his or her beneficiary is paid a cash benefit based on prior earnings—usually one-half to two-thirds of the worker's average weekly wage, per week of employment. In most states there is a set time limit—such as 500 weeks—for which benefits can be paid. If the injury causes a specific loss (such as loss of an arm), the employee may receive additional benefits based on a statutory list of losses, even though he or she may return to work. In addition to these cash benefits, employers must furnish medical, surgical, and hospital services needed by the employee.

For an injury or illness to be covered by workers' compensation, the employee need only prove that it arose while he or she was on the job. It does not matter that the employee may have been at fault or disregarded instructions: If he or she was on the job when the injury occurred, he or she is entitled to workers' compensation.

Hospitalization, Medical, and Disability Insurance   Most employers—about 77% of medium and large firms—make available to their employees some type of hospitalization, medical, and disability insurance; along with life insurance, these benefits form the cornerstone of almost all benefit programs.[73] Many offer membership in a health maintenance organization (HMO) as a hospital/medical option. The

HMO is a medical organization consisting of numerous specialists (surgeons, psychiatrists, etc.) operating out of a community-based health care center.[74]

Preferred provider organizations (PPOs) have been defined as a cross between HMOs and the traditional physician/patient arrangement.[75] Unlike an HMO, with its relatively limited list of health care providers often concentrated in one health care center, PPOs let employees select providers (such as participating physicians) who agree to provide price discounts and submit to certain utilization controls, such as on the number of diagnostic tests that can be ordered.[76]

The Pregnancy Discrimination Act   The Pregnancy Discrimination Act (PDA) is aimed at prohibiting sex discrimination based on "pregnancy, childbirth, or related medical conditions."[77] Before enactment of this law in 1978, temporary disability benefits for pregnancies were generally paid in the form of either sick leave or disability insurance, if at all. However, although most employers provide temporary disability income to their employees for up to 26 weeks for most illnesses, those that provided benefits for pregnancy usually limited benefits to only 6 weeks for normal pregnancies. Many believed that the shorter duration of pregnancy benefits constituted discrimination based on sex.

The act requires employers to treat women affected by pregnancy, childbirth, or related medical conditions the same as any employees not able to work, with respect to all benefits, including sick leave and disability benefits, and health and medical insurance. Thus, it is illegal for most employers to discriminate against women by providing benefits of lower amount or duration for pregnancy, childbirth, or related medical conditions. For example, if an employer provides up to 26 weeks of temporary disability income to employees for all illnesses, it is also required to provide up to 26 weeks for pregnancy and childbirth.

COBRA Requirements   The ominously titled COBRA—Comprehensive Omnibus Budget Reconciliation Act—requires most private employers to make available to terminated or retired employees and their families continued health benefits for a period of time, generally 18 months. The former employee must pay for this coverage, if it is desired, as well as pay a small fee for administrative costs.

Care must be taken in administering COBRA, especially with respect to informing employees of their COBRA rights. For example, you don't want a terminated or retired employee to be injured and come back and claim she didn't know her insurance coverage could have been continued. Therefore, when a new employee first becomes eligible for your company's insurance plan, an explanation of COBRA rights should be received and acknowledged. More important, all employees separated from the company for any reason should sign a form acknowledging that they have received and understand their COBRA rights.

Long-Term Care   Today, the oldest group of baby boomers is reaching the age of 50, and as a result, long-term care insurance—care to support older persons in their old age—is reportedly "emerging as the key new employee benefit of the 90s."[78]

There are several types of long-term care for which employers can provide insurance benefits for their employees. For example, adult day care facilities offer structured programs including social and recreational activities. Assisted living facilities offer shared housing and supervision for those who cannot function independently. Custodial care is assistance given by people who have no medical skills to help individuals perform daily living activities such as bathing. Home care is care received at home from a nurse, an aide, or another specialist. Hospice care includes health care and support services for terminally ill patients. An informal care provider is a nonlicensed caregiver, such as a relative or friend, who provides care at home. Respite care is care provided by a temporary caregiver, which allows the primary caregiver (such as a son or spouse) to take some time off. Nursing homes offer all levels of care, from custodial to skilled.[79]

Retirement Benefits

Social Security   Many people assume that Social Security provides income only when they are old, but it actually provides three types of benefits. First are the familiar retirement benefits, which provide an income if the employee retires at age 62 or thereafter and is insured under the Social Security Act. Second, survivor's, or death benefits, provide monthly payments to dependents regardless of the employee's age at death, again assuming that the employee was insured under the Social Security Act. Finally, disability payments provide monthly payments to an employee and his or her dependents if the employee becomes totally disabled for work and meets certain specified work requirements.[80] The Medicare program, which provides a wide range of health services to people 65 and over, is also administered through the Social Security system.

Pension Plans[81]   Pension plans may be classified as defined benefit pension plans or as defined contribution benefit plans.[82] A **defined benefit pension plan** contains a formula for determining retirement benefits so that the actual benefits to be received are defined ahead of time. For example, the plan might include a formula that designates a dollar amount or a percentage of the last five years' annual salary as the basis for the person's eventual pension. A **defined contribution plan** specifies what contribution the employer will make to a retirement or savings fund set up for the employee. The defined contribution plan does not define the eventual benefit amount, only the periodic contribution to the plan. In a defined benefit plan, the employee knows ahead of time what his or her retirement benefits will be upon retirement. With a defined contribution plan, the employee cannot be sure of his or her retirement benefits. Those benefits depend on both the amounts contributed to the fund and the retirement fund's investment earnings. Changes in federal laws have made defined contribution plans more popular among employers.

Under the 401(k) plan, based on Section 401(k) of the Internal Revenue Code, employees can have the employer place a portion of their compensation, which would otherwise be paid in cash, into a company profit-sharing or stock bonus plan. This results in a pretax reduction in salary, so the employee isn't taxed on those set-aside dollars until after he or she retires (or removes the money from the pension fund). Some employers also match a portion of what the employee contributes to the 401(k) plan. One attraction of 401(k) is that employees may have a range of investment options for the 401(k) funds, including mutual stock funds and bond funds.

The Employee Retirement Income Security Act (ERISA) is aimed at protecting the pensions of workers and in stimulating the growth of pension plans.[83] Before enactment of ERISA, pension plans often failed to deliver expected benefits to employees. Any number of reasons, such as business failure and inadequate funding, could result in employees losing their expected pensions and facing the prospect of being unable to retire.

Under ERISA, pension rights had to be **vested**—guaranteed to the employee—under one of three formulas, such as 100% vesting after 10 years of service (often referred to as cliff vesting).[84] However, the Tax Reform Act of 1986 further tightened these vesting rules. Today, participants in a pension plan must have a nonforfeitable right to 100% of their accrued benefits after 5 years of service. As an alternative, the employer may choose to phase in vesting over a period of 3 to 7 years.

Among other things, the Pension Benefits Guarantee Corporation (PBGC) was established under ERISA to ensure that pensions meet vesting obligations; PBGC also insures pensions should a plan terminate without sufficient funds to meet its vested obligations.[85]

Employee Services Benefits

Although an employer's time off, insurance, and retirement benefits account for the main part of its benefits costs, most employees also provide a range of services, including personal services (such as legal and personal counseling), job-related services (such as subsidized child care facilities), educational subsidies, and executive perquisites (such as company cars and planes for its executives). Companies today are also offering more and more convenient workplace benefits aimed at "easing family conflicts and time pressures."[86] The staggering array of convenience benefits offered or under consideration today include flexible work hour scheduling, compressed workweek, telecommuting, sabbatical leave, on-site fitness centers, employee discounts for health centers, athletic teams, discounts for social events, wellness programs, on-site ATM or check cashing, direct paycheck deposit, cafeteria on premises, on-site gift store, on-site dry cleaning, on-site postal service, on-site medical care, time off for children's school activities, child care referral, elder care referral (for the employee's parents), paternity leaves, and coffee carts.[87]

Employee Assistance Programs (EAPs)   An EAP is a formal employer program for providing employees with counseling and/or treatment programs for problems such as alcoholism, gambling, and stress. It is estimated that 50% to 75% of employers with 3,000 or more employees offer EAPs,[88] often offered by contracting for services through large "one-stop shops."

The Cafeteria Approach

Flexible benefits plans were initially called cafeteria plans because (as in a cafeteria) employees could spend their benefits allowances on a choice of benefits options. Over the years, *flexible* has replaced *cafeteria*, although under the Internal Revenue Code regulations, the term *cafeteria* continues to be used.[89]

The idea is to allow the employee to put together his or her own benefit package, subject to two constraints. First, the employer must carefully limit total cost for each benefit package. Second, each benefit plan must include certain nonoptional items, including, for example, Social Security, workers' compensation, and unemployment insurance.

Although most employees favor flexible benefits, many don't like to spend time choosing among available options, and many choose the wrong ones. The administrative costs can be reduced somewhat with packaged flexible benefit programs such as FlexSelect, from Towers, Perrin, Forster, and Crosby of New York; it is a user-friendly interactive program for personal computers that helps employees make flexible benefits choices.[90]

Benefits and Employee Leasing

Employee leasing firms arrange to have all the employer's employees transferred to the employee leasing firm's payroll. *Employee leasing* means the employee leasing firm becomes the legal employer and handles all employee-related paperwork. This usually includes recruiting, hiring, paying tax liabilities (Social Security payments, unemployment insurance, etc.), and handling day-to-day details such as performance appraisals (with the assistance of the on-site supervisor). However, it is with respect to benefits management that employee leasing is often most advantageous.

Getting insurance is often the most serious personnel problem smaller employers face. Even group rates for life or health insurance can be high when only 20 or 30 employees are involved. This is where employee leasing comes in. Remember that the leasing firm is the legal employer of the other company's employees. Therefore, the employees are absorbed into a much larger insurable group (along with other employers' former employees). The employee leasing company can therefore often offer benefits smaller companies can't obtain at nearly such a cost. A small business may thereby be able to get insurance for its employees that it couldn't otherwise afford. In fact, there are some instances in which an employee leasing arrangement actually costs an employer virtually nothing. The leasing firm's fee may be more than outweighed by the reduced benefits cost to the employer, plus the in-house labor cost savings gained by letting the leasing company handle human resource management.[91]

Employee leasing may sound too good to be true, and it sometimes is. Many employers are understandably uncomfortable letting a third party become the legal employer of their employees (who are actually terminated by the employer and rehired by the leasing firm). Some employee leasing firms have a somewhat erratic history, and a number have gone out of business after apparently growing successfully for several years. Such a business failure means that the original employer has to hire back all its employees and find new insurance carriers to insure these "new" employees. Furthermore, Congress is continually tinkering with the tax code in such a way as to reduce the attractiveness of employee leasing's insurance benefits.

Computerizing Benefits Administration

Administering the benefit plan for even a small company with 25 to 30 employees can be a chore. For example, consider the paperwork involved when an employee says "Can I take my vacation next week?" Answering may require digging through time cards, spreadsheets, and HR folders, and then considering whether the request falls under Family and Medical Leave Act or COBRA. Even smaller firms thus often use software like HROffice, from Ascentis Software Corporation. HROffice includes over 100 built-in reports on matters ranging from attendance and benefits to performance reviews and bonuses.[92]

REVIEW

Summary

1. Establishing pay rates involves five steps: conduct salary survey, evaluate jobs, develop pay grades, use wage curves, and fine-tune pay rates.

2. Job evaluation is aimed at determining the relative worth of a job. It compares jobs to one another based on their content, which is usually defined in terms of compensable factors such as skills, effort, responsibility, and working conditions.

3. Most managers group similar jobs into wage or pay grades for pay purposes. These grades are composed of jobs of approximately equal difficulty or importance as determined by job evaluation.

4. Developing a compensation plan for executive, managerial, and professional personnel is complicated by the fact that factors such as performance and creativity must take precedence over static factors such as working conditions. Market rates, performance, and incentives and benefits thus play a much greater role than does job evaluation for these employees.

5. Broadbanding means collapsing salary grades and ranges into just a few wide levels or bands, each of which then contains a relatively wide range of jobs and salary levels.

6. Piecework is the oldest type of incentive plan; a worker is paid a piece rate for each unit he or she produces. With a straight piecework plan, workers are paid on the basis of the number of units produced. With a guaranteed piecework plan, each worker receives his or her base rate (such as the minimum wage) regardless of how many units he or she produces.

7. Profit sharing and the Scanlon plan are examples of organizationwide incentive plans. The problem with such plans is that the link between a person's efforts and rewards is sometimes unclear. On the other hand, such plans may contribute to developing a sense of commitment among employees. Gain-sharing and merit plans are two other popular plans.

8. Supplemental pay benefits provide pay for time not worked. They include unemployment insurance, vacation and holiday pay, severance pay, and supplemental unemployment benefits.

9. Insurance benefits are another type of employee benefit. Workers' compensation, for example, is aimed at ensuring prompt income and medical benefits to work accident victims or their dependents, regardless of fault. Most employers also provide group life insurance and group hospitalization, accident, and disability insurance.

10. Two types of retirement benefits are Social Security and pensions. Social Security does not just cover retirement benefits, but survivors and disability benefits as well. There are three basic types of pension plans: group, deferred profit sharing, and savings plans. One of the critical issues in pension planning is vesting the money that employer and employee have placed in the latter's pension fund, which cannot be forfeited for any reason. ERISA ensures that pension rights become vested and protected after a reasonable amount of time.

Key Terms

Davis-Bacon Act
Walsh-Healey Public
  Contract Act
Fair Labor Standards Act
Equal Pay Act
Civil Rights Act
salary survey
job evaluation
compensable factors
ranking method
wage curve
comparable worth

incentive plan
piecework
stock option
merit pay (merit raise)
profit-sharing plan
employee stock
  ownership plan
  (ESOP)
Employee Retirement
  Income Security Act
  (ERISA)
Scanlon plan

gain-sharing plan
benefits
severance pay
workers' compensation
defined benefit pension
  plan
defined contribution
  plan
vested
flexible benefits plan

Discussion Questions and Exercises

1. What is the difference between exempt and nonexempt jobs?

2. What is the relationship between compensable factors and job specifications?

3. Working individually or in groups, conduct salary surveys for the following positions: entry-level accountant and entry-level chemical engineer. What sources did you use, and what conclusions did you reach? If you were the HR manager for a local engineering firm, what would you recommend that you pay for each job?

4. Working individually or in groups, use published wage surveys to determine local area earnings for the following positions: file clerk I, accounting clerk II, and secretary V. How do the published figures compare with comparable jobs listed in your Sunday newspaper? What do you think accounts for any discrepancy?

5. Working individually or in groups, use the ranking method to evaluate the relative worth of the jobs listed in question 4. (You may use the U.S. Government's *Dictionary of Occupational Titles* as an aid.) To what extent do the local area earnings for these jobs correspond to your evaluations of the jobs?

6. Working individually or in groups, develop an incentive plan for the following positions: chemical engineer, plant manager, and used-car salesperson. What factors did you have to consider in reaching your conclusions?

7. A state university system in the Southeast recently instituted a Teacher Incentive Program (TIP) for its faculty. Faculty committees within each university's college were told to award $5,000 raises (not bonuses) to about 40% of their faculty members based on how good a job they did teaching undergraduates and how many they taught per year. What are the potential advantages and pitfalls of such an incentive program? How well do you think it was accepted by the faculty? Do you think it had the desired effect?

8. What is merit pay? Do you think it's a good idea to award employees merit raises? Why or why not?

9. Working individually or in groups, compile a list of the perks available to the following individuals: the head of your local airport, the president of your college or university, and the president of a large company in your area. Do they all have certain perks in common? What do you think accounts for any differences?

10. You are the HR consultant to a small business with about 40 employees. At the present time the business offers only five days of vacation, five paid holidays, and legally mandated benefits such as unemployment insurance payments. Develop a list of other benefits you believe the firm should offer, along with your reasons for suggesting them.

APPLICATION EXERCISES

Case Incident: Salary Inequities at Acme Manufacturing[93]

Joe Blackenship was trying to figure out what to do about a problem salary situation he had in his plant. Blackenship recently took over as president of Acme Manufacturing. The founder, Bill George, had been president for 35 years. The company was family owned and located in a small eastern Arkansas town. It had approximately 250 employees and was the largest employer in the community. Blackenship was a member of the family that owned Acme, but he had never worked for the company prior to becoming president. He had an MBA and a law degree, plus 15 years of management experience with a large manufacturing organization, where he was senior vice president for human resources when he made his move to Acme.

A short time after joining Acme, Blackenship started to notice that there was considerable inequity in the pay structure for salaried employees. A discussion with the human resources director led him to believe that salaried employees' pay was very much a matter of individual bargaining with the past president. Hourly paid factory employees were not part of the problem because they were unionized and their wages were set by collective bargaining. An examination of the salaried payroll showed that there were 25 employees, ranging in pay from that of the president to that of the receptionist. A closer examination showed that 14 of the salaried employees were female. Three of these were front-line factory supervisors and one was the personnel director. The other 10 were nonmanagement.

This examination also showed that the human resources director appeared to be underpaid, and that the three female supervisors were paid somewhat less than any of the male supervisors. However, there were no similar supervisory jobs in which there were both male and female job incumbents. When asked, the HR director said she thought the female supervisors may have been paid at a lower rate mainly because they were women, and perhaps George did not think that women needed as much money because they had working husbands. However, she added the thought that they were paid less because they supervised less skilled employees than did male supervisors. Blackenship was not sure that this was true.

The company from which Blackenship had moved had a good job evaluation system. Although he was thoroughly familiar and capable with this compensation tool, Blackenship did not have time to make a job evaluation study at Acme. Therefore, he decided to hire a compensation consultant from a nearby university to help him. Together they decided that all 25 salaried jobs should be in the job evaluation cluster, that a modified ranking method of job evaluation should be used, and that the job descriptions recently completed by the personnel director were current, accurate, and usable in the study.

The job evaluation showed that there was no evidence of serious inequities or discrimination in the nonmanagement jobs, but that the HR director and the three female supervisors were being underpaid relative to comparable male salaried employees.

Blackenship was not sure what to do. He knew that if the underpaid female supervisors took the case to the local EEOC office, the company could be found guilty of sex discrimination and then have to pay considerable back wages. He was afraid that if he gave these women an immediate salary increase large enough to bring them up to where they should be, the male supervisors would be upset and the female supervisors might comprehend the total situation and want back pay. The HR director told Blackenship that the female supervisors had never complained about pay differences, and they probably did not know the law to any extent.

The HR director agreed to take a sizable salary increase with no back pay, so this part of the problem was solved. Blackenship believed he had four choices relative to the female supervisors:

1. To do nothing
2. To gradually increase the female supervisors' salaries

3. To increase their salaries immediately

4. To call the three supervisors into his office, discuss the situation with them, and jointly decide what to do

Questions

1. What would you do if you were Blackenship?

2. How do you think the company got into a situation like this in the first place?

3. Why would you suggest Blackenship pursue the alternative you suggested?

Source: This case was prepared by Professor James C. Hodgetts of the Fogelman College of Business and Economics of the University of Memphis. All names are disguised. Used by permission.

Experiential Exercise

Purpose: The purpose of this exercise is to give you experience in performing a job evaluation using the ranking method.

Required Understanding: You should be thoroughly familiar with the ranking method of job evaluation and try to obtain job descriptions for your college's dean, department chairperson, and your professor.

How to Set Up the Exercise/Instructions: Divide the class into groups of four or five students. The groups will perform a job evaluation of the positions of dean, department chairperson, and professor using the ranking method.

1. Perform a job evaluation by ranking the jobs. You may use one or more compensable factors.

2. If time permits, a spokesperson from each group can put his or her group's ratings on the board. Did the groups end up with about the same results? How did they differ? Why do you think they differed?

TAKE IT TO THE WEB

For Internet exercises, updates to chapter material, and more, visit the Dessler Web site at

www.prenhall.com/dessler

ENDNOTES

1. Richard Melcher, "Warm and Fuzzy, Meet Rough and Tumble," *Business Week* (January 26, 1998): 38.

2. Based on Richard Henderson, *Compensation Management* (Reston, VA: Reston, 1980); and Kenneth Sovereign, *Personnel Law* (Englewood Cliffs, NJ: Prentice Hall, 1994): 130–36, 202–29.

3. "State Minimum Wage Rates," *BNA Bulletin to Management* (September 26, 1996): 308–309.

4. A complete description of exemption requirements as found in U.S. Department of Labor, *Executive, Administrative, Professional and Outside Salesmen Exempted from the Fair Labor Standards Act* (Washington, DC: U.S. Government Printing Office, 1973).

5. "Employer Ordered to Pay $2 Million in Overtime," *BNA Bulletin to Management* (December 5, 1996): 391.

6. *HR in Practice* feature from Michael Wolfe, "That's Not an Employee, That's an Independent Contractor," *Compensation and Benefits Review* (July/August 1996): 61.

7. Robert Nobile, "How Discrimination Laws Affect Compensation," *Compensation and Benefits Review* (July/August 1996): 38–42.

8. Henderson, *Compensation Management*, pp. 101–27.

9. Joseph Famularo, *Handbook of Modern Personnel Administration* (New York: McGraw-Hill, 1972), pp. 27–29. See also Bruce Ellig, "Strategic Pay Planning," *Compensation and Benefits Review* 19, no. 9 (July/August 1987): 28–43; and Thomas Robertson, "Fundamental Strategies for Wage and Salary Administration," *Personnel Journal* 65, no. 11 (November 1986): 120–32. One expert cautions against conducting salary surveys based on job title alone. He recommends job-content salary surveys that examine the content of jobs according to the size of each job so that, for instance, the work of the president of IBM and that of a small clone manufacturer would not be inadvertently compared. See Robert Sahl, "Job Content Salary Surveys: Survey Design and Selection Features," *Compensation and Benefits Review* (May/June 1991): 14–21.

10. "Annual Pay Levels and Growth in Pay by State," *BNA Bulletin to Management* (October 30, 1997): 350.

11. "Use of Wage Surveys," *BNA Policy and Practice Services* (Washington, DC: Bureau of National Affairs, 1976), pp. 313–14. A survey of compensation professionals reported use of salary survey data. The surveys were used most often to adjust the salary structure and ranges. Other uses included determining the merit budget, adjusting individual job rates, and maintaining pay leadership. D. W. Belcher, N. Bruce Ferris, and John O'Neill, "How Wage Surveys Are Being Used," *Compensation and Benefits Review* (September/October 1985): 34–51. For further discussion, see, for example, John Yurkutat, "Is 'The End of Jobs' the End of Surveys Too?" *Compensation and Benefits Review* (July/August 1997): 24–29.

12. Mark Meltzer and Howard Goldsmith, "Executive Compensation for Growth Companies, *Compensation and Benefits Review* (November/December 1997): 41–50.

13. "Supplemental Executive Retirement Plans Lead of Top Executive Perks," *Compensation and Benefits Review* (September/October 1998): 13.

14. Douglas Tormey, "Executive Compensation: Creating a 'Legal' Checklist," *Compensation and Benefits Review* (July/August 1996): 21–30.

15. Gerald Ledford Jr., "Three Case Studies on Skill-Based Pay: An Overview," *Compensation and Benefits Review* (March/April 1991): 11–23.

16. Gerald Ledford Jr., "Paying for the Skills, Knowledge, and Competencies of Knowledge Workers," *Compensation and Benefits Review* (July/August 1995): 56.

17. Edward Lawler III, "Competencies: A Poor Foundation for the New Pay," *Compensation and Benefits Review* (November/December 1996): 20–22.

18. Ledford, "Paying for the Skills, Knowledge, and Competencies of Knowledge Workers," p. 55.

19. *Ibid.*, p. 58. See also Melvyn Stark, Warren Luther, and Steve Valvano, "Jaguar Cars Drives Toward Competency-Based Pay," *Compenation and Benefits Review* (November/December 1996): 34–40.

20. Brian Murray and Barry Gerhard, "An Empirical Analysis of a Skill-Based Pay Program and Plant Performance and Outcomes," *Academy of Management Journal* 41, no. 1 (1998): 68–78.

21. Duncan Brown, "Broadbanding: A Study of Company Practices in the United Kingdom," *Compenation and Benefits Review* (November/December 1996): 43.

22. David Hofrichter, "Broadbanding: A 'Second Generation' Approach," *Compenation and Benefits Review* (September/October 1993): 53–58. See also Gary Bergel, "Choosing the Right Pay Delivery System to Fit Banding," *Compensation and Benefits Review* 25, no. 4 (July/August 1994): 34–38.

23. *Ibid.*, p. 55.

24. "Broadbanding Pay Structures Do Not Receive Flat-Out Support from Employers, Survey Finds," *BNA Bulletin to Management* (January 13, 2000): 11.

25. Patricia Zingheim and Jay Schuster, "Introduction: How Are the New Pay Tools Being Deployed?" *Compenation and Benefits Review* (July/August 1995): 10–14.

26. Edward Lawler III, "Pay Strategy: New Thinking for the New Millennium," *Compensation and Benefits Review* (January/February 2000): 7–12.

27. Howard Risher, "Dow Chemical's Salary Program: A Model for the Future," *Compensation and Benefits Review* (May/June 2000): 26–34.

28. Jack Anderson, "Compensating Your Overseas Executives, Part II: Europe in 1992," *Compenation and Benefits Review* (July/August 1990): 28. See also Marc Baranski, "Think Globally, Pay Locally: Finding the Right Mix," *Compensation and Benefits Review* (July/August 1999): 15–24.

29. Based on Anderson, *op. cit.*, pp. 29–31.

30. Helen Remick, "The Comparable Worth Controversy," *Public Personnel Management Journal* (winter 1981): 371–83.

31. *Ibid.*, p. 377.

32. *Ibid.*, p. 380.

33. *Ibid.*, p. 38; U.S. Department of Labor, *Perspectives on Working Women: A Data Book* (October 1980).

34. Paul Platten and Carl Weinberg, "Shattering the Myths About Dot.Com Employee Pay," *Compensation and Benefits Review* (January/February 2000): 21–27.

35. *Ibid.*

36. *Ibid.*

37. Except as noted, this section is based on Bureau of National Affairs, "Non-Traditional Incentive Pay Programs," *Personnel Policies Forum Survey*, no. 148 (May 1991).

38. *Ibid.*, p. 3.

39. Henderson, *Compensation Management*, p. 363. For a discussion of the increasing use of incentives for blue-collar employees, see, for example, Richard Henderson, "Contract Concessions: Is the Past Prologue?" *Compensation and Benefits Review* 18, no. 5 (September/October 1986): 17–30. See also A. J. Vogl, "Carrots, Sticks and Self-Deception," *Across-the-Board*, no. 1 (January 1994): 39–44.

40. Richard Seaman, "Rejuvenating and Organization with Team Pay," *Compensation and Benefits Review* (September/October 1997): 25–30.

41. James Thompson, L. Murphy Smith, and Alicia Murray, "Management Performance Incentives: Three Critical Issues," *Compensation and Benefits Review* 18, no. 5 (September/October 1986): 41–47; Baron Gerhart and Charlie Trevour, "Employment Variability Under Different Managerial Compensation Systems," *Academy of Management Journal* 39, no. 6 (1996): 1692–712; and Ira Sager, "Stock Options: Lou Takes a Cue from Silicon Valley," *Business Week* (March 30, 1998): 34.

42. Bureau of National Affairs, *Bulletin to Management* (January 6, 1983): 1; and Christopher Young, "Trends in Executive Compensation," *Journal of Business Strategy* 19, no. 2 (March/April, 1998): 21–25.

43. James Brinks, "Executive Compensation: Crossroads of the 80s," *Personnel Administrator* 26 (December 1981): 24.

44. "Long-Term Incentives: Trends and Approaches," *Personnel* 57 (July/August 1982): 60–61; and Pearl Meyer, "Stock is No Longer Optional," *Journal of Business Strategy* 19, no. 2 (March/April, 1998): 28–31.

45. "Short-Term Incentives Considered Ineffective, Survey Reveals," *Society for Human Resource Management* (January 2000): 5.

46. Don Delves, "Practical Lessons for Designing an Economic Value Incentive Plan," *Compensation and Benefits Review* (March/April 1999): 61–70.

47. Bill O'Connell, "Dead Solid Perfect: Achieving Sales Compensation Alignment," *Compenation and Benefits Review* (March/April 1996): 46–47.

48. S. Scott Sands, "Ineffective Quotas: The Hidden Threat to Sales Compensation Plans," *Compensation and Benefits Review* (March/April 2000): 35–42.

49. Bill Weeks, "Setting Sells Force Compensation in the Internet Age," *Compensation and Benefits Review* (March/April 2000): 25–34.

50. Fay Hanson, "Currents in Compensation and Benefits," *Compensation and Benefits Review* (November/December 1998): 6.

51. See, for example, Herbert Meyer, "The Pay for Performance Dilemma," *Organizational Dynamics* (winter 1975): 39–50; Thomas Patten Jr., "Pay for Performance or Placation?" *Personnel Administrator* 24 (September 1977): 26–29; and William Kearney, "Pay for Performance? Not Always," *MSU Business Topics* (spring 1979): 5–16. See also Hoyt Doyel and Janet Johnson, "Pay Increase Guidelines with Merit," *Personnel Journal* 64 (June 1985): 46–50; and Jeffrey Pfeffer, "Six Dangerous Myths About Pay," *Harvard Business Review* (May/June, 1998): 109–19.

52. Alfie Kohn, "Challenging Behaviorist Dogma: Myths About Money and Motivation," *Compensation and Benefits Review* (March/April 1998): 27–32.

53. James Brinks, "Is There Merit in Merit Increases?" *Personnel Administrator* 25 (May 1980): 60. See also Dan Gilbert and Glenn Bassett, "Merit Pay Increases Are a Mistake," *Compensation and Benefits Review* 26, no. 2 (March/April 1994): 20–25.

54. Bert Metzger and Jerome Colletti, "Does Profit Sharing Pay?" (Evanston, IL: Profit Sharing Research Foundation, 1971), quoted in David Belcher, *Compensation Administration* (Englewood Cliffs, NJ: Prentice Hall, 1973): 353. See also D. Keith Denton, "An Employee Ownership Program That Rebuilt Success," *Personnel Journal* 66, no. 3 (March 1987): 114–18; and Edward Shepard, "Profit Sharing and Productivity: Further Evidence from the Chemicals Industry," *Industrial Relations* 33, no. 4 (October 1994): 452–66.

55. "Employers Expanding Stock Options to All," *HRMagazine* (October 1999): 30.

56. Based on Randy Swad, "Stock Ownership Plans: A New Employee Benefit," *Personnel Journal* 60 (June 1981): 453–55; and Sager, "Stock Options: Lou Takes a Cue from Silicon Value," p. 34.

57. See James Brockardt and Robert Reilly, "Employee Stock Ownership Plans After the 1989 Tax Law: Valuation Issues," *Compenation and Benefits Review* (September/October 1990): 29–36.

58. Donald Sullivan, "ESOPs," *California Management Review* 20, no. 1 (fall 1979): 55–56. For a discussion of the effects of employee stock ownership on employee attitudes, see

Katherine Klein, "Employee-Stock Ownership and Employee Attitudes: A Test of Three Models," *Journal of Applied Psychology* 72, no. 2 (May 1987): 319–31.

59. Everett Allen, Jr., Joseph Melone, and Jerry Rosenbloom, *Pension Planning* (Homewood, IL: Irwin, 1981), p. 316; and John Gamble, "ESOPs: Financial Performance and Federal Tax Incentives," *Journal of Labor Research* 9, no. 3 (summer 1998): 529–42.

60. Brian Moore and Timothy Ross, *The Scanlon Way to Improved Productivity: A Practical Guide* (New York: Wiley, 1978), p. 2. See also Woodruff Imberman, "Is Gainsharing the Wave of the Future?" *Management Accounting* (November 1995): 35–38.

61. Based in part on Steven Markham, K. Dow Scott, and Walter Cox, Jr., "The Evolutionary Development of a Scanlon Plan," *Compensation and Benefits Review* (March/April 1992): 50–56.

62. *Ibid.*, p. 51.

63. Moore and Ross, *The Scanlon Way to Improved Productivity*, pp. 1–2.

64. Barry W. Thomas and Madeline Hess Olson, "Gainsharing: The Design Guarantees Success," *Personnel Journal* (May 1988): 73–79. See also "Aligning Compensation with Quality," *BNA Bulletin to Management* (April 1, 1993): 97.

65. Robert McNutt, "Sharing Across the Board: DuPont's Achievement Sharing Program," *Compensation and Benefits Review* (July/August 1990): 17–24.

66. Based on Frederick Hills, Thomas Bergmann, and Vida Scarpello, *Compensation Decision Making* (Fort Worth, TX: Dryden Press, 1994), p. 424. See also L. Kate Beatty, "Pay and Benefits Break Away from Tradition," *HRMagazine* 39, no. 11 (November 1994): 63–68.

67. "Benefit Costs Posted Biggest Jump Since 1992, B.L.S. says," *BNA Bulletin to Management* (February 10, 2000): 45.

68. "Vacation Allowances are Far More General Abroad," *Compensation and Benefits Review* (September/October 1998): 15.

69. Henderson, *Compensation Management*, p. 555.

70. Miriam Rothman, "Can Alternatives to Sick Pay Plans Reduce Absenteeism?" *Personnel Journal* 60 (October 1981): 788–91; Richard Bunning, "A Prescription for Sick Leave," *Personnel Journal* 67, no. 8 (August 1988): 44–49; and Carl Quintanilla, "A Sick Leave Policy Backfires at Cincinnati's Public Schools," *Wall Street Journal* (July 14, 1998): A1.

71. Famularo, *Handbook of Modern Personnel Administration*, pp. 51–62; and Sovereign, *Personnel Law*, pp. 231–47.

72. Henderson, *Compensation Management*, p. 250. For an explanation of how to reduce workers' compensation costs, see Betty Strigel Bialk, "Cutting Workers' Compensation Costs," *Personnel Journal* 66, no. 7 (July 1987): 95–97; and "Workers' Compensation Outlook: Cost Control Persists," *BNA Bulletin to Management* (January 30, 1997): 33.

73. "Employee Benefits in Medium and Large Firms," *BNA Bulletin to Management* (September 4, 1997): 284–85.

74. *Ibid.*, pp. 284–85.

75. Hills, Bergmann, and Scarpello, *Compensation Decision Making*, p. 137.

76. George Milkovich and Jerry Newman, *Compensation* (Burr Ridge, IL: Irwin, 1993), p. 445.

77. Based on Paul Greenlaw and Diana Foderaro, "Some Practical Implications of the Pregnancy Discrimination Act," *Personnel Journal* 58 (October 1979): 677–81. See also Commerce Clearing House, "Supreme Court Says Giving Women Pregnancy Leave Is Lawful Even in the Case Where Men Receive No Disability Leave Whatsoever," *Ideas and Trends in Personnel* (January 23, 1987): 9–10.

78. James Weil, "Baby Boomer Needs Will Spur Growth of Long-Term Care Plans," *Compensation and Benefits Review* (March/April 1996): 49.

79. *Ibid.*, p. 51.

80. Jerome B. Cohen and Arthur Hanson, *Personal Finance* (Homewood, IL: Irwin, 1964), pp. 312–20. See also *BNA Bulletin to Management* (January 14, 1988): 12–13. This article explains changes in the Social Security law and presents an exhibit showing how to estimate Social Security benefits.

81. See, for example, Henderson, *Compensation Management*, pp. 289–90; and Famularo, *Handbook of Modern Personnel Administration*, pp. 37.1–37.9.

82. Avy Graham, "How Has Vesting Changed Since Passage of Employee Retirement Income Security Act?" *Monthly Labor Review* (August 1988): 20–25.

83. Robert Paul, "The Impact of Pension Reform on American Business," *Sloan Management Review* 18 (Fall 1976): 59–71. See also John M. Walbridge, Jr., "The Next Hurdle for Benefits Manager: Section 89," *Compensation and Benefits Review* 20, no. 6 (November/December 1988): 22–35.

84. Henderson, *Compensation Management*, p. 292. ERISA applies not just to pensions but to various other benefits including retiree medical benefits as well. For a discussion, see Michael Langan, "ERISA After Twenty Years: Past, Present, and Future," *Benefits Law Journal* 7, no. 3 (Autumn 1994): 225–70.

85. James Benson and Barbara Suzaki, "After Tax Reform, Part III: Planning Executive Benefits," *Compensation and Benefits Review* 20, no. 2 (March/April 1988): 45–57; and "Post-Retirement Benefits Impact of FASB New Accounting Rule" (February 23, 1989): 57.

86. Don Bohl, "Mini Survey: Companies That Tend to Create the 'Convenient Work Place,' " *Compenation and Benefits Review* (May/June 1996): 23–26.

87. *Ibid.*, pp. 24–25.

88. Richard T. Hellan, "Employee Assistance: An EAP Update: A Perspective for the '80s," *Personnel Journal* 65, no. 6 (1986): 51; and Michael Prince, "EAPs Becoming Part of Larger Programs," *Business Insurance* 32, no. 24 (June 15, 1998): 14–16.

89. Henderson, *Compensation Management*, p. 568. See also "Couples Want Flexible Leave, Benefits," *BNA Bulletin to Management* (February 19, 1998): 53.

90. For information about this program, contact Towers, Perrin, Forster, and Crosby, 245 Park Avenue, New York, NY 10167. Hewitt Associates similarly has a program called FlexSystem (New York: Hewitt Associates). See also Michael Sturman, John Hannon, and George Milkovich, "Computerized Decision Aids for Flexible Benefits Decisions: The Effects of an Expert System and Decision Support System on Employee Intentions and Satisfaction with Benefits," *Personnel Psychology* 49 (1996): 883–908.

91. For a discussion see, for example, Marvin Selter, "On the Plus Side of Employee Leasing," *Personnel Journal* (April 1986): 87–91; and "Employee Leasing Raises Questions," *BNA Bulletin to Management* (August 22, 1996): 272.

92. Jim Meade, "Affordable HRIS Strong on Benefits," *HRMagazine* (April 2000): 132–35.

93. Raymond L. Hilgert and Cyril C. Ling, *Cases and Experiential Exercises in Human Resource Management*, 2nd ed. (Upper Saddle River, NJ: Prentice Hall, 1996), pp. 214–15. Case prepared by Professor James C. Hodgetts, Fogelman College of Business and Economics, University of Memphis. Used by permission.

Managing Labor Relations and Collective Bargaining

➤ The Labor Movement
➤ Unions and the Law
➤ The Union Drive and Election
➤ The Collective Bargaining Process
➤ What's Next for Unions?

When you finish studying this chapter, you should be able to:

■ *Discuss* the nature of the major federal labor relations laws.

■ *Describe* the process of a union drive and election.

■ *Discuss* the main steps in the collective bargaining process.

INTRODUCTION

FedEx had long been known for excellent labor relations, so the concerns expressed by its pilots had many people wondering if more of FedEx's pilots would join the Pilots Union. Its pilots—concerned about relatively high pay hikes won by their counterparts at UPS, and by less flexible work schedules at their own firm—had rejected a proposed contract backed by their own union leaders.[1] What's worse, the dissatisfaction may spread to the company's ground workers, allowing the Teamsters to improve their bid to unionize FedEx's 100,000 ground workers. At FedEx, said one pilot, "There was a trust relationship that has deteriorated."[2]

THE LABOR MOVEMENT

Today, more than 16 million U.S. workers—around 14% of the total number of men and women working in the United States—belong to unions.[3] Many are still traditionally blue-collar workers, but unions increasingly appeal to white-collar workers, too. For instance, federal, state, and local governments employ almost 7 million union members, or about 37% of total government employees.

Yet such figures mask the fact that dramatic changes are taking place in unions today: U.S. union membership peaked at about 34% in 1955. It has consistently fallen since then due to factors such as the shift from manufacturing to service jobs, and new legislation (such as occupational safety laws) that provide the sorts of protections that workers could once only obtain from their unions.

Even with such declines, however, it would be a mistake to write off unions.[4] In the United States, for instance, a growing and very significant number of government and white-collar employees are turning to unions. In some industries—including transportation and public utilities, where more than 26% of employees are union members—it's still relatively difficult to get a job without joining a union.[5] Union membership also varies widely by state, from a high of 26.8% in New York to a low of 3.7% in South Carolina, for instance.[6] Furthermore, although union membership around the world is also declining, union membership as a percentage of employment is still very high in most countries of the world: 37% in Canada, 43% in Mexico, 44% in Brazil, 29% in Germany, 33% in the United Kingdom, 44% in Italy, and 24% in Japan.[7]

Even in the United States, membership may be stabilizing, with a wide range of workers including doctors, psychologists, graduate teaching assistants, and even fashion models forming or joining unions.[8]

Why Do Workers Organize?

Much time has been spent trying to discover why workers unionize, and many theories have been proposed. There is no simple answer, partly because each worker probably joins for his or her own reasons.

It seems clear that workers do not unionize just to get more pay or better working conditions. These are important factors, and, in fact (for whatever reason), the weekly earnings of union members are much higher than those of nonunion workers: about $50 per week more in service jobs, $60 in manufacturing, $130 in government, and as much as $300 per week more in construction jobs, for instance.[9]

Yet the urge to unionize more often seems to boil down to the workers' belief that it is only through unity that they can get their fair share of the pie and also protect themselves from the arbitrary whims of management.[10] In practice, this often means that low morale, fear of job loss, and poor communication foster unionization.

In one case, for example, a butcher was hired by Wal-Mart, and says he was told he would be able to start management training and possibly move up to supervisor. He started work and bought a new car for the commute. However, he says his supervisor never mentioned the promotion again after the employee hurt his back at work and was out for five weeks. Faced with high car payments and feeling cheated, the butcher went to the Grocery Workers Union, which quickly sent an organizer to speak with the employee near the Wal-Mart store. The store's meat cutters eventually voted to unionize, but didn't celebrate for long. A week later Wal-Mart announced it would switch to completely prepackaged meat. Henceforth, the meat suppliers would do all the cutting at their factories, and the stores' meat cutters would no longer be required.[11]

What Do Unions Want? What Are Their Aims?

We can generalize by saying that unions have two sets of aims, one for union security and one for improved wages, hours, working conditions, and benefits for their members.

Union Security   First and probably foremost, unions seek to establish security for themselves. They fight hard for the right to represent a firm's workers and to be the *exclusive* bargaining agent for all employees in the unit. (As such, they negotiate contracts for all employees, including those who are not members of the union.) Five types of union security are possible:

1. *Closed shop.*[12] The company can hire only union members. This was outlawed in 1947 but still exists in some industries (such as printing).
2. *Union shop.* The company can hire nonunion people but they must join the union after a prescribed period of time and pay dues. (If not, they can be fired.)
3. *Agency shop.* Employees who do not belong to the union still must pay union dues on the assumption that the union's efforts benefit *all* the workers.
4. *Open shop.* It is up to the workers whether they join the union—those who do not do not pay dues.
5. *Maintenance of membership arrangement.* Employees do not have to belong to the union. However, union members employed by the firm must maintain membership in the union for the contract period.

Improved Wages, Hours, Working Conditions, and Benefits for Members
Once their security is assured, unions fight to better the lot of other members—to improve their wages, hours, and working conditions, for example. The typical labor agreement also gives the union a role in other HR activities, including recruiting, selecting, compensating, promoting, training, and discharging employees.

The AFL-CIO

The American Federation of Labor and Congress of Industrial Organizations **(AFL-CIO)** is a voluntary federation of about 100 national and international labor unions in the United States. It was formed by the merger of the AFL and CIO in 1955, with the AFL's George Meany as its first president. For many people, it has become synonymous with the word *union* in the United States.

Approximately 2.5 million workers belong to unions that are not affiliated with the AFL-CIO. Of these workers, about one-half belong to the largest independent union, the United Auto Workers (about 1 million members).[13]

UNIONS AND THE LAW

Until about 1930, there were no special labor laws. Employers didn't have to engage in collective bargaining with employees and were virtually unrestrained in their behavior toward unions: The use of spies, blacklists, and the firing of agitators was widespread. "Yellow dog" contracts, whereby management could require nonunion membership as a condition for employment, were widely enforced. Most union weapons—even strikes—were illegal.

This one-sided situation lasted in the United States from the Revolution to the Great Depression (around 1930). Since then, in response to changing public attitudes, values, and economic conditions, labor law has gone through three clear changes: from "strong encouragement" of unions, to "modified encouragement coupled with regulation," to "detailed regulation of internal union affairs."[14]

Period of Strong Encouragement: The Norris-LaGuardia Act (1932) and the National Labor Relations Act (1935)

The **Norris-LaGuardia Act** set the stage for an era in which union activity was encouraged. It guaranteed to each employee the right to bargain collectively "free from interference, restraint, or coercion." It declared yellow dog contracts unenforceable. It limited the courts' abilities to issue injunctions for activities such as peaceful picketing and payment of strike benefits.[15]

Yet this act did little to restrain employers from fighting labor organizations by whatever means they could muster. Therefore, the National Labor Relations Act (or **Wagner Act**) was passed in 1935 to add teeth to the Norris-LaGuardia Act. It did this by banning certain unfair labor practices, providing for secret-ballot elections and majority rule for determining whether a firm's employees were to unionize, and creating the **National Labor Relations Board (NLRB)** for enforcing these two provisions.

In addition to activities like overseeing union elections, the NLRB periodically issues interpretive rulings. For example, about 6 million employees fall under the "contingent" or "alternative" employee umbrella today. The NLRB therefore recently ruled that temporary employees could join the unions of permanent employees in the companies where their employment agencies assign them to work.[16]

Unfair Employer Labor Practices   The Wagner Act deemed as "statutory wrongs" (but not crimes) five unfair labor practices used by employers:

1. It is unfair for employers to "interfere with, restrain, or coerce employees" in exercising their legally sanctioned right of self-organization.
2. It is an unfair practice for company representatives to dominate or interfere with either the formation or the administration of labor unions. Among other management actions found to be unfair under practices 1 and 2 are bribing employees, using company spy systems, moving a business to avoid unionization, and blacklisting union sympathizers.
3. Companies are prohibited from discriminating in any way against employees for their legal union activities.
4. Employers are forbidden to discharge or discriminate against employees simply because the latter file unfair practice charges against the company.
5. Finally, it is an unfair labor practice for employers to refuse to bargain collectively with their employees' duly chosen representatives.

An unfair labor practice charge may be filed (see Figure 8.1) with the NLRB. The board then investigates the charge and determines whether formal action should be

FORM NLRB 501
(2 81)

FORM EXEMPT UNDER
44 U.S.C. 3512

UNITED STATES OF AMERICA
NATIONAL LABOR RELATIONS BOARD
CHARGE AGAINST EMPLOYER

INSTRUCTIONS: File an original and 4 copies of this charge with NLRB Regional Director for the region in which the alleged unfair labor practice occurred or is occurring.	DO NOT WRITE IN THIS SPACE	
	CASE NO.	DATE FILED

1. EMPLOYER AGAINST WHOM CHARGE IS BROUGHT

a. NAME OF EMPLOYER	b. NUMBER OF WORKERS EMPLOYED

c. ADDRESS OF ESTABLISHMENT *(street and number, city, State, and ZIP code)*	d. EMPLOYER REPRESEN-TATIVE TO CONTACT	e. PHONE NO.

f. TYPE OF ESTABLISHMENT *(factory, mine, wholesaler, etc.)*	g. IDENTIFY PRINCIPAL PRODUCT OR SERVICE

h. THE ABOVE-NAMED EMPLOYER HAS ENGAGED IN AND IS ENGAGING IN UNFAIR LABOR PRACTICES WITHIN THE MEANING OF SECTION 8(a), SUBSECTIONS (1) AND _____ OF THE NATIONAL
(list subsections)
LABOR RELATIONS ACT, AND THESE UNFAIR LABOR PRACTICES ARE UNFAIR LABOR PRACTICES AFFECTING COMMERCE WITHIN THE MEANING OF THE ACT.

2. BASIS OF THE CHARGE *(be specific as to facts, names, addresses, plants involved, dates, places, etc.)*

BY THE ABOVE AND OTHER ACTS, THE ABOVE-NAMED EMPLOYER HAS INTERFERED WITH, RESTRAINED, AND COERCED EMPLOYEES IN THE EXERCISE OF THE RIGHTS GUARANTEED IN SECTION 7 OF THE ACT.

3. FULL NAME OF PARTY FILING CHARGE *(if labor organization, give full name, including local name and number)*

4a. ADDRESS *(street and number, city, State, and ZIP code)*	4b. TELEPHONE NO.

5. FULL NAME OF NATIONAL OR INTERNATIONAL LABOR ORGANIZATION OF WHICH IT IS AN AFFILIATE OR CONSTITUENT UNIT *(to be filled in when charge is filed by a labor organization)*

6. DECLARATION

I declare that I have read the above charge and that the statements therein are true to the best of my knowledge and belief.

By _____   _____
(signature of representative or person filing charge)   (title, if any)

Address _____   _____   _____
(telephone number)   (date)

WILLFULLY FALSE STATEMENTS ON THIS CHARGE CAN BE PUNISHED BY FINE AND IMPRISONMENT
(U.S. CODE, TITLE 18, SECTION 1001)

FIGURE 8.1   NLRB Form 501: Filing an Unfair Labor Practice Charge

taken. Possible actions include dismissal of the complaint, request for an injunction against the employer, and an order that the employer cease and desist.

From 1935 to 1947   Union membership increased quickly after passage of the Wagner Act in 1935. Other factors such as an improving economy and aggressive union leadership contributed to this as well. But by the mid-1940s, the tide had begun to turn. Largely because of a series of massive postwar strikes, public policy began to shift against what many viewed as the union excesses of the times. The stage was set for passage of the Taft-Hartley Act of 1947.

Period of Modified Encouragement Coupled with Regulation: The Taft-Hartley Act (1947)

The **Taft-Hartley** (or Labor Management Relations) **Act** reflected the public's less enthusiastic attitudes toward unions. It amended the Wagner Act with provisions aimed at limiting unions in four ways: by prohibiting unfair union labor practices; by enumerating the rights of employees as union members; by enumerating the rights of employers; and by allowing the president of the United States to temporarily bar national emergency strikes.

Unfair Union Labor Practices   The Taft-Hartley Act enumerated several labor practices that unions were prohibited from engaging in:

1. Unions were banned from restraining or coercing employees from exercising their guaranteed bargaining rights.
2. It is an unfair labor practice for a union to cause an employer to discriminate in any way against an employee in order to encourage or discourage his or her membership in a union.
3. It is an unfair labor practice for a union to refuse to bargain in good faith with the employer about wages, hours, and other employment conditions.

Rights of Employees   The Taft-Hartley Act also protected the rights of employees against their unions. For example, many people felt that compulsory unionism violated the basic U.S. right of freedom of association. New right-to-work laws sprang up in 19 states (mainly in the South and Southwest); these outlawed labor contracts that made union membership a condition for keeping one's job. (Recall that even today, union membership varies widely by state, from a high of 26.8% in New York to a low of 3.7% in South Carolina, for instance.) Other representative membership figures include California, 16.5%; Florida, 7.4%; Texas, 6.5%; Michigan, 23.9%; Arizona, 5.8%; and Ohio, 19.4%.[17]

Rights of Employers   The Taft-Hartley Act also explicitly gave employers certain rights. For example, it gave them full freedom to express their views concerning union organization. Thus, a manager can tell his or her employees that in his or her opinion unions are worthless, dangerous to the economy, and immoral. A manager can even, generally speaking, hint that unionization and subsequent high-wage demands might result in the permanent closing of the plant but not its relocation. Employers can set forth the union's record in regard to violence and corruption, if appropriate, and can play on the racial prejudices of workers by describing the union's philosophy toward integration. In fact, the only major restraint is that there can be no threat of reprisal or force or promise of benefit.[18]

The employer also cannot meet with employees on company time within 24 hours of an election or suggest to employees that they vote against the union while they are at home or in the employer's office, although he or she can do so while in their work area or where they normally gather.

National Emergency Strikes   The Taft-Hartley Act also allows the U.S. president to intervene in **national emergency strikes**, which are strikes (for example, on the part of steel firm employees) that might imperil the national health and safety. The president may appoint a board of inquiry and, based on its report, apply for an injunction restraining the strike for 60 days. If no settlement is reached during that time, the injunction can be extended for another 20 days. During this period, employees are polled in a secret ballot to ascertain their willingness to accept the employer's last offer.

Period of Detailed Regulation of Internal Union Affairs: The Landrum-Griffin Act (1959)

In the 1950s, senate investigations revealed unsavory practices on the part of some unions, and the result was the **Landrum-Griffin Act** (officially, the Labor Management Reporting and Disclosure Act). An overriding aim of this act was to protect union members from possible wrongdoing on the part of their unions. It was also an amendment to the Wagner Act.

The Landrum-Griffin Act contains a bill of rights for union members. Among other things, this provides for certain rights in the nomination of candidates for union office. It also affirms a member's right to sue his or her union and ensures that no member can be fined or suspended without due process, which includes a list of specific charges, time to prepare defense, and a fair hearing.

The act also laid out rules regarding union elections. For example, national and international unions must elect officers at least once every five years, using some type of secret-ballot mechanism.

The senate investigators also discovered flagrant examples of employer wrongdoing. The Landrum-Griffin Act therefore also greatly expanded the list of unlawful employer actions. For example, companies can no longer pay their own employees to entice them not to join the union.

THE UNION DRIVE AND ELECTION

It is through the union drive and election that a union tries to be recognized to represent employees.[19] This process has five basic steps: initial contact, authorization cards, hearing, campaign, and the election.

Step 1: Initial Contact

During the initial contact stage, the union determines the employees' interest in organizing, and an organizing committee is established.

The initiative for the first contact between the employees and the union may come from the employees, from a union already representing other employees of the firm, or from a union representing workers elsewhere. Sometimes, a union effort starts with a disgruntled employee's contacting the local union to learn how to organize his or her place of work (as at Wal-Mart). Sometimes, though, the campaign starts when a union decides it wants to expand to representing other employees in the firm or when the company looks like an easy one to organize. (For instance, the Teamsters Union—already firmly in place at UPS—began an intensive organizing campaign at FedEx.) In any case, there is an initial contact between a union representative and a few employees.

When an employer becomes a target, a union official usually assigns a representative to assess employee interest. The representative visits the firm to determine whether enough employees are interested to make a union campaign worthwhile. He or she also identifies employees who would make good leaders in the organizing campaign and calls them together to create an organizing committee. The objective is to "educate the committee about the benefits of forming a union, the law and procedures involved in forming a local union, and the issues management is likely to raise during a campaign."[20]

The union must follow certain guidelines when it starts contacting employees. The law allows union organizers to solicit employees for membership as long as it doesn't endanger the performance or safety of the employees. Therefore, much of the contact takes place off the job, perhaps at home or at eating places near work. Organizers can also safely contact employees on company grounds during off hours (such as lunch or break time). Under some conditions, union representatives may solicit employees at their workstations, but this is rare. In practice, there will be much informal organizing going on at the workplace as employees debate the merits of organizing. In any case, this initial contact stage may be deceptively quiet. In some instances the first inkling management has of a union campaign is the distribution or posting of a handbill soliciting union membership.

Technology, in the form of e-mail is of course affecting the union organizing process. However, preventing union employees from sending pro-union e-mail messages on company e-mail systems can be a tricky matter. Prohibiting only union e-mail has been found to violate NLRB decisions, for instance. And instituting a rule barring workers from using e-mail for all non–work-related topics may similarly be ineffective if the company actually does little to stop e-mail other than pro-union messages.[21]

One expert says an employer's main goal shouldn't be to win representation elections, but to avoid them altogether. He says doing so means taking fast action when the first signs of union activity appear. His advice in a nutshell: Don't just ignore the union's efforts while it spreads pro-union rumors, such as "If we had a union, we wouldn't have to work so much overtime." Retain an attorney and react at once.[22]

Labor relations consultants are increasingly influencing the unionization process, with both management and unions using outside advisors. The use by management of consultants (who are often referred to disparagingly by unions as *union busters*) has apparently grown tremendously. A study by the AFL-CIO's Department of Organization and Field Services concluded, for example, that management consultants were involved in 85% of the elections they surveyed.[23]

Unions are not without creative ways to win elections, one of which is called union salting. **Union salting** refers to a union organizing tactic by which workers who are in fact employed full-time by a union as undercover union organizers are hired by unwitting employers. A 1995 U.S. Supreme Court decision, in *NLRB* v. *Town and Country Electric*, held the tactic to be legal.[24]

Step 2: Authorization Cards

For the union to petition the NLRB for the right to hold an election, it must show that a sizable number of employees may be interested in being organized. The next step is thus for union organizers to try to get the employees to sign **authorization cards** (see Figure 8.2). Thirty percent of the eligible employees in an appropriate bargaining unit must sign before an election can be petitioned.

During this stage, both union and management typically use various forms of propaganda. The union claims it can improve working conditions, raise wages, increase benefits, and generally get the workers better deals. Management need not be silent; it can attack the union on ethical and moral grounds and cite the cost of union membership, for example. Management can also explain its track record, express facts and opinions, and explain to its employees the law applicable to organizing campaigns and the meaning of the duty to bargain in good faith (if the union should win the election). However, neither side can threaten, bribe, or coerce employees. Further, an employer may not make promises of benefit to employees or make unilateral changes in terms and conditions of employment that were not planned to be implemented prior to the onset of union organizing activity. Managers also should not look through signed authorization cards if confronted with them by union representatives. Doing so could be construed as an unfair labor practice by the NLRB, which could view it as spying on those who signed.

During this stage, unions can picket the company, subject to three constraints: the union must file a petition for an election within 30 days after the start of picketing,

---

UNITED GLASS AND CERAMIC WORKERS
OF NORTH AMERICA, AFL-CIO, CLC

OFFICIAL MEMBERSHIP APPLICATION AND AUTHORIZATION

I, hereby apply for membership in the United Glass and Ceramic Workers of North America, AFL-CIO, CLC. I hereby designate and authorize the United Glass and Ceramic Workers of North America, AFL-CIO, CLC, as my collective bargaining representative in all matters pertaining to wages, rates of pay, and other conditions of employment. I also authorize the United Glass and Ceramic Workers of North America, AFL-CIO, CLC, to request recognition from my employer as my bargaining agent.

SIGNATURE OF APPLICANT _____

EMPLOYED BY _____

APPLICATION RECEIVED BY _____

DATE _____

FIGURE 8.2 Sample Authorization Card

Source: © 1982 by CCH Incorporated. All rights reserved. Reprinted with permission from *Human Resources Management Ideas and Trends Newsletter.*

the firm cannot already be lawfully recognizing another union, and there cannot already have been a valid NLRB election during the past 12 months.

Step 3: The Hearing

After the authorization cards have been collected, one of three things can occur. If the employer chooses not to contest union recognition, no hearing is needed and a consent election is held immediately. If the employer chooses not to contest the union's *right* to an election (and/or the scope of the bargaining unit, or which employees are eligible to vote in the election), no hearing is needed and the parties can stipulate an election. If an employer does wish to contest the union's right, it can insist on a hearing to determine those issues. An employer's decision about whether to insist on a hearing is a strategic one based on the facts of each case and whether it feels it needs additional time to develop a campaign to try to persuade a majority of its employees not to elect a union to represent them.

Most companies contest the union's right to represent their employees, and thus decline to voluntarily recognize the union: They claim that a significant number of their employees do not really want the union. It is at this point that the U.S. Labor Department's NLRB gets involved. The NLRB is usually contacted by the union, which requests a hearing. Based on this, the regional director of the NLRB sends a hearing officer to investigate. (For example, did 30% or more of the employees in an appropriate bargaining unit sign the authorization cards?) The examiner sends both management and the union a notice of representation hearing that states the time and place of the hearing.

The **bargaining unit** is one decision to come out of the hearing; it is the group of employees that the union will be authorized to represent and bargain for collectively.

Finally, if the results of the hearing are favorable for the union, the NLRB directs that an election be held. It issues a Decision and Direction of Election notice to that effect, and NLRB Form 666 (Figure 8.3) is sent to the employer to post.

Step 4: The Campaign

During the campaign that precedes the election, the union and employer appeal to employees for their votes. The union emphasizes that it will prevent unfairness, set up a grievance/seniority system, and improve unsatisfactory wages. Union strength, they'll say, will give employees a voice in determining wages and working conditions. Management emphasizes that improvements such as those the union promises don't require unionization, and that wages are equal to or better than they would be with a union contract. Management also emphasizes the financial cost of union dues; the fact that the union is an "outsider"; and that if the union wins, a strike may follow.[25] It can even attack the union on ethical and moral grounds, while insisting that employees will not be as well off and may lose freedom. But neither side can threaten, bribe, or coerce employees.

Step 5: The Election

Finally, the election can be held within 30 to 60 days after the NLRB issues its Decision and Direction of Election. The election is by secret ballot; the NLRB pro-

Form NLRB 666
(7–72)

★ NOTICE TO EMPLOYEES

FROM THE

National Labor Relations Board

A PETITION has been filed with this Federal agency seeking an election to determine whether certain employees want to be represented by a union.

The case is being investigated and NO DETERMINATION HAS BEEN MADE AT THIS TIME by the National Labor Relations Board. IF an election is held Notices of Election will be posted giving complete details for voting.

It was suggested that your employer post this notice so the National Labor Relations Board could inform you of your basic rights under the National Labor Relations Act.

YOU HAVE THE RIGHT under Federal Law

- To self-organization
- To form, join, or assist labor organizations
- To bargain collectively through representatives of your own choosing
- To act together for the purposes of collective bargaining or other mutual aid or protection
- To refuse to do any or all of these things unless the union and employer, in a state where such agreements are permitted, enter into a lawful union security clause requiring employees to join the union.

It is possible that some of you will be voting in an employee representation election as a result of the request for an election having been filed. While NO DETERMINATION HAS BEEN MADE AT THIS TIME, in the event an election is held, the NATIONAL LABOR RELATIONS BOARD wants all eligible voters to be familiar with their rights under the law IF it holds an election.

The Board applies rules which are intended to keep its elections fair and honest and which result in a free choice. If agents of either Unions or Employers act in such a way as to interfere with your right to a free election, the election can be set aside by the Board. Where appropriate the Board provides other remedies, such as reinstatement for employees fired for exercising their rights, including backpay from the party responsible for their discharge.

FIGURE 8.3   NLRB Form 666: Notice to Employees

NOTE:

The following are examples of conduct which interfere with the rights of employees and may result in the setting aside of the election.

- Threatening loss of jobs or benefits by an Employer or a Union

- Misstating important facts by a Union or an Employer where the other party does not have a fair chance to reply

- Promising or granting promotions, pay raises, or other benefits, to influence an employee's vote by a party capable of carrying out such promises

- An Employer firing employees to discourage or encourage union activity or a Union causing them to be fired to encourage union activity

- Making campaign speeches to assembled groups of employees on company time within the 24-hour period before the election

- Incitement by either an Employer or a Union of racial or religious prejudice by inflammatory appeals

- Threatening physical force or violence to employees by a Union or an Employer to influence their votes

Please be assured that IF AN ELECTION IS HELD every effort will be made to protect your right to a free choice under the law. Improper conduct will not be permitted. All parties are expected to cooperate fully with this agency in maintaining basic principles of a fair election as required by law. The National Labor Relations Board as an agency of the United States Government does not endorse any choice in the election.

NATIONAL LABOR RELATIONS BOARD
an agency of the
UNITED STATES GOVERNMENT

THIS IS AN OFFICIAL GOVERNMENT NOTICE AND MUST NOT BE DEFACED BY ANYONE

FIGURE 8.3 (continued)

vides the ballots (see Figure 8.4), voting booth, and ballot box and counts the votes and certifies the results of the election.

The union becomes the employees' representative if it wins the election, and winning means getting a majority of the votes cast, not a majority of the workers in the bargaining unit. (It is also important to keep in mind that when an employer commits an unfair labor practice, a "no union" election may be reversed. As representatives of their employer, supervisors must therefore be very careful not to commit such unfair practices.)

The Supervisor's Role

Supervisors must be knowledgeable about what they can and can't do to legally hamper organizing activities, lest they commit unfair labor practices. Such practices could cause a new election to be held after the company has won a previous election

UNITED STATES OF AMERICA
National Labor Relations Board
OFFICIAL SECRET BALLOT
FOR CERTAIN EMPLOYEES OF

Do you wish to be represented for purposes of collective bargaining by —

MARK AN "S" IN THE SQUARE OF YOUR CHOICE

YES □   NO □

DO NOT SIGN THIS BALLOT. Fold and drop in ballot box.
If you spoil this ballot return it to the Board Agent for a new one.

FIGURE 8.4 Sample NLRB Ballot

or cause the company to forfeit the second election and go directly to contract negotiation. (In one case, a plant superintendent reacted to a union's initial organizing attempt by prohibiting distribution of union literature in the plant's lunchroom. Because solicitation of off-duty workers in nonwork areas is generally legal, the company subsequently allowed the union to post union literature on the company's bulletin board and to distribute union literature in nonworking areas inside the plant. However, the NLRB still ruled that the initial act of prohibiting distribution of the literature was an unfair labor practice, one that was not "made right" by the company's subsequent efforts. The NLRB used the superintendent's action as one reason for invalidating an election that the company won.[26] To avoid such problems, employers should have rules governing distribution of literature and solicitation of workers and train supervisors in how to apply them.[27]

Rules Regarding Literature and Solicitation   An employer can take a number of steps to legally restrict union organizing activity.[28] For example:

- Nonemployees can always be barred from soliciting employees during their work time—that is, when the employee is on duty and not on a break.
- Employers can usually stop employees from soliciting other employees for any purpose if one or both employees are on paid-duty time and not on a break.
- Most employers (not including retail stores, shopping centers, and certain other

employers) can bar nonemployees from the building's interiors and work areas as a right of private property owners. In certain cases, nonemployees can also be barred from exterior private property such as parking lots—if there is a business reason (such as safety) and the reason is not just to interfere with union organizers.

■ Whether or not employers must allow union representatives permission to organize on employer-owned property at shopping malls is a matter of legal debate. In 1992, the U.S. Supreme Court ruled in *Lechmere, Inc.*, v. *National Labor Relations Board* that nonemployees may be barred from an employer's property if they have reasonable alternative means of communicating their message to the intended audience. On the other hand, if the employer permits other organizations such as the Salvation Army to set up at their workplaces, discriminating against the union organizers may be viewed as an unfair labor practice.[29]

Such restrictions are valid only if they are not imposed in a discriminatory manner. For example, if employees are permitted by company policy to collect money for a wedding shower and baby gifts, to sell Avon-type products or Tupperware, or to engage in other solicitation during their working time, the employer will not be able to lawfully prohibit them from union soliciting during work time.

Finally, remember that there are many more ways to commit unfair labor practices than just keeping union organizers off your private property. For example, one employer decided to have a cookout and paid day off two days before a union representation election. The NLRB held that this was too much of a coincidence and represented coercive conduct. The union had lost the first vote but won the second vote as a result.[30]

Decertification Elections: When Employees Want to Oust Their Union

Winning an election and signing an agreement do not necessarily mean that the union is in the company to stay—quite the opposite. The same law that grants employees the right to unionize also gives them a way to legally terminate the union's right to represent them. The process is known as *decertification*. Around 450 to 500 decertification elections are typically held each year, of which the unions win 30%.[31] (In 1999, 2,976 union representation elections were held, of which unions won 1,526, or 51.3%.)[32]

Decertification campaigns don't differ much from certification campaigns (those leading up to the initial election).[33] The union organizes membership meetings and house-to-house visits, mails literature to the homes, and uses phone calls, NLRB appeals, and (sometimes) threats and harassment to win the election.[34] Managers use meetings—including one-on-one meetings, small-group meetings, and meetings with entire units—as well as legal or expert assistance, letters, improved working conditions, and subtle or not-so-subtle threats in its attempts to win a decertification vote. Employers are also increasingly turning to consultants.

THE COLLECTIVE BARGAINING PROCESS

What Is Collective Bargaining?

When and if the union is recognized as a company's employees' representative, a day is set for meeting at the bargaining table. Representatives of management and the union meet to negotiate a labor agreement that contains agreements on specific provisions covering wages, hours, and working conditions.

What exactly is **collective bargaining**? According to the National Labor Relations Act:

> For the purpose of (this act) to bargain collectively is the performance of the mutual obligation of the employer and the representative of the employees to meet at reasonable times and confer in good faith with respect to wages, hours, and terms and conditions of employment, or the negotiation of an agreement, or any question arising thereunder, and the execution of a written contract incorporating any agreement reached if requested by either party, but such obligation does not compel either party to agree to a proposal or require the making of a concession.

In plain language, this means that both management and labor are required by law to negotiate wages, hours, and terms and conditions of employment "in good faith." In a moment we will see that the specific terms that are negotiable (because wages, hours, and conditions of employment are too broad to be useful in practice) have been clarified by a series of court decisions.

What Is Good Faith?

Good faith bargaining is the cornerstone of effective labor management relations. It means that both parties communicate and negotiate. It means that proposals are matched with counterproposals and that both parties make every reasonable effort to arrive at an agreement.[35] It does not mean that either party is compelled to agree to a proposal. Nor does it require that either party make any specific concessions (although as a practical matter, some may be necessary).

When Is Bargaining Not in Good Faith?   As interpreted by the NLRB and the courts, examples of a violation of the requirements for good faith bargaining may include:

1. *Surface bargaining.* This involves going through the motions of bargaining without any real intention of completing a formal agreement.
2. *Concession.* Although no one is required to make a concession, the courts' and NLRB's definitions of *good faith* suggest that a willingness to compromise is an essential ingredient in good faith bargaining.
3. *Proposals and demands.* The NLRB considers the advancement of proposals as a positive factor in determining overall good faith.
4. *Dilatory tactics.* The law requires that the parties meet and "confer at reasonable times and intervals." Obviously, refusal to meet at all with the union does not satisfy the positive duty imposed on the employer.
5. *Imposing conditions.* Attempts to impose conditions that are so onerous or unreasonable as to indicate bad faith are scrutinized by the board.
6. *Unilateral changes in conditions.* This is viewed as a strong indication that the employer is not bargaining with the required intent of reaching an agreement.
7. *Bypassing the representative.* An employer violates its duty to bargain when it refuses to negotiate with the union representative.

The Negotiating Team

Both union and management send a negotiating team to the bargaining table, and both teams usually go into the bargaining sessions having done their homework. Union representatives have sounded out union members on their desires and conferred with union representatives of related unions.

Similarly, management uses several techniques to prepare for bargaining. For example, pay and benefit data are compiled and include comparisons to local pay rates and rates paid for similar jobs within the industry. Management also "costs" the current labor contract and determines the increased cost—total, per employee, and per hour—of the union's demands. It also tries to identify probable union demands. It uses information from grievances and feedback from supervisors to determine ahead of time what the union's demands might be and thus prepare counteroffers and arguments ahead of time.[36]

Bargaining Items

Labor law sets out categories of items that are subject to bargaining: These are *mandatory, voluntary,* and *illegal items.*

Voluntary (or permissible) **bargaining items** are neither mandatory nor illegal; they become a part of negotiations only through the joint agreement of both management and union. Neither party can be compelled against its wishes to negotiate over voluntary items. An employee cannot hold up signing a contract because the other party refuses to bargain on a voluntary item.

Illegal bargaining items are forbidden by law. The clause agreeing to hire "union members exclusively" would be illegal in a right-to-work state, for example.

About 70 **mandatory bargaining items** exist, some of which are shown in Figure 8.5. They include wages, hours, rest periods, layoffs, transfers, benefits, and severance pay. Others are added as the law evolves. For instance, drug testing evolved into a mandatory item as a result of court decisions in the 1980s.[37]

Bargaining Stages[38]

Bargaining typically goes through several stages of development.[39] First, each side presents its demands. At this stage, both parties are usually quite far apart on some issues. Second, there is a reduction of demands. At this stage, each side trades off some of its demands to gain others. Third come the subcommittee studies: The parties form joint subcommittees to try to work out reasonable alternatives. Fourth, an informal settlement is reached and each group goes back to its sponsor. Union representatives check informally with their superiors and the union members; management representatives check with top management. Finally, when everything is in order, a formal agreement is fine-tuned and signed.

Negotiating guidelines are summarized in the following *HR in Practice* box.

Impasses, Mediation, and Strikes[40]

Impasses   In collective bargaining, an impasse occurs when the parties are not able to move further toward settlement. An impasse usually occurs because one

MANDATORY	PERMISSIBLE	ILLEGAL
Rates of pay	Indemnity bonds	Closed shop
Wages	Management rights as to union affairs	Separation of employees based on race
Hours of employment	Pension benefits of retired employees	Discriminatory treatment
Overtime pay		
Shift differentials	Scope of the bargaining unit	
Holidays		
Vacations	Including supervisors in the contract	
Severance pay		
Pensions	Additional parties to the contract such as the international union	
Insurance benefits		
Profit-sharing plans		
Christmas bonuses	Use of union label	
Company housing, meals, and discounts	Settlement of unfair labor charges	
	Prices in cafeteria	
Employee security	Continuance of past contract	
Job performance		
Union security	Membership of bargaining team	
Management–union relationship		
Drug testing of employees	Employment of strikebreakers	

FIGURE 8.5   Bargaining Items

Source: From *Collective Bargaining and Labor Relations: Cases, Practice, and Law* by Michael R. Carrell and Christina Heavrin, p. 127. Reprinted with permission of Prentice Hall, Upper Saddle River, New Jersey.

party demands more than the other offers. Sometimes an impasse can be resolved through a third party, a disinterested person such as a mediator or arbitrator. If the impasse is not resolved in this way, a work stoppage, or *strike*, may be called by the union to pressure management.[41]

Third-Party Involvement   Three types of third-party interventions are used to overcome an impasse: mediation, fact-finding, and arbitration. With **mediation**, a neutral third party tries to assist the principals in reaching agreement. The mediator usually holds meetings with each party to determine where each stands regarding its position, and then this information is used to find common ground for further bargaining. The mediator is always a go-between. As such, he or she communicates assessments of the likelihood of a strike, the possible settlement packages available, and the like. The mediator does not have the authority to insist on a position or make a concession.

In certain situations, as in a national emergency dispute in which the president of the United States determines that it would be a national emergency for a strike to

HR in Practice

Negotiating Guidelines

1. Be sure you have *set clear objectives* for every bargaining item and you understand on what grounds the objectives are established.[42]
2. *Do not hurry.*
3. When in doubt, *caucus* with your associates.
4. Be *well prepared* with firm data supporting your position.
5. Always strive to keep some *flexibility* in your position. Don't get yourself out on a limb.
6. Don't just concern yourself with what the other party says and does; *find out why*. Remember that economic motivation is not the only explanation for the other party's conduct and actions.
7. Respect the importance of *face saving* for the other party.
8. Constantly be alert to the *real intentions* of the other party with respect not only to goals but also priorities.
9. Be a good *listener*.
10. Build a reputation for *being fair but firm*.
11. Learn to *control your emotions*; don't panic. Use emotions as a tool, not an obstacle.
12. Be sure as you make each bargaining move that you know its *relationship* to all other moves.
13. Measure each move against your *objectives*.
14. Pay close attention to the *wording* of every clause renegotiated; words and phrases are often a source of grievances.
15. Remember that collective bargaining negotiations are, by their nature, part of a *compromise* process. There is no such thing as having all the pie.
16. Learn to *understand* people and their personalities.
17. Consider the impact of present negotiations on those in *future years*.

occur, a fact-finder may be appointed. A **fact-finder** is a neutral party who studies the issues in a dispute and makes a public recommendation of what a reasonable settlement ought to be.[43] For example, presidential emergency fact-finding boards have successfully resolved impasses in certain critical transportation disputes.

Arbitration is the most definitive type of third-party intervention because the arbitrator may have the power to decide and dictate settlement terms. Unlike mediation and fact-finding, arbitration can guarantee a solution to an impasse. With binding arbitration, both parties are committed to accepting the arbitrator's award. With nonbinding arbitration, they are not. Arbitration may also be voluntary or compulsory (in other words, imposed by a government agency). In the United States, voluntary binding arbitration is the most prevalent.

Strikes   A strike is a withdrawal of labor; there are four main types of strikes. An *economic strike* results from a failure to agree on the terms of a contract—from an impasse, in other words. *Unfair labor practice strikes*, on the other hand, are aimed at protesting illegal conduct by the employer. A **wildcat strike** is an unauthorized strike occurring during the term of a contract. A **sympathy strike** occurs when one union strikes in support of the strike of another. There were 29 major U.S. work stoppages in 1997 pulling 339,000 employees off their jobs for a total of 4.9 million days of lost work.[44]

Picketing is one of the first activities occurring during a strike. The purpose of picketing is to inform the public about the existence of the labor dispute and often to encourage others to refrain from doing business with the employer against whom the employees are striking.

Employers can make several responses when they become the object of a strike. One is to shut down the affected area and thus halt their operations until the strike is over. A second alternative is to contract out work during the duration of the strike in order to blunt the effects of the strike on the employer. A third alternative is for the employer to continue operations, perhaps using supervisors and other nonstriking workers to fill in for the striking workers. A fourth alternative is the hiring of replacements for the strikers. In an economic strike, such replacements can be deemed permanent and would not have to be let go to make room for strikers who decided to return to work. If the strike were an unfair labor practice strike, the strikers would be entitled to return to their jobs if the employer makes an unconditional offer for them to do so.

Other Alternatives Management and labor may both use other weapons to try to break an impasse and achieve their aims. The union, for example, may resort to a *corporate campaign*, which is an organized effort by the union that exerts pressure on the corporation by pressuring the company's other unions, shareholders, directors, customers, creditors, and government agencies, often directly. Thus, individual members of the board of directors might be shocked by picketing of their homes, political figures might be pressured to agree to union demands, and the company's banks might become targets of a union member **boycott**, a removal of patronage.[45]

Inside games are another union tactic, one often used in conjunction with corporate campaigns. *Inside games* are union efforts to convince employees to impede or to disrupt production, for example, by slowing the work pace, refusing to work overtime, filing mass charges with governmental agencies, refusing to do work without receiving detailed instructions from supervisors (even though such instruction has not previously been required), and engaging in other disruptive activities such as castigating management and holding sick outs.[46] Although the employees are at work and being paid, they are essentially "on strike." Inside games can thus be viewed as essentially de facto strikes, albeit "strikes" in which the employees are being supported by the company, which continues to pay them. In one inside game at Caterpillar's Aurora, Illinois, plant, United Auto Workers' grievances in the final stage before arbitration rose from 22 to 336. The effect, of course, was to clog the grievance procedure and tie up workers and management in unproductive endeavors on company time.[47]

Employers can try to break an impasse with lockouts. A **lockout** is a refusal by the employer to provide opportunities to work. The employees are (sometimes literally) locked out and prohibited from doing their jobs (and thus from getting paid).

A lockout is not generally viewed as an unfair labor practice by the NLRB. For example, if your product is a perishable one (such as vegetables), then a lockout may be a legitimate tactic to neutralize or decrease union power. A lockout is viewed as an unfair labor practice by the NLRB only when the employer acts for a prohibited purpose. It is not a prohibited purpose to try to bring about a settlement of negotiations on terms favorable to the employer. Lockouts are not widely used today, though; employers are usually reluctant to cease operations when employees are willing to continue working (even though there may be an impasse at the bargaining table).[48]

Both employers and unions can seek injunctive relief if they believe the other side is taking actions that could cause irreparable harm to the other party. To obtain such relief, the NLRB must show the district court that an unfair labor practice—such as interfering with the union organizing campaign—if left unremedied, will irreparably harm the other party's statutory rights. (For example, if the employer is interfering with the union's organization campaign, or if the union is retaliating against employees for trying to gain access to the NLRB, the other side might press the NLRB for 10(j) injunctive relief.) Such relief is requested after the NLRB issues an unfair labor practices complaint. The injunctive relief is a court order compelling a party or parties either to resume or to desist a certain action.[49]

The Contract Agreement

The contract agreement may be 20 or 30 pages long or longer. It may contain just general declarations of policy or a detailed specification of rules and procedures. The tendency today is toward the longer, more detailed contract. This is largely a result of the increased number of items the agreements cover.

The main sections of a typical contract cover subjects such as:

1. Management rights
2. Union security and automatic payroll dues deduction
3. Grievance procedures
4. Arbitration of grievances
5. Disciplinary procedures
6. Compensation rates
7. Hours of work and overtime
8. Benefits such as vacation, holidays, insurance, and pension
9. Health and safety provisions
10. Employee security seniority provisions
11. Contract expiration date

WHAT'S NEXT FOR UNIONS?

Why the Union Decline?

Several factors contributed to the decline in union membership in the 1980s and 1990s. Unions have traditionally appealed mostly to blue-collar workers, and the proportion of blue-collar jobs has been decreasing as service-sector and white-collar service jobs have increased. Furthermore, several economic factors, including intense international competition (see the *Global Issues in HR* Box), outdated equipment and factories, mismanagement, new technology, and government regulation, have hit those industries (such as mining and manufacturing) that have traditionally been unionized. The effect of all this has been the permanent layoff of hundreds of thou-

International Labor Relations

Firms opening subsidiaries abroad find substantial differences in labor relations practices among the world's countries and regions. The following synopsis illustrates some of these differences by focusing on Europe. However, keep in mind that similarly significant differences exist in, say, South and Central America and Asia. Some important differences between labor relations practices in Europe and the United States include:[50]

- *Centralization.* In general, collective bargaining in Western Europe is likely to be industrywide or regionally oriented, whereas U.S. collective bargaining generally occurs at the enterprise or plant level.

- *Union structure.* Because collective bargaining is relatively centralized in most European countries, local unions in Europe tend to have much less autonomy and decision-making power than in the United States, and they basically concentrate on administrative and service functions.

- *Employer organization.* Due to the prevalence of industrywide bargaining, the employer's collective bargaining role tends to be performed primarily by employer associations in Europe; individual employers in the United States generally (but not always) represent their own interests in bargaining collectively with unions.

- *Union recognition.* Union recognition for collective bargaining in Western Europe is much less formal than in the United States. For example, in Europe there is no legal mechanism requiring an employer to recognize a particular union; even if a union claims to represent 80% of an employer's workers, another union can try to organize and bargain for the other 20%.

- *Union security.* Union security in the form of formal closed-shop agreement is largely absent in continental Western Europe.

- *Labor–management contracts.* As in the United States, most European labor–management agreements are legally binding documents, except in Great Britain, where such collective agreements are viewed as "gentlemen's agreements" existing outside the law.

- *Content and scope of bargaining.* U.S. labor–management agreements tend to focus on wages, hours, and working conditions. European agreements, on the other hand, tend to be brief and simple and to specify minimum wages and employment conditions, with employers free to institute more favorable terms. The relative brevity of the European agreements is a function of two things: Industrywide bargaining makes it difficult to write detailed contracts applicable to individual enterprises, and in Europe government is much more heavily involved in setting terms of employment such as vacations and working conditions.

- *Grievance handling.* In Western Europe, grievances occur much less frequently than in the United States; when raised, they are usually handled by a legislated machinery outside the union's formal control.

(continued)

International Labor Relations (continued)

- *Strikes.* Generally speaking, strikes occur less frequently in Europe than in the United States. This is probably due to industrywide bargaining, which generally elicits less management resistance than in the United States, where demands "cut deeper into the individual enterprise's revenues."[51]

- *Government's role.* In Europe governments generally do not regulate the bargaining process but are much more interested in directly setting the actual terms of employment than is the case in the United States.

- *Worker participation.* Worker participation has a long and relatively extensive history in Western Europe, where it tends to go far beyond matters such as pay and working conditions. The aim is to create a system by which workers can participate in a meaningful way in the direct management of the enterprise. Determining wages, hours, and working conditions is not enough; employees should participate in formulating all management decisions. In many countries in Western Europe works councils are required; a *works council* is a committee in which plant workers consult with management about certain issues or share in the governance of the workplace.[52] Codetermination is a second form of worker participation in Europe; *codetermination* means that there is mandatory worker representation on an enterprise's board of directors. It is especially prevalent in Germany.

sands of union members, the permanent closing of company plants, the relocation of companies to nonunion settings (either in the United States or overseas), and mergers and acquisitions that have eliminated union jobs and affected collective bargaining agreements. Other changes, including the deregulation of trucking, airlines, and communications, have helped to erode union membership as well.[53]

How Unions Are Changing

Does all this mean that unions will disappear? Probably not. It does mean a change in the way unions operate and the role they see for themselves.

First, unions are increasingly going after a piece of the pie in terms of ownership and control of corporations. As a United Steelworkers Union president put it, "We are not going to sit around and allow management to louse things up like they did in the past."[54] Today, more than 8 million workers own a piece of their employers through employee stock ownership plans. Recall that these ESOPs are basically pension plans through which a company's employees accumulate shares of their company's stock. As a result, nonmanagement employees now sit on boards of directors at more than 300 firms in their role as representatives of the firm's employee stock ownership plans.

Second, unions are becoming both more aggressive and more sophisticated in the way they present themselves to the public. The AFL-CIO has a program to train

1,000 unionists in the fundamentals of how to come across well on television, for instance.

Third, during the past 10 years or so, the major union effort has been aimed at organizing white-collar workers. Service-oriented industries such as insurance, banking, retail trade, and government are now being organized by unions. More than 10% of white-collar workers have already become unionized. The number is increasing rapidly, particularly among professionals, many of whom work in the public sector.[55]

Fourth, unions are entering into more cooperative pacts with employers—for instance, working with them in developing team–based employee participation programs. About half the collective bargaining agreements signed recently encouraged cooperative labor–management relationships. *Cooperative clauses* cover things like joint committees to review drug problem, health care, and safety issues.[56]

Such programs can have positive effects. For many years, for instance, Scott Paper Company "was the most struck company in the primary mill segment of the paper industry." With poor labor–management relations undermining the firm's competitiveness, management approached the United Paperworkers International Union to try to build a more cooperative relationship. Joint labor–management committees were established at each site; the committees shared information regarding the company's performance and competition. The workers themselves gradually became heavily involved in redesigning their jobs; and the teams were soon leading cost improvement projects and helping to set budgets. By then, the company was producing more products with 22% fewer hourly paid employees. And, the employees were among the best paid in the industry and were working in participative, self-directed teams.[57]

Are Employee Participation Programs Unfair Labor Practices?

The proliferation of employee participation programs—team-based quality improvement programs and so on—has added urgency to a question that's been debated in labor relations circles for more than 50 years: Are employee participation programs like these "sham unions" and therefore illegal under the National Labor Relations Act? At present, they are "subject to serious legal challenge under the National Labor Relations Act"[58] for unfair labor practices. For example, a program giving employees more input in how they perform their jobs at UPS faced strong opposition from the Teamsters Union. Under this program, hourly employees work together in self-directed teams establishing priority on how work is to be done. UPS argues that the program recognizes that such employee involvement and teamwork can translate into higher productivity. For its part, the Teamsters Union (which represents the company's drivers and other hourly workers) is suspicious that the program is merely a tactic for subverting the union's influence on its members.[59]

Whether or not an employer's participation program will be viewed as an impermissible labor organization revolves around two main criteria: If the company dominates the union, and if the employees participating in the program become involved in traditionally union-type matters such as wages and working conditions, then the program might be interpreted as a sham union.[60] Thus, in the *Electromation Corporation* case decided in 1992 by the NLRB, the firm set up action committees to advise management regarding matters such as absenteeism/infractions, pay progression, and the attendance bonus plan. When a Teamsters local lost a certification election at this firm, the union filed an unfair labor practice suit with the NLRB. It claimed, in part, that the action committees were unlawfully dominated labor organizations. The NLRB decided in favor of the union but did not really clarify when and under what conditions participation programs might be acceptable. The matter continues to move through the courts.

REVIEW

Summary

1. In addition to improve wages and working conditions, unions seek security when organizing. There are five possible arrangements, including the closed shop, the union shop, the agency shop, the open shop, and maintenance of membership.

2. The AFL-CIO is a national federation comprising 109 national and international unions. It can exercise only the power it is allowed to exercise by its constituent national unions.

3. During the period of strong encouragement of unions, the Norris-LaGuardia Act and the NLRA were passed; these marked a shift in labor law from repression to strong encouragement of union activity. They did this by banning certain types of unfair labor practices, by providing for secret-ballot elections, and by creating the NLRB.

4. The Taft-Hartley Act reflected the period of modified encouragement coupled with regulation. It enumerated the rights of employees with respect to their unions, enumerated the rights of employers, and allowed the U.S. president to temporarily bar national emergency strikes. Among other things, it also enumerated certain union unfair labor practices. For example, it banned unions from restraining or coercing employees from exercising their guaranteed bargaining rights. And employers were explicitly given the right to express their views concerning union organization.

5. The Landrum-Griffin Act reflected the period of detailed regulation of internal union affairs. It grew out of discoveries of wrongdoing on the part of both management and union leadership and contained a bill of rights for union members. (For example, it affirms a member's right to sue his or her union.)

6. There are four steps in a union drive and election: the initial contact, obtaining authorization cards, holding a hearing with the NLRB, and the election itself. Remember that the union need only win a majority of the votes cast, *not* a majority of the workers in the bargaining unit.

7. Bargaining collectively in good faith is the next step if and when the union wins the election. Good faith means that both parties communicate and negotiate, and that proposals are matched with counterproposals. Some hints on bargaining include do not hurry, be prepared, find out why, and be a good listener.

8. An impasse occurs when the parties aren't able to move further toward settlement. Third-party involvement—namely, arbitration, fact-finding, or mediation—is one alternative. Sometimes, though, a strike occurs. Responding to the strike involves such steps as shutting the facility, contracting out work, or possibly replacing the workers. Boycotts and lockouts are two other anti-impasse weapons sometimes used by labor and management.

Key Terms

closed shop
union shop
agency shop
open shop
AFL-CIO
Norris-LaGuardia Act
Wagner Act
National Labor Relations
  Board (NLRB)
Taft-Hartley Act

national emergency
  strikes
Landrum-Griffin Act
union salting
authorization cards
bargaining unit
collective bargaining
good faith bargaining
voluntary bargaining
  items

illegal bargaining items
mandatory bargaining
  items
mediation
fact-finder
arbitration
wildcat strike
sympathy strike
boycott
lockout

Discussion Questions and Exercises

1. Discuss the steps in an NLRB election.
2. Describe important tactics you would expect the union to use during the union drive and election.
3. Briefly explain why labor law has gone through a cycle of repression and encouragement.
4. What is meant by good faith bargaining? When is bargaining not in good faith?
5. Define impasse, mediation, and strike, and explain the techniques that are used to overcome an impasse.

APPLICATION EXERCISES

Case Incident: Seeds of Mistrust at AA?[61]

Former American Airlines (AA) chairman Bob Crandall is widely acclaimed as an airline executive who not only made American Airlines a success, but changed the whole airline dramatically. While he was chairman, for instance, American harnessed technology to distribute tickets through its SABRE system of travel agents, entered into several important alliances, instituted new "yield control" capacity controls to price airline seats, and implemented the airline's first big frequent flyer program.

Yet in 1997, people were asking whether Crandall was less than successful in dealing with his own employees and labor relations. The "seeds of mistrust," according to one article at the time, included a two-tier wage scale for pilots, belittling pilots to analysts and to the press, threatening to shut down the airline unless the pilots agreed to further concessions, and letting "his combative personality become the focus of labor talks."[62] As a result, said one business writer at the time, pilots "speak of him with outright contempt." The public, concerned about a possible pilot walkout, curtailed their AA ticket buying for a time, a step that even the airline estimated cost it at least $100 million in lost bookings. On the other hand, "pilots are a difficult bunch to manage, especially when compared with other unionized workers." Part of the problem seemed to lay in the two-tier pay system that Crandall had pushed: Current AA pilots continued at a relatively high pay scale, whereas new pilots hired in (and who might be sitting next to the higher-priced pilots and doing much the same jobs) made considerably less. A whole subclass of resentful pilots may have inadvertently been created. Now, though, the airline's management had to figure out how to reach an agreement with the pilots as a group.

Questions

1. Based on what you know from this chapter, what factors at AA do you think might encourage more pilots to join their union and become resistant to management's overtures?

2. Because pilots can't be replaced quickly, a strike by pilots can effectively shut down the airline immediately. How would you handle the threat of a strike if you were Crandall? Why?

3. If you were advising AA's management, how would you suggest they go about extricating themselves from this situation and ensuing that it doesn't happen again? Is that feasible?

Experiential Exercise

Purpose: The purpose of this exercise is to give you practice in dealing with some of the elements of a union organizing campaign.

Required Understanding: You should be familiar with the material covered in this chapter, as well as the following incident, "An Organizing Question on Campus."

How to Set Up the Exercise/Instructions: Divide the class into groups of four or five students. Assume that you are labor relations consultants retained by the college to identify the problems and issues involved and to advise Art Tipton about what to do next. Each group will spend about 45 minutes discussing the issues and outlining those issues as well as an action plan for Tipton.

If time permits, a spokesperson from each group should list on the board the issues involved and the group's recommendations.

An Organizing Question on Campus[63]

Art Tipton is a human resources director of Pierce University, a private university located in a large urban city. Ruth Ann Zimmer, a supervisor in the maintenance and housekeeping services division of the university, has just come into your office to discuss her situation. Zimmer's division of the university is responsible for maintaining and cleaning physical facilities of the university. Zimmer is one of the department supervisors who supervises employees who maintain and clean on-campus dormitories.

In the next several minutes, Zimmer proceeds to express her concerns about a union-organizing campaign that has begun among her employees. According to Zimmer, a representative of the Service Workers Union has met with a number of the employees, urging them to sign union authorization cards. She has observed several of her employees "cornering" other employees to talk to them about joining the union and urge them to sign union authorization (or representation) cards. Zimmer even observed this during the working hours as employees were going about their normal duties in the dormitories. Zimmer reports that a number of her employees have come to her asking for her opinions about the union. They reported to her that several other supervisors in the department had told their employees not to sign any union authorization cards and not to talk about the union at any time while they were on campus. Zimmer also reports that one of her fellow supervisors told his employees in a meeting that anyone who was caught talking about the union or signing a union authorization card would be disciplined and perhaps terminated.

Zimmer says that the employees are very dissatisfied with their wages and many of the conditions that they have endured from students, supervisors, and other staff people. She says that several employees told her that they had signed union cards because they believed that the only way university administration would pay attention to their concerns was if the employees had a union to represent them. Zimmer says that she made a list of employees whom she felt had joined or were interested in the union, and she could share these with Tipton if he wanted to deal with them personally. Zimmer closes her presentation with the comment that she and other department supervisors need to know what they should do in order to stomp out the threat of unionization in their department.

TAKE IT TO THE WEB

 For Internet exercises, updates to chapter material, and more, visit the Dessler Web site at

www.prenhall.com/dessler

ENDNOTES

1. Nicole Harris, "Flying Into a Rage?" *Business Week* (April 27, 1998): 119.
2. *Ibid.*, p. 119.
3. "Union Numbers Up, but Membership Rate Down Again," *BNA Bulletin to Management* (February 4, 1999): 37.
4. "Union Membership Falls Again in 1997," *BNA Bulletin to Management* (February 26, 1998): 61; see also Sharon Leonard, "Union Could be Staging a Comeback," *HRMagazine* (December 1999): 207.
5. *Ibid.*, p. 61.
6. "Union Membership by State and Industry," *BNA Bulletin to Management* (May 29, 1997): 172–73.
7. "Union Membership Around the World," *BNA Bulletin to Management* (November 13, 1997): 364–65.
8. Stephen Greenhouse, "Labor, Revitalized with New Recruiting, Has Regained Power and Prestige," *New York Times* (October 9, 1999): A10.
9. "Union Membership and Earnings," pp. 52–53.
10. Michael E. Gordon and Angelo DeNis, "An Examination of the Relationship Between Union Membership and Job Satisfaction," *Industrial and Labor Relations Review* 48, no. 2 (January 1995): 222–36.
11. Ann Zimmerman, "Pro-Union Butchers at Wal-Mart Win a Union Battle but Lose War," *Wall Street Journal* (April 11, 2000): A14.
12. Based on Richard Hodgetts, *Introduction to Business* (Reading, MA: Addison-Wesley, 1977), pp. 213–14. See also Benjamin Taylor and Fred Witney, Labor Relations Law (Englewood Cliffs, NJ: Prentice Hall, 1992): 157–84.
13. "Boardroom Reports," *The Conference Board*, New York, December 15, 1976, p. 6. See also "Perspectives on Employment," *Research Bulletin #194, The Conference Board* (1986).
14. The following material is based on Arthur Sloane and Fred Witney, *Labor Relations* (Englewood Cliffs, NJ: Prentice Hall, 2001), pp. 63–120.
15. *Ibid.*, p. 106.
16. Karen Robinson, "Temp Workers Gain Union Access," *HR News*, Society for Human Resource Management 19, no. 10 (October 2000): 1.
17. "Union Membership by State and Industry," *BNA Bulletin to Management* (May 29, 1997): 172–73.

18. Sloane and Witney, *Labor Relations*, pp. 102–106.

19. See William J. Glueck, "Labor Relations and the Supervisor," in M. Jean Newport, *Supervisory Management: Tools and Techniques* (St. Paul, MN: West, 1976), pp. 207–34. See also "Big Labor Tries the Soft Sell," *Business Week* (October 13, 1986): 126.

20. William Fulmer, "Step by Step Through a Union Election," *Harvard Business Review* 60 (July/August 1981): 94–102. For an interesting description of contract negotiations, see Peter Cramton and Joseph Tracy, "The Determinants of U.S. Labor Disputes," *Journal of Labor Economics* 12, no. 2 (April 1994): 180–209.

21. "Desktop Organizers: Unions Gained Access to Workers Via Employers' E-Mail Systems," *BNA Bulletin to Management* (September 30, 1999): 305.

22. Jonathan Segal, "Expose the Unions Underbelly," *HR Magazine* (June 1999): 166–76.

23. *Labor Relations Consultants: Issues, Trends, Controversies* (Rockville, MD: Bureau of National Affairs, 1985), p. 7.

24. For a discussion, see Cory Fine, "Beware the Trojan Horse," *Workforce* (May 1998): 45– 51.

25. Fulmer, "Step by Step Through a Union Election," p. 94. See also "An Employer May Rebut Union Misrepresentations," *BNA Bulletin to Management* (January 16, 1986): 17.

26. Frederick Sullivan, "Limiting Union Organizing Activity Through Supervisors," *Personnel* 55 (July/August 1978): 55–65. Richard Peterson, Thomas Lee, and Barbara Finnegan, "Strategies and Tactics in Union Organizing Campaigns," *Industrial Relations* 31, no. 2 (spring 1992): 370–81. See also Alan Story, "Employer Speech, Union Representation Elections, and the First Amendment," *Berkeley Journal of Employment and Labor Law* 16, no. 2 (1995): 356–457.

27. Sullivan, "Limiting Union Activity Through Supervisors," p. 60.

28. *Ibid.*, pp. 62–65.

29. "Union Access to Employer's Customers Restricted," *BNA Bulletin to Management* (February 15, 1996): 49; "Workplace Access for Unions Hinges on Legal Issues," *BNA Bulletin to Management* (April 11, 1996): 113.

30. B&D Plastics, Inc. 302 NLRB No. 33, 1971, 137 LRRM 1039; discussed in "No Such Things as a Quote Free Lunch," *BNA Bulletin to Management* (May 23, 1991): 153–54.

31. "Unions Decertifications up in First Half of 1998," *BNA Bulletin to Management* (December 24, 1998): 406.

32. BNA Bulletin to Management, *"Fewer Elections, Same Result in Win Rate for 1999"* (June 1, 2000).

33. William Fulmer, "When Employees Want to Oust Their Union," *Harvard Business Review*, 56 (March/April 1978): 163–70; Francis T. Coleman, "Once a Union, Not Always a Union," *Personnel Journal* 64, no. 3 (March 1985): 42–45. See also "Decertification: Fulfilling Unions Destiny?" *Personnel Journal* 66 (June 1987): 144–48.

34. Fulmer, "When Employees Want to Oust Their Union," p. 167. See also David Meyer and Trevor Bain, "Union Decertification Election Outcomes: Bargaining Unit Characteristics and Union Resources," *Journal of Labor Research* 15, no. 2 (spring 1994): 117–36.

35. Dale Yoder, *Personnel Management* (Englewood Cliffs, NJ: Prentice Hall, 1972), p. 486. See also Michael Ballot, *Labor-Management Relations in a Changing Environment* (New York: Wiley, 1992), pp. 169–425.

36. Boulwareism is the name given to a strategy, now generally held in disfavor, by which the company, based on an exhaustive study of what it thought its employees wanted, made but one offer at the bargaining table and then refused to bargain any further unless convinced by the union on the basis of new facts that its original position was wrong. The NLRB subsequently found that the practice of offering the same settlement to all units, insisting that certain parts of the package could not differ among agreements, and com-

municating to the employees about how negotiations were going amounted to an illegal pattern. John Fossum, *Labor Relations* (Dallas, TX: Business Publications, 1982), p. 267. See also William Cooke, Aneil Mishra, Gretchen Spreitzer, and Mary Tschirhart, "The Determinants of NLRB Decision-Making Revisited," *Industrial and Labor Relations Review* 48, no. 2 (January 1995): 237–57.

37. Commerce Clearing House, "Drug Testing/Court Rulings," *Ideas and Trends* (January 25, 1988): 16.

38. Bargaining items based on Reed-Richardson, *Collective Bargaining by Objectives* (Englewood Cliffs, NJ: Prentice Hall, 1997), pp. 113–15; bargaining stages based on William Glueck, "Labor Relations and the Supervisor," in M. Gene Newport, *Supervisory Management* (St. Paul, MN: West, 1976); pp. 200–34; and Sloane and Witney, *op. cit.*, pp. 214–56.

39. Yoder, *Personnel Management*, pp. 517–18.

40. Fossum, *Labor Relations*, pp. 298–322.

41. Although considerable research has been done on the subject, it's not clear what sorts of situations precipitate impasses. At times, however, it seems that the prospect of having the impasse taken to an arbitrator actually "chills" the negotiation process. Specifically, if neither the union nor the management negotiators want to make the tough choices, they might consciously or unconsciously opt to declare an impasse knowing that the arbitrator will then have to take the heat. See Linda Babcock and Craig Olson, "The Causes of Impasses in Labor Disputes," *Industrial Relations* 31, no. 2 (spring 1992): 348–60.

42. Richardson, *Collective Bargaining*, p. 150.

43. Fossum, *Labor Relations*, p. 312. See also Thomas Watkins, "Assessing Arbitrator Competence," *Arbitration Journal* 47, no. 2 (June 1992): 43–48.

44. *Ibid.*, p. 317. See also "Number of Major Strikes and Lockouts Hit New Low in 1997," *BNA Bulletin to Management* (March 12, 1998): 77.

45. For a discussion see Herbert Northrup, "Union Corporate Campaigns and Inside Games as a Strike Form," *Employee Relations Law Journal* 19, no. 4 (spring 1994): 507–49.

46. *Ibid.*, p. 513.

47. *Ibid.*, p. 518.

48. For a discussion of the cost of a strike, see Woodruff Imberman, "Strikes Cost More Than You Think," *Harvard Business Review* 57 (May/June 1979): 133–38. The NLRB held in 1986 in Charter Equipment, Inc., 280 NLRB No. 71, that an employer could lawfully hire temporary replacements during the course of a lockout, in the absence of proof of specific antiunion motivation, in order to bring economic pressure to bear upon a union to support a legitimate bargaining position.

49. Clifford Koen Jr., Sondra Hartmen, and Dinah Payne, "The NLRB Wields a Rejuvenated Weapon," *Personnel Journal* (December 1996): 85–87.

50. Robert Sauer and Keith Voelker, *Labor Relations: Structure and Process* (New York: Macmillan, 1993), pp. 510–25.

51. *Ibid.*, p. 516. See also Marino Regini, "Human Resource Management and Industrial Relations in European Companies," *International Journal of Human Resource Management* 4, no. 3 (September 1993): 555–68.

52. Quoted from *ibid.*, 559.

53. "AFL-CIO Launching New Strategy to Win Over Nonunion Workers," *Compensation and Benefits Review* 18, no. 5 (September/October 1986): 8; Shane R. Premeaux, R. Wayne Moody, and Art Bethke, "Decertification: Fulfilling Unions' 'Destiny'?" *Personnel Journal* 66, no. 6 (June 1987): 144; and Peter A. Susser, "The Labor Impact of Deregulation," *Employment Relations Today* 13, no. 2 (summer 1986): 117–23.

54. "The Battle for Corporate Control," *Business Week* (May 18, 1987): 107.

55. Sar Levitan and Frank Gallo, "Collective Bargaining and Private Sector Employment," *Monthly Labor Review* (September 1989): 24–33; Charles Craver, "The American Labor Movement in the Year 2000," *Business Horizons* (November/December 1993): 64–69; and Barbara Ettoree, "Will Unions Survive?" *Management Review* (August 1993): 9–15; and Stephanie Overman, "Unions Demand a Voice," *HRMagazine* 42, no. 7 (July 1992): 112–18; Bill Leonard, "The New Fact of Organized Labor," *HRMagazine* (July 1999): 56.

56. "Contracts Call for Greater Labor Management Teamwork," *BNA Bulletin to Management* (April 29, 1999): 133.

57. John Nee, Pamela Kennedy, and Donald Langham, "Increasing Manufacturing Effectiveness Through Joint Union/Management Cooperation," *Human Resource Management* 38, no. 1 (spring 1999): 77–85.

58. Based on Kenneth Jenero and Christopher Lyons, "Employee Participation Programs: Prudent or Prohibited?" *Employee Relations Law Journal* 17, no. 4 (spring 1992): 535–66. See also Edward Cohen-Rosenthal and Cynthia Burton, "Improving Organizational Quality by Forging the Best Union-Management Relationship," *National Productivity Review* 13, no. 2 (spring 1994): 215–31.

59. "Union Fights Team Program at UPS," *BNA Bulletin to Management* (March 14, 1996): 88.

60. Jenero and Lyons, "Employee Participation Programs," p. 539.

61. This case incident and all quotes are based on Ronald Lieber, "Bob Crandall's Boo-Boos," *Fortune* (April 28, 1997): 365–68.

62. *Ibid.*, p. 367.

63. Raymond L. Hilgert and Cyril C. Ling, *Cases and Experiential Exercises in Human Resource Management* (Upper Saddle River, NJ: Prentice Hall, 1996), pp. 291–92.

Managing Careers and Fair Treatment

When you finish studying this chapter, you should be able to:

■ *Explain* in detail techniques for building two-way communications in organizations.

■ *Discuss* in detail how to discipline employees.

■ *Define* wrongful discharge and explain its importance.

■ *List* important HR considerations in adjusting to downsizings and managing careers.

INTRODUCTION

Under the federal **plant closing law**, large employers generally must give employees 60 days' notice before closing a facility or starting a layoff of 50 or more people. But when Levi Strauss announced a few years ago that it was firing almost 7,000 factory workers in North America and shutting 11 of its factories, it went far beyond giving 60 days' notice.[1] Among other things, Levi's gave its workers eight months' notice, agreed to spend $31,000 on each to help them find jobs, and agreed that even those laid off would get a bonus of one year's pay if Levi's meets various financial targets by 2001. Some critics think that Levi's CEO, Robert Haas, is being too soft. Haas believes that employees are the core of any company and that treating them unfairly is just short-sighted. At least one business writer agrees: "In an age where human capital is becoming increasingly important, it is hard to believe that [Robert Haas] has it wrong."[2]

THE BUILDING BLOCKS OF FAIRNESS

Why Treat Employees Fairly?

Two researchers writing in *Harvard Business Review* answer that question this way:

> Never has the idea of fair process been more important for managers than it is today. Fair process turns out to be a powerful management tool for companies struggling to make the transition from a production-based to a knowledge-based company, in which value creation depends increasingly on ideas and innovation. Fair process profoundly influences attitudes and behaviors critical to high performance. It builds trust and unlocks ideas. With it, managers can achieve even the most painful and difficult goals while gaining the voluntary cooperation of the employees affected. Without fair process, even outcomes that employees might favor can be difficult to achieve.[3]

Treating employees fairly is therefore not just for altruists. Instead, it makes sense for employers to be fair, for several reasons. For one thing, an increasingly litigious workforce makes it almost a necessity that employers institute disciplinary and discharge procedures that will survive the scrutiny of arbitrators and the courts. Employees who believe they're being treated fairly also seem more willing to "go the extra mile" in carrying out their jobs.[4] Studies suggest that large, centralized organizations may have to work particularly hard to institute procedures that make the workplace seem fair to employees.[5]

How do you measure "fair treatment" in practice? In practice, fair treatment reflects underlying elements such as "employees are trusted," "employees are treated with respect," and "employees are treated fairly"(see Figure 9.1).[6]

Workplace unfairness can be blatant. For example, some supervisors are "workplace bullies," yelling or ridiculing subordinates, humiliating them, and sometimes even implying threats. Such extreme behavior should of course be prohibited, and many firms have general anti-harassment policies. For example, the policy at the Oregon Department of Transportation is that "it is the policy of the department that all employees, customers, contractors and visitors to the work site are entitled to a positive, respectful and productive work environment, free from behavior, actions, language constituting workplace harassment."[7] Not surprisingly, employees of abusive supervisors are more likely to quit their jobs, and to report lower job and life satisfaction and higher stress if they remain in those jobs.[8]

How can HR systems and policies enhance the perceived fairness of an organization? Actions include building two-way communications, implementing "guaranteed fair treatment" employee discipline processes, protecting employees' privacy, and doing a better job of managing career-related matters including dismissals. We'll address these topics in this chapter.

BUILDING TWO-WAY COMMUNICATIONS

Whether you are an irate customer, student, or employee, having the other person listen to what you're saying helps signal that you've been treated fairly. For example,

What is your organization like most of the time? Circle YES if the item describes your organization, NO if it does not describe your organization, and ? if you cannot decide.

IN THIS ORGANIZATION . . .

1. Employees are praised for good work. . . . . .Yes	?	No
2. Supervisors yell at employees (R)[a]. . . . . .Yes	?	No
3. Supervisors play favorites (R)[a]. . . . . .Yes	?	No
4. Employees are trusted[a]. . . . . .Yes	?	No
5. Employees' complaints are dealt with effectively[a]. . . . . .Yes	?	No
6. Employees are treated like children (R)[a]. . . . . .Yes	?	No
7. Employees are treated with respect[a]. . . . . .Yes	?	No
8. Employees' questions and problems are responded to quickly[a]. . . . . . . Yes	?	No
9. Employees are lied to (R)[a]. . . . . .Yes	?	No
10. Employees' suggestions are ignored (R)[a] . . . . Yes	?	No
11. Supervisors swear at employees (R)[a]. . . . . Yes	?	No
12. Employees' hard work is appreciated[a]. . . . . Yes	?	No
13. Supervisors threaten to fire or lay off employees (R). . . . . Yes	?	No
14. Employees are treated fairly[a]. . . . . .Yes	?	No
15. Co-workers help each other out . . . . .Yes	?	No
16. Co-workers argue with each other (R) . . . . Yes	?	No
17. Co-workers put each other down (R) . . . . .Yes	?	No
18. Co-workers treat each other with respect[a] . . . . .Yes	?	No

Note: R = the item is reverse scored.
[a]Item included in the 12-item version of the scale administered to the midwestern university.

FIGURE 9.1 Perceptions of Fair Interpersonal Treatment Scale

Source: Michelle A. Donovan et al., "The Perceptions of Their Interpersonal Treatment Scale: Development and Validation of a Measure of Interpersonal Treatment in the Workplace," *Journal of Applied Psychology* 83, no. 5 (1998): 692. Copyright © (1997) by Michelle A. Donovan, Fritz Drasgow, and Liberty J. Munson at the University of Illinois at Urbana-Champaign. All rights reserved.

two researchers found that at least three principles contributed to perceived fairness in business settings: *engagement* (involving individuals in the decisions that affect them by asking for their input and allowing them to refute the merits of one another's ideas and assumptions); *explanation* (ensuring that everyone involved and affected should understand why final decisions are made as they are and of the thinking that underlies the decisions); and *expectation clarity* (making sure everyone knows up front by what standards they will be judged and the penalties for failure).[9] Given communication's link to fairness, many firms have established programs like those described next to foster communications.

"Speak Up!" Programs

Some programs aim to encourage upward communications. In other words, they aim to encourage employees to "speak up" about concerns that run the gamut from malfunctioning vending machines to unlit parking lots to a manager spending too much of the department's money on travel.

Toyota Motor Manufacturing company in Lexington, Kentucky, is one example. At Toyota a hotline gives Toyota employee-team members an anonymous method of bringing questions or problems to management's attention. The hotline is available 24 hours per day. Employees are instructed to pick up any phone, dial the hotline extension (the number is posted on the plant bulletin boards), and deliver their messages to the recorder. Toyota guarantees that all hotline inquiries will be reviewed by the HR manager and thoroughly investigated.

What's Your Opinion?

Many firms also administer periodic **opinion surveys**: The FedEx Survey Feedback Action (SFA) program is typical. SFA includes an anonymous survey that lets employees express feelings about the company and their managers, and to some extent about service, pay, and benefits. Each manager then has an opportunity to discuss the anonymous department results with his or her subordinates, and thus design a blueprint for improving work group commitment. Sample questions include:

> I can tell my manager what I think.
>
> My manager tells me what is expected.
>
> My manager listens to my concerns.
>
> My manager keeps me informed.
>
> Upper management listens to ideas from my level.
>
> FedEx does a good job for the customers.
>
> In my environment we use safe work practices.
>
> I am paid fairly for this kind of work.

Top-Down Programs

Saturn uses several **top-down programs** to get data to all employees. "The communication is excellent," says one assembler. "We get information continuously via the internal television network, and from financial documents." One union leader says, "We have 'town hall' meetings once per month and usually have at least 500 to 700 people attending. That plus the broadcasts usually make sure that everyone's knowledge base is up—you better know the facts if you want to work here."[10]

The process aims to build trust: "They must trust you to do the job," says one Saturn employee," and they therefore trust you with a lot of confidential information, for instance, on the financials of our firm. They tell you 'here is the problem, what would you do about it?' "

EMPLOYEE DISCIPLINE AND PRIVACY

Handling Grievances

The potential for grievances and discontent is always present at work. Just about any factor involving wages, hours, or conditions of employment has and will be used as the basis of a grievance in most firms. Discipline cases and seniority problems (including promotions, transfers, and layoffs) would probably top the list. Others would include grievances growing out of job evaluations and work assignments, overtime, vacations, incentive plans, and holidays.

Whatever the source of grievances, many firms today (and virtually all unionized ones) give employees channels through which to air grievances. Grievance procedures help ensure that employees' grievances are heard and treated fairly, and unionized firms don't hold a monopoly on fair treatment. Even in nonunionized firms, such procedures can help ensure that labor–management peace prevails.

In unionized companies, grievance handling is often called *contract administration* because no labor contract can ever be so complete that it covers all contingencies and answers all questions. (For example, suppose the contract says you can discharge an employee only for "just cause." You subsequently discharge someone for speaking back to you in harsh terms. Was it within your rights to discharge this person? Was speaking back to you harshly "just cause"?)

Problems like this are usually handled and settled through the labor contract's grievance procedure. The procedure provides an orderly system whereby employer and union determine whether the contract has been violated.[11] It is the vehicle for administering the contract on a day-to-day basis. This day-to-day collective bargaining should involve interpretation only; it usually does not involve negotiating new terms or altering existing ones.[12]

Grievance procedures are typically multistep processes. For example, the grievant might first be required to work out an agreement with his or her supervisor, perhaps with a union officer or colleague present. Appeals may then be taken successively to the supervisor's boss, then that person's boss, and perhaps finally to a special master or arbitrator.

Guidelines for Handling Grievances   The best way to handle a grievance is to develop a work environment in which grievances don't occur in the first place:[13] Doing so depends first on your ability to recognize, diagnose, and correct the causes of potential employee dissatisfaction (causes such as unfair appraisals, inequitable wages, or poor communications) before they become formal grievances. Some guidelines for handling a grievance should one occur are presented in the *HR in Practice* box.

The FedEx Guaranteed Fair Treatment Program

Grievance procedures aren't limited to unionized firms. In fact, (nonunionized) FedEx's **guaranteed fair treatment** program goes beyond most grievance procedures: Special, easily available forms make filing the grievance easy, employees are encouraged to use the system, and the highest levels of top management are routinely involved in reviewing complaints.

Steps   The FedEx guaranteed fair treatment procedure includes three steps. In step 1, *management review*, the complainant submits a written complaint to a member of management (manager, senior manager, or managing director) within seven calendar days of the occurrence of the eligible issue. Then the manager, senior manager, and managing director of the employee's group review all relevant information; hold a telephone conference and/or meeting with the complainant; make a decision to either uphold, modify, or overturn management's action; and communicate their decision in writing to the complainant and the department's personnel representative.

In step 2, *officer complaint*, the complainant submits a written appeal to an officer (vice president or senior vice president) of the division within seven calendar days of the step 1 decision. The vice president and senior vice president then review all rele-

DO

- Investigate and handle each and every case as though it may eventually result in an arbitration hearing.
- Talk with the employee about his or her grievance; give the person a good and full hearing.
- Require the union to identify specific contractual provisions allegedly violated.
- Comply with the contractual time limits of the company for handling the grievance.
- Visit the work area of the grievance.
- Determine whether there were any witnesses.
- Examine the grievant's personnel record.
- Fully examine prior grievance records.
- Treat the union representative as your equal.
- Hold your grievance discussion privately.
- Fully inform your own supervisor of grievance matters.

DON'T

- Discuss the case with the union steward alone—the grievant should definitely be there.
- Make arrangements with individual employees that are inconsistent with the labor agreement.
- Hold back the remedy if the company is wrong.
- Admit to the binding effect of a past practice.
- Relinquish to the union your rights as a manager.
- Settle grievances on the basis of what is "fair." Instead, stick to the labor agreement, which should be your only standard.
- Bargain over items not covered by the contract.
- Treat as subject to arbitration claims demanding the discipline or discharge of managers.
- Give long, written grievance answers.
- Trade a grievance settlement for a grievance withdrawal (or try to make up for a bad decision in one grievance by bending over backward in another).
- Deny grievances on the premise that your "hands have been tied by management."
- Agree to informal amendments in the contract.

vant information; conduct an additional investigation, when necessary; make a decision to either uphold, overturn, or modify management's action, or initiate a board of review; and communicate their decision in writing to the complainant with copies to the department's personnel representative and the complainant's management.

Finally, in step 3, *executive appeals review*, the complainant submits a written complaint within seven calendar days of the step 2 decision to the employee relations department. This department then investigates and prepares a case file for the executive review appeals board. The appeals board—the CEO, the COO, the chief personnel officer, and three senior vice presidents—then reviews all relevant information and makes a decision to uphold, overturn, or initiate a board of review or to take other appropriate action.

Fairness in Disciplining

The purpose of **discipline** is to encourage employees to behave sensibly at work (where *sensible* is defined as adhering to rules and regulations). In an organization, rules and regulations serve about the same purpose that laws do in society; discipline is called for when one of these rules or regulations is violated.[15] A fair and just discipline process is based on three pillars: rules and regulations, a system of progressive penalties, and an appeals process.

A set of clear rules and regulations is the first pillar. These rules address issues such as theft, destruction of company property, drinking on the job, and insubordination. Examples of rules include:

> *Poor performance is not acceptable.* Each employee is expected to perform his or her work properly and efficiently and to meet established standards of quality.

> *Alcohol and drugs do not mix with work.* The use of either during working hours and reporting for work under the influence of either are both strictly prohibited.

> *The vending of anything in the plant without authorization is not allowed, nor is gambling in any form permitted.*

The purpose of these rules is to inform employees ahead of time what is and is not acceptable behavior. Employees must be told, preferably in writing, what is not permitted. This is usually done during the employee's orientation. The rules and regulations are usually listed in the employee orientation handbook.

A system of progressive penalties is a second pillar of effective discipline. Penalties may range from oral warnings to written warnings to suspension from the job to discharge. The severity of the penalty is usually a function of the type of offense and the number of times the offense has occurred. For example, most companies issue warnings for the first unexcused lateness. However, for a fourth offense, discharge is the usual disciplinary action.

Finally, an appeals process should be part of the disciplinary process; this helps to ensure that discipline is meted out fairly and is equitable. Discipline guidelines are summarized in the *HR in Practice* box.

Discipline without Punishment

Traditional discipline has two major potential flaws. First, no one ever feels good about being punished (although fairness guidelines like those previously mentioned can take the edge off this). A second shortcoming is that forcing your rules on employees may gain their short-term compliance, but not their cooperation when you are not around to enforce the rules.

Discipline without punishment (or nonpunitive discipline) is aimed at avoiding

Discipline Guidelines

- *Make sure the evidence supports the charge of employee wrongdoing.* In one study, "the employer's evidence did not support the charge of employee wrongdoing" was the reason arbitrators gave most often for reinstating discharged employees or for reducing disciplinary suspensions.[16]
- *Ensure that the employees' due process rights are protected.* Arbitrators normally reverse discharges and suspensions that are imposed in a manner that violates basic notions of fairness or employee due process procedures.[17] For example, follow established progressive discipline procedures, and don't deny the employee an opportunity to tell his or her side of the story.[18]
- *The discipline should be in line with the way management usually responds to similar incidents.*[19]
- *Adequately warn the employee of the disciplinary consequences of his or her alleged misconduct.*
- *The rule that allegedly was violated should be "reasonably related" to the efficient and safe operation of the particular work environment.* Employees, in other words, are usually allowed by arbitrators to question the reason behind any rule or order.
- *Management must fairly and adequately investigate the matter before administering discipline.*
- *The investigation should produce substantial evidence of misconduct.*
- *Applicable rules, orders, or penalties should be applied evenhandedly and without discrimination.*
- *The penalty should be reasonably related to the misconduct and to the employee's past work history.*
- *Maintain the employee's right to counsel.* All union employees have the right to bring help when they are called in for an interview that they reasonably believe might result in disciplinary action.[20]
- *Don't rob your subordinate of his or her dignity.*[21] Discipline your subordinate in private (unless he or she requests counsel).
- *Remember that the burden of proof is on you.* In U.S. society, a person is always considered innocent until proven guilty.
- *Get the facts.* Don't base your decision on hearsay evidence or on your general impression.
- *Don't act while angry.* Very few people can be objective and sensible when they are angry.

these disciplinary problems. This is accomplished by gaining the employees' acceptance of your rules and by reducing the punitive nature of the discipline itself. In summary[22]:

1. *Issue an oral reminder.* As a supervisor, your goal is to get the employee to agree to solve the problem.
2. *Should another incident arise within six weeks, issue the employee a formal written reminder, a copy of which is placed in the personnel file.* In addition, privately hold a second discussion with the employee, again without any threats.

3. *Give a paid one-day "decision-making leave."* If another incident occurs after the written warning in the next six weeks or so, the employee is told to take a one-day leave with pay to stay home and consider whether the job is right for him or her and whether he or she wants to abide by the company's rules. When the employee returns to work, he or she meets with you and gives you a decision regarding whether he or she will follow the rules.
4. *If no further incidents occur in the next year or so, the one-day paid suspension is purged from the person's file.* If the behavior is repeated, dismissal (see later discussion) is required.[23]

The process must of course be changed in exceptional circumstances. Criminal behavior or in-plant fighting might be grounds for immediate dismissal, for instance. And if several incidents occurred at very close intervals, step 2—the written warning—might be skipped.

Electronic Trespassing and Employee Privacy

Electronic monitoring and searches of employees have become quite widespread. For example, in a survey of 906 companies by the American Management Association, 35% said they've recorded employees' telephone calls or voice mail, checked computer files and electronic mail, or videotaped employees' performance.[24] At least half the companies recently surveyed track individual employees' Internet connections; many (such as the *New York Times*, which fired 23 employees for mailing each other off-color messages) punish e-mail policy offenders.[25]

Electronic eavesdropping is legal—at least to a point. For example, federal law and most states' laws allow employers to monitor their employees' phone calls "in the ordinary course of business," according to one legal expert, but they must stop listening once it becomes clear that a conversation is personal rather than business related.[26] E-mail service can also apparently be (and is) intercepted under federal law when it is to protect the property rights of the provider.[27] However, just to be safe, more employers today are issuing e-mail and on-line services usage policies to, for instance, forewarn employees that those systems are intended to be used for business purposes only. They are having employees sign e-mail monitoring and telephone monitoring acknowledgment statements like the one in Figure 9.2. One reason for explicit policy statements is the risk that employers may be held liable for illegal acts committed by their employees via e-mail: For example, messages sent by supervisors that contain sexual innuendo or ones defaming an employee can cause problems for the employer if the employer hasn't taken steps to prohibit such e-mail system misuse.[28]

Videotaping in the workplace seems to call for more legal caution. In one case, one U.S. Court of Appeals ruled that an employer's continuous video surveillance of employees in an office setting did not constitute an unconstitutional invasion of privacy.[29] Yet, a Boston employer recently had to pay over $200,000 to five workers it secretly videotaped in an employee locker room, after they sued in state court.[30]

MANAGING DISMISSALS

Dismissal is the most drastic disciplinary step and one that must be taken with deliberate care.[31] Specifically, the dismissal should be *just* in that sufficient cause exists for it. Furthermore, the dismissal should occur only after all reasonable steps to

I understand that my telephone and e-mail communications will be monitored periodically by my supervisor and other [Company] management staff. I understand that the purpose of this monitoring is to improve:

- The quality of customer service provided to policyholders and prospective customers
- My product knowledge and presentation skills

_____
Signature   Date

_____
Print Name   Department

FIGURE 9.2   Sample Monitoring Acknowledgment Statement

Source: Reprinted with permission from *Bulletin to Management* (*BNA Policy and Practice Series*) 48, no. 14, Part II, p. 7 (April 3, 1997). Copyright 1997 by The Bureau of National Affairs, Inc. (800-372-1033), http://www.bna.com.

rehabilitate or salvage the employee have failed. However, there are undoubtedly times when dismissal is required, perhaps at once, and in these instances it should be carried out forthrightly.[32]

Of course, the best way to "handle" a dismissal is to avoid it in the first place, when possible. Many dismissals start with bad hiring decisions. Using sound selection practices including assessment tests, reference and background checks, drug testing, and clearly defined jobs can reduce the need for many dismissals.[33]

For more than 100 years, the prevailing rule in the United States has been that without an employment contract, either the employer or the employee can **terminate at will** the employment relationship. In other words, the employee could resign for any reason, at will, and the employer could similarly dismiss an employee for any reason, at will. Today, however, dismissed employees are increasingly taking their cases to court, and in many cases employers are finding that they no longer have a blanket right to fire. Instead, federal equal employment opportunity and other laws and various state laws and court rulings increasingly limit management's right to dismiss employees at will.

Grounds for Dismissal

There are four bases for dismissal: unsatisfactory performance, misconduct, lack of qualifications for the job, and changed requirements of (or elimination of) the job. *Unsatisfactory performance* may be defined as a persistent failure to perform assigned duties or to meet prescribed standards on the job.[34] Specific reasons include excessive absenteeism, tardiness, a persistent failure to meet normal job requirements, or an adverse attitude toward the company, supervisor, or fellow employees. *Misconduct* can be defined as deliberate and willful violation of the employer's rules and may include stealing, rowdy behavior, and insubordination. *Lack of qualifications* for the job is defined as an employee's inability to do the assigned work although he or she is diligent. Because in this case the employee may be trying to do the job, it is especially important that every effort be made to salvage him or her—perhaps by assigning the employee to another job, or training the person. *Changed requirements of the job* may be defined as an employee's incapability of doing the work assigned after the nature of the job has been changed. Similarly, an employee may have to be dismissed when his or her job is eliminated. Again, the employee may be industrious, so every effort should be made to retrain or transfer this person, if possible.

Insubordination, a form of misconduct, is sometimes the grounds for dismissal. Stealing, chronic tardiness, and poor-quality work are fairly concrete grounds for dismissal, but insubordination is sometimes harder to translate into words. To that end, it may be useful to remember that some acts are or should be considered insubordinate whenever and wherever they occur. These include, for instance, direct disregard of the boss's authority, and disobedience of, or refusal to obey, the boss's orders—particularly in front of others.

Dismissing employees is never easy, but at least the employer can try to ensure the process is perceived as fair. One recent study found, for instance, that "individuals who reported that they were given full explanations of why and how termination decisions were made were more likely to (1) perceive their layoff as fair, (2) endorse the terminating organization, and (3) indicate that they did not wish to take the past employer to court.[35]

Avoiding Wrongful Discharge Suits

Wrongful discharge occurs when an employee's dismissal does not comply with the law or with the contractual arrangement stated or implied by the firm via its employment application forms, employee manuals, or other promises. The time to protect against such suits is before mistakes have been made and suits have been filed.

Avoiding wrongful discharge suits requires at least a two-prong strategy. First is to follow employment policies and dispute resolution procedures (such as those outlined in this chapter) that make employees feel that they are treated fairly.[36] People who are fired and who walk away with the feeling that they've been embarrassed, stripped of their dignity, or treated unfairly financially (for instance, in terms of severance pay) are more likely to seek retribution in the courts. There is probably no way to make a termination pleasant, but an employer's first line of defense is to at least make sure it is fair.

The second way to avoid wrongful discharge suits is to lay the groundwork— starting with the employment application—that will help avoid such suits before they get started. Steps to take include the following:

- Have applicants sign the employment application and make sure it contains a clearly worded statement that employment is for no fixed term and that the employer can terminate at any time. In addition, the statement should inform the job candidate that "nothing on this application can be changed."
- Review your employee manual to look for and delete statements that could prejudice your defense in a wrongful discharge case. For example, delete any reference to the fact that "employees can be terminated only for just cause" (unless you really mean that).
- Have clear written rules listing infractions that may require discipline and discharge, and then make sure to follow the rules.
- If a rule is broken, get the worker's side of the story in front of witnesses, and preferably get it signed. Then make sure to check out the story, getting both sides of the issue.
- Be sure that employees are appraised at least annually. If an employee shows evidence

of incompetence, give that person a warning and provide an opportunity to improve. All evaluations should be put in writing and signed by the employee.[37]

■ Keep careful confidential records of all actions such as employee appraisals, warnings or notices, memos outlining how improvement should be accomplished, and so on.

■ A 10-step checklist to prevent exposure to wrongful discharge litigation would include: (1) Is employee covered by any type of written agreement, including a collective bargaining agreement? (2) Have written or oral representations been made to form a contract? (3) Is a defamation claim likely? (4) Is there a possible discrimination allegation? (5) Is there any workers' compensation involvement? (6) Have reasonable rules and regulations been communicated and enforced? (7) Has employee been given an opportunity to explain any rule violations or to correct poor performance? (8) Have all monies been paid within 24 hours after separation? (9) Has employee been advised of his or her rights under COBRA? (10) Has employee been advised of what the employee will tell a prospective employer in response to a reference inquiry?[38]

If humanitarianism and wrongful discharge suits aren't enough to encourage you to be fair in dismissing, consider this: One study found that managers run double their usual risk of suffering a heart attack during the week after they fire an employee.[39] Between 1989 and 1994, physicians interviewed 791 working people who had just undergone heart attacks to find out what might have triggered them. The researchers concluded that the stress associated with firing someone doubled the usual risk of a heart attack for the person doing the firing, during the week following the dismissal.

The Termination Interview

Dismissing an employee is one of the most difficult tasks you can face at work.[40] The dismissed employee, even if warned many times in the past, may still react with disbelief or even violence. Guidelines for the **termination interview** itself are as follows:

1. *Plan the interview carefully.* According to experts at Hay Associates, this includes:
   ■ Make sure the employee keeps the appointment time.
   ■ Never inform an employee over the phone.
   ■ Allow 10 minutes as sufficient time for the interview.
   ■ Use a neutral site, never your own office.
   ■ Have employee agreements, the human resource file, and a release announcement (internal and external) prepared in advance.
   ■ Be available at a time after the interview in case questions or problems arise.
   ■ Have phone numbers ready for medical or security emergencies.

2. *Get to the point.* Do not beat around the bush by talking about the weather or making other small talk. As soon as the employee enters your office, give the person a moment to get comfortable and then inform him or her of your decision.

3. *Describe the situation.* Briefly, in three or four sentences, explain why the person is being let go. For instance, "Production in your area is down 4%, and we are continuing to have quality problems. We have talked about these problems several times in the past three months, and the solutions are not being following through. We have to make a change."[41] Remember to describe the situation rather than attack the employee personally by saying things like, "Your production is just not up to par." Also emphasize that the decision is final and irrevocable.

4. *Listen.* Continue the interview until the person appears to be talking freely and reasonably calmly about the reasons for his or her termination and the support package (including severance pay).

5. *Review all elements of the severance package.* Describe severance payments, benefits, access to office support people, and the way references will be handled. However, under no conditions should any promises or benefits beyond those already in the support package be implied.
6. *Identify the next step.* The terminated employee may be disoriented and unsure what to do next. Explain where the employee should go next, upon leaving the interview.

Outplacement Counseling[42]   **Outplacement counseling** is a systematic process by which a terminated person is trained and counseled in the techniques of conducting a self-appraisal and securing a new job that is appropriate to his or her needs and talents.[43] As the term is generally used, *outplacement* does not imply that the employer takes responsibility for placing the terminated person in a new job. Instead it is a counseling service whose purpose is to provide the person with advice, instructions, and a sounding board to help formulate career goals and successfully execute a job search. Outplacement counseling thus might more accurately (but more ponderously) be called "career counseling and job search skills for terminated employees." The outplacement counseling is considered part of the terminated employee's support or severance package.

Outplacement counseling is usually conducted by outplacement firms such as Drake Beam Morin, Inc., or Right Associates, Inc. Managers who are let go typically have office space and secretarial services they can use at local offices of such firms, in addition to the counseling services.

Exit Interviews   Many employers conduct final exit interviews with employees who are leaving the firm. These are usually conducted by the HR department. They aim at eliciting information about the job or related matters that might give the employer a better insight into what is right—or wrong—about the company.

Exit interview questions to ask include: How were you recruited? Why did you join the company? Was the job presented correctly and honestly? Were your expectations met? What was the workplace environment like? What was your supervisor's management style like? What did you like most/least about the company? Were there any special problems areas? Why did you decide to leave, and how was the departure handled?[44]

The assumption, of course, is that because the employee is leaving, he or she will be candid. Based on one survey, though, the quality of information you can expect to get from exit interviews is questionable. The researchers found that at the time of separation, 38% of those leaving blamed salary and benefits, and only 4% blamed supervision. Followed up 18 months later, however, 24% blamed supervision and only 12% blamed salary and benefits. Getting to the real problem during the exit interview may thus require some heavy digging.[45]

MANAGING CAREERS: FROM HIRING TO RETIREMENT

A *career* may be defined as the occupational positions a person has had over many years. Many people look back on their careers with satisfaction, knowing that what they might have achieved they did achieve, and that their career hopes were satisfied. Others are less fortunate and feel that, at least in their careers, their lives and their potential were not fulfilled.

Employers can, of course, have a significant impact on their employees' careers, and thereby on their career satisfaction and success. Recruiting, selecting, placing, training, rewarding, promoting, and separating the employee from the firm all affect the person's career, and therefore his or her career satisfaction and success. Some firms institute relatively formal career management processes—in other words, a process for enabling the employees to better understand and develop their career skills and interests and to use these skills and interests most effectively both within the company and, if necessary, after they leave the firm. Other firms do relatively little.

Software programs are available for improving the organizational career-planning process. For example, *workforce vision* from Criterion, Inc., in Irving, Texas, helps the company analyze an employee's training needs. Clicking on the employee's name launches his or her work history, competencies, career path, and other information. For each competency (such as leadership and customer focus), a "gap analysis" is shown graphically on a bar chart, highlighting the person's strengths and weaknesses. Developmental activities can then be organized around the person's needs.[46]

Managing the Early Steps in the Career Management Process

Employers can take many steps to help make a new employee's introduction to the job more rewarding. Before hiring, realistic job previews can help prospective employees more accurately gauge whether the job is indeed for them, and particularly whether a job's demands are a good fit with a candidate's skills and interests. Especially for recent college graduates, the first job can be crucial for building confidence and a more realistic picture of what he or she can and cannot do: Providing challenging first jobs (rather than relegating new employees to "jobs where they can't do any harm"), as well as an experienced mentor who can help the person learn the ropes, can be important. Some refer to this as preventing *reality shock*, a phenomenon that occurs when a new employee's high expectations and enthusiasm confront the reality of a boring, unchallenging job.

After the person has been on the job for a while, an employer can take many steps to contribute in a positive way to the employee's career. Career-oriented appraisals—in which the manager is trained not just to appraise the employee but to also match the person's strengths and weaknesses with a feasible career path and required development work—is one important step. Similarly, providing periodic, planned job rotation and job pathing can help the person develop a more realistic picture of what he or she is (and is not) good at, and thus the sort of future career moves that might be best. Many employers, such as Saturn Corporation, provide employees with career planning workshops in which they can use tests and similar exercises to learn more about what careers might be best for them.

Formal career development programs don't just benefit the individual employee. For example, Sun Microsystems maintains a career development center staffed by seven certified counselors for helping employees fill in the gaps in their development and to choose internal career opportunities at Sun. The firm believes its program helps explain why their average employee tenure of four years is more than twice what it is estimated to be at other Silicon Valley firms.[47]

Mentoring   Mentoring can have positive effects on the younger person's career, including faster promotions and salary progression and reduced anxiety. Mentoring relationships can be two-edged swords, though. For example, personality problems or an unrealistically high sense of entitlement on the part of the protégé (regarding access to the mentor's time and advice) can adversely affect the mentor and protégé.[48]

Mentors don't have to be formally assigned, and there's evidence that informal mentoring may actually be superior. In one study, protégés with informal mentors reported their mentors provided more career development and support than did those with formal mentors. Employees with histories of informal mentors also earned significantly more than did those with histories of formal mentors. Employees with both formal and informal mentors received more compensation and promotions than did those without mentors, however.[49]

Managing Promotions and Transfers

How promotions are managed can also affect not just employees' careers but the perceived fairness of the process. In making promotion decisions, several policy decisions should be addressed.

For example, competence rather than seniority is today normally the basis for promotions, although in many organizations civil service requirements and similar constraints still give an edge to more senior applicants. Furthermore, if competence is to be the basis for promotion, how should it be measured? Defining past performance is usually fairly straightforward; however, many employers also choose to use tests and assessment centers (as well as past performance) to decide who to promote. Whether to establish a formal job-posting and promotions process is important, too: Employers, such as FedEx, increasingly use sophisticated job-posting processes to give current employees the best possible opportunity to be considered for open jobs. With more firms downsizing and flattening their organizations, "promotions" may often mean lateral moves or transfers. In such situations, the promotion may take the form of an opportunity to take on new (but same-level) responsibilities, such as a salesperson moving into HR, or increased, enriched decision-making responsibilities within the same job.

A transfer is a move from one job to another, usually with no change in salary or grade. Employees may seek transfers not just for advancement, but for noncareer reasons, such as better hours, location of work, and so on. One familiar question is whether transferring employees from locale to locale upsets the employee's family life. Studies suggest that "mobile" families are no less satisfied with their family lives than "stable" ones; however, approximately 50% of top managers are reluctant to relocate.[50]

Women and men face different challenges as they advance through their careers. Women report greater barriers (such as being excluded from informal networks) than do men, and report greater difficulty getting developmental assignments and geographic mobility opportunities. Men are more likely to have been given developmental opportunities, while women had to be more proactive to get such assignments. Because developmental experiences like these are so important, "organizations that are interested in helping female managers advance should focus on breaking down the barriers that interfere with women's access to development experiences."[51]

Career Planning and the Web

Many people use the Web today to help analyze and advance their careers. For example, anyone can use the Web to take a career interests inventory from the comfort of their home. Well-known Web-based career assessment tools include: self-directed-search.com; review.com/birkman; keirsey.com; and careerdiscovery.com. Some firms have created their own internal career development Web sites. For example, Unisys's Web-based career center helps its employees identify their strengths and improve their career understanding and progress.[52]

While many people do so, posting your résumé on the Web can be problematic. "Once I put my résumé on the Internet, I couldn't do anything to control it," said one technical consultant after his boss had stumbled across the fact he was job hunting several months before. If you post your résumé on the Web, experts suggest taking several precautions. At a minimum, date your résumé (in case it lands on your boss's desk two years from now); insert a disclaimer forbidding unauthorized transmission by head-hunters; check ahead of time to see who has access to the database on which you're posting your résumé; and try to cloak your anonymity by listing your capabilities but not your name or employer—just an anonymous e-mail account to receive inquiries.[53]

Layoffs and the Plant Closing Law

Nondisciplinary separations are a fact of life at work and may be initiated by either employer or employee. For the employer, reduced sales or profits or the desire for more productivity may require layoffs or downsizings; employees may leave to retire or to seek better jobs. As explained in Chapter 7, the Worker Adjustment and Retraining Notification Act (popularly known as the plant closing law) requires employers of 100 or more employees to give 60 days' notice before closing a facility or starting a layoff of 50 or more people.

A **layoff**, in which workers are sent home for a time, is a situation in which three conditions are present: There is no work available for the employees, management expects the no-work situation to be temporary and probably short term, and management intends to recall the employees when work is again available.[54] A layoff is therefore not a termination, which is a permanent severing of the employment relationship. However, some employers use the term *layoff* as a euphemism for discharge or termination. (See the *Global Issues in HR* Box)

Adjusting to Downsizings and Mergers

Downsizing—reducing, usually dramatically, the number of people employed by the firm—is being done by more and more employers.[55] Yet many firms find that their operating earnings don't improve after major staff cuts are made. In one survey only 43% of the surveyed downsized firms saw operating earnings rise.[56]

Several things probably contribute to this anomaly. For one thing, many firms that downsize don't actually eliminate all the employees that they claim were let go, but instead retain them either as consultants, or temporary workers, or as "redeployees" who are shifted to other jobs with the firm.[57]

Immediately rehiring dozens or hundreds of employees whom you have just fired is not as irrational as it might seem, particularly when the morale aspects of any

Employment Contracts

Businesses expanding abroad soon discover that hiring employees in Europe requires much more stringent communication than does hiring people in the United States. For example, the European Union (EU) has a directive that requires employers to provide employees with very explicit contracts of employment, usually within two months of their starting work.[58]

How employers must comply with this law varies by country. For example, in the United Kingdom the employee must be given a written contract specifying, among other things, name of employer, grievance procedure, job title, rate of pay, disciplinary rules, pension plan, hours of work, vacation and sick-leave policies, pay periods, and date when employment began. In Germany, the contracts need not be in writing, although they customarily are, given the amount of detail they must cover, including minimum notice prior to layoff, wages, vacations, maternity/paternity rights, equal pay, invention rights, noncompetition clause, and sickness pay. The contract need not be in writing in Italy, but again, it usually is. Items covered include start date, probationary period, working hours, job description, place of work, basic salary, and a noncompetition clause. In France, the contract must be in writing, and specify information such as the identity of the parties, place of work, type of job or job descriptions, notice period, dates of payment, and work hours.

Although employment contract requirements differ from one European country to another, one thing can be said with certainty: When it comes to outlining the nature of the employment relationship, employers can't take fair treatment lightly, but instead must be very explicit about what the nature of the employer–employee relationship is to be.

downsizing are considered. Downsizing employers understand that the impact of any downsizing on the morale of the employees "left behind" must be considered, lest low morale drive productivity down. As a result, many employers take pains to ensure that those "downsized out" are treated fairly, even to the point of trying to rehire them into other jobs.[59] But, of course, many are actually let go.

From a practical point of view, additional steps should be and often are taken to reduce the remaining employees' uncertainty and to address their concerns. In that regard, a postdownsizing program instituted at Duracell, Inc., provides an illustration. These included a postdownsizing announcement and an activities program including: a full staff meeting at the facility; immediate follow-up in which remaining employees were split into groups with senior managers to express their concerns and have their questions answered; and encouraging supervisors to meet with their employees frequently and informally to encourage an open-door atmosphere. Other companies, such as the Diners Club subsidiary of Citicorp, use attitude surveys to help management monitor how the new postdownsizing push for customer service progresses with the remaining employees.[60]

Ironically, today's emphasis on "human capital" notwithstanding, layoffs and downsizings, if anything, are up. For example, layoffs reached a 10-year high of almost 690,000 in 1998, and almost 440,000 just for the first seven months of 1999. Numbers like these have prompted experts to suggest considering alternatives to reducing employee head counts. Suggestions include: finding volunteers who are interested in reduced hours or part-time work; using attrition; opting for voluntary early retirement packages; and networking with local employers concerning temporary or permanent redeployments.[61]

Retirement

Retirement, for many employees, is bittersweet: The employee may be free of the daily requirements of his or her job, but at the same time slightly adrift as a result of not having a job to go to. About 30% of the employers in one survey, therefore, said they offered formal **preretirement counseling** aimed at easing the passage of their employees into retirement. The most common preretirement practices were:

> Explanation of Social Security benefits (reported by 97% of those with preretirement education programs)
> Leisure-time counseling (86%)
> Financial and investment counseling (84%)
> Health counseling (82%)
> Psychological counseling (35%)
> Counseling for second careers outside the company (31%)
> Counseling for second careers inside the company (4%)

Among employers that did not have preretirement education programs, 64% believed that such programs were needed, and most of these said their firms had plans to develop them within two or three years.

Another important trend is granting part-time employment to employees as an alternative to outright retirement. Several recent surveys of blue- and white-collar employees showed that about half of all employees over age 55 would like to continue working part time after they retire.[62]

REVIEW

Summary

1. Firms give employees vehicles through which to express opinions and concerns. For example, Toyota's hotline provides employees with an anonymous channel through which they can express concerns to top management. Firms such as IBM and FedEx engage in periodic anonymous opinion surveys.

2. Guaranteed fair treatment programs, such as the one at FedEx, help to ensure that grievances are handled fairly and openly. Steps include management review, officer complaint, and executive appeals review.

3. A fair and just discipline process is based on three prerequisites: rules and regulations, a system of progressive penalties, and an appeals process. A number of discipline guidelines are important, including that discipline should be in line with the way management usually responds to similar incidents; that management must adequately investigate the matter before administering discipline; and that managers should not rob a subordinate of his or her dignity.

4. The basic aim of discipline without punishment is to gain an employee's acceptance of

the rules by reducing the punitive nature of the discipline itself. In particular, an employee is given a paid day off to consider his or her infraction before more punitive disciplinary steps are taken.

5. Managing dismissals is an important part of any supervisor's job. Among the reasons for dismissal are unsatisfactory performance, misconduct, lack of qualifications, changed job requirements, and insubordination. In dismissing one or more employees, however, remember that termination at will as a policy has been weakened by exceptions in many states. Furthermore, great care should be taken to avoid wrongful discharge suits.

6. Dismissing an employee is always difficult, and the termination interview should be handled properly. Specifically, plan the interview carefully (for instance, early in the week), get to the point, describe the situation, and then listen until the person has expressed his or her feelings. Then discuss the severance package and identify the next step.

7. Nondisciplinary separations such as layoffs and retirement occur all the time. The plant closing law (the Worker Adjustment and Retraining Notification Act) outlines requirements to be followed with regard to official notice before operations with 50 or more people are to be closed down.

8. Disciplinary actions are one big source of grievances. Discipline should be based on rules and adhere to a system of progressive penalties, and it should permit an appeals process.

Key Terms

plant closing law	dismissal	outplacement counseling
opinion surveys	terminate at will	layoff
top-down programs	insubordination	downsizing
guaranteed fair treatment	wrongful discharge	retirement
discipline	termination interview	preretirement counseling

Discussion Questions and Exercises

1. Explain the role of communications and guaranteed fair treatment in fostering employee initiative.

2. Describe specific techniques you would use to foster top-down communication in an organization.

3. Describe the similarities and differences between a program such as FedEx's guaranteed fair treatment program and a typical union grievance procedure.

4. Explain how you would ensure fairness in disciplining, discussing particularly the prerequisites to disciplining, disciplining guidelines, and the discipline without punishment approach.

5. Why is it important in our highly litigious society to manage dismissals properly?

6. What techniques would you use as alternatives to traditional discipline? What do such alternatives have to do with "organizational justice"? Why do you think alternatives like these are important, given industry's need today for highly committed employees?

7. Working individually or in groups, interview managers or administrators at your employer or college in order to determine the extent to which the employer or college builds two-way communications, and the specific types of programs (such as speak up! programs) that are used. Do the managers think they are effective? What do the employees (or faculty members) think of the programs if they are in use at the employer or college?

8. Working individually or in groups, obtain copies of the student handbook for your college and determine to what extent there is a formal process through which students can air grievances. Do you think the process should be an effective one? Based on your contacts with other students, has it been an effective grievance process?

9. Working individually or in groups, determine the nature of the academic discipline process in your college. Do you think it is an effective one? Based on what you read in this chapter, would you recommend any modification of the student discipline process?

APPLICATION EXERCISES

Case Incident: Job Insecurity at IBM

For more than 50 years IBM was known for its policy of job security. Throughout all those years, it had never laid off any employees, even as the company was going through wrenching changes. For example, in the late 1970s and 1980s, IBM had to close its punch card manufacturing plants and division, but the thousands of employees who worked in those plants were given an opportunity to move to comparable jobs in other IBM divisions.

Unfortunately, IBM's full-employment policy evaporated quickly when its computer industry market share dropped throughout the 1980s; both its sales revenue and profits began to erode. By 1991 it had become apparent that a drastic restructuring was needed. The firm therefore accelerated its downsizing efforts, instituting various early retirement and incentive plans aimed at getting employees to voluntarily leave IBM. Various imaginative schemes were introduced, including spinning off certain operations to groups of employees who then quit IBM while becoming independent consultants, doing tasks very similar to those they used to do while employees of IBM. By 1992, however, at least 40,000 more employees still had to be trimmed, and by 1993 it had become apparent that IBM's cherished full employment policy had to be discarded. For the first time, IBM began laying off employees, and eventually tens of thousands more employees were let go, beginning with about 300 employees of the firm's Armonk, New York, headquarters.

Questions

1. What do you think accounts for the fact that a company like IBM can have high job security but still lose market share, sales, and profitability? In other words, why do you think job security did not translate into corporate success as well as it might have at IBM?

2. What sorts of steps do you think IBM could have taken in order to continue to avoid layoffs? If you don't think any such steps were feasible, explain why.

3. Given IBM's experience with avoiding dismissals, what do you think are the implications for other companies thinking of similar policies of their own?

Experiential Exercise

Purpose: The purpose of this exercise is to provide you with some experience in analyzing and handling an actual grievance.

Required Understanding: Students should be thoroughly familiar with the following case, titled "Botched Batch." However, *do not read the "Award" or "Discussion" sections until after the groups have completed their deliberations.*

How to Set Up the Exercise/Instructions: Divide the class into groups of four or five students. The group should take the arbitrator's point of view and assume that they are to analyze the case and make the arbitrator's decision. Review the case again at this point, but please do not read the answer.

Each group should answer the following questions:

1. What would your decision be if you were the arbitrator? Why?
2. Do you think that following their experience in this arbitration the parties will be more or less inclined to settle grievances by themselves without resorting to arbitration?

Botched Batch

Facts: A computer department employee made an entry error that botched an entire run of computer reports. Efforts to rectify the situation produced a second set of improperly run reports. As a result of the series of errors, the employer incurred extra costs of $2,400, plus a weekend of overtime work by other computer department staffers. Management suspended the employee for three days for negligence, and also revoked a promotion for which the employee had previously been approved.

Protesting the discipline, the employee stressed that she had attempted to correct her error in the early stages of the run by notifying the manager of computer operations of her mistake. Maintaining that the resulting string of errors could have been avoided if the manager had followed up on her report and stopped the initial run, the employee argued that she had been treated unfairly because the manager had not been disciplined even though he compounded the problem, whereas she was severely punished. Moreover, citing her "impeccable" work record and management's acknowledgment that she had always been a "model employee," the employee insisted that the denial of her previously approved promotion was "unconscionable.'

(*Please do* not *read beyond this point until after you have completed the experiential exercise.*)

Award: The arbitrator upholds the three-day suspension, but decides that the promotion should be restored.

Discussion: "There is no question," the arbitrator notes, that the employee's negligent act "set in motion the train of events that resulted in running two complete sets of reports reflecting improper information." Stressing that the employer incurred substantial cost because of the error, the arbitrator cites "unchallenged" testimony that management had commonly issued three-day suspensions for similar infractions in the past. Thus, the arbitrator decides, the employer acted with just cause in meting out an "evenhanded" punishment for the negligence.

Turning to the denial of the already approved promotion, the arbitrator says that this action should be viewed "in the same light as a demotion for disciplinary reasons." In such cases, the arbitrator notes, management's decision normally is based on a pattern of unsatisfactory behavior, an employee's inability to perform, or similar grounds. Observing that management had never before reversed a promotion as part of a disciplinary action, the arbitrator says that by tacking on the denial of the promotion in this case, the employer substantially varied its disciplinary policy from its past practice. Because this action on management's part was not "evenhanded," the arbitrator rules, the promotion should be restored.

TAKE IT TO THE WEB

 For Internet exercises, updates to chapter material, and more, visit the Dessler Web site at

www.prenhall.com/dessler

ENDNOTES

1. *"The Quiet American," The Economist* (November 8, 1997): 76.

2. *Ibid.*, p. 76.

3. W. Chan Kim and Rene Mauborgne, "Fair Process: Managing in the Knowledge Economy," *Harvard Business Review* (July/August 1997): 65–66.

4. Daniel Skarlicki and Gary Latham, "Increasing Citizenship Behavior Within a Labor Union: A Test of Organizational Justice Theory," *Journal of Applied Psychology* 81, no. 2 (1996): 161–69.

5. Marshall Schminke et al., "The Effect of Organizational Structure on Perceptions of Procedural Fairness," *Journal of Applied Psychology* 85, no. 2 (2000): 294–304.

6. Michelle Donovan et al., "The Perceptions of Their Interpersonal Treatment Scale: Development and Validation of a Measure of Interpersonal Treatment in the Workplace," *Journal of Applied Psycology* 83, no. 5 (1998): 683–92.

7. Rudy Yandrick, "Lurking in the Shadows," *HRMagazine* (October 1999): 61–68.

8. Bennett Tepper, "Consequences of Abusive Supervision," *Academy of Management Journal,* 43, no. 2 (2000): 178–90.

9. Kim and Mauborgne, "Fair Process: Managing in the Knowledge Economy," pp. 65–75.

10. Gary Dessler, *Winning Commitment: How Top Companies Get and Keep Employee Commitment* (New York: McGraw-Hill, 1993), pp. 37–52.

11. Arthur Sloane and Fred Witney, *Labor Relations* (Englewood Cliffs, NJ: Prentice Hall, 1977), pp. 229–31.

12. Reed Richardson, *Collective Bargaining* (Englewood Cliffs, NJ: Prentice Hall, 1977), p. 184.

13. See, for example, Clyde Summers, "Protecting All Employees Against Unjust Dismissal," *Harvard Business Review* 58 (January/February 1980): 132–39; and George Bohlander and Harold White, "Building Bridges: Non-Union Employee Grievance Systems," *Personnel* (July 1988): 62–66.

14. Walter Baer, Grievance Handling: 101 Guides for Supervisors (New York: American Management Association, 1970).

15. Lester Bittel, *What Every Supervisor Should Know* (New York: McGraw-Hill, 1974), p. 308; see also Paul Falcone, "The Fundamentals of Progressive Discipline," *HRMagazine* (February 1997): 90–92.

16. For an example of a peer review appeals process see, for example, Dawn Anfuso, "Coors Taps Employment Judgement," *Personnel Journal* (February 1994): 50–59.

17. George Bohlander, "Why Arbitrators Overturn Managers in Employee Suspension and Discharge Cases," *Journal of Collective Negotiations* 23, no. 1 (1994): 76–77.

18. *Ibid.*, p. 82.

19. *Ibid.*, p. 82. See also Ahman Karim, "Arbitration Considerations in Modifying Discharge Decisions in the Public Sector," *Journal of Collective Negotiations* 22, no. 3 (1993): 245–51; and Joseph Martocchio and Timothy Judge, "When We Don't See Eye to Eye: Discrepancies Between Supervisors and Subordinates in Absence Disciplinary Decisions," *Journal of Management* 21, no. 2 (1995): 251–78.

20. Commerce Clearing House, "One Thing Unions Offer Is Fair Discipline—But Management Can Offer That Too," *Ideas and Trends in Personnel* (September 3, 1982): 168. See also Brian Klass and Daniel Feldman, "The Impact of Appeal System Structure on Disciplinary Decisions," *Personnel Psychology* 47, no. 1 (spring 1994): 91–108.

21. Commerce Clearing House, "Non-Union Employees, NLRB Rules, Have the Right to

Help During Questioning by Management," *Ideas and Trends in Personnel* (August 6, 1982): 151.

22. Based on George Odiorne, *How Managers Make Things Happen* (Englewood Cliffs, NJ: Prentice Hall, 1961), pp. 132–43; see also Bittel, *What Every Supervisor Should Know*, pp. 285–98. See also Cynthia Fukami and David Hopkins, "The Role of Situational Factors in Disciplinary Judgments," *Journal of Organizational Behavior* 14, no. 7 (December 1993): 665–76.

23. Nonpunitive discipline discussions based on David Campbell et al., "Discipline Without Punishment—At Last," *Harvard Business Review* (July/August 1995): 162–78; Gene Milbourne, Jr., "The Case Against Employee Punishment," *Management Solutions* (November 1986): 40–45; Mark Sherman and Al Lucia, "Positive Discipline and Labor Arbitration," *Arbitration Journal* 47, no. 2 (June 1992): 56–58; Michael Moore, Victor Nichol, and Patrick McHugh, "No-Fault Programs: A Way to Cut Absenteeism," *Employment Relations Today* (winter 1992/1993): 425–32; and " 'Positive Discipline' Replaces Punishment," *BNA Bulletin to Management* (April 27, 1995): 136.

24. "Electronic Monitoring and Surveillance," *BNA Bulletin to Management* (June 19, 1997): 196–97.

25. Larry Armstrong, "Someone to Watch Over You," *Business Week* (July 10, 2000): 189.

26. "Surveillance of Employees," *BNA Bulletin to Management* (April 25, 1996): 136.

27. "Telephone and Electronic Monitoring: A Special Report on the Issues and the Law," *BNA Bulletin to Management* (April 3, 1997): 2.

28. "Curbing the Risks of E-mail Use," *BNA Bulletin to Management* (April 10, 1997): 120.

29. *Vega-Rodriduez* v. *Puerto Rico Telephone Company*. CAL,#,962061,4/8/97, discussed in "Video Surveillance Withstands Privacy Challenge," *BNA Bulletin to Management* (April 17, 1998): 121.

30. "Secret Videotaping Leads to $200,000 Settlement," *BNA Bulletin to Management* (January 22, 1998): 17.

31. Joseph Famularo, *Handbook of Modern Personnel Administration* (New York: McGraw-Hill, 1982), 65.3–65.5.

32. *Ibid.*, p. 65.3.

33. Andrea Poe, "Make Foresight 20/20," *HRMagazine* (February 20, 2000): 74–80.

34. *Ibid.*, p. 65.4.

35. Connie Wanderg et al., "Perceived Fairness of Layoffs Among Individuals Who Have Been Laid Off: A Longitudinal Study," *Personnel Psychology* 52 (1999): 59–84.

36. "Fairness to Employees Can Stave Off Litigation," *BNA Bulletin to Management* (November 27, 1997): 377.

37. Note, however, that under recent court rulings at least one U.S. court of appeals (for the Seventh Circuit) has held that employee handbooks distributed to long-term employees before employers began amending their handbooks to contain "no contract" and "at-will employment" disclaimers may still be viewed by the court as contracts with these employees. The case was *Robinson* v. *Ada S. McKinley Community Services, Inc.*, 19F.3d 359 (7th Cir. 1994); see Kenneth Jenero, "Employers Beware: You May Be Bound By the Terms of Your Old Employee Handbooks," *Employee Relations Law Journal* 20, no. 2 (autumn 1994): 299–312.

38. Kenneth Sovereign, *Personnel Law* (Upper Saddle River, NJ: Prentice Hall, 1999), p. 185.

39. "One More Heart Risk: Firing Employees," *The Miami Herald* (March 20, 1998): C1, C7.

40. Based on James Coil, III, and Charles Rice, "Three Steps to Creating Effective Employee Releases," *Employment Relations Today* (spring 1994): 91–94.

41. William J. Morin and Lyle York, *Outplacement Techniques* (New York: AMACOM, 1982), pp. 101–31; F. Leigh Branham, "How to Evaluate Executive Outplacement Services," *Personnel Journal* 62 (April 1983): 323–26; and Sylvia Milne, "The Termination Interview," *Canadian Manager* (spring 1994): 15–16. There is debate regarding what is the "best day of the week" on which to terminate an employee. Some say Friday to give the employee a few days to "cool off," others suggest midweek, in order to allow employees "who remain in the department or in the immediate work group some time to process the change and to talk with each other to sort it out." See Jeffrey Connor, "Disarming Terminated Employees," *HRMagaizne* (January 2000): 113–14.

42. Morin and York, *Outplacement Techniques*, p. 117. See also Sonny Weide, "When You Terminate an Employee," *Employment Relations Today* (August 1994): 287–93.

43. Commerce Clearing House, *Ideas and Trends in Personnel* (July 9, 1982): 132–46.

44. Paul Brada, "Before You Go . . . ," *HRMagazine* (December 1998): 89–102.

45. Joseph Zarandona and Michael Camuso, "A Study of Exit Interviews: Does the Last Word Count?" *Personnel* 62, no. 3 (March 1981): 47–48.

46. Jim Meade, "Boost Careers and Succession Planning," *HRMagazine* (October 2000): 175–78

47. "Career Guidance Steers Workers Away From Early Exits," *BNA Bulletin of Management* (September 7, 2000): 287.

48. Daniel Feldman, "Toxic Mentor or Toxic Protégés? A Critical Reexamination of Dysfunctional Mentoring," *Human Resource Management Review* 9, no. 3 (1999): 247–78.

49. Belle Rose Ragins and John Cotton, "Mentor Functions and Outcomes: A Comparison of Men and Women in Formal and Informal Mentoring Relationships," *Journal of Applied Psychology* 84, no. 4 (1999): 529–50. This section based on Gary Dessler, *Human Resource Management* (Upper Saddle River, New Jersey: Prentice Hall, 1997), pp. 392–401.

50. Richard Chanick, "Career Growth for Baby Boomers," *Personnel Journal* 71, no. 1 (January 1992): 40–46.

51. Karen Lyness and Donna Thompson, "Climbing the Corporate Ladder: Do Female and Male Executives Follow the Same Route?" *Journal of Applied Psychology* 85, no. 1 (2000): 86–101.

52. Gina Imperato, "Get Your Career in Site," *Fast Company* (March 2000): 318–34.

53. "Read This Before You Put a Resume Online ," *Fortune* (May 24, 1999): 290–91.

54. Quoted from Commerce Clearing House, *Ideas and Trends* (August 9, 1988): 133. See also Bureau of National Affairs, "Plant Closing Notification Rules: A Compliance Guide," *Bulletin to Management* (May 18, 1989); and Nancy Ryan, "Complying with the Worker Adjustment and Retraining Notification Act (WARNACT)," *Employee Relations Law Journal* 18, no. 1 (summer 1993): 169–76.

55. See, for example, "Mass Layoffs, Third Quarter, 1996," *BNA Bulletin to Management* (April 17, 1997): 124–25.

56. Eric Greenberg, "Upswing in Downsizings to Continue," *Management Review* (February 1993): 5.

57. See, for example, "Downsizing: Working Through the Pain," *BNA Bulletin to Management* (June 6, 1996): 184; and Jennifer Laabs, "Create Job Orders, Not Pink Slips," *Personnel Journal* (June 1996): 97–99.

58. See, for example, "Cushioning the Blow of Layoffs," *BNA Bulletin to Management* (July 3, 1997): 216; and "Levi Strauss Cushions Blow of Plant Closings," *BNA Bulletin to Management* (November 20, 1997): 370.

59. Alan Chesters, "Employment Contracts—In Writing or Not?" *Global Workforce* (April 1997): 12–13.

60. Les Feldman, "Duracell's First Aid for Downsizing Survivors," *Personnel Journal* (August 1989): 94; James Emshoff, "How to Increase Employee Loyalty While You Downsize," *Business Horizons* (March/April 1994): 49–57.

61. Marlene Piturro, "Alternatives to Downsizing," *Management Review* (October 1999): 37–42; see also "Companies Rang in New York with More Mass Layoffs," *BNA Bulletin of Management* (August 19, 1999): 261.

62. "Preretirement Education Programs," *Personnel* 59 (May/June 1982): 47. For a discussion of why it is important for retiring employees to promote aspects of their lives aside from their careers, see Daniel Halloran, "The Retirement Identity Crisis—and How to Beat It," *Personnel Journal* 64 (May 1985): 38–40. For an example of a program aimed at training preretirees to prepare for the financial aspects of their retirement, see, for example, Silvia Odenwald, "Pre-Retirement Training Gathers Steam," *Training and Development Journal* 40, no. 2 (February 1986): 62–63; "Pay Policies," *BNA Bulletin to Management* (March 29, 1990): 103; and Maureen Minehan, "The Aging of America Will Increase Elder Care Responsibilities," *HRMagazine* 42, no. 7 (July 1997): 184.

Chapter 10

Protecting Safety and Health

➤ Employee Safety and Health: An
Introduction
➤ What Causes Accidents?
➤ How to Prevent Accidents
➤ Employee Health: Problems and
Remedies

When you finish studying this chapter, you should be able to:

■ *Discuss* OSHA and how it operates.

■ *Describe* the supervisor's role in safety.

■ *Explain* in detail three basic causes of accidents.

■ *Explain* how to prevent accidents at work.

■ *Discuss* major health problems at work and how to remedy them.

INTRODUCTION

In a case appealed to the 7th Circuit (which covers Illinois, Indiana, and Wisconsin), a worker fell to his death after stepping onto a corroded fire escape platform that collapsed.[1] The Occupational Safety and Health Administration (OSHA) charged the employer with criminally violating a federal safety standard requiring adequate fire and emergency exits. The federal jury who first heard the case ruled against the company on the assumption that it should have known about the unsafe conditions at the site. The 7th Circuit Appeals Court subsequently reversed that ruling, however, saying that the jury would have to find that the company actually knew about the corroded fire escape to be held liable. Regardless of the legal technicalities, though, one fact remains: A worker lost his life because of a safety hazard at work.

EMPLOYEE SAFETY AND HEALTH: AN INTRODUCTION

Why Employee Safety and Health Are Important

Providing a safe and accident-free work environment is important for several reasons, one of which is the staggering nature of work-related safety and accident figures. In one recent year, more than 6,100 deaths and 6.7 million incidences of nonfatal injuries and illnesses resulted from accidents at work—roughly 8.4 cases per 100 full-time workers in the United States per year.[2] Many safety experts believe such figures seriously underestimate the actual number of workplace injuries and illnesses. One study said workers actually suffer an estimated 13.2 million nonfatal injuries and 862,200 illnesses annually, for a total cost of $171 billion each year.[3] Many injuries and accidents, one theory goes, may just go unreported.

But even figures like these don't tell the full story. They don't reflect the human suffering incurred by the injured workers and their families.[4] They don't reflect the fact that incident rates vary from industry to industry, from a high of 9.7 in manufacturing to a low of 1.9 in finance, insurance, and real estate.[5] And they don't reflect the legal implications of not providing a safe workplace, which under the Occupational Safety and Health Act and other laws, can be considerable.

A Manager's Briefing on Occupational Law

The **Occupational Safety and Health Act**[6] was passed by Congress in 1970 "to assure so far as possible every working man and woman in the nation safe and healthful working conditions and to preserve our human resources." The only employers not covered by the act are self-employed persons, farms in which only immediate members of the employer's family are employed, and certain workplaces that are already protected by other federal agencies or under other statutes. Federal agencies are covered by the act, although provisions of the act usually don't apply to state and local governments in their role as employers.

Under the act's provisions, the **Occupational Safety and Health Administration (OSHA)** was created within the Department of Labor. OSHA's basic purpose is to administer the act and to set and enforce the safety and health standards that apply to almost all workers in the United States. The standards are enforced through the Department of Labor; OSHA has inspectors working out of branch offices throughout the country to ensure compliance.

OSHA Standards OSHA operates under the general standard that each employer:

> shall furnish to each of his [or her] employees employment and a place of employment which are free from recognized hazards that are causing or are likely to cause death or serious physical harm to his [or her] employees.

To carry out this basic mission, OSHA is responsible for promulgating legally enforceable standards. These are contained in five volumes covering general industry standards, maritime standards, construction standards, other regulations and procedures, as well as a field operations manual. The standards are very complete and cover just about every conceivable hazard in great detail. For example, a small part of the standard governing handrails for scaffolds is presented in Figure 10.1.

Extensive as the standards are, many believe they're not enough. For example, some experts contend that OSHA's permissible exposure limits for about 500 chemical-type substances are out of date. Meeting the limits may still expose employees to adverse health effects.[7]

OSHA Record-Keeping Procedures   Employers with 11 or more employees must maintain records of occupational injuries and illnesses, and report both occupational injuries and occupational illnesses. All occupational illnesses must be reported.[8] Similarly, most occupational injuries also must be reported, specifically those injuries that result in medical treatment (other than first aid), loss of consciousness, restriction of work (one or more lost workdays), restriction of motion, or transfer to another job.[9] A form used to report occupational injuries or illness is shown in Figure 10.2.

Inspections and Citations   OSHA standards are enforced through inspections and (if necessary) citations. However, OSHA may not conduct warrantless inspections without an employer's consent. It may, however, inspect after acquiring a judicially authorized search warrant or its equivalent.[10]

Like many government agencies, OSHA has wide-ranging compliance responsibilities but relatively limited funds for accomplishing its aims. As a result, over the past few years OSHA has tried to encourage cooperative safety programs rather than rely only on inspections and citations.[11] For example, its Cooperative Compliance Program targets a limited number of employers in a state, and then sends them notices asking that they work with OSHA to develop voluntary plans for addressing workplace safety and health problems.[12]

Such efforts notwithstanding, OSHA does of course still make extensive use of inspections and has a list of inspection priorities. Imminent danger situations get top priority. These are conditions in which it is likely that a danger exists that can immediately cause death or serious physical harm. Second priority is given to catastrophes, fatalities, and accidents that have already occurred. (Such situations must be reported to OSHA within 48 hours.) Third priority is given to valid employee complaints of alleged violation of standards. Next in priority are periodic, special-emphasis inspections aimed at high-hazard industries, occupations, or substances. Finally, random inspections and reinspections generally have last priority. Most inspections result from employee complaints.

Guardrails not less than 2″ × 4″ or the equivalent and not less than 36″ or more than 42″ high, with a midrail, when required, of a 1″ × 4″ lumber or equivalent, and toeboards, shall be installed at all open sides on all scaffolds more than 10 feet above the ground or floor. Toeboards shall be a minimum of 4″ in height. Wire mesh shall be installed in accordance with paragraph (a)(17) of this section.

FIGURE 10.1   OSHA Standards Example

Source: General Industry Standards and Interpretations, U.S. Department of Labor, OSHA (Volume 1: Revised 1989, Section 1910.28(b)(15)), p. 67.

```
OSHA No. 101                                          Form approved
Case or File No. _____                       OMB No. 44R 1453

        Supplementary Record of Occupational Injuries and Illnesses

EMPLOYER
    1. Name _____
    2. Mail address _____
                      (No. and street)        (City or town)        (State)
    3. Location, if different from mail address _____
INJURED OR ILL EMPLOYEE
    4. Name _____ Social Security No. _____
           (First name)  (Middle name)    (Last name)
    5. Home address _____
                      (No. and street)        (City or town)        (State)
    6. Age _____    7. Sex: Male _____ Female _____ (Check one)
    8. Occupation_____
                  (Enter regular job title, not the specific activity he/she was performing at time of injury.)
    9. Department_____
                  (Enter name of department or division in which the injured person is regularly employed, even
                  though he/she may have been temporarily working in another department at the time of injury.)
THE ACCIDENT OR EXPOSURE TO OCCUPATIONAL ILLNESS
    10. Place of accident or exposure _____
                      (No. and street)        (City or town)        (State)
        If accident or exposure occurred on employer's premises, give address of plant or establishment in
        which it occurred. Do not indicate department or division within the plant or establishment. If accident
        occurred outside employer's premises at an identifiable address, give that address. If it occurred on a
        public highway or at any other place which cannot be identified by number and street, please provide
        place references locating the place of injury as accurately as possible.
    11. Was place of accident or exposure on employer's premises? _____(Yes or No)
    12. What was the employee doing when injured? _____
                              (Be specific. If he/she was using tools or equipment or handling
    _____
                  material, name them and tell what he/she was doing with them.)
    _____
    13. How did the accident occur?_____
                              (Describe fully the events which resulted in the injury or occupational illness. Tell what
    _____
    happend and how it happened. Name any objects or substances involved and tell how they were involved. Give
    _____
    full details on all factors which led or contributed to the accident. Use separate sheet for additional space.)
OCCUPATIONAL INJURY OR OCCUPATIONAL ILLNESS
    14. Describe the injury or illness in detail and indicate the part of body affected. _____
                                                          (e.g.: amputation of right index finger
    _____
              at second joint; fracture of ribs; lead poisoning; dermatitis of left hand, etc.)
    15. Name the object or substance which directly injured the employee. (For example, the machine or thing
        he/she struck against or which struck him/her; the vapor or poison inhaled or swallowed; the chemical or
        radiation which irritated the skin; or in cases of strains, hernias, etc., the thing he/she was lifting, pulling,
        etc.)
    _____
    _____
    16. Date of injury or initial diagnosis of occupational illness_____
                                                          (Date)
    17. Did employee die? _____ (Yes or No)
OTHER
    18. Name and address of physician _____
    19. If hospitalized, name and address of hospital _____
    _____
        Date  of  report  _____  Prepared  by  _____
        Official position _____
```

FIGURE 10.2   Form Used to Record Occupational Injuries and Illnesses

OSHA inspectors look for violations of all types, but some potential problem areas—such as scaffolding and fall protection—seem to grab more of their attention. Figure 10.3 summarizes the 10 most frequent OSHA inspection violation areas.[13]

OSHA no longer follows up every employee complaint with an inspection.[14] Under its priority system, OSHA conducts an inspection within 24 hours when a complaint indicates an immediate danger, and within 3 working days when a serious hazard exists. For a nonserious complaint filed in writing by a worker or a union, OSHA responds within 20 working days. Other nonserious complaints are handled by writing to the employer and requesting corrective action.

After the inspection report has been submitted to the local OSHA office, the area director determines what citations, if any, will be issued. The **citations** inform the employer and employees of the regulations and standards that have been violated and of the time set for rectifying the problem.

OSHA can also impose penalties. In general, OSHA calculates these based on the gravity of the violation and usually takes into consideration such factors as the size of the business, the firm's compliance history, and the employer's good faith. Penalties generally range from $5,000 to up to $70,000 for willful or repeat serious violations, although in practice the penalties can be far higher. For example, in one settlement negotiated between OSHA and A. K. Steel, Inc., willful and serious viola-

Inspectors are expected to look for violations of all types, but violations OSHA deems serious are the ones inspectors are likeliest to target. In fiscal 1998, the 10 most frequently found serious violations related to problems with the following areas:

Rank	Area of Concern	No. of Serious Violations
1	Scaffolding	5,539
2	Fall protection	3,862
3	Hazard communication	3,274
4	Lockout/tagout	3,532
5	Machine guarding	2,266
6	Power presses	2,230
7	Mechanical power	2,151
8	Electrical	1,902
9	Excavation (construction)	1,399
10	Machine guarding (abrasive wheels)	1,338

Lockout/tagout refers to electrical repairs, during which switches for power must be shut off, locked, and tagged so power cannot be turned on while someone is repairing an electrical system. Hazard communication means proper use of material data safety sheets for chemical products at a worksite.

FIGURE 10.3 The OSHA Inspection Hit List
Source: Occupational Safety and Health Administration.

tions of OSHA rules that resulted in one death and serious injuries to two workers prompted OSHA to propose a $1 million penalty for the company's steel plant in Middletown, Ohio.[15] In fact, many cases are settled with OSHA before litigation in what attorneys call *precitation settlements*. The citation and agreed-on penalties are issued simultaneously, after the employers initiate negotiation settlements with OSHA.[16]

In practice, OSHA must have a final order from the independent Occupational Safety and Health Review Commission (OSHRC) to enforce a penalty. Although that appeals process has been sped up of late, an employer who files a notice of contest can still drag out an appeal for years.[17]

Today inspectors and their superiors don't look just for specific hazards, but also evidence of a comprehensive approach. For example, factors contributing to a firm's OSHA liability include: lack of a systematic safety approach; sporadic or irregular safety meetings; a lack of responsiveness to safety audit recommendations; not following up on employee safety complaints; and failure to regularly inspect the workplace, for instance, through employer walk-throughs and self-inspections.[18]

While some employers understandably view OSHA inspections with some trepidation, the inspection tips summarized in Figure 10.4—such as a "check the inspectors credentials," and "accompany the inspector and take detailed notes"—can help ensure the inspection goes smoothly.[19]

Responsibilities and Rights of Employers and Employees   Both employers and employees have responsibilities and rights under the Occupational Safety and Health Act. For example, employers are responsible for providing "a workplace free from recognized hazards," for being familiar with mandatory OSHA standards, and for examining workplace conditions to make sure they conform with applicable standards.

Employees also have rights and responsibilities but cannot be cited for violations of their responsibilities. They are responsible, for example, for complying with all applicable OSHA standards, for following all employer safety and health rules and regulations, and for reporting hazardous conditions to the supervisor. Employees have a right to demand safety and health on the job without fear of punishment. Employers are forbidden to punish or discriminate against workers who complain to OSHA about job safety and health hazards.

Getting employees to wear personal protective equipment can be a famously difficult chore. Including the employees in planning the program, reinforcing appropriate behaviors, and addressing comfort issues can smooth the way for more widespread use of protective equipment.[20]

WHAT CAUSES ACCIDENTS?

Accidents occur for three main reasons: chance occurrences, unsafe working conditions, and unsafe acts by employees. Chance occurrences (such as walking past a window just as someone hits a ball through it) contribute to accidents but are more or less beyond management's control; we will therefore focus on unsafe conditions and unsafe acts.

Initial Contact

- Refer the inspector to your OSHA coordinator.
- Check the inspector's credentials.
- Ask the inspector why he is inspecting your workplace. Is it a complaint? Programmed visit? Fatality or accident follow-up? Imminent danger investigation?
- If the inspection is the result of a complaint, the inspector won't identify the complainant, but you are entitled to know whether the person is a current employee.
- Notify your OSHA counsel, who should review all requests from the inspector for documents and information. Your counsel also should review the documents and information you provide to the inspector.

Opening Conference

- Establish the focus and scope of the planned inspection: Does the inspector want to inspect the premises or simply study your records?
- Discuss the procedures for protecting trade-secret areas, conducting employee interviews, and producing documents.
- Show the inspector that you have safety programs in place. He or she may not go to the work floor if paperwork is complete and up-to-date.

Walk-Around Inspection

- Accompany the inspector and take detailed notes.
- If the inspector takes a photo or video, you should too.
- Ask the inspector for duplicates of all physical samples and copies of all test results.
- Be helpful and cooperative, but don't volunteer information.
- To the extent possible, immediately correct any violation the inspector identifies.

FIGURE 10.4 OSHA Inspection Tips

Unsafe Conditions

Unsafe conditions are one main cause of accidents. These include such obvious factors as:

- Improperly guarded equipment
- Defective equipment
- Unsafe storage, such as congestion or overloading
- Improper illumination, such as glare or insufficient light
- Improper ventilation, such as insufficient air change or impure air source[21]

The basic remedy here is to eliminate or minimize the unsafe conditions. OSHA standards address the mechanical and physical working conditions that cause accidents. A checklist of unsafe conditions can be useful for spotting problems; one

Checklist of Mechanical or Physical Accident-Causing Conditions

I. GENERAL HOUSEKEEPING

Adequate and wide aisles—no materials protruding into aisles

Parts and tools stored safely after use—not left in hazardous positions that could cause them to fall

Even and solid flooring—no defective floors or ramps that could cause falling or tripping accidents

Waste and trash cans—safely located and not overfilled

Material piled in safe manner—not too high or too close to sprinkler heads

All work areas clean and dry

All exit doors and aisles clean of obstructions

Aisles kept clear and properly marked; no air lines or electric cords across aisles

II. MATERIAL HANDLING EQUIPMENT AND CONVEYANCES

On all conveyances, electric or hand, check to see that the following items are all in sound working conditions:

Brakes—properly adjusted

Not too much play in steering wheel

Warning device—in place and working

Wheels—securely in place; properly inflated

Fuel and oil—enough and right kind

No loose parts

Cables, hooks or chains—not worn or otherwise defective

Suspended chains or hooks conspicuous

Safely loaded

Properly stored

III. LADDERS, SCAFFOLD, BENCHES, STAIRWAYS, ETC.

The following items of major interest to be checked:

Safety feet on straight ladders

Guardrails or handrails

Treads, not slippery

No splintered, cracked, or rickety

Properly stored

Extension ladder ropes in good condition

Toeboards

IV. POWER TOOLS (STATIONARY)

Point of operation guarded

Guards in proper adjustment

Gears, belts, shafting, counterweights guarded

Foot pedals guarded

Brushes provided for cleaning machines

Adequate lighting

Properly grounded

Tool or material rests properly adjusted

Adequate work space around machines

Control switch easily accessible

Safety glasses worn

Gloves worn by persons handling rough or sharp materials

No gloves or loose clothing worn by persons operating machines

V. HAND TOOLS AND MISCELLANEOUS

In good condition—not cracked, worn, or otherwise defective

Properly stored

Correct for job

Goggles, respirators, and other personal protective equipment worn where necessary

(continued)

checklist is presented in the *HR in Practice* box. The new *Occupational Hazards* magazine Web site (occupationalhazards.com) is a good source for safety, health, and industrial hygiene information.

Although accidents can happen anywhere, there are some high-danger zones. About one-third of industrial accidents occur around forklift trucks, wheelbarrows, and other handling and lifting areas, for example. The most serious accidents usually occur near metal and woodworking machines and saws, or around transmission machinery such as gears, pulleys, and flywheels.[22]

Other Working Condition-Related Causes of Accidents   Some working condition–related causes of accidents are less obvious because they involve the psychology of the workplace. For example, one researcher observed the official hearings regarding fatal accidents suffered by offshore oil workers in the British sector of the North Sea.[23] From this and similar studies, it's apparent that several basically psychological aspects of the work environment can set the stage for subsequent unsafe acts. A strong pressure to complete the work as quickly as possible, employees who are under stress, and a poor safety climate—for instance, supervisors who never mention safety—are some of the not-so-obvious working conditions that can set the stage for accidents.

Furthermore, some jobs are inherently more dangerous than others. According to one study, for example, the job "crane operator" results in about three times more accident-related hospital visits than does the job "supervisor."

Work schedules and fatigue also affect accident rates. Accident rates usually don't increase too noticeably during the first five or six hours of the workday, but after six hours the accident rate accelerates. This is due partly to fatigue and partly to the fact that accidents occur more often during night shifts.

Accidents also occur more frequently in plants with a high seasonal layoff rate and where there is hostility among employees, garnished wages, and blighted living conditions. Temporary stress factors such as high workplace temperature, poor illumination, and a congested workplace are also related to accident rates. Workers who work under stress and time pressures, or who feel their jobs are threatened or insecure, have more accidents than those who do not.[24]

Unsafe Acts

Most safety experts and managers know that it's impossible to eliminate accidents just by reducing unsafe conditions. People cause accidents, and no one has found a sure-fire way to eliminate **unsafe acts** such as:

- Throwing materials
- Operating or working at unsafe speeds—either too fast or too slow
- Making safety devices inoperative by removing, adjusting, or disconnecting them
- Lifting improperly[25]

There is no one explanation for why an employee may behave in an unsafe manner. In some cases (as noted above) the working conditions may set the stage for unsafe acts: For instance, employees who are under a great deal of stress, or who believe there's a strong pressure to complete the work as quickly as possible, or who believe the climate of the firm places less emphasis on safety than on productivity or profits may behave in an unsafe manner even if he or she knows better.[26] Sometimes, employees aren't adequately trained in safe work methods; some companies don't provide employees with the correct safe procedures to use, and employees may simply develop their own (often bad) work habits. On the other hand, it's often the employee and his or her attitudes, personality, and skills that accounts for the bad behavior.

What Traits Characterize "Accident-Prone" People?   Psychologists have tried for years—to no avail—to determine what package of traits distinguishes those who are accident prone from those who are not.[27]

It may be intuitively obvious that some people are accident prone, but years of research has failed to unearth any set of traits that accident repeaters seemed to have in common. Today, most experts doubt that accident proneness is universal—that there are some people who will have many accidents no matter what situation they are put in—although some researchers believe that accident proneness is a type of deviant behavior characterized by impulsiveness.[28] Instead, the consensus is that the person who is accident prone on one job may not be on a different job—that accident proneness is situational. For example, lack of motor skills may characterize accident-prone workers on jobs involving coordination. In fact, many human traits have been found to be related to accident repetition in specific situations, as explained below.[29]

HOW TO PREVENT ACCIDENTS

How can you prevent accidents at work? One thing to remember is that it's not always the employees that are causing the accidents: "Although it is clear that individual behavior influences accidents, starting and ending one's investigation at this level ignores the broader contextual influence on behavior in organizations."[30] Certainly, screening out or firing impulsive employees will reduce the incidence of unsafe behaviors, as will mopping up oil spills and placing guardrails around machines. However (as noted previously), psychological factors such as reducing stress and pressure are important, too, and must be addressed if accidents are to be prevented. In practice, there is usually no one single cause—whether acts or conditions—of workplace injuries; instead, accident causes tend to be multifaceted.[31]

Reduce Unsafe Conditions

Reducing unsafe conditions is an employer's first line of defense. Employers working with safety engineers have to "engineer out" potentially hazardous conditions, for instance, by placing guardrails around moving machines.

Reduce Unsafe Acts

Accidents are similar to other types of poor performance, and psychologists have had success in screening out individuals who might be accident prone for some specific job. The basic technique is to identify the human trait (such as visual skill) that might be related to accidents on the specific job. Then determine whether scores on this trait are related to accidents on the job.[32] For example:

> *Emotional stability and personality tests.* Psychological tests—especially tests of emotional stability—have been used to screen out accident-prone taxi drivers. In this case, researchers found that taxi drivers who made five or more errors on such tests averaged three accidents, whereas those who made fewer than five errors averaged only 1.3 accidents.[33]

> *Measures of muscular coordination.* We also know that coordination is a predictor of safety for certain jobs. In one study, more than 600 employees were divided into two groups according to test scores on coordination tests. It was found that the poorest quarter had 51 percent more accidents than those in the better three-quarters.[34]

> *Tests of visual skills.* Good vision plays a part in preventing accidents in many occupations, including driving and operating machines. In a study in a paper mill, 52 accident-free employees were compared with 52 accident-prone employees. The researcher found that 63 percent of the no-accident group passed a vision test, whereas only 3.3 percent of the accident group passed it.[35]

> *Genetic screening.* In the face of considerable ethical concerns, some have proposed using genetic screening to reduce injuries and disease at work. This approach, which uses genetic tests, is based on the belief that individual differences in susceptibility to toxic exposure exist—in other words, some people are genetically more susceptible to, say, chemical pollutants than are others. Genetic tests might provide information that is predictive of an individual's health status on the job.[36]

> *Employee selection.* Experts suggest at least asking several safety-related questions during the selection interview—for instance, "What would you do if you saw a fellow employee working in an unsafe way?" "What would you do if your supervisor gave you a task, but didn't provide any training on how to safely perform it?"[37]

Use Posters and Other Propaganda

Propaganda such as safety posters can help reduce unsafe acts. In one study, their use apparently increased safe behavior by more than 20 percent.[38] However, posters are no substitute for a comprehensive safety program; instead, they should be combined with other techniques such as screening and training to reduce unsafe conditions and acts. The posters should also be changed often to maintain workers' interest.[39]

Provide Safety Training

Safety training can also reduce accidents. Such training is especially appropriate with new employees. It is important to instruct them in safe practices and procedures, warn them of potential hazards, and work on developing their predisposition toward safety.

Use Incentives and Positive Reinforcement

Some firms use incentives (such as cash bonuses) if particular safety goals are met. However, some contend that programs like these are misguided. OSHA has argued, for instance, that such plans don't actually cut down on injuries or illnesses but only on injury and illness *reporting*. One option is to emphasize "nontraditional" incentives, for instance, by giving employees recognition awards for attending safety meetings, identifying hazards, or for demonstrating their safety and health proficiency.[40]

Safety programs based on positive reinforcement can also improve safety at work.[41] One program was instituted in a wholesale bakery that bakes, wraps, and transports pastry products to retail outlets nationwide.[42] The program stressed positive reinforcement and training. A reasonable goal (in terms of observed behaviors performed safely) was set and communicated to workers to ensure that they knew what was expected of them in terms of good performance. Employees were then presented with safety information and examples of safety do's and don'ts during a 30-minute training session.

At the conclusion of training, the employees were shown a graph plotting their pretraining safety record (in terms of observed incidents performed safely). They were encouraged to increase their performance to the new safety goal for their own protection, to decrease costs for the company, and to help the plant get out of last place in the safety ranking of the parent company. Then the graph and a list of safety do's and don'ts were posted in a conspicuous place in the work area. Workers could thus compare their current safety performance with both their previous performance and their assigned goal. Supervisors also praised employees when they performed selected incidents safely. Safety in the plant subsequently improved markedly.[43]

Safety incentives needn't be complicated. One organization uses a suggestion box; employees make suggestions for improvements regarding unsafe acts or conditions. The employer follows up on all suggestions, the best of which result in gift certificates for their authors.[44]

Yet, relying solely on behavior-based safety isn't the only or (necessarily) the best option. Programs like these should not take the place of eliminating hazards, providing personal protective equipment, and using training and warnings to reduce safety misbehaviors.[45]

Emphasize Top-Management Commitment

Safety programs require a strong and obvious management commitment to safety.[46] This manifests itself, for instance, in top management's: being personally involved in safety activities; giving safety matters high priority in company meetings and production scheduling; giving the company safety officer high rank and status; and including safety training in new employees' training. Here's an example:

One of the best examples I know of in setting the highest possible priority for safety takes place at a DuPont Plant in Germany. Each morning at the DuPont Polyester and Nylon Plant the director and his assistants meet at 8:45 to review the past 24 hours. The first matter they discuss is not production, but safety. Only after they have examined reports of accidents and near misses and satisfied themselves that corrective action has been taken do they move on to look at output, quality, and cost matters.[47]

Emphasize Safety

Supervisors also have to instill in their employees the desire to work safely. This involves more than talking up safety or enforcing safety rules, although such actions are important.[48] As important (or more) than what you say is what you do: In other words, it's crucial to show by word and deed that safety is very important. Some employers link managers' bonuses to safety improvements. For example, Georgia-Pacific has reduced its workers' compensation costs through an HR policy that forces managers to cut accidents in half or forfeit 30 percent of their bonuses.[49]

Creating the right safety climate isn't just theoretical. One study assessed safety climate in terms of items such as "my supervisor says a good word whenever he sees the job done according to the safety rules," and "my supervisor approaches workers during work to discuss safety issues." The study found that (1) employees did develop consistent perceptions concerning supervisory safety practices, and (2) safety climate perceptions predicted safety records in the months following the survey.[50]

Establish a Safety Policy

A safety policy should emphasize that the firm will do everything practical to eliminate or reduce accidents and injuries. It should also emphasize the fact that accident and injury prevention is not just important but of the utmost importance at your firm.

Set Specific Loss Control Goals

Analyze the number of accidents and safety incidents and then set specific safety goals to be achieved. For example, safety goals can be set in terms of frequency of lost-time injuries per number of full-time employees.[51]

Conduct Safety and Health Inspections Regularly

Routinely inspect all premises for possible safety and health problems using checklists such as those in the *HR in Practice* box (on pages 279–280) as aids. Similarly, investigate all accidents and "near misses" and have a system in place for letting employees notify management about hazardous conditions.[52] *Safety audits* measure several things, such as injury and illnesses statistics, workers' compensation costs, and vehicle accident statistics.[53]

Similarly, employee safety committees can improve workplace safety. Typical committee activities include evaluating safety adequacy, monitoring safety audit findings, and suggesting strategies for improving health and safety performance.[54]

Monitor Work Overload and Stress

In one recent study, "role overload" (the degree to which the employee's performance was seen as being affected by inadequate time, training, and resources) was significantly associated with unsafe behaviors.[55] Other researchers have suggested that as work overload increases, workers are more likely to adopt shortcuts and somewhat more risky work methods. Therefore, supervisors should monitor employees (and particularly those in relatively hazardous jobs) for signs of stress and overload. These and other safety steps are summarized in Figure 10.5.

EMPLOYEE HEALTH: PROBLEMS AND REMEDIES[56]

Various health-related substances and problems can undermine employee performance at work. These include alcoholism, stress, asbestos, video displays, AIDS, and workplace violence.

Alcoholism and Substance Abuse

Alcoholism and substance abuse are serious and widespread workplace problems.[57] Although the percentage of full-time U.S. workers engaging in illegal drug use has reportedly dropped by more than half since 1985, about 15% of employees still report having used illicit drugs "in the past year," 7.3% report currently using illicit drugs, and 7.4% report "continued heavy alcohol use."[58] Average figures can be somewhat misleading, however: For instance, drug use among nonsupervisory construction workers was about 17%, but only 1% among police and detectives.[59]

Recognizing the alcoholic on the job can be a problem. The early symptoms such as tardiness can be similar to those of other problems and thus difficult to classify. The supervisor is not a psychiatrist, and without specialized training, identifying and dealing with the alcoholic is difficult. For many employers, dealing with alcohol and substance abuse begins with substance abuse testing. For example, more than one-third of businesses recently reported testing applicants and/or employees for alcohol.[60]

- Reduce unsafe conditions.
- Reduce unsafe acts.
- Use posters and other propaganda.
- Provide safety training.
- Use positive reinforcement.
- Emphasize top-management commitment.
- Emphasize safety.
- Establish a safety policy.
- Set specific loss control goals.
- Conduct safety and health inspections regularly.
- Monitor work overload and stress.

FIGURE 10.5 Steps to Take to Reduce Workplace Accidents

A chart showing observable behavior patterns that indicate alcohol-related problems is presented in Table 10.1. As you can see, alcohol-related problems range from tardiness in the earliest stages of alcohol abuse to prolonged, unpredictable absences in its later stages.[61]

The Problems of Job Stress and Burnout

Problems such as alcoholism and drug abuse sometimes result from stress, especially *job stress*. Job-related factors such as overwork, relocation, and problems with customers eventually put the person under such stress that a pathological reaction such as drug abuse occurs. Eighty-eight percent of managers in one recent survey reported elevated stress levels, with most reporting feeling under more stress than they could ever remember.

The effect of the stress depends on its source. In this study, for instance, challenge-related stress was positively related to job satisfaction and negatively related to searching for a new job. Hindrance-related stress was negatively related to job satisfaction and positively related to job search and turnover.[62]

A variety of external—environmental—factors can lead to job stress.[63] These include work schedule, pace of work, job security, route to and from work, workplace noise, and the number and nature of customers or clients.[64]

However, no two people react the same because personal factors also influence stress. For example, those with Type A personalities—people who are workaholics and who feel driven to always be on time and meet deadlines—normally place themselves under greater stress than do others.

Job stress has serious consequences for both the employee and the organization. The human consequences of job stress include anxiety, depression, anger, and various physical consequences, such as cardiovascular disease, headaches, and accidents. Stress also has serious consequences for the organization, including reductions in the quantity and quality of job performance, increased absenteeism and turnover, and increased grievances and health care costs.[65] A study of 46,000 employees concluded that health care costs of the high-stress workers were 46% higher than those of their less-stressed co-workers.[66] Yet stress is not necessarily dysfunctional. Some people, for example, find that they are more productive as a deadline approaches.

Reducing Your Own Job Stress   A person can do several things to alleviate stress, ranging from commonsense remedies such as getting more sleep and eating better to more exotic remedies such as biofeedback and meditation. Finding a more suitable job, getting counseling, and planning and organizing each day's activities are other sensible responses.[67] In his book *Stress and the Manager*, Dr. Karl Albrecht suggests, for example, the following to reduce job stress:[68]

- Build rewarding, pleasant, cooperative relationships with as many of your colleagues and employees as you can.
- Don't bite off more than you can chew.
- Build an especially effective and supportive relationship with your boss.
- Understand the boss's problems and help him or her to understand yours.
- Negotiate with your boss for realistic deadlines on important projects. Be prepared to propose deadlines yourself, instead of having them imposed on you.

TABLE 10.1 Observable Alcohol-Related Behavior Patterns

Stage	Absenteeism	General Behavior	Job Performance
I Early	Tardiness Quits early Absence from work situations	Complaints from fellow employees for not doing his or her share Overreaction Complaints of not "feeling well"	Misses deadlines Commits errors (frequently) Lower job efficiency
II Middle	("I drink to relieve tension") Frequent days off for vague or implausible reasons ("I feel guilty about sneaking drinks"; "I have tremors")	Makes untrue statements Marked changes Undependable statements Avoids fellow employees Borrows money from fellow employees Exaggerates work accomplishments Frequent hospitalization Minor injuries on the job (repeatedly)	Criticism from the boss General deterioration Cannot concentrate Occasional lapse of memory Warning from boss
III Late Middle	Frequent days off; several days at a time Does not return from lunch ("I don't feel like eating"; "I don't want to talk about it"; "I like to drink alone")	Aggressive and belligerent behavior Domestic problems interfere with work Financial difficulties (garnishments, etc.) More frequent hospitalization Resignation: does not want to discuss problems Problems with the laws in the community	Far below expectation Punitive disciplinary action
IV Approaching Terminal Stage	Prolonged unpredictable absences ("My job interferes with my drinking")	Drinking on the job (probably) Completely undependable Repeated hospitalization Serious financial problems Serious family problems: divorce	Uneven Generally incompetent Faces termination or hospitalization

Note: Based on content analysis of files of recovering alcoholics in five organizations. From *Managing and Employing the Handicapped: The Untapped Potential,* by Gopal C. Pati and John I. Adkins, Jr., with Glenn Morrison (Lake Forest, IL: Brace-Park, Human Resource Press, 1981).

Source: From "The Employer's Role in Alcoholism Assistance" by Gopal C. Pati and John I. Adkins, Jr., copyright July 1983. Used by permission of ACC Communications Inc./*Personnel Journal* (now known as *Workforce*), Costa Mesa, CA. All rights reserved.

- Find time every day for detachment and relaxation.
- Get away from your office from time to time for a change of scene and a change of mind.
- Don't put off dealing with distasteful problems.
- Make a constructive "worry list." Write down the problems that concern you, and beside each write down what you're going to do about it.

What the Employer Can Do   The employer and its HR specialists and supervisors can also play a role in identifying and reducing job stress:

■ Monitor each employee's performance to identify symptoms of stress.
■ Use attitude surveys to identify organizational sources of stress, selection, and placement procedures to ensure effective person–job match.
■ Reduce personal conflicts on the job.
■ Reduce the amount of red tape for employees.
■ Provide employee assistance programs including professional counseling help.[69]

Giving employees more control over their jobs can also mediate the effects of job stress, as illustrated by a recent study[70] in which the psychological strain caused by job stress was reduced by giving workers more control over their jobs. The jobs perceived as less stressful actually had high demands in terms of workload and pressure. However, the jobs apparently *felt* less stressful because they also ranked high in task clarity, job control, supervisory support, and employee skill utilization.[71]

Burnout is a phenomenon closely associated with job stress, and has been defined as the total depletion of physical and mental resources caused by excessive striving to reach an unrealistic work-related goal.[72] Burnout manifests itself in emotional exhaustion, depersonalization (a feeling that you can't get close to others), and feelings of diminished personal accomplishment.[73] Basically, a person burns out when the stress of trying to attain unattainable work-related goals becomes too great.

The burnout victim is usually a workaholic—a person for whom the constant stress of seeking an unattainable goal to the exclusion of other activities can lead to physical and perhaps mental collapse. This needn't be limited to upwardly mobile executives: For instance, social-work counselors caught up in their clients' problems are often burnout victims. Some signs of possible impending burnout include:[74]

■ You are unable to relax.
■ You identify so closely with your activities that when they fall apart, you do too.
■ Your need for a particular crutch such as smoking, alcohol, or tranquilizers is increasing.
■ You are constantly irritable, and family and friends are often commenting that you don't look well.
■ You would describe yourself as a workaholic and constantly strive to obtain your work-related goals to the exclusion of almost all outside interests.

What can a burnout candidate do? Here are some suggestions:

Break patterns. First, survey how you spend your time. The more well rounded your life is, the better protected you are against burnout.

Get away from it all periodically. Schedule occasional periods of introspection during which you can get away from your usual routine, perhaps alone, to seek a perspective on where you are and where you are going.

Reassess your goals in terms of their intrinsic worth. Are the goals you've set for yourself attainable? Are they really worth the sacrifices you'll have to make?

Think about your work. Could you do as good a job without being so intense or by also pursuing outside interests?

Reduce stress. Organize your time more effectively, build a better relationship with your boss, negotiate realistic deadlines, find time during the day for detachment and relaxation, reduce unnecessary noise around your office, and limit interruption.

Asbestos Exposure at Work

There are four major sources of occupational respiratory diseases: asbestos, silica, lead, and carbon dioxide. Of these, asbestos has become a major concern, in part because of publicity surrounding asbestos in buildings such as schools constructed before the mid-1970s. Major efforts are now under way to rid these buildings of the cancer-causing asbestos.

OSHA standards require several actions with respect to asbestos. They require that companies monitor the air whenever an employer expects the level of asbestos to rise to one-half the allowable limit. (A company would therefore have to monitor if it expected asbestos levels of 0.1 fibers per cubic centimeters in this case.) Engineering controls—walls, special filters, and so forth—are required to maintain an asbestos level that complies with OSHA standards. Respirators can only be used if additional efforts are then still required to achieve compliance.

Computer Monitor Health Problems and How to Avoid Them

The fact that many workers today spend hours each day working in front of computer screens is creating health problems at work. According to a study by the National Institute for Occupational Safety and Health (NIOSH), short-term eye problems such as burning, itching, and tearing, as well as eyestrain and eye soreness are common complaints among video monitor users.

Backaches and neckaches are also widespread. These often occur because employees try to compensate for monitor problems (such as glare) by maneuvering into awkward body positions. There may also be a tendency for computer users to suffer from cumulative motion disorders, such as carpal tunnel syndrome, caused by repetitive use of the hands and arms at uncomfortable angles.[75]

NIOSH has therefore provided general recommendations regarding the use of computer monitors. These can be summarized as follows:

1. *Give employees rest breaks.* NIOSH recommends a 15-minute rest break after 2 hours of continuous work for operators under moderate workloads and 15-minute breaks every hour for those with heavy workloads.
2. *Design the maximum flexibility into the workstation so that it can be adapted to the individual operator.* For example, use movable keyboards, adjustable chairs with midback supports, and a video display in which screen height and position are independently adjustable.
3. *Reduce glare with devices such as shades over windows, terminal screen hoods properly positioned, antiglare screen filters, and recessed or indirect lighting.* Special "personal glare screen" eyeglasses can also lower the effect of glare.[76]
4. *Give workers a complete preplacement vision exam to ensure properly corrected vision for reduced visual strain.*

Many computer-related health problems can be reduced by using the right equipment and a little common sense. For example:

1. Place the keyboard in front of the employee, tilted away with the rear portion lower than the front.
2. Place the computer mouse and mousepad as close to the user as possible, and ensure that there are no obstructions on the desk that impede mouse movement.[77]
3. The height of the table or chair should allow wrists to be positioned at the same level as the elbow.
4. The monitor and typing material should be at or just below eye level, and the monitor should be a distance 18 to 30 inches from the eyes.
5. The wrists should be able to rest lightly on a pad for support.
6. The feet should be flat on the floor, or on a footrest.[78]

AIDS in the Workplace

Some of the most crucial AIDS-related issues employers must deal with concern their legal responsibilities in dealing with AIDS sufferers. Although case law is still evolving, several tentative conclusions are warranted. First, you cannot single out an employee to be tested for AIDS, because to do so would be to subject the person to discriminatory treatment under the Americans with Disabilities Act (ADA). Similarly, although you can probably require a physical exam that includes an AIDS test as a condition of employment, refusing to hire the person because of positive test results could put you at risk of a disability discrimination suit. Mandatory leave cannot be required of a person with AIDS unless work performance has deteriorated. Preemployment inquiries about AIDS (such as inquiries about any other illnesses or disabilities) would not be advisable given the prohibitions of the ADA. Providing sympathy and support and making reasonable accommodations to persons with AIDS, and using education and counseling to deal with the fears of the person's co-workers seem to be among the only concrete prescriptions for dealing with the concerns this disease elicits at work.[79]

Workplace Smoking

The Nature of the Problem   Smoking is a serious problem for employees and employers. For instance, the congressional Office of Technology Assessment estimates that each employee-smoker costs an employer between $2,000 and $5,000 yearly.[80] These costs derive from higher health and fire insurance, as well as increased absenteeism and reduced productivity (which occurs when, for instance, a smoker takes a 10-minute break to finish a cigarette down the hall).

What You Can and Cannot Do   In general, you can deny a job to a smoker as long as you do not use smoking as a surrogate for some other kind of discrimination. The EEOC, in other words, says that a policy of not hiring smokers is legal as long as the rules apply to all applicants and employees.[81] A "no-smokers hired" policy does not, according to one expert, violate the ADA because smoking is not considered a disability, and, in general, "employers' adoption of a 'no-smokers-hired' policy is not illegal under federal law."[82] Therefore, you can probably institute a policy against hiring people who smoke.

The problem arises, of course, when you try to implement smoking restrictions in a facility where you already have smokers. The best advice seems to be to proceed with aid of counsel one step at a time, starting with restrictions that are not too confining.

Smoking Policies   Employer smoking bans are on the rise because of health concerns, economic concerns, or the fear that nonsmoking employees will sue for a workplace free of secondhand smoke. In one survey of 283 employers, one-quarter of the organizations polled prohibited smoking anywhere on company premises—up from 14% the previous year.[83]

Dealing with Violence at Work

The Nature of the Problem   Violence against employees is an enormous problem at work. Fifty-seven percent of the employers in one recent poll said they had at least one violent threat or incident in their places between January 1996 and July 1999. These ranged from verbal threats (41%) to bomb threats (7%).[84] Homicide is the second leading cause of job-related deaths, accounting for about 17% of fatal injuries to workers.[85] Although in one study robbery was the primary motive for homicide at work, roughly one of seven workplace homicide victims was killed by a co-worker or personal associate.[86] For example, 29 U.S. Postal Service supervisors and colleagues were slain by disgruntled postal workers in a recent 10-year period.[87] Workplace violence isn't always aimed just at people. It can also manifest itself in sabotaging the firm's property, software, or information databases.[88]

Reducing Workplace Violence   HR managers can take several concrete steps to reduce the incidence of workplace violence. They include:

Heighten security measures   Heightened security measures are an employer's first line of defense against workplace violence, whether that violence derives from co-workers, customers, or outsiders. These measures include[89] improve external lighting; use drop safes to minimize cash on hand and post signs noting that only a limited amount of cash is on hand; install silent alarms and surveillance cameras; increase the number of staff on duty; provide staff training in conflict resolution and nonviolent response; close establishments during high-risk hours late at night and early in the morning;[90] issue a weapons policy that states, for instance, that regardless of their legality, firearms or other dangerous or deadly weapons cannot be brought onto the facility either openly or concealed.[91]

Improve employee screening   With about 30% of workplace attacks committed by co-workers, screening out potentially explosive internal and external applicants is the employer's next line of defense. Obtain a detailed employment application and solicit an applicant's employment history, education background, and references.[92] Sample interview questions to ask might include, for instance, "What frustrates you?" and "Who was your worst supervisor and why?"[93] Certain background circumstances, such as the following, may provide a red flag indicating the need for a more in-depth background investigation of the applicant:[94]

- An unexplained gap in employment
- Incomplete or false information on the résumé or application
- A negative, unfavorable, or false reference
- Prior insubordinate or violent behavior on the job
- A criminal history involving harassing or violent behavior
- A prior termination for cause with a suspicious (or no) explanation
- A history of drug or alcohol abuse

- Strong indications of instability in the individual's work or personal life as indicated, for example, by frequent job changes or geographic moves
- Lost licenses or accreditations[95]

Use workplace violence training   Supervisors can be trained to identify the clues that typically precede violent incidents. Common clues include:[96]

Verbal threats. Individuals often talk about what they may do. An employee might say, "Bad things are going to happen to so-and-so."

Physical actions. Troubled employees may try to intimidate others, gain access to places where they do not belong, or flash a concealed weapon in the workplace to test reactions.

Frustration. Most cases do not involve a panicked individual; a more likely scenario would involve an employee who has a frustrated sense of entitlement to a promotion, for example.

Obsession. An employee may hold a grudge against a co-worker or supervisor, and some cases stem from romantic interest.[97]

The following are telltale signs of a potentially violent employee:[98]

- An act of violence on or off the job.
- Erratic behavior evidencing a loss of perception or awareness of actions.
- Overly confrontational or antisocial behavior
- Sexually aggressive behavior
- Isolationist or loner tendencies
- Insubordinate behavior with a suggestion of violence
- Tendency to overreact to criticism
- Exaggerated interest in war, guns, violence, mass murders, catastrophes, and so on
- The commission of a serious breach of security
- Possession of weapons, guns, knives, or like items in the workplace
- Violation of privacy rights of others, such as searching desks or stalking
- Chronic complaining and the raising of frequent, unreasonable grievances
- A retributory or get-even attitude

The U.S. Postal Service recently took steps to reduce workplace threats and assaults. The steps include more background checks, drug testing, a 90-day probationary period for new hires, more stringent security (including a hotline that allows employees to report threatening situations), a zero tolerance policy for reporting and recording potentially violent incidents, and training managers to create a healthier workplace culture.[99]

Violence Toward Women at Work   While there are more fatal occupational injuries to men than to women, the proportion of women who are victims of assault is much higher. Of all women who die on the job, 39% are the victims of assault, for instance, whereas only 18% of males who die at work have been murdered. Violence against women in the workplace is therefore a particularly serious problem.[100]

Fatal workplace violence against women has three main sources. Of all females murdered at work, more than three-fourths are victims of random criminal violence carried out by an assailant unknown to the victim, as might occur during a robbery. The remaining criminal acts are carried out either by co-workers, family members, or previous friends or acquaintances.

Crime and Punishment Abroad

Maintaining a healthy and safe environment for expatriates—employees who are posted overseas—presents some unique concerns.[101] For example, international terrorists sometimes target the facilities and executives of multinational enterprises and the incidence of such attacks—although still low—has increased regularly.

Protecting overseas executives (and their families) has therefore fostered a thriving anti-terrorist securities industry. For example, securities consultants provide advice (such as fortify executives' homes and don't use the same schedule and route to work every day) as well as provide trained chauffeurs, guards, and armored vehicles.

Crime and imprisonment are safety issues while you're abroad as well. Theft and pickpocketing are always potential problems for travelers from abroad, for instance, but it's not always others' criminal behavior the traveler must watch out for. For example, "Travelers have been thrown in jail for exceeding a credit card limit, buying artifacts from an unlicensed dealer, entering an Islamic country with alcohol, or failing to meet a contract deadline," so that knowingly or innocently breaking local laws can be a major concern, too.[102]

Particularly when traveling in areas where medical facilities may not meet developed-country standards, dramatic events—sudden illnesses or serious accidents, for instance—can also be particularly serious abroad. Language difficulties, cultural misunderstandings, lack of normal support and infrastructure systems (such as telephones) can all combine to make an accident or illness that may be manageable in one country a disaster in another. As a result, many multinationals brief their business travelers and expatriates about what to expect and how to react when confronted with a health or safety problem abroad, others also make use of insurance programs (such as that of the MEDEX Assistance Corporation) to help their overseas travelers and their families if assistance is required.

There's nothing typical about workplace violence, but research sheds some light on the typical female victim. The typical female assault victim is a white female (79%), in her early 30s (mean age approximately 31), working as a salesperson (31%) in a convenience store (46%), and is shot by an unknown assailant (88%) at about 11:00 P.M.[103] Concrete security improvements including better lighting, cash drop-boxes, and similar steps are especially pertinent in reducing such violent acts against women. The box above provides a global perspective.

REVIEW

Summary

1. The area of safety and accident prevention is of concern to managers at least partly because of the staggering number of deaths and accidents occurring at work. There are three main reasons for safety programs: moral, legal, and economic.

2. The purpose of OSHA is to ensure every working person a safe and healthful workplace. OSHA standards are very complete and detailed and are enforced through a system of workplace inspections. OSHA inspectors can issue citations and recommend penalties to their area directors.

3. There are three basic causes of accidents: chance occurrences, unsafe conditions, and unsafe acts on the part of employees. In addition, three other work-related factors—the job itself, the work schedule, and the psychological climate—also contribute to accidents.

4. Unsafe acts on the part of employees are a second basic cause of accidents. Such acts are to some extent the result of certain behavior tendencies on the part of employees, and these tendencies are possibly the result of certain personal characteristics.

5. Most experts doubt that there are accident-prone people who have accidents regardless of the job. Instead, the consensus seems to be that the person who is accident prone in one job may not be on a different job. For example, vision is related to accident frequency for drivers and machine operators, but might not be for other workers, such as accountants.

6. There are several approaches to preventing accidents. One is to reduce unsafe conditions. The other approach is to reduce unsafe acts—for example, through selection and placement, training, positive reinforcement, propaganda, and top-management commitment.

7. Alcoholism, drug addiction, stress, and emotional illness are four important and growing health problems among employees. Alcoholism is a particularly serious problem that can drastically lower the effectiveness of your organization. Techniques including disciplining, discharge, in-house counseling, and referrals to an outside agency are used to deal with these problems.

8. Stress and burnout are other potential health problems at work. An employee can reduce job stress by getting away from work for a while each day, delegating, and developing a worry list.

9. Violence against employees is an enormous problem at work. Steps that can reduce workplace violence include improved security arrangements, better employee screening, and violence-reduction training.

Key Terms

Occupational Safety and   citations   unsafe acts
   Health Act   unsafe conditions   burnout
Occupational Safety and
   Health Administration
   (OSHA)

Discussion Questions and Exercises

1. How would you go about providing a safer work environment for your employees?

2. Discuss how you would go about minimizing the occurrence of unsafe acts on the part of your employees.

3. Discuss the basic facts about OSHA—its purpose, standards, inspection, and rights and responsibilities.

4. Explain the supervisor's role in safety.

5. Explain what causes unsafe acts.

6. Answer the question, "Is there such a thing as an accident-prone person?"

7. Describe at least five techniques for reducing accidents.

8. Explain how an employee could reduce stress at work.

APPLICATION EXERCISES

Case Incident: The New Safety Program

Employees' safety and health are very important matters in the laundry and cleaning business. Each facility is a small production plant in which machines, powered by high-pressure steam and compressed air, work at high temperatures washing, cleaning, and pressing garments often under very hot, slippery conditions. Chemical vapors are continually produced, and caustic chemicals are used in the cleaning process. High-temperature stills are almost continually "cooking down" cleaning solvents in order to remove impurities so that the solvents can be reused. If a mistake is made in this process—such as injecting too much steam into the still—a boilover occurs, in which boiling chemical solvent erupts out of the still, onto the floor, and onto anyone who happens to be standing in its way.

As a result of these hazards and the fact that chemically hazardous waste is continually produced in these stores, several government agencies (including OSHA and the Environmental Protection Agency) have instituted strict guidelines regarding the management of these plants. For example, posters have to be placed in each store notifying employees of their right to be told what hazardous chemicals they are dealing with and what is the proper method for handling each chemical. Special waste-management firms must be used to pick up and properly dispose of the hazardous waste.

A chronic problem the owners have is the unwillingness on the part of the cleaning–spotting workers to wear safety goggles. Not all the chemicals they use require safety goggles, but some—like the hydrofluorous acid used to remove rust stains from garments—are very dangerous. The latter is kept in special plastic containers because it dissolves glass. Some of the employees feel that wearing safety goggles can be troublesome; they are somewhat uncomfortable, and they also become smudged easily and thus cut down on visibility. As a result, it is sometimes almost impossible to get employees to wear their goggles.

Questions

1. How should a laundry go about identifying hazardous conditions that should be rectified?

2. Would it be advisable for a firm to set up a procedure for screening out accident-prone individuals?

3. How would you suggest that owners get all employees to behave more safely at work? Also, how would you advise them to get those who should be wearing goggles to do so?

Experiential Exercise

Purpose: The purpose of this exercise is to give you practice in identifying unsafe conditions.

Required Understanding: You should be familiar with material covered in this chapter, particularly that on unsafe conditions and that in the first *HR in Practice* box.

How to Set Up the Exercise/Instructions: Divide the class into groups of four or five students.

Assume that you are a safety committee retained by your school to identify and report on any possible unsafe conditions in and around the school building.

Each group will spend about 45 minutes in and around the building you are now in for the purpose of identifying and listing possible unsafe conditions. (*Hint*: Make use of the *HR in Practice* checklist.)

Return to the class in about 45 minutes, and a spokesperson for each group should list on the board the unsafe conditions you think you have identified. How many were there? Do you think these also violate OSHA standards? How would you go about checking?

TAKE IT TO THE WEB

 For Internet exercises, updates to chapter material, and more, visit the Dessler Web site at

www.prenhall.com/dessler

ENDNOTES

1. "Criminal Violation Depends on Knowledge," *BNA Bulletin to Management* (March 5, 1998): 68.

2. 'Occupational Injuries and Illnesses," *BNA Bulletin to Management* (January 18, 1996): 20–21; "Workplace Fatalities—1997," *BNA Bulletin to Management* (August 28, 1997): 276–77. The Workplace injury and illnesses rate, while still high, has actually declined in the last few years. The overall rate was 6.7 injuries or illnesses per 100 workers in private industry in 1998, 7.1% in 1997, and 8.4% in 1994. "Injuries, Illnesses Lowest on Record," *Occupational Hazards* (February 2000): 33.

3. "Workplace Injuries Cost $171 Billion, Cause 66,500 Deaths, Study Says," *BNAC Communicator* (winter 1998): 9.

4. *Workers' Compensation Manual for Managers and Supervisors* (Chicago: Commerce Clearing House, Inc., 1992), p. 12. See also Guy Toscano and Janice Windau, "The Changing Character of Fatal Work Injuries," *Monthly Labor Review* 117, no. 10 (October, 1994): 17–28.

5. "One the Job Injuries, Illnesses Continue Steady Decline," *BNA Bulletin in Management* (January 20, 2000): 21.

6. Occupational Safety and Health Administration; much of this is based on *All About OSHA* (revised) (Washington, DC: U.S. Department of Labor, 1980).

7. Todd Nighswonger, "Where Do You Set the Standard?" *Occupational Hazards* (May 2000): 59–60.

8. Bureau of National Affairs, "OSHA Hazard Communication Standard Enforcement," *Bulletin to Management* (February 23, 1989): 13.

9. Bureau of Labor Statistics, "What Every Employer Needs to Know About OSHA Record Keeping" (Washington, DC: U.S. Department of Labor, 1978), p. 3; and "Is It a Recordable Injury? Depends on the Treatment," *BNA Bulletin to Management* (September 29, 1999): 284.

10. "Supreme Court Says OSHA Inspectors Need Warrants," *Engineering News Record* (June 1, 1978): 9–10; and W. Scott Railton, "OSHA Gets Tough on Business," *Management Review* 80, no. 12 (December 1991): 28–29.

11. "Safety Program Rule Called Top OSHA Priority," *BNA Bulletin to Management* (October 31, 1996): 345.

12. "OSHA Seeks 'Cooperative Compliance,' " *BNA Bulletin to Management* (September 4, 1997): 288; and "OSHA's Cooperative Program Shoves Off," *BNA Bulletin to Management* (December 25, 1997): 416.

13. William Atkinson, "When OSHA Comes Knocking," *HRMagazine* (October 1999): 35–38.

14. Michael Verespej, "OSHA Revamps Its Inspection Policies," *Industry Week* (September 17, 1979): 19–20. See also Horace E. Johns, "OSHA's Impact," *Personnel Journal* 67, no. 11 (November 1988): 102–107.

15. "Employers Hit with Megafines for OSHA Violations," *BNA Bulletin to Management* (May 9, 1996): 146.

16. "Settling Safety Violations Has Benefits," *BNA Bulletin to Management* (July 31, 1997): 248.

17. Bureau of National Affairs, "OSHA Instruction on Penalties," *Bulletin to Management* (February 7, 1991): 33; Commerce Clearing House, "OSHA Will Begin Higher Fines March 1st," *Ideas and Trends in Personnel* (January 23, 1991): 14; John Bruening, "OSHRC on the Comeback Trail," *Occupational Hazards* (January 1991): 33–36. OSHA is also stressing record-keeping violations. See, for example, Brian Jackson and Jeffrey Myers, "Just When You Thought You Were Safe: OSHA Record-Keeping Violations," *Management Review* 83, no. 5 (May 1994): 63.

18. Jim Lastowka, "Ten Keys to Avioding OSHA Liability," *Occupational Hazards* (October 1999): 163–70.

19. Robert Grossman, "Handling Inspections: Tips from Insiders," *HRMagazine* (October 1999): 41–50.

20. Tom Andrews, "Getting Employees Comfortable with PPE," *Occupational Hazards* (January 2000): 35–38.

21. "A Safety Committee Man's Guide," Aetna Life and Casualty Insurance Company, Catalog 872684. See also Todd Nighswonger, "Get a Grip on Slips," *Occupational Hazards* (September 2000): 47–50.

22. *Ibid.*, see also "Workplace Fatalities," *BNA Bulletin to Management* (August 28, 1997): 276–77.

23. For a discussion of this see David Hofmann and Adam Stetzer, "A Cross-Level Investigation of Factors Influencing Unsafe Behaviors and Accidents," *Personnel Psychology* 49 (1996): 307–308.

24. Willard Kerr, "Complementary Theories of Safety Psychology," in Edwin Fleishman and Alan Bass, *Industrial Psychology* (Homewood, IL: Dorsey Press, 1974), pp. 493–500; and Alan Fowler, "How to Make the Workplace Safer," *People Management* 1, no. 2 (January 1995): 38–39. See also Hofmann and Stetzer, "A Cross-Level Investigation of Factors Influencing Unsafe Behaviors and Accidents," pp. 307–10.

25. List of unsafe acts from "A Safety Committee Man's Guide," Aetna Life and Casualty Insurance Company.

26. See, for example, Hofmann and Stetzer, *op. cit.*, pp. 307–308; C. Wright, "Routine Deaths: Fatal Accidents in the Oil Industry," *Sociological Review* 4 (1986): 265–89; D. E. Embrey, "Incorporating Management and Organizational Factors into Probabilistic Safety Assessment," *Reliability Engineering and System Safety* 38 (1992): 199–208.

27. A. G. Arbous and J. E. Kerrich, "The Phenomenon of Accident Proneness," *Industrial Medicine and Surgery* 2 (1953): 141–48, reprinted in Fleishman and Bass, *Industrial Psychology*, p. 485.

28. John Miner and J. Frank Brewer, "Management of Ineffective Performance," in Marvin Dunnette (ed.), *Handbook of Industrial and Organizational Psychology* (Chicago: Rand McNally, 1976), pp. 1004–1005.

29. Ernest McCormick and Joseph Tiffin, *Industrial Psychology* (Engewood Cliffs, NJ: Prentice Hall, 1974), pp. 522–23; Norman Maier, *Psychology and Industrial Organization* (Boston: Houghton-Mifflin, 1965), pp. 458–62; Milton Blum and James Nayler, *Industrial Psychology* (New York: Harper & Row, 1968), pp. 519–31. For an example, see David DeJoy, "Attributional Processes and Hazard Control Management in Industry," *Journal of Safety Research* 16 (summer 1985): 61–71.

30. R. House, D. M. Rousseau, and M. Thomas-Hunt, "The Meso Paradigm: A Framework for the Integration of Micro and Macro Organizational Behavior," in L. L. Cummings, B. M. Staw (eds.), *Research in Organizational Behavior* Vol. 17 (Greenwich, CT: JAI Press, 1995), pp. 71–114.

31. Michael Frone, "Predictors of Work Injurys Among Employed Adolescents," *Journal of Applied Psychology* 83, no. 4 (1998): pp. 565–76.

32. Maier, *Psychology and Industrial Organization*, pp. 463–67; McCormick and Tiffin, Industrial Psychology, pp. 533–36; and Blum and Nayler, *Industrial Psychology*, pp. 525–27.

33. D. Weschler, "Test for Taxicab Drivers," *Journal of Personnel Research* 5 (1926): 24–30, quoted in Maier, *Psychology and Industrial Organization*, p. 64. See also Leo DeBobes, "Psychological Factors in Accident Prevention," *Personnel Journal* 65 (January 1986). See also Curtiss Hansen, "A Causal Model of the Relationship Among Accidents, Biodata Personality, and Cognitive Factors," *Journal of Applied Psychology* 74, no. 1 (February 1989): 81–90.

34. Maier, *Psychology and Industrial Organization*, p. 463.

35. S. E. Wirt and H. E. Leedkee, "Skillful Eyes Prevent Accidents," *Annual Newsletter*, National Safety Council, Industrial Nursing Section, November 1945, pp. 10–12, quoted in Maier, *Psychology and Industrial Organization*, p. 466.

36. Judy D. Olian, "Genetic Screening for Employment Purposes," *Personnel Psychology* 37, no. 3 (autumn 1984): 423–38.

37. Dan Hartshorn, "The Safety Interview," *Occupational Hazards* (October 1999): 107–11.

38. S. Laner and R. J. Sell, "An Experiment on the Effect of Specially Designed Safety Posters," *Occupational Psychology* 34 (1960): 153–69, in McCormick and Tiffin, *Industrial Psychology*, p. 536.

39. McCormick and Tiffin, *Industrial Psychology*, p. 537. A group of international experts met in Belgium in 1986 and concluded that a successful safety poster must be simple and specific and reinforce safe behavior rather than negative behavior. See "What Makes an Effective Safety Poster," *National Safety and Health News* 134, no. 6 (December 1986): 32–34.

40. James Nash, "Rewarding the Safety Process," *Occupational Hazards* (March 2000): 29–34.

41. OSHA has published two useful training manuals: *Training Requirements of OSHA Standards* (February 1976) and *Teaching Safety and Health in the Work Place*, U.S. Department of Labor, Occupational Safety and Health Administration (1976); see also J. Surry, "Industrial Accident Research: Human Engineering Approach" (Toronto: University of Toronto, Department of Industrial Engineering, June 1968), Chapter 4, quoted in McCormick and Tiffin, *Industrial Psychology*, p. 534. For an example of a very successful incentive program aimed at boosting safety at Campbell Soup Company, see Frederick Wahl, Jr., "Soups on for Safety," *National Safety and Health News*, no. 6 (December 1986): 49–53. For a discussion of how employee involvement can impact job redesign and employee safety, see Douglas May and Catherine Schwoerer, "Employee Health by Design: Using Employee Involvement Teams in Ergonomics Job Redesign," *Personnel Psychology*, no. 4 (winter 1994): 861–76.

42. Judi Komaki, Kenneth Barwick, and Lawrence Scott, "A Behavioral Approach to

Occupational Safety: Pinpointing and Reinforcing Safe Performance in a Food Manufacturing Plant," *Journal of Applied Psychology* 63 (August 1978): 434–45. See also Robert Reber, Jerry Wallin, and David Duhon, "Preventing Occupational Injuries Through Performance Management," *Public Personnel Management*, no. 2 (summer 1993): 301–11; Anat Arkin, "Incentives to Work Safely," *Personnel Management*, no. 9 (September 1994): 48–52; and Peter Makin and Valerie Sutherland, "Reducing Accidents Using a Behavioral Approach," *Leadership and Organizational Development Journal*, no. 5 (1994): 5–10.

43. Judi Komaki, Arlene Heinzmann, and Lorealie Lawson, "Effect of Training and Feedback: Component Analysis of a Behavioral Safety Program," *Journal of Applied Psychology* 65 (June 1980): 261–70. See also Jorma Sari, "When Does Behavior Modification Prevent Accidents," *Leadership and Organizational Development Journal*, no. 5 (1994): 11–15.

44. J. Nigel Ellis and Susan Warner, "Using Safety Awards to Promote Fall Prevention," *Occupational Hazards* (June 1999): 59–62.

45. Gerald Wagner, "The Hierarchy of Controls: An Alternative to Behavior Based Safety," *Occupational Hazards* (May 1999): 95–97; John Grubbs, "Exploring Your Behavior Based Safety Options," *Occupational Hazards* (July 1999): 36–40.

46. Dov Zohar, "Safety Climate in Industrial Organizations Theoretical and Implied Implications," *Journal of Applied Psychology* 65 (February 1980): 97. For a discussion of the importance of getting employees involved in managing their own safety program, see John Lutness, "Self-Managed Safety Program Gets Workers Involved," *Safety and Health* 135, no. 4 (April 1987): 42–45. See also Frederick Streff, Michael Kalsher, and E. Scott, "Developing Efficient Workplace Safety Programs: Observations of Response Co-Variations," *Journal of Organizational Behavior Management* 13, no. 2 (1993).

47. Willie Hammer, *Occupational Safety Management and Engineering* (Englewood Cliffs, NJ: Prentice Hall, 1985): pp. 62–63.

48. Lester Bittel, *What Every Supervisor Should Know* (New York: McGraw-Hill, 1974), p. 25. For an example of an effective safety training program, see Michael Pennacchia, "Interactive Training Sets the Pace," *Safety and Health*, no. 1 (January 1987): 24–27; and Philip Poynter and David Stevens, "How to Secure an Effective Health and Safety Program at Work," *Professional Safety*, no. 1 (January 1987): 32–41. Appointing a safety committee can also be useful. See for example, Neville Tompkins, "Getting the Best Help from Your Safety Committee," *HRMagazine*, no. 4 (April 1995): 76.

49. "With Pay on the Line, Managers Improve Safety," *BNA Bulletin to Management* (March 20, 1997): 89.

50. Dov Zohar, "A Group Level Model of Safety Climate: Testing the Effect of a Group Climate on Microtek Students in Manufacturing Jobs," *Journal of Applied Psychology* 85, no. 4 (2000): 587–96. See also Judith Erickson, "Corporate Culture: The Key to Safety Performance," *Occupational Hazards* (April 2000): 45–50.

51. *Workers' Compensation Manual for Managers and Supervisors,* p. 24. James Frierson, "An Analysis of ADA Provisions on Denying Employment Because of a Risk of Future Injury," *Employee Relations Law Journal*, no. 4 (spring 1992): 603–22.

52. Bureau of National Affairs, "Workplace Safety: Improving Management Practices," *Bulletin to Management* (February 9, 1989) 42, 47; see also Marlene Morgenstern, "Workers' Compensation: Managing Costs," *Compensation and Benefits Review* (September/October 1992): 30–38. See also Linda Johnson, "Preventing Injuries: The Big Payoff," *Personnel Journal* (April 1994): 61–64; and David Webb, "The Bathtub Effect: Why Safety Programs Fail," *Management Review* (February 1994): 51–54.

53. Howard Street, "Getting Full Value From Auditing and Metrics," *Occupational Hazards* (August 2000): 33–36.

54. Lisa Cullen, "Safety Committees: A Smart Business Decision," *Occupational Hazards* (May 1999): 99–104.

55. Hofmann and Stetzer, *op. cit.*, p. 329.

56. This section based largely on Miner and Brewer, "Management of Ineffective Performance," p. 1005.

57. "Drug Use Among Employees," *BNA Bulletin to Management* (May 2, 1996): 140–41.

58. *Ibid.*

59. *Ibid.*

60. "Employee Alcohol Testing on the Rise," *BNA Bulletin to Management* (August 20, 1998): 261.

61. Gopal Pati and John Adkins Jr., "The Employer's Role in Alcoholism Assistance," *Personnel Journal* 62, no. 7 (July 1983): 568–72. See also Commerce Clearing House, "How Should Employees Respond to Indications an Employee May Have an Alcohol or Drug Problem?" *Ideas and Trends* (April 6, 1989): 53–57.

62. Marice Cavanaugh et al., "An Empirical Examination of Self-Reported Work Stress Among U.S. Managers," *Journal of Applied Psychology* 85, no. 1 (2000): 65–74.

63. This is based on Terry Beehr and John Newman, "Organizational Stress, Employer Health, and Organizational Effectiveness: A Factor Analysis, Model, and Literature Review," *Personnel Psychology* 31 (winter 1978): 665–99. See also Shailendra Singh, "Managing Stress Through Empowerment: A Brief Literature Survey," *Management and Labor Studies*, 22, no. 1 (January 1997): 26–32.

64. Eric Sundstrom et al., "Office Noise, Satisfaction, and Performance," *Environment and Behavior*, no. 2 (March 1994): 195–222.

65. Michael Manning, Conrad Jackson, and Marcelline Fusilier, "Occupational Stress, Social Support, and the Costs of Health Care," *Academy of Management Journal* 39, no. 3 (1996): 738–50.

66. "Stress, Depression Cost Employers," *Occupational Hazards* (December 1998): 24.

67. John Newman and Terry Beehr, "Personnel and Organizational Strategies for Handling Job Stress: A Review of Research and Opinion," *Personnel Psychology* (spring 1979): 1–43. See also "Work Place Stress: How to Curb Claims," *BNA Bulletin to Management* (April 14, 1988): 120.

68. Karl Albrecht, *Stress and the Manager*, 1979, pp. 253–55. Reprinted by permission of Prentice Hall, Upper Saddle River, NJ. For a discussion of the related symptoms of depression see James Krohe, Jr., "An Epidemic of Depression?" *Across-the-Board* (September 1994): 23–27.

69. "Managing Stress in the Workplace," *BNA Bulletin to Management* (January 18, 1996): 24. Reprinted with permission from *Bulletin to Management (BNA Policy and Practice Series)* (January 18, 1996): 24. Copyright 1996 by The Bureau of National Affairs, Inc. (800-372-1033), http://www.bna.com.

70. Pascale Carayon, "Stressful Jobs and Non-Stressful Jobs: A Cluster Analysis of Office Jobs," *Ergonomics*, no. 2 (1994): 311–23.

71. *Ibid.*, pp. 319–20.

72. Harvey Freudenberger, *Burn-out* (Toronto: Bantam Books, 1980).

73. Raymond Lee and Blake Ashforth, "A Meta-Analytic Examination of the Correlates of the Three Dimensions of Job Burnout," *Journal of Applied Psychology* 81, no. 2 (1996): 123–33.

74. Freudenberger, *op. cit.*, pp. 16–18. See also Raymond Lee and Blake Ashforth, "A Further Examination of Managerial Burnout: Toward an Integrated Model," *Journal of Organizational Behavior* 14, (1993): 3–20.

75. J. A Savage, "Are Computer Terminals Zapping Workers' Health?" *Business and Society Review* (1994).

76. Anne Chambers, "Computervision Syndrome: Relief is in Sight," *Occupational Hazards* (October 1999): 179–84.

77. These are based on "Inexpensive Ergonomic Innovations," *BNA Bulletin to Management* (February 1, 1996): 40.

78. Sondra Lotz Fisher, "Are Your Employees Working Ergosmart?" *Personnel Journal* (December 1996): 91–92. See also William Kincaid, "Office Ergonomics for Maximum Performance," *Occupational Hazards* (May 1999): 85–88.

79. Bureau of National Affairs, "AIDS and the Workplace: Issues, Advice, and Answers," *Bulletin to Management* (November 14, 1985): 1–6. See also David Ritter and Ronald Turner, "AIDS: Employer Concerns and Options," *Labor Law Journal*, no. 2 (February 1987): 67–83; and Bureau of National Affairs, "How Employers Are Responding to AIDS in the Workplace," *Fair Employment Practices* (February 18, 1988): 21–22. For a complete guide to services and information regarding "The Work Place and AIDS," see *Personnel Journal*, no. 10 (October 1987): 65–80. See also William H. Wager, "AIDS: Setting Policy, Educating Employees at Bank of America," *Personnel*, no. 8 (August 1988): 4–10. See also Margaret Magnus, "AIDS: Fear and Ignorance," *Personnel Journal*, no. 2 (February 1988): 28–32, for poll regarding major workplace comments associated with AIDS, and Maureen Minehan, "New Aids Survival Rates Mean Patients Returning to Work," *HRMagazine* 42, no. 10 (October 1997): 208.

80. Marco Colossi, "Do Employees Have the Right to Smoke?" *Personnel Journal* (April 1988): 72–79.

81. Jim Collison, "Workplace Smoking Policies: Sixteen Questions and Answers," *Personnel Journal* (April 1988): 81. See also Daniel Warner, "We Do Not Hire Smokers: May Employers Discriminate Against Smokers?" *Employee Responsibilities and Rights*, no. 2 (June 1994): 129–40.

82. Warner, "We Do Not Hire Smokers," p. 138.

83. Bureau of National Affairs, "Smoking Bans on the Rise," *Bulletin to Management* (March 16, 1989): 82.

84. "An Ounce of Workplace Violence Prevention Could Save Employers from a World of Hurt," *BNA Bulletin to Management* (November 18, 1999).

85. Gus Toscano and Janice Windau, "The Changing Character of Fatal Work Injuries," *Monthly Labor Review* (October 1994): 17–28. See also "Workplace Violence," *BNA Bulletin to Management* (October 31, 1996): 348–49.

86. *Ibid.*, p. 17.

87. Based on Louis DiLorenzo and Darren Carroll, "The Growing Menace: Violence in the Workplace," *New York State Bar Journal* (January 1995): 24.

88. Jennifer Laabs, "Employees Sabotage," *Workforce* (July 1999): 33–42.

89. "Workplace Violence: Sources and Solutions," *BNA Bulletin to Management* (November 4, 1993): 345.

90. *Ibid.*

91. "Weapons in the Workplace: A Review of Employer Policies," *BNA Bulletin to Management* (June 5, 1996): 1–7; Lloyd Nigro and William Waugh, Jr., "Violence in the American Workplace: Challenges to the Public Employer," *Public Administration Review* (July/August 1996): 326–33. "OSHA Addresses Top Homicide Risk," *BNA Bulletin to Management* (May 14, 1998): 148.

92. Alfred Feliu, "Workplace Violence and the Duty of Care: The Scope of an Employer's

Obligation to Protect Against the Violent Employee," *Employee Relations Law Journal* 20, no. 3 (winter 1994/95): 395.

93. Dawn Anfuso, "Workplace Violence," *Personnel Journal* (October 1994): 66–77.

94. Feliu, "Workplace Violence and the Duty of Care," p. 395.

95. Quoted from Feliu, "Workplace Violence and the Duty of Care," p. 395.

96. "Preventing Workplace Violence," *BNA Bulletin to Management* (June 10, 1993): 177. See also Jenny McCune, "Companies Grapple with Workplace Violence," *Management Review*, no. 3 (March 1994): 52–57.

97. Quoted or paraphrased from *ibid.*, p. 177 and based on recommendations from Chris Hatcher.

98. Feliu, "Workplace Violence and the Duty of Care," pp. 401–402.

99. "Employers Battling Workplace Violence Might Consider Postal Service Plan," *BNA Bulletin to Management* (August 5, 1999): 241.

100. This is based on Beverly Younger, "Violence Against Women in the Workplace," *Employee Assistance Quarterly*, no. 3/4 (1994): 113–33.

101. This is based on Dennis Briscoe, *International Human Resource Management* (Englewood Cliffs, NJ: Prentice Hall, 1995): 167–69.

102. *Ibid.*, p. 168.

103. *Ibid.*, p. 120.

Glossary

A

action learning A training technique by which management trainees are allowed to work full time analyzing and solving problems in other departments. [146]

adverse impact The overall impact of employer practices that result in significantly higher percentages of members of minorities and other protected groups being rejected for employment, placement, or promotion. [39]

affirmative action Steps that are taken for the purpose of eliminating the present effects of past discrimination. [28]

AFL-CIO A voluntary federation in the United States of about 100 national and international (ie, with branches in Canada) unions. [219]

Age Discrimination in Employment Act of 1967 The act prohibiting arbitrary age discrimination and specifically protecting individuals over 40 years old. [28]

agency shop A form of union security in which employees who do not belong to the union must still pay union dues on the assumption that union efforts benefit all workers. [219]

Albemarle Paper Company v. Moody Supreme Court case in which it was ruled that the validity of job tests must be documented and that employee performance standards must be unambiguous. [34]

alternation ranking method Ranking employees from best to worst on a particular trait. [168]

Americans with Disabilities Act (ADA) The act requiring employers to make reasonable accommodations for disabled em- ployees, it prohibits discrimination against disabled persons. [36]

application form The form that provides information on education, prior work record, and skills. [91]

appraisal interview An interview in which the supervisor and subordinate review the appraisal and make plans to remedy deficiencies and reinforce strengths. [174]

arbitration The most definitive type of third-party intervention, in which the arbitrator usually has the power to determine and dictate the settlement terms. [234]

authority The right to make decisions, direct others' work, and give orders. [3]

authorization cards In order to petition for a union election, the union must show that at least 30% of employees may be interested in being unionized. Employees indicate this interest by signing authorization cards. [225]

B

bargaining unit The group of employees the union will be authorized to represent. [226]

behavior modeling A training technique in which trainees are first shown good management techniques in a film, are then asked to play roles in a simulated situation, and are then given feedback and praise by their supervisor. [150]

benefits Indirect financial payments given to employees. They may include health and life insurance, vacation, pension, education plans, and discounts on company products, for instance. [201]

bona fide occupational qualification (BFOQ) Requirement that an employee be of a certain religion, sex, or national origin where that is reasonably necessary to the organization's normal operation. Specified by the 1964 Civil Rights Act. [41]

boycott The combined refusal by employees and other interested parties to buy or use the employer's products. [235]

burnout The total depletion of physical and mental resources caused by excessive striving to reach an unrealistic work-related goal. [288]

business necessity Justification for an otherwise discriminatory employment practice, provided there is an overriding legitimate business purpose. [41]

C

case study method A development method in which the manager is presented with a written description of an organizational problem to diagnose and solve. [147]

central tendency A tendency to rate all employees the same way, such as rating them all average. [176]

citations Summons informing employers and employees of the regulations and standards that have been violated in the workplace. [276]

Civil Rights Act of 1964, Title VII Rights guaranteed by the Constitution of the United States that makes it unlawful practice for an employer to discriminate against any individual with respect to hiring, compensation, terms, conditions, or privileges of employment because of race, color, religion, sex, or nation. [187]

Civil Rights Act of 1991 (CRA 1991) It places burden of proof back on employers and permits compensatory and punitive damages. [35]

closed shop A form of union security in which the company can hire only union members. This was outlawed in 1947 but still exists in some industries (such as printing). [219]

collective bargaining The process through which representatives of management and the union meet to negotiate a labor agreement. [231]

comparable worth The concept by which women who are usually paid less than men can claim that men in comparable rather than strictly equal jobs are paid more. [195]

compensable factor A fundamental, compensable element of a job, such as skills, effort, responsibility, and working conditions. [189]

competitive advantage The basis for superiority over competitors and thus for hoping to claim certain customers. [13]

content validity A test that is *content valid* is one in which the test contains a fair sample of the tasks and skills actually needed for the job in question. [104]

controlled experimentation Formal methods for testing the effectiveness of a training program, preferably with before-and-after tests and a control group. [153]

criterion validity A type of validity based on showing that scores on the test *(predictors)* are related to job performance *(criterion)*. [104]

critical incident method Keeping a record of uncommonly good or undesirable examples of an employee's work-related behavior and reviewing it with the employee at predetermined times. [170]

D

Davis-Bacon Act A law passed in 1931 that sets wage rates for laborers employed by contractors working for the federal government. [186]

defined benefit pension plan A plan that contains a formula for determining retirement benefits. [205]

defined contribution plan A plan in which the employer's contribution to employees' retirement or savings funds is specified. [205]

discipline A procedure that corrects or punishes a subordinate because a rule or procedure has been violated. [253]

dismissal Involuntary termination of an employee's employment with the firm. [255]

disparate impact Means there is an unintentional disparity between the proportion of a protected group applying for a position and the proportion getting the job. [39]

disparate treatment Means there is an intentional disparity between the proportion of a protected group and the proportion getting the job. [39]

downsizing Refers to the process of reducing, usually dramatically, the number of people employed by the firm. [262]

E

employee orientation A procedure for providing new employees with basic background information about the firm. [135]

Employee Retirement Income Security Act (ERISA) Signed into law by President Ford in 1974 to require that pension rights be vested, and protected by a government agency, PBGC. [200]

employee stock ownership plan (ESOP) A corporation contributes shares of its own stock to a trust in which additional contributions are made annually. The trust distributes the stock to employees on retirement or separation from service. [200]

Equal Employment Opportunity Commission (EEOC) The commission, created by Title VII, is empowered to investigate job discrimination complaints and sue on behalf of complainants. [27]

Equal Pay Act of 1963 An amendment to the Fair Labor Standards Act designed to require equal pay for women doing the same work as men. [28,187]

F

Fair Labor Standards Act Congress passed this act in 1936 to provide for minimum wages, maximum hours, overtime pay, and child labor protection. The law has been amended many times and covers most employees. [186]

federal agency guidelines Guidelines issued by federal agencies charged with ensuring compliance with equal employment federal legislation explaining recommended employer procedures in detail. [29]

flexible benefits plan Individualized plans allowed by employers to accommodate employee preferences for benefits. [206]

forced distribution method Similar to grading on a curve; predetermined percentages of ratees are placed in various performance categories. [170]

G

gain-sharing plan An incentive plan that engages employees in a common effort to achieve productivity objectives and share the gains. [201]

good faith bargaining A term that means both parties are communicating and negotiating and that proposals are being matched with counterproposals with both parties making every reasonable effort to arrive at agreements. It does not mean that either party is compelled to agree to a proposal. [231]

good faith effort strategy Employment strategy aimed at changing practices that have contributed in the past to excluding or underutilizing protected groups. [50]

graphic rating scale A scale that lists a number of traits and a range of performance for each. The employee is then rated by identifying the score that best describes his or her level of performance for each trait. [168]

Griggs v. The Duke Power Company Case heard by the Supreme Court in which the plaintiff argued that his employer's requirement that coal handlers be high school graduates was unfairly discriminatory. In finding for the plaintiff, the Court ruled that discrimination need not be overt to be illegal, that employment practices must be related to job performance, and that the burden of proof is on the employer to show that hiring standards are job related. [34]

guaranteed fair treatment Employer programs that are aimed at ensuring that all employees are treated fairly, generally by providing formalized, well-documented, and highly publicized vehicles through which employees can appeal any eligible issues. [251]

H

halo effect In performance appraisal, the problem that occurs when a supervisor's rating of a subordinate on one trait biases the rating of that person on other traits. [176]

human resource management The policies and practices one needs to carry out the "people" or human resource aspects of a management position, including recruiting, screening, training, rewarding, and appraising. [2]

I

illegal bargaining items Items in collective bargaining that are forbidden by law; for example, the clause agreeing to hire "union members exclusively" would be illegal in a right-to-work state. [232]

incentive plan A plan in which a production standard is set for a specific work group, and its members are paid incentives if the group exceeds the production standard. [196]

in-house development centers A company-based method for exposing prospective managers to realistic exercises to develop improved management skills. [150]

insubordination Willful disregard or disobedience of the boss's authority or legitimate orders; criticizing the boss in public. [257]

interview A procedure designed to solicit information from a person's oral responses to oral inquiries. [111]

J

job analysis The procedure for determining the duties and skill requirements of a job and the kind of person who should be hired for it. [62]

job description A list of a job's duties, responsibilities, reporting relationships, working conditions, and supervisory responsibilities—one product of a job analysis. [62]

job evaluation A formal and systematic comparison of jobs to determine the worth of one job relative to another. [188]

job posting Posting notices of job openings on company bulletin boards is an effective recruiting method. [75]

job rotation A management training technique that involves moving a trainee from department to department to broaden his or her experience and identify strong and weak points. [146]

job specification A list of a job's "human requirements," that is, the requisite education, skills, personality, and so on—another product of a job analysis. [62]

L

Landrum-Griffin Act The law aimed at protecting union members from possible wrongdoing on the part of their unions. [223]

layoff A situation in which there is a temporary shortage of work and employees are told there is no work for them but that management intends to recall them when work is again available. [262]

learning organization An organization "skilled at creating, acquiring, and transferring knowledge and at modifying its behavior to reflect new knowledge and insights." [152]

line manager A manager who is authorized to direct the work of subordinates and responsible for accomplishing the organization's goals. [3]

lockout A refusal by the employer to provide opportunities to work. [235]

M

management assessment centers A situation in which management candidates are asked to make decisions in hypothetical situations and are scored on their performance. It usually also involves testing and the use of management games. [110]

management by objectives (MBO) Involves setting specific measurable goals with each

employee and then periodically reviewing the progress made. [171]

management development Any attempt to improve current or future management performance by imparting knowledge, changing attitudes, or increasing skills. [145]

mandatory bargaining items Items in collective bargaining that a party must bargain over if they are introduced by the other party—for example, pay. [232]

mediation Intervention in which a neutral third party tries to assist the principals in reaching agreement. [233]

merit pay (merit raise) Any salary increase awarded to an employee based on his or her individual performance. [199]

N

national emergency strikes Strikes that might "imperil the national health and safety." [223]

National Labor Relations Board (NLRB) The agency created by the Wagner Act to investigate unfair labor practice charges and to provide for secret-ballot elections and majority rule in determining whether or not a firm's employees want a union. [220]

Norris-LaGuardia Act This law marked the beginning of the era of strong encouragement of unions and guaranteed to each employee the right to bargain collectively "free from interference, restraint, or coercion." [220]

O

Occupational Safety and Health Act The law passed by Congress in 1970 "to assure so far as possible every working man and

woman in the nation safe and healthful working conditions and to preserve our human resources." [273]

Occupational Safety and Health Administration (OSHA) The agency created within the Department of Labor to set safety and health standards for almost all workers in the United States. [273]

Office of Federal Contract Compliance Programs (OFCCP) This office is responsible for implementing the executive orders and ensuring compliance of federal contractors. [28]

on-the-job training (OJT) Training a person to learn a job while working at it. [139]

open shop Perhaps the least attractive type of union security from the union's point of view, the workers decide whether or not to join the union; and those who join must pay dues. [219]

opinion surveys Communication devices that use questionnaires to regularly ask employees their opinions about the company, management, and work life. [250]

organizational development (OD) A method aimed at changing the attitudes, values, and beliefs of employees so that employees can improve the organization. [151]

outplacement counseling A systematic process by which a terminated person is trained and counseled in the techniques of self-appraisal and securing a new position. [259]

P

paired comparison method Ranking employees by making a

chart of all possible pairs of the employees for each trait and indicating which is the better employee of the pair. [168]

performance analysis Verifying that there is a performance deficiency and determining whether that deficiency should be rectified through training or through some other means (such as transferring the employee). [137]

personnel replacement charts Company records showing present performance and promotability of inside candidates for the most important positions. [74]

piecework A system of pay based on the number of items processed by each individual worker in a unit of time, such as items per hour or items per day. [196]

plant closing law The Worker Adjustment and Retraining Notification Act, which requires notifying employees in the event an employer decides to close its facility. [247]

Pregnancy Discrimination Act (PDA) An amendment to Title VII of the Civil Rights Act that prohibits sex discrimination based on "pregnancy, childbirth, or related medical conditions." [29]

Preretirement counseling Employer-sponsored counseling aimed at providing information to ease the passage of employees into retirement. [264]

profit-sharing plan A plan whereby most employees share in the company's profits. [199]

protected class Persons such as minorities and women protected by equal opportunity laws including Title VII. [34]

Q

qualifications inventories Manual or computerized systematic records listing employees' education, career and development interests, languages, special skills, and so on to be used in forecasting inside candidates for promotion. [74]

quota strategy Employment strategy aimed at mandating the same results as the good faith effort strategy through specific hiring and promotion restrictions. [50]

R

ranking method The simplest method of job evaluation that involves ranking each job relative to all other jobs, usually based on overall difficulty. [189]

ratio analysis A forecasting technique for determining future staff needs by using ratios between sales volume and number of employees needed. [73]

reliability The characteristic which refers to the consistency of scores obtained by the same person when retested with the identical or equivalent tests. [104]

retirement The point at which a person gives up one's work, usually between the ages of 60 to 65, but increasingly earlier today due to firms' early retirement incentive plans. [264]

S

salary survey A survey aimed at determining prevailing wage rates. A good salary survey provides specific wage rates for specific jobs. Formal written questionnaire surveys are the most comprehensive, but telephone surveys and newspaper ads are also sources of information. [188]

Scanlon plan An incentive plan developed in 1937 by Joseph Scanlon and designed to encourage cooperation, involvement, and sharing of benefits. [200]

sensitivity training A method for increasing employees' insights into their own behavior by candid discussions in groups led by special trainers. [151]

severance pay A one-time payment some employers provide when terminating an employee. [203]

sexual harassment Harassment on the basis of sex that has the purpose or effect of substantially interfering with a person's work performance or creating an intimidating, hostile, or offensive work environment. [30]

simulated training Training employees on special off-the-job equipment, as in airplane pilot training, whereby training costs and hazards can be reduced. [139]

speak up! programs Communications programs that allow employees to register questions, concerns, and complaints about work-related matters. [249]

staff manager A manager who assists and advises line managers. [3]

stock option The right to purchase a stated number of shares of a company stock at today's price at some time in the future. [198]

strategic human resource management The "linking of HRM with strategic goals and objectives in order to improve business performance and develop organizational cultures." [15]

survey feedback A method that involves surveying employees' attitudes and providing feedback to department managers so that problems can be solved by the managers and employees. [151]

sympathy strike A strike that takes place when one union strikes in support of the strike of another. [235]

T

Taft-Hartley Act Also known as the Labor Management Relations Act, this law prohibited union unfair labor practices and enumerated the rights of employees as union members. It also enumerated the rights of employers. [222]

task analysis A detailed study of a job to identify the skills required so that an appropriate training program may be instituted. [136]

team building Improving the effectiveness of teams such as corporate officers and division directors through use of consultants, interviews, and team-building meetings. [151]

terminate at will The idea, based in law, that the employment relationship can be terminated at will by either the employer or the employee for any reason. [256]

termination interview The interview in which an employee is informed of the fact that he or she has been dismissed. [258]

test validity The accuracy with which a test, interview, and so on measures what it purports to measure or fulfills the function it was designed to fill. [103]

Title VII of the 1964 Civil Rights Act The section of the act that says an employer cannot discriminate on the basis of race, color, religion, sex, or national origin with respect to employment. [27]

top-down programs Communications activities including in-house television centers, frequent roundtable discussions, and in-house newsletters that provide continuing opportunities for the firm to let all employees be updated on important matters regarding the firm. [250]

training The process of teaching new employees the basic skills they need to perform their jobs. [135]

trend analysis Study of a firm's past employment needs over a period of years to predict future needs. [73]

U

union salting A union organizing tactic by which workers who are in fact employed full-time by a union as undercover union organizers are hired by unwitting employers. [224]

union shop A form of union security in which the company can hire nonunion people but they must join the union after a prescribed period of time and pay dues. (If they do not, they can be fired.) [219]

unsafe acts Behavior tendencies and undesirable attitudes that cause accidents. [281]

unsafe conditions The mechanical and physical conditions that cause accidents. [278]

V

vesting Provision that money placed in a pension fund cannot be forfeited for any reason. [206]

Vietnam Era Veterans' Readjustment Act of 1974 An act requiring that employers with government contracts take affir-

mative action to hire disabled veterans. [29]

Vocational Rehabilitation Act of 1973 The act requiring certain federal contractors to take affirmative action for disabled persons. [29]

voluntary bargaining items Items in collective bargaining over which bargaining is neither illegal nor mandatory—neither party can be compelled against its wishes to negotiate over those items. [232]

W

wage curve Shows the relationship between the value of the job and the average wage paid for this job. [190]

Wagner Act This law banned certain types of unfair labor practices and provided for secret-ballot elections and majority rule for determining whether or not a firm's employees want to unionize. [220]

Walsh-Healey Public Contract Act A law enacted in 1936 that requires minimum-wage and working conditions for employees working on any government contract amounting to more than $10,000. [186]

Wards Cove v. Atonio U.S. Supreme Court decision that makes it difficult to prove a case of unlawful discrimination against an employer. [35]

wildcat strike An unauthorized strike occurring during the term of a contract. [234]

worker involvement programs Programs that aim to boost organizational effectiveness by getting employees to participate in planning, organizing, and managing their jobs. [145]

worker's compensation Provides income and medical benefits to work-related accident victims or their dependents regardless of fault. [203]

wrongful discharge An employee dismissal that does not comply with the law or does not comply with the contractual arrangement stated or implied by the firm via its employment application forms, employee manuals, or other promises. [257]

Index

Page numbers followed by f indicate figure: those followed by t indicate table.

recruitment and, 85–91
of workforce, 5
diversity management, 47–50
diversity training, 144–145
dot-com companies, employee
compensation for, 196, 197f
Dow and Ciba-Geigy, 149
downsizing, 262–264
drug screening, during employee
selection, 125–126
Duracell, Inc., 263

E

Electromation Corporation case,
239–240
electronic monitoring, 255, 256f
electronic performance monitoring (EPM), 173–174
electronic performance support
systems (EPSS), 10
Employee Appraiser, 173
employee assistance programs
(EAPs), 206
employee commitment, human
resources and, 11
employee compensation,
185–207
benefits, 201–207 (*See also* benefits)
broadbanding, 194
comparable worth, 195–196
competency-based pay, 193
current trends in, 193–196
for dot-com companies, 196,
197f
equity and, 188
establishing pay rates,
188–193 (*See also* pay
rates, setting)
globalization and, 195f
incentive plans, 196–201 (*See
also* incentive plans)
"new pay," 194
employee compensation laws,
186–188
Civil Rights Act, 1964, 187
Davis-Bacon Act, 1931, 186
Equal Pay Act, 1963, 187
Fair Labor Standards Act,
1938, 186

Walsh-Healey Public Contract
Act, 1936, 186
employee contracts, in foreign
countries, 263f
employee discipline, 253–255,
254f
guidelines for, 254f
without punishment, 253–255
employee health, 285–286
AIDS, 290
alcoholism, 285–286, 287f
asbestos, 289
burnout, 288–289
computers and, 289–290
job stress, 286–289
smoking in the workplace,
290–291
substance abuse, 285–286
employee leasing
benefits and, 207
defined, 207
employee orientation, 135
employee participation programs, National Labor
Relations Act and, 239–240
employee privacy, 255, 256f
employee referral programs, 82,
84
Employee Retirement Income
Security Act (ERISA), 200,
205–206
employee selection, 102–126 (*See
also* selection interviews)
accident prevention and, 282
*Albemarle Paper Company v.
Moody,* 34–35
applications, 44
arrest records, 44
background investigations,
118–123
discriminatory practices,
43–44
drug screening, 125–126
educational requirements, 43
graphology, 123–124
Griggs v. Duke Power Company,
34
honesty testing, 123, 124f
immigration laws, 126
importance of, 103
legal implications of, 103

physical characteristics, 43–44
physical examinations,
124–125
recruitment and, 72–73
reference checks, 118–123
testing applicants, 43, 103–111
(*See also* testing applicants)
Uniform Guidelines on
Employee Selection
Procedures, 29–30
violence in the workplace
and, 291–292
employee services benefits, 206
employee stock ownership incentive plans, 199–200
employers, smaller, insurance
and, 207
employment agencies
recruitment, 78, 80
temporary workers and, 80
employment discrimination (*See
discrimination; equal
employment opportunity
(EEO) laws)
employment planning (*See* workforce planning)
empowerment training, 145
Enterprise Information Portals
(EIPs), 143
environmental scanning,
defined, 17
Equal Employment Opportunity
Commission (EEOC),
27–28
employee charge, 44–45
employer response to charge,
44–4545–46, 45f
Guidelines, 30
mandatory arbitration, 47
mediation program, 45
equal employment opportunity
(EEO) laws, 27–39, 40t
affirmative action and, 49
Age Discrimination in
Employment Act, 1967,
28
Americans with Disabilities
Act, 36–38
applicant testing and, 105
application forms and, 91, 94

V

vacation benefits, 202
values training, 144
vested, defined, 206
vestibule training, 140
veterans, Vietnam Era Veteran's
    Readjustment Act, 1974,
    29, 40t
videoconferencing, for distance
    learning, 140–141
Vietnam Era Veteran's
    Readjustment Act, 1974,
    29, 40t
violence in the workplace,
    291–293
    nature of, 291
    reduction of, 291–293
    toward women, 292–293
    training about, 291–292
Vocational Rehabilitation Act,
    1973, 29, 40t

W

wage curves, 190
Wagner Act (*See* National Labor
    Relations Act (NLRA),
    1935)
Wal-Mart, 14, 218
walk-ins, for recruitment, 82, 84
Walsh-Healey Public Contract
    Act, 1936, 186
*Wards Cove Packing Company v.
    Atonio*, 35, 40t
web (*See also* internet)
    career planning and, 261–262
web-based performance
    appraisal, 173
welfare-to-work programs, 89–91
Western Airlines v. Criswell, 41
women
    reciting, 89
    violence in the workplace
        and, 292–293

work, nature of, 8–9
work overload, accident preven-
    tion and, 285
Worker Adjustment and
    Retaining Act, 1989, 203, 262
worker involvement programs, 145
worker stress, accident preven-
    tion and, 285
workers' compensation laws, 203
workforce
    boosting diversity, 48–49
    contingent, 80
    defined, 73
    diversity of, 5
workforce planning, 73–77
    external candidates, 77–91
    internal candidates, 74–77
    managerial judgment, 73–74
    ratio analysis, 73
    trend analysis, 73
wrongful discharge, 257–258